No Remorse

No Remorse

Psychopathy and Criminal Justice

Jacqueline B. Helfgott

Foreword by Robert D. Hare

To Laura –
What would I do
without you? :)
Love,
Jackie
11-19-18

PRAEGER™

An Imprint of ABC-CLIO, LLC
Santa Barbara, California • Denver, Colorado

Library of Congress Cataloging-in-Publication Data

Names: Helfgott, Jacqueline B., author.
Title: No remorse : psychopathy and criminal justice / Jacqueline B. Helfgott ; foreword by Robert D. Hare.
Description: 1 Edition. | Santa Barbara : Praeger, [2019] | Includes bibliographical references and index.
Identifiers: LCCN 2018027983 (print) | LCCN 2018038035 (ebook) | ISBN 9781440865756 (eBook) | ISBN 9781440865749 (hardback : alk. paper)
Subjects: LCSH: Psychopaths. | Criminals. | Criminal justice, Administration of.
Classification: LCC HV6133 (ebook) | LCC HV6133 .H45 2019 (print) | DDC 364.3/8—dc23
LC record available at https://lccn.loc.gov/2018027983

ISBN: 978-1-4408-6574-9 (print)
978-1-4408-6575-6 (ebook)

23 22 21 20 19 1 2 3 4 5

This book is also available as an eBook.

Praeger
An Imprint of ABC-CLIO, LLC

ABC-CLIO, LLC
130 Cremona Drive, P.O. Box 1911
Santa Barbara, California 93116-1911
www.abc-clio.com

This book is printed on acid-free paper ∞

Manufactured in the United States of America

Portions of the following works have been adapted for use in this book:

Jacqueline B. Helfgott, "Primitive Defenses in the Language of the Psychopath: Considerations for Forensic Practice," *Journal of Forensic Psychology Research and Practice*, 4:3, 2004, 1–29. Reprinted by permission of Taylor & Francis Ltd.

Jacqueline B. Helfgott, "Criminal Behavior and the Copycat Effect: Literature Review and Theoretical Framework for Empirical Investigation," *Aggression and Violent Behavior*, 22, May–June 2015, 46–64. Reprinted by permission of Elsevier.

DEDICATED TO WILLIAM H. PARSONAGE

~ Professor, Mentor, Colleague, Friend ~

Who taught me to never forget

that crime, justice, and psychopathy

are about being human

Contents

Foreword

I am pleased and honored to write the Foreword for *No Remorse: Psychopathy and Criminal Justice*. In 1989, Jacqueline Helfgott, then a graduate student at Penn State, asked if she could use the PCL-R for her master's thesis and doctoral dissertation. Although I had sent out copies of an early draft of the PCL-R items to a number of interested researchers in 1985, the instrument was in the early stages of development, and there were no formal training opportunities for those who wanted to use it for research purposes. I was happy to hear from her and sent her several large cardboard boxes of coded institutional files and VHS videotapes of offenders we had rated on the PCL-R items. She used the material to score the PCL-R and returned the data to me for an interrater reliability check. The reliability of her scores was high. She completed her graduate work on psychopathic cognitive style and defensive process in 1992. Her work was among the relatively few studies that used the PCL-R before its formal publication in 1991.

It was unusual in 1989 to learn that a criminology/criminal justice student was interested in the empirical study of psychopathy. Most of the research on the construct at that time took place in psychology departments with a clinical or forensic program. (Ironically, I was, and continue to be, an *experimental* psychologist.) Yet, in those early years, the construct of psychopathy and its measurement were relevant and central to the theories and precepts of criminology and criminal justice, although few theoreticians and researchers in criminology made the connection. Upon graduating with her PhD in 1992, Dr. Helfgott went on to teach and chair the Department of Criminal Justice at Seattle University, where she remains to this day, as professor and director of the Crime & Justice Research Center. Over the years, she has taught a course on psychopathy to criminal justice students. This book is the product of her work: teaching about psychopathy to criminology and criminal justice students and criminal justice professionals; and focusing on topics and issues of critical importance to criminology and criminal justice and to all of us who care about how the construct of psychopath affects issues of individual liberty, crime control, and public safety.

No Remorse: Psychopathy and Criminal Justice is a much-needed book. It discusses how and why the construct of psychopathy is important for criminology and criminal justice students, professionals, and provides a general understanding of why psychopathy is central to crime and justice. Dr. Helfgott is a longtime psychopathy scholar and criminologist, and a member of the Society of the Scientific Study of Psychopathy, which I cofounded. She has conducted applied research in criminal justice, with emphasis on issues that span the entirety of the criminal justice system. She is an ideal person to write this book. Her applied research in law enforcement, public safety, criminal profiling and police-community relations, prison subculture and prisoner reentry, restorative-community justice, and victimology/victim services and her theoretical work on criminal psychology, criminal behavior, and typologies of crime are impressive and bring a unique and important perspective to the study and understanding of psychopathy. The book is a valuable contribution to the field and important for any social scientist, criminal justice or mental health professional, or anyone interested in learning about how and why psychopathy matters in thinking about crime and the administration of justice.

I have written extensively on the importance of the construct of psychopathy for criminal justice, noting that "Psychopathy is one of the best-validated clinical constructs in the realm of psychopathology, and arguably the single most important clinical construct in the criminal justice system" (Hare, 1998, p. 189). Yet, until recently, most of the published books on psychopathy were texts and edited volumes written by theorists and researchers in psychology and psychiatry. *No Remorse: Psychopathy and Criminal Justice* is among the first texts of its kind, with a primary focus on the importance of psychopathy for criminology and criminal justice.

Psychologists and psychiatrists are concerned mainly with theory, research, assessment, diagnosis, and treatment. *No Remorse: Psychopathy and Criminal Justice* reflects on the role and function of a psychological construct, its diagnosis, its meaning to people, the impact it has on individuals, the harm it can potentially cause, and the ultimate benefit knowledge about its nature offers to society. The book situates the construct of psychopathy within the broader issues with which criminology and criminal justice students must grapple. These include the intersection of science, law, ethics, media and popular culture, the social construction of crime, the gendered nature of crime, and issues of due process and crime control in the administration of justice. These are issues that affect everyone. It is crucial for the public to understand the impact that psychopathic individuals have on our everyday lives and on our experiences as voters, jurors, neighbors, professionals, and humans.

No Remorse: Psychopathy and Criminal Justice is a must-read for anyone who wants to understand why psychopathy matters in understanding crime, how the construct of psychopathy is intertwined with the criminal law and legal decisions about legal competence and insanity, and the myriad ways in which psychopathy has made its way into the criminal justice system in policing, courts, corrections, juvenile justice, and victim services. I had the opportunity in 2012 to be involved in the multiauthored *FBI Law Enforcement Bulletin: Special Issue on Psychopathy*. Dr. Helfgott has actively been involved in advancing the issues outlined in the bulletin and in helping us all make better sense of how the construct of psychopathy affects criminological thinking and criminal justice practice. I hope that this book will be read not just by students, scholars, and practitioners of criminology and criminal justice, but by psychology. sociology, and behavioral science students and scholars, mental health practitioners, medical professionals, voters, jurors, and anyone who wants to learn and think more broadly about the profound effects of psychopathy on justice-involved individuals, victims and survivors of crime, and criminal justice professionals. I also hope the book will stimulate new directions for future theory and research that will advance our understanding of the criminal justice implications of the psychopathy construct.

Robert D. Hare, PhD
March 29, 2018
www.hare.org

Preface

I have taught a course called "The Psychopath" every year since I began my academic career 26 years ago, and have been struck by the lack of availability of textbooks written for criminology/criminal justice students on the subject. Over the years, I have included additional content in the course beyond the focus of traditional texts on psychopathy to teach students about how theory and research on psychopathy fits within criminological theory, and about why knowing about psychopathy matters for their future roles as police officers, federal agents, corrections officers, correctional counselors, probation and parole officers, defense attorneys, prosecutors, judges, forensic psychologists, forensic scientists, death investigators, crime analysts, juvenile justice case managers, victim advocates, academic scholars, and the other positions they may hold as criminal justice graduates.

Absent a text on psychopathy written for criminology/criminal justice students, I set out to educate students about the ways in which the psychopathy construct has historically made its way into criminology and criminal justice—in law enforcement, criminal law and the courts, corrections, juvenile justice, and victim services. *No Remorse: Psychopathy and Criminal Justice* is written for my students, for students in criminology/criminal justice and other social or behavioral sciences, and for criminal justice professionals and others who come into contact with the criminal justice system and the intersection of criminal justice and mental health, and for anyone who wants to learn about how the construct of psychopathy impacts criminal justice policy and practice.

It has special significance for me that I am completing this book in my 26th year as a university professor. I run marathons (slowly) for fun and like the idea of being able to wake up on any given day and run 26.2 miles if I want to. Completing this book has been much more difficult than running a marathon, but I can't help but view the experience through the marathon lens. Just as each mile in a marathon has special meaning and the person you are at the finish is never the same person you were at the start, each year of accumulated research on psychopathy incorporated into this book has had a profound impact on our understanding of psychopathy. Scientific advances over the years have brought us to a very different place than we were 26 plus years ago. When I was an undergraduate student at the University of Washington in the 1980s, I double-majored in society and justice and psychology, and I took a class on psychopathy taught by Dr. Dale Smith who had done work with Dr. Hans Toch on inmate adaptation. The required reading for the course was Cleckley's (1941) *Mask of Sanity*, Jack Olsen's (1983) *Son: A Psychopath and His Victims*, and Yochelson and Samenow's (1977) *Criminal Personality*. I instantly became fascinated by the subject and wanted to know what a psychopath was, what it was like to treat psychopaths, and how to determine who was and who was not a psychopath. I conducted a senior project with Dr. Smith in which I interviewed psychologists who treated psychopaths in the Seattle area about their experience treating psychopaths. As someone who second-guesses just about everything I do, I was consumed by the notion that there were people who could do anything they wanted without remorse or guilt or second-guessing. I went to the library sometime around 1987 to do research on the topic and remember going outside to sit on the front steps in frustration because after reading article after article I could not find a single definition that told me what a psychopath was. Every book and article I read defined psychopathy differently and confused me even more.

While I was in college, the stories of Kevin Coe, Spokane Washington's "South Hill Rapist" and subject of Jack Olsen's book *Son: A Psychopath and His Victims* and Diane Downs who had shot her three children in Oregon and was the subject of Ann Rule's (1988) book *Small Sacrifices* were all over the local news. Watching them on TV and reading about their cases cemented my interest in psychopathy—it boggled my mind how they spoke to reporters and presented themselves in court, and how they did what they did, with seemingly no remorse. In my last year of college, Dr. Smith took me and my fellow University of Washington society and justice major and friend Michelle Harmon (who also went on to get her PhD in criminology and criminal justice at the University of Maryland) to the Washington State Penitentiary in Walla Walla. During our tour of the prison, we saw Kevin Coe just feet away from us. It was an impactful experience to see Kevin Coe as a real person amid learning about him through a true-crime novel and the nightly news. I was hooked on my quest to find out what could possibly make Kevin Coe, or any person, harm someone else with no remorse and be oblivious to the pain and suffering he had caused, and even though he was in prison, I wondered, what now?

When I went to graduate school, I knew what I wanted to study. I applied to programs in clinical psychology and indicated I wanted to study psychopathy and criminal behavior. I received a call from Penn State University where

I had applied to the Psychology Department and was asked if I would consider accepting an offer for admission to Penn State's graduate program in administration of justice. The offer was a full ride teaching and research assistantship and difficult to pass up. So rather than ending up in a psychology department, I found myself studying psychopathy in a criminology/criminal justice department with a graduate minor in psychology. In my first year of graduate school, I still remember the day in the library at Penn State when I discovered Gacono and Meloy's (1988) article "The Relationship between Cognitive Style and Defensive Process in the Psychopath." A huge light went off for me reading that article, and I set off to empirically test their "levels hypothesis" for my master's thesis and doctoral work. My program shift from psychology to criminal justice required me to think much more broadly about psychopathy than I would have in a psychology department. In the Administration of Justice Department at Penn State at the time, the faculty were psychologists, lawyers, sociologists, organizational theorists, historians, and retired criminal justice practitioners turned academics. I was required to think beyond the etiology, diagnosis, and treatment of psychopathy—about the role and function of the label "psychopath" in culture; the implications of a psychopathy diagnosis for individual due process; how psychopathy impacts public safety; the sex-typed origins of DSM classifications and the myth of mental illness; injustices that have occurred historically when psychologists and psychiatrists held too much power in correctional contexts; the broad implications of a diagnosis of psychopathy for individuals and society; interactions between the mental health and the criminal justice systems, and the theoretical connections across psychology, sociology, criminology, and behavioral sciences that explain crime and criminal behavior. I had a faculty member from the Penn State Psychology Department (Dr. Juris Draguns) on my doctoral committee, and my dissertation chair Dr. Lynne Goodstein was a psychologist. However, within the Administration of Justice Department, my work studying psychopathy was not seen as central to criminology and criminal justice and for the entire time I was in my doctoral program I was questioned and warned by multiple faculty about the dangers of locating criminal behavior in personality. When I completed my dissertation, one of the criminal justice faculty members (not on my committee) shook my hand and said, "Congratulations, but I wish you would have done your dissertation on something else."

Fast forward 30 years and I can barely keep up with the research explosion on the topic of psychopathy. Every time I teach my psychopath course, I tell students my story about being on the steps of the library as an undergraduate, in complete frustration not being about to find a single straightforward definition of psychopathy—and about how lucky they are with the incredible amount of research available today, the *Psychopathy Checklist–Revised* that got everyone on the same page, and the multiple lines of research examining psychopathy from every angle. As I write, I know there are studies being conducted and findings that will be published that I would have loved to include and that will help to answer the questions left unanswered in this book.

My goal in writing this book is to provide a new lens through which to make sense of psychopathy that centralizes psychopathy in criminological theory and examines the ways in which psychopathy has made its way into criminal justice practice. Chapter 1, "Psychopathy and Its Relevance to Crime and Justice," provides an overview of psychopathy with discussion of the importance of the topic to criminology and criminal justice. Chapter 2, "Theory and Research on Psychopathy," reviews key research findings. Chapter 3, "The Mental Mechanisms of Psychopathy: Unconscious Defensive Process and Conscious Cognitive Style," examines and reports research findings on the relationship between levels of personality—unconscious primitive defenses, cognitive thinking errors, and antisocial behavior—and provides illustration of the mental mechanisms of the psychopath. Chapter 4, "Psychopathy from an Interdisciplinary Perspective," makes connections between theories that have been developed in psychology, criminology, and social and behavioral sciences to explain psychopathy. Chapter 5, "The Psychopath in Popular Culture," examines the ways in which psychopathy has been depicted in popular culture and its importance in thinking about how the construct of psychopathy is used in criminal justice practice. Chapter 6, "Psychopathy and Criminal Justice Practice," provides a comprehensive overview of how the construct of psychopathy has made its way into criminal justice practice in law enforcement, criminal law and the courts, corrections, reentry, juvenile justice, and victim services. Chapter 7, "New Research and Emerging Issues," discusses recent research findings on psychopathy, crime, and gender and the neuroscience of psychopathy and implications for assessment, treatment, and criminal responsibility. Chapter 8, "Future Implications of the Psychopathy Construct for Criminology and Criminal Justice Policy and Practice," focuses on key research areas of importance for the future, raises ethical-legal issues, and questions left unresolved. I hope *No Remorse: Psychopathy and Criminal Justice* helps move forward the idea that psychopathy is of great importance to criminological theory and criminal justice practice and that topics and ideas in the book plant seeds to inspire students to take the theory and research further. We are at a place in the evolution of theory and research on psychopathy where we know more than we ever have. We have accumulated vast amounts of knowledge about what psychopathy is. We know how to define psychopathy. We know about the etiology, development, and manifestation of psychopathy. We have research findings that tell us about the neuroscience of psychopathy and about the psychopath's unconscious defensive process and cognitive thinking errors and information-processing deficits. We know about how pop cultural depictions of psychopathy influence the public conception that influences laws and juror decision making and about the ways in which psychopathy has made its way into components of the criminal justice system. However, there are many questions left unanswered, and/or under- or unexplored, in areas such as gender and psychopathy, ethical-legal-philosophical perspectives on psychopathy that may shape how we view psychopathy as a mitigating versus aggravating factor in criminal justice decision making, and there are technological advances in artificial intelligence and affective computing that may offer new possibilities for psychopathy treatment. I look forward to the research to come.

Acknowledgments

No project can get off the ground without the help of a community of people. I have been fortunate to have an incredible community of mentors, colleagues, family, and friends who have made this book possible.

First, thanks to my family. My daughter Zalia. She is the best thing that ever happened to me. She grew up hearing me talk about psychopaths, helping me select scenes from *The Bad Seed* for my classes, and I'll never forget the look on her face when she first saw little Rhoda Penmark. She is now a college student majoring in theoretical physics and applied mathematics. She is extraordinary, and I know she will change the world.

Thanks to my mom, Dr. Esther Helfgott, the strongest woman I know, who taught me what it means to be a true scholar. Thanks to my incredible brothers, Ian and Scott Helfgott, to my late dad Oscar Feit and Grandma Anna Helfgott both of whom are still always with me, and to the rest of my family who provide the love and stability and support necessary to make it through a project like this. Thanks to my friends—Laura, Macy, Jill, Sharon, Zach, and Brian, and others who have supported me in different areas of life, including my fellow Marathon Maniacs and Seattle Urban Sketchers who provided me an outlet besides studying and writing about psychopaths. And thanks to my daughter's friends Lillian and Bridget who grew up driving around in the back of my car listening to my stories of all the bad things that have happened on every corner, and I'm pretty sure are tired of hearing me talk about psychopaths.

Thanks to my professional colleagues who have supported me—my doctoral committee chair, Dr. Lynne Goodstein, and committee members professors William Parsonage and Dan Katkin from the Penn State Administration of Justice Department, and Dr. Juris Draguns from the Penn State Psychology Department whose work has influenced my thinking about the influence of culture on manifestations of psychopathy and who took me under his wing to teach me the Rorschach.

I have dedicated this book to William Parsonage, who has been my mentor, professor, colleague, coauthor, and friend since I was assigned to be his teaching and research assistant in graduate school nearly 30 years ago who, as a former police and probation officer turned academic, taught me how to conduct research in criminal justice with great respect for criminal justice practitioners, concern for the needs of justice-involved individuals and victims of crime, and the importance of asking questions that matter and of conducting primary data collection to find answers. Bill threw me into the fire to teach his probation and parole course my first days as a graduate student, opened doors for me to get data collection access in the prisons, took me into prisons to meet prisoners and correctional staff, brought me into his family to meet his wife, Sue Parsonage, who inspired my interest in prison art, and has been in my corner cheerleading me ever since, and served on my dissertation committee. I am now the same age as Bill was in 1989 when I started graduate school. I hope I can be half the mentor to my students that he has been to me over the years.

Thanks to my long-time colleague Dr. Faith Lutze who has been my friend since we were grad students together at Penn State and Dr. Fran Bernat who started as a professor at Penn State when I got there as a grad student and has become a lifelong friend, colleague, and mentor. Faith and Fran—the nights chatting in conference hotel rooms with you have made me a better person and a better scholar. Thanks to my Seattle University criminal justice faculty colleagues—the best faculty colleagues a person could dream up—Drs. Matt Hickman, Steve Rice, Pete Collins, and Will Parkin, and especially Elaine Gunnison who has been the most incredible friend and colleague a person could ask for. Elaine—you are one of the most incredible people I know, and I don't know what I would do without your daily "You got this" texts telling me to get off my e-mail and get back to work. Thanks also to Dr. David Connor whose tips about waking up at 4 a.m. got me through the final stages of this project, although in the course of writing this book, I'm pretty sure I went to sleep at 4 a.m. more times than I ever actually woke up at 4 a.m. I would also like to acknowledge friend and colleague Jerry Westby, for many years of support and encouragement for this project.

Much appreciation to the psychopathy scholars who have influenced my work. To Dr. Robert Hare whose work on psychopathy and developing the PCL-R set the groundwork for the enormous research surge on the topic. To Dr. Reid Meloy whose theories have been a major force driving my thinking and research, whose work I naturally gravitate toward, and whose name is imprinted on the brain of every student who ever completes one of my classes. And to Drs. Adrian Raine, Philip Jenkins, Mary Ellen O'Toole, Dave Kosson, Stanton Samenow, Carl Gacono, and others who have inspired me and whose work is cited throughout this book. A final warm gratitude to the late true-crime author Jack Olsen whose book *Son: A Psychopath and His Victims* was a first and forever spark for me. I will never forget the first time I met Jack when he came to Seattle University to do a guest presentation with his arms full of his books to give me and the e-mails he would send with the greeting "Yo Jack!" Jack Olsen was and still is the best true-crime writer of all time.

I have been fortunate to have had the opportunity to conduct research in a range of criminal justice contexts and to interact with criminal justice professionals in law enforcement, the courts, corrections, and victim services. I have had the opportunity to work with prisoners and victims and survivors of crime who have given me the opportunity to understand the tragedy and harm and human resilience at the center of crime and its aftermath. Thanks to my criminal justice practitioner colleagues, who have taught me so much about the inner workings of the criminal justice system, and to the prisoners and formerly incarcerated, and crime victims who have shared their stories and experiences with me to help me understand what crime and justice is from the inside.

Special thanks to the students who have taken my psychopathy course and the research assistants who assisted me with this book. The questions you have asked and issues you have raised have made this a much better book than it would have been had I written it early in my career. To the research assistants who assisted me with this book and have gone on to do important work—Carol Woods (now Dr. Woods, psychologist at Atascadero State Hospital in California), Matt Willms (now a forensic assessment clinician), Karolyn Kukoski (now ombudsman at the Washington State Special Commitment Center at McNeil Island), Megan Moshe (now cotreasurer of Aftermath: Surviving Psychopathy), and students from my most recent psychopath class—Mary Dillon and Nicollette Rhindero—who were a huge help on the section on psychopath films, and others—thank you for all you have done to help me get this project completed. And to former student Loren Atherley (now a researcher with the Seattle Police Department), who for many years was designated as my backup to complete this book in the event something happened to me before it was finished.

Finally, an enormous and warm thank you to Acquisitions Editor Debbie Carvalko, Senior Production Editor Mark Kane, and the editorial staff at Praeger/ABC-CLIO for their support, encouragement, and opportunity to publish this book, and for making the process such a smooth and rewarding experience. Thanks also to Praeger/ABC-CLIO graphic designers and to Westchester Publishing Services Project Manager Nitesh Sharma and the copyediting staff for their care in the editing and production process to create the final product. It is an honor to publish this book with Praeger/ABC-CLIO.

Even with this lengthy acknowledgment, I'm sure I'm forgetting someone, so if I forgot you, you know who you are—Thank you!

CHAPTER ONE

Psychopathy and Its Relevance to Crime and Justice

I would have liked him at some point in the process to take responsibility, to show remorse. . . . We didn't get any of that tonight.

—Bob Meyers, brother of Dean Meyers, one of 10 victims of the 2002 DC sniper shootings committed by John Allen Muhammad and Lee Boyd Malvo, after witnessing Muhammad's execution ("D.C. Sniper John Allen Muhammad Executed," 2009)

Psychopathy is one of the best-validated clinical constructs in the realm of psychopathology, and arguably the single most important clinical construct in the criminal justice system.

—Robert D. Hare (1998, p. 189)

In 1993, Richard Allen Davis kidnapped 12-year-old Polly Klaas from a slumber party at her home in California. Polly had been playing a game with friends while her mother and sister were sleeping in a room down the hall when Davis abducted her at knifepoint. Her body was found two months later 25 miles from her home after Davis, arrested for drunk driving, confessed to her murder when his fingerprints were identified as those of the kidnapper. At the time of Polly Klaas's murder, Davis was on parole after serving 8 years on a 16-year sentence for a prior kidnapping. On August 5, 1996, a jury decided that Richard Allen Davis should be executed. Following the guilty verdict, Davis turned to the courtroom audience and TV cameras, and with a glaring smirk, gestured with his middle fingers without a flicker of remorse. Later, Polly's father, Marc Klaas, said in a television interview that he hoped the verdict would send a message to "all of the other psychopaths out there" (King 5 News, 1996, August 5). Davis now sits on San Quentin's death row seeking pen pals through his personal website.[1]

---

[1] Davis's website is provided through the *Canadian Coalition against the Death Penalty* and has generated much controversy. It is available at http://www.ccadp.org/richarddavis.htm.

Although it did not seem to be difficult for Marc Klaas to make the determination that a psychopath was to blame for the death of his daughter, psychologists and criminologists have long struggled to understand psychopathy, to identify psychopathic individuals, and to use scientific knowledge about the condition to explain, predict, and control criminal behavior. The term "psychopath" is common in everyday language, media, and pop culture. Images of psychopaths are projected through news media, television, film, music, literature, art, myth, fairy tale, and the Bible. We all know who Marc Klaas was talking about. We may not know the scientific terms or how to clinically diagnose a personality disorder, but we know what it feels like when someone makes the hair rise on the backs of our necks. When it comes to making decisions about crime, it is this feeling that drives us.

And nothing makes the hair rise off the back of our necks more than an offender like Davis who so blatantly defies the needs of the court, the community, and the distraught family of his young victim by refusing to show remorse for the harm caused by his actions. Apology, expression of remorse, is a fundamental need expressed by victims and the community after a crime has occurred (Brooks & Reddon, 2003; Helfgott, Lovell, & Lawrence, 2000; Helfgott, Lovell, Lawrence, & Parsonage, 1999; Lovell, Helfgott, & Lawrence, 2002a; Lovell, Helfgott, & Lawrence, 2002b; Spice, Viljoen, Douglas, & Hart, 2015; Weisman, 2008, 2009). Sanctions such as a prison or death sentence are the formal and expected community response to crime, but expression of remorse is what we want and need in the aftermath of crime.

Psychopaths don't show remorse. Human beings who have psychopathic personalities are characterized in the academic literature as having "defect in affect" (Cleckley, 1941), as being "without conscience" (Hare, 1993) and "reptilian" (Meloy, 1988), and in popular culture as "cold blooded" and "evil." Psychopaths epitomize the antihuman who is incapable of caring about anyone. And in virtually every newscast of a courtroom where an offender is sentenced, the reporter will offer those familiar parting words, "He (or she) showed no remorse," as the offender is hauled off to prison.

It is no wonder why the terms "criminal" and "psychopath" have been synonymous for much of history in popular culture, the academic literature, and the criminal justice system. We now know after more than 200 years of academic study that all criminals are not psychopaths and all psychopaths are not criminals. However, psychopathy is historically, theoretically, and practically important to the study of criminal behavior. Research on the links between psychopathy, criminal behavior, and violence has grown at an enormous pace over the past 30 years and has made its way into the criminal justice system at a number of critical junctures in the criminal justice process. There is a large and growing body of literature indicating that psychopathy is highly predictive of recidivism, treatability, and violence (Babiak, et al., 2012; Gacono, 2016; Hare, 2016; Hare & Neumann, 2006; Patrick, 2013, 2018; Scott, 2014). "Indices of psychopathy are rapidly becoming a routine part of assessment batteries used to make decisions about competency, sentencing, diversion, placement, suitability for treatment, and risk for recidivism and violence" (Hare, 1998, p. 205). In law enforcement, determining whether or not a suspect is psychopathic is useful in criminal profiling (Hare & O'Toole, 2006; O'Toole, 2007; Turvey, 2002) and hostage negotiations (Babiak et al., 2012; Greenstone, Kosson, & Gacono, 2000). Identifying psychopathy in incarcerated offenders is important in correctional classification, management, and treatment (Wong & Hare, 2005; Young, Justice, Gacono, & Kivisto, 2000, 2016), and expert testimony on psychopathy has been introduced in a broad range of court cases, including sexually violent predator determinations, in capital sentencing, determinations of competency and insanity, juvenile transfers to adult court, and in making predictions of dangerousness for sentencing and release decisions (DeMatteo & Edens, 2006; Lyon & Ogloff, 2000; Lyon, Ogloff, & Shepherd, 2016; Venables & Hall, 2013) and has been found to be associated with general criminal behavior, violence (Douglas, Vincent, & Edens, 2018), and specific criminal types such as serial murder (Hickey et al., 2018), sexual assault and rape (Knight & Guay, 2018; Seto, Harris, & Lalumière, 2016), computer criminal behavior (Seigfried-Spellar, Villacís-Vukadinović, & Lynam, 2017), and white-collar crime (Cox, Edens, Rulseh, & Clark, 2016).

The concepts of criminality, delinquency, antisocial personality, sociopathy, and psychopathy have been intertwined and misunderstood throughout history. Much of the research conducted on criminal and antisocial behavior overlaps with the literature on psychopathy. Research on criminal behavior conducted prior to the last 30 years utilized heterogeneous offender samples with no clear distinction between "criminals" and "psychopaths." In 1991, the first edition of the *Psychopathy Checklist–Revised* (PCL-R), developed by Robert Hare (Hare, 1991), was published by Multi-Health Systems. The second edition of the PCL-R was published in 2003 (Hare, 1991, 2003). As the first standardized, valid, and reliable tool to assess psychopathy, the PCL-R offered researchers a tool to measure psychopathy to ensure all studies were measuring the same clinical entity. Since publication of the PCL-R there has been a surge in research on psychopathy and attempts to practically apply the concept in North America and internationally to make critical criminal justice decisions, and the PCL-R is now considered the "gold standard of psychopathy" (Vitacco, Neumann, & Jackson, 2005, p. 466).

Research conducted since the publication of the PCL-R has shown that psychopathy is a robust predictor of violent recidivism, dangerousness, and treatment outcome (Douglas, Vincent, & Edens, 2006; Douglas, Vincent, & Edens, 2018; Hare, 1998; Hare 2003; Hemphill, Hare, & Wong, 1998) leading to the contention that psychopathy is the "single most important clinical construct in the criminal justice system" (Hare, 1998, p. 189). California's three-strikes law requiring mandatory life sentences for repeat felony offenders was, in part, motivated by the murder of Polly Klaas and by the notion of the "6 percent solution" that hypothesizes that incarcerating a small number of dangerous offenders will significantly reduce the crime rate and protect public safety. This theory, derived from criminologist Marvin Wolfgang's cohort studies of career criminals in the 1940s and 1950s, showed that six-percent of the cohort was responsible for more than 50 percent of total crime (Beres & Griffith, 1998; Vaughn & DeLisi, 2008). Based on this notion, the three strikes should enhance public safety by identifying and incarcerating those inclined to reoffend. Along these lines, psychopathy can be viewed as a scientific reconceptualization of evil that has been used to contain and control threatening and unexplainable behavior. "Get tough" laws are enacted through the image of the psychopathic predator (Helfgott, 2008)—three- and two-strikes legislation, sexual psychopath/predator laws, capital punishment, the federal Violent Crime Control and Law Enforcement Act of 1994—have all been championed as weapons with which the incorrigible criminal will be aggressively attacked. In the public mind, the incorrigible criminal is the psychopath.

Defining Psychopathy

If you asked "What is a psychopath?" 30, 40, or 50 years ago, you would have had a hard time finding a simple answer. Hervey Cleckley, in his classic work *The Mask of Sanity*, called the psychopath "the forgotten man of psychiatry" (Cleckley, 1941, 1988, p. 16) because the term has historically represented a "loose and variously understood" heterogeneous group, and a "wastebasket" category with no clear definition. The terms "sociopath," "psychopath," and "antisocial personality" (and sometimes even "psychotic") have been confused and used interchangeably over the years in science and popular culture by researchers, clinicians, criminal justice professionals, news reporters, filmmakers, and the general public (Dinwiddie, 2015; Helfgott, 2013c; Keesler & DeMatteo, 2017; Smith, Edens, Clark, & Rulseh, 2014). However, today, "psychopathy has journeyed beyond its confusing origins and a mismatch of labels into an empirically measurable syndrome" (Gacono, 2016, p. 10). Research conducted over the past several decades suggests that psychopathy is a unique clinical condition characterized by the "juxtaposition of affective interpersonal traits with antisocial behavior" (Hare & Neumann, 2006, p. 84) that is empirically associated with criminal behavior and violent recidivism (Hare, Neumann, & Mokros, 2018). However, even today there is controversy over the appropriate scope and definition of the psychopathy construct (Patrick, Fowles, & Krueger, 2009) and whether and when psychopathy should be viewed dimensionally or as a taxon (Gacono, 2016; Patrick, 2018b) and from variable and person-centered approaches (Neumann, Vitacco, & Mokros, 2016).

Given the negative connotations of the term "psychopath" and the association of the condition with antisocial and criminal behavior, it is important to think about what psychopathy means beyond the clinical construct. *What function does the label "psychopath" serve in society and culture? Is the term "psychopath" used as a clinical, sterilized, modernized, scientized stand-in when we really mean "evil"? Can a person be a little bit psychopathic—just enough to be able to employ psychopathic character traits necessary to engage in behavior that harms others without the downside of feeling guilt and remorse? Why are people so fascinated with psychopaths in media and popular culture? Is there something enjoyable or necessary about hearing stories about human monsters who feel no remorse? Does knowing about the "psychopaths out there" remind us of the ultimate boundary of human behavior?*

These questions compel exploration of the psychopathy beyond the clinical condition. Most of the research on psychopathy has been conducted within the fields of psychology and psychiatry with limited attention to the broader implications and meaning of the term. Thinking about the broader implications of the psychopathy construct is critical in any discussion of the ways in which the construct has made its way into the criminal justice system. When clinical diagnoses and psychological constructs are used in practical ways to make decisions about how to interrogate suspects, to link serial crimes and scene evidence, to inform trial and sentencing juries, as selection or exclusion criteria for treatment programs, or to make prison release or civil commitment decisions, the cultural context in which these decisions are made and the meaning the term "psychopath" holds for people (e.g., criminal justice practitioners, news reporters, jurors, moviegoers) is just as important to understand as the clinical features of the psychopathy construct.

Psychopathy as a Clinical Disorder of Personality

Psychopathy is a personality disorder characterized by an inability to form human attachment, aggressive narcissism, and antisocial behavior (Meloy, 1992). A personality disorder is "*an enduring pattern of inner experience and behavior that deviates markedly from the expectations of the individual's culture, is pervasive and inflexible, has an onset in adolescence or early adulthood, is stable over time, and leads to distress or impairment*" (APA, 2013, DSM-5, p. 645). The psychopathic personality disorder is comprised by a constellation of interpersonal, affective, lifestyle, and antisocial characteristics characterized by two essential features: *aggressive narcissism* and *antisocial lifestyle*.[2] The aggressive narcissism

[2] This view of psychopathy as comprised of aggressive narcissism and antisocial behavior is one of a number of conceptualizations of psychopathy that offers an explanatory framework to understand the two-factor construct comprised of personality and behavioral components. In recent

component of the psychopathic personality (see Figure 1.1) involves a deceitful and arrogant interpersonal style and deficient affective experience. The antisocial lifestyle component of the psychopathic personality (see Figure 1.2) involves criminal and noncriminal antisocial behavior.

The disordered pattern of experience and behavior of the psychopath originates in early infancy prior to 36 months of age. In his book *The Psychopathic Mind*, Meloy (1988) explains the early developmental origins of the disorder describing psychopathy as:

> a deviant developmental disturbance characterized by an inordinate amount of instinctual aggression and the absence of the object relational capacity to bond. Psychopathy is a process: a continuous interplay of factors and operations that are implicitly progressing or regressing toward a particular end point . . . a fundamental disidentification with humanity. (Meloy, 1988, p. 5)

This fundamental disidentification with humanity is what makes individuals who have psychopathic personality disorder more likely than those who do not to engage in behaviors that harm others. This is also what makes the construct of psychopathy so important to understand in terms of the role it plays in criminal behavior and criminal justice policy and practice. If an individual is fundamentally unable to identify with and form human attachment, it makes it possible, and easy, to harm others with no remorse. And when it comes to responding to criminal behavior in the criminal justice system, remorse is a key factor at every stage of the criminal justice system.

Robert Hare, creator of the PCL-R and author of *Without Conscience: The Disturbing World of the Psychopaths among Us*, describes psychopathy as a personality disorder defined by a constellation of affective, interpersonal, and behavioral characteristics most of which society views as pejorative (Hare, 1993; Hare, 1998). According to Hare:

> Psychopaths are social predators who charm, manipulate, and ruthlessly plow their way through life leaving a broad trail of broken hearts, shattered expectations, and empty wallets. Completely lacking in conscience and feelings for others, they selfishly take what they want and do as they please, violating social norms and expectations without the slightest sense of guilt or regret. (Hare, 1993, p. xi)

---

years the four-factor model of psychopathy—interpersonal, affective, lifestyle, and antisocial behavior—has been empirically supported as a framework for understanding the structure of the psychopathy construct (Hare, Neumann, & Mokros, 2018).

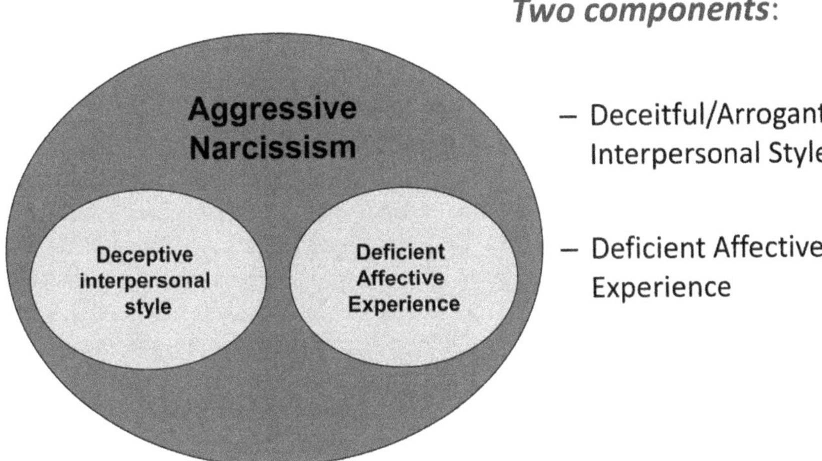

Figure 1.1 Aggressive Narcissism

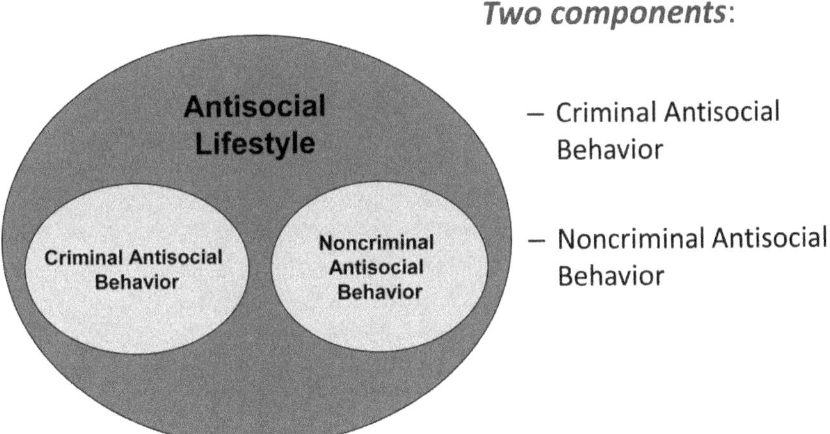

Figure 1.2 Antisocial Lifestyle

Psychopaths are hardwired to commit antisocial and criminal behavior because they have an emotional dysfunction that interferes with their ability to feel (Blair, Mitchell, & Blair, 2005; Igoumenou et al., 2017; Kosson, Vitacco, Swagger, & Steuerwald, 2016). One of the most distinctive features of psychopathy is the "mask," first described by Cleckley (1941) in the *Mask of Sanity*, that enables untrustworthy and reckless individuals to appear psychologically normal (Patrick, 2018a).

The clarity and consensus regarding the meaning the term "psychopath" in recent years can be largely attributed to the development and standardization of the *Psychopathy Checklist–Revised*, known as the PCL-R, a 20-item scale that assesses psychopathy using a semistructured interview, file, and collateral information that measures personality traits and behaviors associated with a widely understood, historical, and traditional conception of psychopathy (Hare, 2003). The PCL-R (Hare, 1991, 2003) has become the standard measure of psychopathy in research, clinical assessment, and criminal justice practice. Researchers consider the PCL-R's ability to predict violence to be unprecedented and unparalleled (Salekin, Rogers, & Sewell, 1996). The PCL-R is a valid and reliable measure of psychopathy that is a strong predictor of violent recidivism and dangerousness (Douglas, Vincent, & Edens, 2006; Hart, 1998; Porter & Porter, 2007),[3] criminal career trajectory (Shaw & Porter, 2012), and determinant of high criminogenic offender risk/needs (Simourd & Hodge, 2000). The PCL-R has gained widespread attention, is now used at various stages of the criminal justice system in Canada and the United States (Hare, 1998), and variations and versions of the instruments have been published including the *Psychopathy Checklist: Screening Version* (PCL:SV) (Hart, Cox, & Hare, 1995), the *Hare P-Scan* (Hare & Hervé, 1999, 2001), the *Psychopathy Checklist: Youth Version* (PCL:YV) (Forth, Kosson, & Hare, 2003), and the *Self-Report Psychopathy Scale* (SRP 4) (Paulhus, Neumann, & Hare, 2017).

The advent and standardization of the PCL-R has made it possible for researchers to distinguish between offenders who are antisocial (the majority of offenders in prison populations) and those whose criminal behavior is psychopathologically rooted. The PCL-R is comprised of two factors consisting of features that distinguish personality features (Factor 1) and behavioral features (Factor 2) of the disorder. Table 1.1 shows the PCL-R items and factors. Factor 1 items are associated with affective and interpersonal personality characteristics derived from Cleckley (1941, 1988) and reflect the aggressive narcissism component of the disorder. Factor 2 items reflect the antisocial behavior/social deviance component of the disorder including antisocial behaviors similar to those included in the antisocial personality disorder classification in the *Diagnostic and Statistical Manual for Mental Disorders* (APA, DSM-5, 2013). Research using item response theory (IRT) has provided support for a four-factor model of psychopathy with specific PCL-R items associated with interpersonal, affective, lifestyle, and antisocial factors (Hare, 2016; Hare & Neumann, 2006; Hare, Neumann, & Mokros, 2018; Neumann, Kosson, & Salekin,

[3] A large body of research on psychopathy and the prediction of violent recidivism has accumulated. For specific findings and review of the research, see Douglas, Vincent, and Edens (2018), Gacono (2000, 2016), Harris, Rice, and Cormier (1991), Hare (2001, 2003), Hemphill, Hare, and Wong (1998), Hodgins (1997), Litwack and Schlesinger (1998), Salekin, Rogers, and Sewell (1996), Serin and Amos (1995), Porter and Porter (2007), and Venables and Hall (2013).

Table 1.1 PCL-R Factors 1 and 2

FACTOR 1	FACTOR 2
Item 1: Glibness/superficial charm	Item 3: Need for stimulation/ proneness to boredom
Item 2: Grandiose sense of self-worth	Item 9: Parasitic lifestyle
Item 4: Pathological lying	Item 10: Poor behavioral controls
Item 5: Conning/manipulative	Item 12: Early behavior problems
Item 6: Lack of remorse or guilt	Item 13: Lack of realistic, long-term goals
Item 7: Shallow affect	Item 14: Impulsivity
Item 8: Callous/lack of empathy	Item 15: Irresponsibility
Item 16: Failure to accept responsibility for own actions	Item 18: Juvenile delinquency
	Item 19: Revocation of conditional release
	Item 20: Criminal versatility
PCL-R items not included in factors:	
Item 17: Many short-term marital relationships	
Item 11: Promiscuous sexual behavior	

2007) (see Figure 1.3, PCL-R Four-Factor Model of Psychopathy).[4] This research has empirically supported the conceptualization of the psychopathy construct as comprised of two superordinate factors—interpersonal/affective and social deviance, and four facets—interpersonal, affective, lifestyle, and antisocial (Hare, 2003).

The four-factor model of psychopathy offers a more complex understanding of the fundamental facets of the disorder. The four-factor model has informed recent research examining the relationship between psychopathy facets and central emotional deficit of psychopathy and its behavioral expression such as the ability to recognize emotion in others (Igoumenou et al., 2017), and some researchers have utilized the model in studies that

[4] Psychological characteristics in individuals cannot be directly observed. Psychological tests are used to make inferences about an individual's level of a characteristic. Psychologists use psychometric tests such as the PCL-R to make inferences about characteristics associated with a particular psychological condition. IRT is a psychometric model used to measure performance on a test item in relation to other items on a test. IRT enables psychologists to measure individuals on the latent trait defined by the set of items while simultaneously scaling each item on the very same dimension.

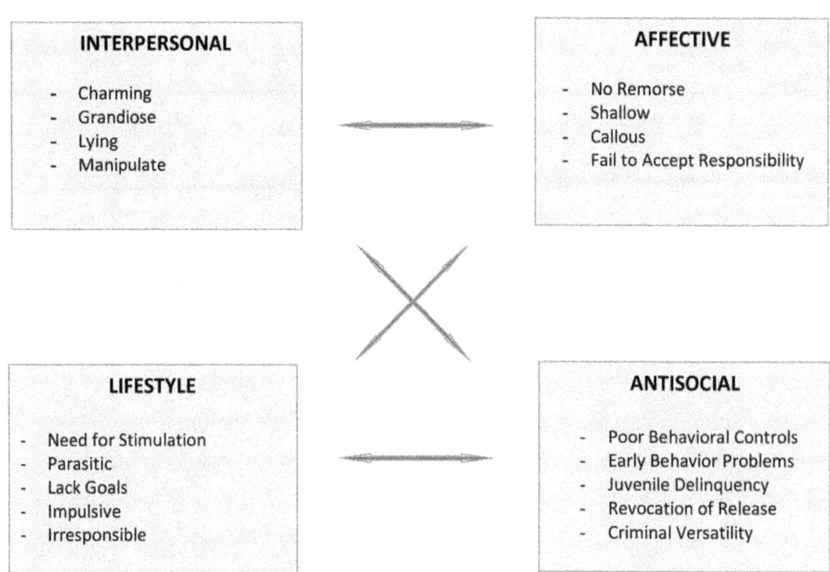

Figure 1.3 PCL-R Four-Factor Model of Psychopathy. (Adapted from Hare, Neumann, & Mokros (2018). "The PCL-R Assessment of Psychopath: Development, Properties, Debates, and New Directions." In C. J. Patrick (Ed.), *Handbook of Psychopathy* (2nd ed., pp. 39–79). New York: Guilford Press).

have called to question the long-standing assumption that antisociality is a core feature of psychopathy rather than a consequence of the condition (e.g., Walters, 2012). Ultimately, psychopaths present significant problems for society, themselves, and people they interact with because they have a pathological interpersonal style, a deficit in emotional experience, a lifestyle that involves a pattern of irresponsibility, and behavior that is antisocial throughout the life course.

Psychopathy and Antisocial Personality Disorder

The term "psychopathic personality" has been used in the academic literature and popular discourse for more than 200 years falling in and out of favor and sometimes replaced with other terms such as "sociopath" and "antisocial personality disorder." "Psychopathic personality" has never been an official classification in any of the editions of the *Diagnostic and Statistical Manual of Mental Disorders* (DSM) but has long been identified as a distinct disorder associated with antisocial personality disorder and other Cluster B disorders in the DSM—histrionic, narcissistic, and borderline personality disorders (Wulach, 1988). However, researchers agree that the psychopathy is a distinct clinical entity that has not been adequately conveyed through the diagnostic categories in the various editions of the DSM (Reid, 1985). Researchers continue to use the term "psychopathy" in discussion and empirical study in reference to a distinct phenomenon that is not necessarily synonymous with associated terms used over time in the DSM (APA, 1952), DSM-II (APA, 1968), DSM-III (APA, 1980), DSM-III-R (APA, 1987), DSM-IV (APA, 1994), DSM-IV-TR (APA, 2000), and DSM-5 (APA, 2013). Research continues to support a clear distinction between antisocial personality disorder (APD)[5] and psychopathy (Ogloff, Campbell, & Shepherd, 2015; Wall, Wygant, & Sellbom, 2015; Walsh & Wu, 2008).

The DSM-III (APA, 1980) and DSM-III-R (APA, 1987) versions of APD were extensively criticized because they were long and cumbersome, overfocused on behaviors, underfocused on personality, and incongruent with international criteria[6] (Hare, Hart, & Harpur, 1991). The criteria were "too descriptive, inclusive, criminally biased, and socioeconomically skewed to be of much clinical or research use" (Meloy, 1988). The DSM-IV (APA, 1994), DSM-IV-TR (APA, 2000), and DSM-5 (APA, 2013) APD classifications are shorter than their predecessors but the criteria remain behaviorally focused, including personality features such as lack of empathy, superficial charm, and inflated and arrogant self-appraisal under the subheading "Associated Features and Disorders."

However, the antisocial personality disorder classification remains the diagnostic category closest to the historical concept of psychopathy. The criteria for diagnosis of APD are:

- A pervasive pattern of disregard for the rights of others, occurring since age 15 years, as indicated by at least three sub-criteria (e.g., failure to conform with respect to lawful behavior, deceitfulness, impulsivity, irritability and aggressiveness, consistent irresponsibility, lack of remorse).
- Individual must be at least 18 years of age.
- Diagnosis of conduct disorder with onset before age 15.

---

[5] Antisocial personality disorder has historically been abbreviated as both "APD" and "ASPD" in the scientific literature. Currently, most authors use ASPD to avoid confusion with avoidant personality disorder. I have used ASPD in my own writing (e.g., Helfgott, 2013a); however, I use APD throughout this text for brevity and for historical consistency because early authors used "APD" in discussions of Cluster B personality disorders—antisocial personality disorder (APD), borderline personality disorder (BPD), histrionic personality disorder (HPD), and narcissistic personality disorder (NPD).

[6] See *International Classification of Diseases* (10th ed.) (World Health Organization, 1992, 2015). The ICD-10 classification "dissocial personality" is considered to represent the classical concept of psychopathy (Coid, 1993).

- Occurrence of antisocial behavior is not exclusively during the course of Schizophrenia or Bipolar Disorder. (DSM-5, APA, 2013, p. 659)

Although the APD is the official classification most resembling the traditional concept of psychopathy, its strict behavioral criteria has led researchers to conclude that the classification is not a useful measurement for empirical study of psychopathy as it has been traditionally defined.

The PCL-R differs from the antisocial personality disorder classification in that its criteria capture both the personality (Factor 1) and behavioral (Factor 2) features of the traditional concept of psychopathy based on the work of Cleckley (1941, 1988). The PCL-R measures a unitary syndrome comprised of two distinct underlying mechanisms—*aggressive narcissism*, the interpersonal/affective (Factor 1) component, and *antisocial behavior,* the social deviance component (Factor 2) (Meloy, 1992). The distinctiveness of these mechanisms and the relationship between them play an important role in differentiating psychopathy from criminality, in understanding the relationship between personality and crime, and in identifying psychopathy independent of cultural influences that shape its manifestation. The two PCL-R factors are correlated with each other (.56 in prison inmates and .53 in forensic patients) (Hare, Hart, & Harpur, 1991). Factor 1 reflects core personality features of the condition and is considered to infer interpersonal style. Factor 1 is positively correlated with clinical ratings of psychopathy, prototypicality ratings of narcissistic and histrionic personality disorder, and self-report measures of Machiavellianism and narcissism, and negatively correlated with measures of empathy and anxiety (Hare, 1991; Harpur, Hare, & Hakstian, 1989; Hart & Hare, 1989). Factor 2 reflects chronically unstable and antisocial lifestyle and is considered to be a measure of social deviance. Factor 2 is positively correlated with criminal behaviors, socioeconomic background, self-report measures of socialization and antisocial behavior, and diagnosis of APD (Hare, 1991, 2003; Harpur, Hare, & Hakstian, 1989).

Psychopathy as a Categorical or Dimensional Construct

Psychopathy can be considered *categorically* as a discrete clinical disorder of personality (or taxon) or *dimensionally* along a continuum as a personality dynamic used to a greater or lesser degree by all individuals as a tool with which to commit immoral acts without remorse or shame. The categorical model of psychopathy holds that a person either is or is not a psychopath. Although psychopathy can be understood from both dimensional and categorical perspectives, researchers have generally used a PCL-R cutoff score of 30 and above as the criterion for classification as a primary or "true" psychopath (Gacono, 2016). However, some researchers suggest that a lower score may

Categorical	***Dimensional***
• Yes/No • Qualitative Difference • Primary or "true"	• More/less • Quantitative/Continuum • Secondary (APD, non-psychopath)

Figure 1.4 Categorical v. Dimensional Models of Psychopathy

differentiate psychopaths from nonpsychopaths (Harris, Rice, & Cormier, 1991; Harris, Rice, & Quinsey, 1994).[7] The dimensional model holds that all human beings possess characteristics of psychopathy to greater or lesser degrees (see Figure 1.4). In other words, a person can be more or less psychopathic with psychopathy level reflecting greater inclination toward criminal behavior and violence.

Research and strong arguments exist to support both models. Gacono and Meloy (2002) and Gacono (2013, 2016) stress the importance of understanding psychopathy as a taxon (PCL-R ≥ 30) for research purposes and as a dimensional construct along a continuum of severity in clinical/forensic settings and recommend that other tests (including assessment of defensive process) be used in conjunction with the PCL-R to further delineate the dimensional aspects (behavioral and intrapsychic characteristics) of antisocial and psychopathic subjects.[8] Wallace, Schmitt, Vitale, and Neman (2000) suggest that PCL-R scores above 30 reflect the categorical phenomenon (e.g., the true or primary psychopath), whereas PCL-R scores below 30 reflect the dimensional construct (e.g., the secondary psychopath or antisocial personality disorder).

---

[7] Gacono (2016) cautions that research findings can be obscured when researchers make categorical differences using data collected with dimensional research designs—e.g., using samples that do not include scores over 29. Thus the issue of what cutoff score should be used in research is an issue of some debate and ongoing discussion and highlights the importance of understanding both the categorical and dimensional perspectives.

[8] While the PCL-R (Factor 1) measures personality features distinguishing psychopathic from non-psychopathic antisocial personality disordered (APD) individuals, Factor 1 ratings depend on clinician inferences about the motives and accuracy of patient self-reports and interpersonal style (Kosson, Gacono, & Bodholdt, 2000; Kosson et al., 2013). With the subjective nature of Factor 1 ratings, aspects of the interpersonal style of the psychopath can be lost. With this in mind, the Interpersonal Measure of Psychopathy (IM-P) was developed as a supplement to the PCL-R to assess the core personality of the psychopath by identifying and coding interpersonal behaviors (Kosson, Gacono, & Bodholdt, 2000; Kosson et al., 2016).

The Mental Mechanisms of Psychopathy Used in Ordinary Life

Enormous progress has been made in the identification of the clinical-categorical condition. However, because knowledge is limited regarding the cultural influences that shape the manifestation of the disorder, drawing a definitive line between psychopaths and nonpsychopaths is problematic. The phenomena of secondary psychopathy and subclinical/adaptive/successful/prosocial psychopathy (Benning, Venables, & Hall, 2018; Dutton, 2012; Galang et al., 2016; Hall & Benning, 2006; Riech, 2014; Smith, 1978) raises issue regarding the dimensional nature of psychopathy and the need for an alternative and complementary conceptualization beyond the clinical construct. Recent criticism of issues associated with instruments such as the PCL-R that have the potential to divide the world up into psychopaths and "psychopath spotters" (Ronson, 2011) suggest that there is some benefit to reflection on the broader cultural meaning and function of the term "psychopath" and the potential commonalities between psychopaths and nonpsychopaths. Along these lines, psychopathy can be viewed, beyond the clinical condition, from a cultural-dimensional perspective. This broader perspective raises this question: *Can psychopathy be viewed as a psychological tool used in ordinary life, by ordinary, nonpsychopathic people, to temporarily and selectively detach from humanity in order to eliminate feelings of guilt associated with a particular antisocial or deviant act?*

Secondary psychopathy can be conceptually distinguished from the primary (clinical-categorical) condition. The secondary psychopath is not a clinical psychopath—he or she has learned to temporarily use psychological mechanisms very similar to those used consistently by the primary psychopath, and as a result, is able to produce behavior that may appear to be "psychopathic." This is not to say that individuals who have been historically associated with the term "secondary psychopath" are not criminal or deviant or psychopathologically disordered in some way. They may or may not be afflicted with any one of a number of conditions, but they are not psychopaths. Individuals who have historically been labeled secondary psychopaths can be distinguished from nonpsychopaths by the presence of some psychopathic traits and behaviors, the ability to form human attachments, the experience of shame (Prado, Treeby, & Crowe, 2016), and in some cases simply the legal and/or social identification as criminal or deviant.

Blackburn's (1988) statement that psychopathy is a "moral judgment masquerading as a clinical diagnosis" is particularly applicable here. If antisocial behavior is socially constructed and shaped by cultural forces, such behavior cannot logically be used as a diagnostic marker with which to identify an underlying disturbance of personality. Assessment of antisocial inclination through antisocial behavior is tautologically meaningless. The secondary psychopath possesses the capacity to bond; thus, the homogeneous element that distinguishes primary psychopathy does not apply, and the classification of secondary psychopathy is dependent on cultural norms that dictate and define and socially construct deviant and criminal behavior. Theoretically, the phenomenon of secondary psychopathy has historically been a subject for deviance theorists and criminologists, *not* psychologists and psychiatrists.[9] The secondary psychopath is the social deviant, the criminal, the unethical businessperson, the existentialist, the gang member, the cult follower, the deadbeat dad, the spouse abuser, the child neglecter, the income tax cheater, the date rapist, the police officer, the corrections officer, the executioner, the racist, the moralist, the name-caller, the backstabber, the freeway curser, the murder mystery enthusiast, the horror film patron, and anyone and everyone who has ever had to detach themselves, temporarily, from another living being in order to engage in a particular activity. The activity (and the traits and behaviors that support it) itself is not sufficiently indicative of psychopathology.

Is it meaningful, useful, or perhaps detrimental to use the term "psychopath" to refer to secondary psychopaths? Is it constructive to think about how or if the mental mechanisms of psychopathy are used by nonpsychopaths to hurt others without having to feel the discomfort associated with remorse? With care not to minimize the existence of and harm caused by the clinical condition, exploration of the ways in which nonpsychopathic people cognitively neutralize feelings of guilt and remorse when engaging in behaviors that may cause them emotional distress may be a useful exercise to understand the mental mechanisms of psychopathy. In other words, what is the difference between a nonpsychopath who is able to internally ignore or block out feelings of guilt when harming another person and a psychopath, who because of the very nature of the condition, utilizes unique mental processes to harm without remorse. Examination of the similarities and differences between the mental mechanisms of nonpsychopaths and psychopaths when engaging in behaviors that harm others can potentially help to determine where the dimensional model leaves off and the point at which psychopathy becomes a categorical phenomenon. For this purpose, the ***mental mechanisms of psychopathy*** can be defined *as traits and behaviors produced through a unique interaction between the unconscious defensive process and conscious cognitive style.* **Psychopathic behavior** can be defined as *behaviors produced through the use of the mental mechanisms of psychopathy that create interpersonal harm with an*

---

[9] Secondary psychopathy may be the product of a psychopathological disturbance other than psychopathy (e.g., neurosis and psychosis), an organic dysfunction (e.g., brain tumor), or any one of a number of underlying conditions. If such were the case, the individual's behavior would be the problem of the psychologist, psychiatrist, neurologist, etc. However, secondary psychopathy, apart from its etiological origins, is a sociocultural construction that has been meaningfully investigated beyond the psychological discourse through deviance, social control, and criminological theories.

apparent lack of remorse. Psychopathic traits and behaviors are produced through the interaction between primitive defensive organization (i.e., the utilization of splitting, projective identification, primitive idealization, devaluation, omnipotence, and denial) and cognitive style (i.e., the "cutting off" of mental representations that would obstruct the commission of an antisocial or immoral act). Primary psychopaths possess a clinical personality disorder characterized by an enduring pattern of perceiving and relating to the world. They use primitive defenses and cognitive thinking errors habitually and consistently throughout their lives. Secondary psychopaths (who engage in antisocial acts as a result of a condition other than psychopathy) and nonpsychopaths (who do not engage in acts that would be deemed antisocial) utilize primitive defenses and cognitive thinking errors on occasion—to commit a crime, to engage in military combat, to execute a criminal, to cheat on a college exam, to enjoy a film about serial murder. And the tendency to use psychopathic dynamics may depend on sociocultural factors.

The similarities between the use of the mental mechanisms of psychopathy by ordinary nonpsychopathic people can be superficially explored by comparing the traits and behaviors of the PCL-R with the traits and behaviors displayed during the commission of an act that would generally not be considered to be psychopathic.[10] For example, most people have found themselves, at one time or another, in the position of wanting to end an unsatisfactory relationship before the other person is ready to do so. What is required to engage in this activity is the use of unconscious defenses (to maintain a positive self-identity), conscious rationalizations (to justify behavior), and antisocial behavior (to execute the plan). This interaction between the levels of personality often produces traits and behaviors similar to those of the psychopath. Table 1.2 illustrates use of the applicable traits and behaviors of the PCL-R in a hypothetical "breakup" scenario.

The use of the mental mechanisms of psychopathy in a situation such as this provides escape from guilt and feelings of attachment that would prohibit dissolution of the relationship. Underlying these traits and behaviors in the nonpsychopath *is able to attach* to others, to use higher-level defense mechanisms (e.g., rationalization, intellectualization, projection, sublimation), and to generate mental representations that would deter the commission of the act. However, certain acts require the use of the mental mechanisms of psychopathy because they involve emotional, physical, or

[10] This illustration is intended as a brief introduction to the similarities between the traits and behaviors produced through mental mechanisms of psychopathy used in ordinary life and those associated with psychopathic personality disorder. Underlying these traits and behaviors is a unique interaction between psychodynamic and cognitive components of personality discussed in depth in Chapter 3 with examples of the mental mechanisms of high PCL-R scoring psychopaths.

Table 1.2 PCL-R Traits and Behaviors Applicable to the Breakup Scenario

1. Glibness/ superficial charm	You attempt to impress upon the unwanted partner that he or she is no longer needed by maintaining distance with an air of charmed nonchalance.
2. Grandiose sense of self-worth	You believe that the unwanted partner is not good enough for you—you've moved onto some higher developmental level while he or she is stuck in a place you grew out of long ago.
3. Need for stimulation	You are bored with the relationship, need some excitement, and are certain that another relationship will provide it.
4. Pathological lying	Instead of telling the truth (e.g., "I'm not attracted to you anymore") you tell your unwanted partner something that will absolve your guilt (e.g., "I've been in relationships my whole life. I need to be alone and to get in touch with myself. It has nothing to do with you.")
5. Conning/ manipulative	You bargain to make the situation go more smoothly (e.g., "I'll give you everything I own if it'll make it easier" or "We'll still be friends. I'll call you next week and we'll go to the movies.") with no intention of following through.
6. Lack of remorse or guilt	You genuinely do not feel a thing for your unwanted partner. You cannot be moved by his or her emotions and experience a general feeling of apathy in your interactions with the person.
7. Shallow affect	In an attempt to detach from your unwanted partner, you control your emotions (which is not difficult to do because you really don't care anymore). Your absence of emotional expression is perceived by the unwanted partner (who is extremely distraught) as cold and empty. You know that he or she is right, and you wonder how you could behave this way.
8. Callous/lack of empathy	You are unable to understand why your unwanted partner is making such a blubbering fool of himself or herself. You have no sympathy for someone who acts like such an idiot.
9. Parasitic lifestyle	Your relationship continued until this point because no one else was around for you to depend on (for any number of things, such as free dinners, back rubs, and someone to call when your car breaks down). You initiate the breakup with the idea that you will find someone who will be better able to satisfy your needs.

(continued)

Table 1.2 *(continued)*

10. Poor behavioral controls	The difficulty of the situation makes you angry, and you impulsively decide to walk out and slam the door before you've said what you'd planned to say or before the unwanted partner comes to a resolution.
11. Promiscuous sexual behavior	You have had thoughts or have engaged in actions that reflect a desire to "play the field."
12. Early behavioral problems	Not applicable.
13. Lack of realistic, long-term goals	You believe that once you are rid of the relationship you will find the "perfect" (unrealistically) idealized mate.
14. Impulsivity	You just woke up this morning and realized that you want out of the relationship. You decide to get out of the situation immediately before your head catches up with your urge.
15. Irresponsibility	Your unconscious lack of concern about relationship has developed into a pattern of thoughtlessness, tardiness, deceit, and carelessness where your partner is concerned.
16. Failure to accept responsibility	You are unable to share blame for the failure of the relationship and mask this inability with overt self-blaming (Item 4) and covert self-talk that justifies your behavior ("He or she has nagged me to death and has been asking for this for a long time.")
17. Many short-term marital relationships	You are constantly searching for the perfect relationship, and your inability to take responsibility for your actions has led to many short-term relationships.
18. Juvenile delinquency	Not applicable.
19. Revocation of conditional release	Not applicable.
20. Criminal versatility	Not applicable.

monetary injury to others. It is difficult, if not impossible, to harm another human being without the ability to emotionally detach—the fundamental component of psychopathy.

Sociologists and criminologists have addressed the relationship between emotional attachment, cognition, and behavior using different terminology and a more general application than have psychologists. In sociological terms, crime is associated with weak or broken social bonds (Hirschi, 1969), defensive techniques (Sykes & Matza, 1957), and linguistic accounts that justify and excuse behavior (Gabor, 1994; Scully & Marolla, 1984). Direct parallels can be drawn between Hirschi's (1969) social bond theory and Meloy's (1992) theory of violent attachments; between Sykes and Matza's (1957) techniques of neutralization and Kernberg's (1987) primitive borderline defenses; and between Scully and Marolla's (1984) findings on the vocabulary of rapists, Gabor's (1994) study of crime by the public, and Rieber and Vetter's (1995) research on the deceptive aberration of language in the psychopath. The similarities across disciplines in the explanations of antisocial behavior reflect an important theoretical link that is necessary to examine the congruence between the psychopathic personality and the psychopathic dynamic used in ordinary life. Few studies have explored the similarities between antisocial behavior committed by the general public and antisocial behavior committed by individuals who have been identified as criminals.[11]

Beyond discussions of the dimensional model of psychopathy, the similarities between the general nonpsychopathic public and individuals diagnosed as psychopaths have only been minimally addressed in the literature though there seems to be an upswing in the research examining psychopathic character traits as adaptive in some contexts. For example, Galang et al. (2016) identified prosocial aspects of psychopathy that creative personalities share with people described as having psychopathic traits. Riech (2014) discusses the overrepresentation of psychopathy in the legal profession, and Lilienfeld et al. (2012) found that boldness associated with psychopathy is a predictor of presidential performance and successful interpersonal behavior in the political leadership sphere. Recent findings by Falkenbach, Mckinley, and Larson (2017) suggest that psychopathic character traits may aid individuals in carrying out police and first-responder work where decreased emotional response, low stress reactivity, and fearlessness may aid in doing one's job.

Because nonpsychopaths have formed attachment in infancy, it makes sense to analyze the ways in which they detach from a sociological, rather than psychological, perspective. The techniques used in ordinary life to detach from others in order to engage in an antisocial act are superficial in the sense that they are not deeply rooted in the psyche and are primarily learned through culture. According to Blackburn (1993):

---

[11] Gabor's (1994) book, *Everybody Does It! Crime by the Public*, is the first to explore in detail crime committed by the general public. Jungian theorists (e.g., Abrahms & Zweig, 1991; Guggenbuhl-Craig, 1980; Hort, 1996; Moore, 1990) have discussed repressed evil (or shadow) that exists in all human beings and is projected onto criminals, psychopaths, "monsters," etc. Garland (1990) notes the relationship between repressed evil and punishment but does not directly focus on the psychological parallels between criminal and noncriminal antisocial behavior.

> Deviant acts may or may not be a consequence of personality characteristics, but they are not in themselves traits, and belong in a different conceptual domain of *social deviance*. . . . Socially deviant behaviors, then are neither necessary nor sufficient criteria of a disorder of personality, and there is no *a priori* reason for expecting those who are homogeneous in terms of social deviance to belong to a single category of personality deviation. (pp. 84–85)

On the other hand, the cultural-dimensional construct of psychopathy as a personality *mechanism* (rather than a clinical-categorical personality *disorder*) can enhance sociological explanations of socially deviant behavior. The integration of sociological theories of deviance and psychological theories of personality facilitates analysis of the homogeneity of socially deviant behavior notwithstanding the heterogeneity of the underlying personality deviations that may or may not support such behavior. From this perspective, the psychopathic mechanism is used by all human beings, regardless of personality organization, to engage in behavior that is harmful to the social group. This conceptualization of psychopathy distinguishes the use of the psychopathic mechanism from the affliction of the psychopathic personality. Theoretical integration also lays foundation for the abandonment of the term "secondary psychopathy," relegation of the study of the group to which the label has been applied to deviance theorists and criminologists, and an interdisciplinary approach to the study of psychopathy as both a personality disorder and a dynamic.

Psychopathy as a Cultural Projection of Evil

Most of what has been written about psychopathy has focused on the clinical condition. However, the historically pejorative association of psychopathy with evil and wickedness (Meloy, 2001) implies that the term "psychopath" holds meaning for people beyond the view of the condition as a disorder of personality. In an ethnographic study of supermax prisoners and the role of psychopathy in their classification and management, Rhodes (2002) quotes a mental health worker who worked with psychopathic prisoners who said she felt like she was "sitting with evil" (p. 451). Richman, Mercer, and Mason (1999) found that extreme crimes committed by persons diagnosed as psychopaths were attributed to evil by forensic nurses presented with vignettes involving crimes committed by schizophrenic, bipolar, and psychopathic patients. Ruffles's (2004) review of Australian judicial decisions found that psychological diagnoses of antisocial personality disorder and psychopathy have "covered the gap in the law's vocabulary left by the absence of evil" (p. 114) and ask, "why not simply drop the scientific charade and embrace evil as a legal concept?" (p. 120). In a study of layperson perceptions of psychopathy, a sample of community members attending jury duty found that layperson perceptions of psychopathy were strongly associated with perceptions of "evil" (Edens et al., 2013).

Examination of the ways in which psychopathy is conceptualized, sanctioned, and generally experienced in society is critical to understanding the implications of the construct for criminal justice. Certain subcultural groups (i.e., minorities and the individuals with lower socioeconomic status) are afforded less social trust, are more likely to come into contact with the criminal justice system, and are more likely to be in a position where they would be diagnosed with antisocial personality disorder, which, in minds of both the public and professionals working in the criminal justice system means a diagnosis of psychopathy (Stevens, 1994). Once in the grips of the criminal justice system, the individual is "transposed into a peculiar juridical reality" whereby he or she is seen as a legal subject who "bears all the attributes of free will, responsibility, and hedonistic psychology which the standard bourgeois individual is deemed to possess, no matter how far the actualities of his or her case depart from this ideal" (Garland, 1990, p. 111). "The defendant's personality and actions are viewed through the prism of this ideological form which is at once *mythical* and *socially effective* [italics mine], so that even the most destitute and desperate victims of market society are deemed to be free and equal and in control of their own destinies once they appear in a court of law" (Garland, 1990, p. 112).

The most extreme criminal defendant is molded through the prism of this mythical and socially effective ideological form into a monster, or as Polly Klaas's father put it, a "psychopath." These are the defendants who, as the news media likes to remind us, "show no remorse" after the jury verdict is read. These are the criminals who are beyond rehabilitation, and therefore, beyond social concern. The diagnosis of psychopathy (whether spoken or unspoken, scientific or not) frees the public from the guilt associated with the thought that a particular criminal justice decision may be racially or socioeconomically biased. To say that someone is a psychopath is to make a determination about one's personality, and personality is not a status protected under law. In contemporary times, the label of "psychopath" is perceived to be gender-, race-, and class-neutral—a "politically correct" social stigma driven (from a Durkheimian perspective)[12] by passion and the collective need for social

---

[12] The Durkheimian perspective refers to the work of French sociologist Emile Durkheim (1858–1917), whose work is widely known and heavily cited in discussions of the social function of crime and punishment. Durkheim theorized that crime is a normal part of social life, that passion is the driving force of punishment, that the recognition of criminality increases social solidarity among law-abiding citizens, and that without the punishment of offenders the law-abiding would be demoralized in their efforts to avoid antisocial conduct. For an in-depth discussion of Durkheim's perspective on the sociology of punishment, see Garland's (1990) *Punishment and Modern Society.*

solidarity. The psychopath is the scapegoat of last resort, and deservedly so, if it were clear where to point the collective finger.

The collective process by which psychopaths (and others) are stigmatized and sanctioned in American culture is remarkably similar to the individual process that permits psychopaths to harm without remorse. Guggenbuhl-Craig (1980) contends that most people fail to recognize the psychopathic places within themselves and believe themselves to be highly developed in those areas where they are most flawed. This sort of self-deception and self-delusion is fundamental to the psychopathic process in both the individual and culture. Psychological defense mechanisms are used collectively to maintain a positive social (and national) identity, just as the individual utilizes defenses to maintain a positive self-identity. According to Goffman (1963), there are three types of identity—social identity (characteristics attributed to an individual as a result of normative expectations), personal identity (unique physical aspects and life history items that come to be attached to an individual), and ego identity (the subjective and reflexive experiencing of oneself in relation to the world). To preserve one's ego identity, personal and social identity are consciously and unconsciously manipulated to present the self in the most positive light. In the case of the primary psychopath whose ego identity is not integrated (in terms of the "good" and "bad" sides of the self), personal and social identity are continually modified through the use of primitive defenses in an attempt to mask (from others and the self) aspects of the self that are socially and psychically experienced as negative.

The psychopath uses defense mechanisms of primitive idealization, projective identification, devaluation, omnipotent control, and denial (Gacono & Meloy, 1988; Kosson, Gacono, Klipfel, & Bodholdt, 2016). These five mechanisms revolve around the fundamental defense that psychodynamic theorists call "splitting." Splitting is the unconscious counterpart to the thinking error "cutoff" used by Yochelson and Samenow (1976), and refers to the primitive dissociation of good and bad aspects of the self and of internal representations of others (Kernberg, Selzer, Koenigsberg, Carr, & Appelbaum, 1989). Splitting results in sudden and complete reversals of feelings and conceptualizations of the self and others. Simply put, splitting is the unconscious mechanism that facilitates a worldview organized in terms of good/bad, black/white, weak/strong, etc., and a complete inability to integrate polar objects (to see gray). These defense mechanisms enable the psychopath to defend against the negative experiencing of the self. Through the combined use of unconscious defenses and cognitive thinking errors, the psychopath is able to see himself or herself as "all good" and others as "all bad" and

---

For a brief, but informative, biography of Durkheim's life and work, see Martin, Mutchnick, and Austin's (1990) *Criminological Thought: Pioneers Past and Present*.

deserving of attack. These defenses are considered "primitive" because they are an unsuccessful means of ego integration.

Nuckolls (1992) compares the psychodynamic splitting of the psyche with the split between the values of materialism and moralism in capitalist society. The contradiction between these competing values has been historically resolved, in part, through the separation and projection of the values onto delegate groups. Women have become delegates for moralism, and men for materialism, allowing the competing values to coexist despite their contradictions, and this collective psychological split has contributed to the gender-specific DSM classifications of antisocial and histrionic personality disorders. Splitting is the cultural solution to conflicting societal values. Nuckolls cites a study by Stein (1989) who proposed that international competition between the superpowers is sustained as nations "project" onto each other the disavowed characteristics of their own identities. For example, "Americans project 'repudiated collectivist dependency wishes' onto the Soviets who then, as delegates, 'act out' such wishes and thus permit Americans [to] 'act out' the reverse fantasy of independence" (Nuckolls, 1992, p. 46). Like the psychopath (and as discussed previously, occasionally the nonpsychopath), American culture defends its ego identity through the use of defense mechanisms similar to those of the psychopath. In fact, the most telling illustration of the cultural manifestation of primitive defenses is the manner in which Americans have conceptualized and responded to crime and to particular conditions and behaviors associated with psychopathy in the public mind (e.g., serial murder, sex offenders, criminal psychotics[13]).

In modern American culture, the psychopath is simultaneously glorified and despised. The popularity of the film noir and neo-noir genre (Miller, 1989; Palmer, 1994) and the films that followed such as *The Silence of the Lambs*, *Natural Born Killers*, *Se7en*, *Basic Instinct*, *Cape Fear*, and *Taxi Driver*,[14] of novels such

---

[13] These categories of offenders are mentioned here because sex offenders and serial murderers are often referred to in everyday communication and the media as psychopaths. Psychopaths are, by definition, *not* psychotic. However, the terms "psychopathy" and "psychosis" are commonly confused in the media, and if asked, "what does the word psychopath mean to you?," most people on the street will say "psycho" or "crazy." One example of this confusion are statements made by various characters in the film *Natural Born Killers*. Mickey and Mallory, the two serial murderers in the film, are referred to as "psychopaths," "psychos," "psychotics," "crazies," and "demons." At one point in the film, a fictional psychologist says that Mickey and Mallory are "psychotic, yes. Insane, no." Although it is unclear whether or not Quentin Tarantino (who wrote the screenplay) or Oliver Stone (the director) purposely included this statement to make a mockery of the psychologist (the entire film was a satire of crime, media, and public fascination with serial murder), the statement certainly confuses the terms given that psychosis is the only condition allowed under the insanity defense, and that psychopaths are (according to the scientific definition of the term) not psychotic.

[14] Film noir (black film) generally refers to a body of films that preceded and followed World War II that displayed dark themes. Films that followed what is considered to be the period of film noir (1940–1959) (Miller, 1987) that reflect noir themes are sometimes referred to as "neo-noir." Copjec

as Capote's (1965) *In Cold Blood* and Dostoyevsky's (1951) *Crime and Punishment,* and of writers such as Jack Olsen and Ann Rule (among others) whose numerous true-crime accounts of psychopaths are best sellers found in every book store and at every grocery checkout, and the more recent depictions of psychopathy in television series such as *Dexter* and books turned into Hollywood films such as *Gone Girl* are evidence of the cultural fascination with the psychopath. Many authors have briefly addressed the roots of this cultural fascination (e.g., Cleckley, 1988; Hare, 1993; Harrington, 1972; Helfgott, 2013c; Rafter, 2006; Rieber & Green, 1989; Smith, 1978). However, much is left unanswered regarding the psychological and sociocultural dynamics of this fascination and of the function of the psychopathic image.

Jungian psychologists have explored the cultural function of shadow and evil, and some have specifically addressed the relationship between psychopathy, shadow, and evil. This body of work offers a deeper understanding as to why human beings are so fascinated with evil and the symbols with which it is associated across time and culture (e.g., vampires, werewolves, witches, communists, whales, sharks, serial murderers, space aliens, criminals, psychopaths). From the beginning of time, cultures have generated stories about evil reflecting a human obsession with the light and the dark sides of nature. Many cultures find ways to make evil evident to the group. In primitive civilizations, jesters were assigned to engage in behaviors that conflicted with group rules—to laugh when everyone else cried and to cry when everyone else laughed. Some North American tribes hold "shadow catharsis festivals" whereby a member of the tribe was elected to perform, ritualistically, shocking acts contrary to group standards (Franz, 1995). Through the arts, media, and political propaganda evil is imagined and "contained" in "others"—evil impulses are projected onto another person, a movie screen, or a character in a novel for the purpose of stimulation and release (Zweig & Abrahms, 1991). This projection of evil can be witnessed in everyday life when movie crowds cheer for on-screen characters who torture and murder, when concertgoers behave violently while listening to rap, heavy metal, and punk music that contains violent lyrics and chaotic rhythmics, and when college students (among others) drink beer on the tailgates of their trucks at "execution parties" held outside local prisons.[15]

(1993) suggests that film noir has reemerged, and that we are obliged to ask why. Psychopathy is the most common psychopathology presented in film noir because the psychopathic personality best captures the noir vision (Miller, 1987). Film noir is an important cultural artifact in the interdisciplinary study of psychopathy.

[15] I draw these examples from personal experience. I attended the film *Natural Born Killers* on its opening night in a university neighborhood in Seattle. Every time the characters Mickey and Mallory brutally murdered someone the crowd whooped and hollered with excitement and laughter. Even more disturbing, while watching the Disney cartoon *The Hunchback of Notre Dame* on a

Cultural images of psychopathy reflect a scientifically sterilized and modernized symbol of evil that serves important functions in society. Myth is a cultural expression of mass consciousness that is as close to absolute truth as can be expressed in words (Hill, 1992). The notion that myth is untrue indicates that our culture is in a state of "mythic denial" and the more modern and removed we are from ancient mythic participation, the less recognizable are our myths. Film and other media representations are modern manifestations of myth that, like ancient myths, reinforce our defenses against what haunts us and, at the same time, make what haunts us more conceivable. The popular culture market enacts a "haunting movement" between our efforts to defend ourselves against what haunts us (shadow and evil) and our desire to confront it (the need for psychic balance) (Natoli, 1994).

Conceptualization of the mass media as modern myth offers insight into the cultural fascination with psychopathy (and violent crime in general) and the function of this fascination. Hare (1993) presents the following theories regarding the function of the psychopathic image in culture: (1) Visual experiencing of the psychopath allows viewers to participate with the psychopath, or as the psychopath, in a manner that is not possible through science. (2) We all identify with and are attracted to psychopaths because we want to understand the internal dynamics we share with them (i.e., we are searching for psychic balance). (3) The psychopathic image reminds psychologically healthy people of the dangers and destructiveness of psychopathy. (4) Psychopaths may recognize themselves through media images and may be compelled to seek help. (5) Media images may serve as role models for individuals with serious psychopathological disturbances

---

Sunday afternoon, I was struck by the way that the small children in the audience reacted to the violent scenes. Children who looked to be no more than five or six years old shrieked and giggled with glee every time the cartoon characters committed a violent act. Having attended a number of concerts over the years, I have witnessed an astonishing amount of destructive behavior committed by audiences while listening to the music of bands such as Guns N' Roses, Slayer, Ted Nugent, Black Sabbath, Alice in Chains and local punk and "grunge" bands. I have seen fist fights, people being thrown through windows, and people urinating on each other during these shows. Several years ago in Seattle a riot ensued and a young man was shot after a rap concert by Ice Cube. Nationwide young men and women are injured, paralyzed, or killed while "moshing" (a type of dance whereby audience members jump up and down banging into and stomping on each other), and "stagediving" (a type of dance conducted in the "pit" in front of the stage whereby audience members climb onto the stage and jump off of it into the audience, which catches the person and passes him or her around above the crowd) at the punk, metal, and grunge concerts. In reference to the last example, I once spoke to a student who drove me to the airport after I interviewed for a position at a university in Texas and was told about the "execution parties" held regularly by the students at the local penitentiary that were described to me as "like tailgating parties at football games, but at prisons instead."

Black (1991) offers evidence to support several of these theories (specifically 1, 2, and 5) in his book *The Aesthetics of Murder: A Study in Romantic Literature and Contemporary Culture,* through analysis of the cases of Mark David Chapman (who was convicted of the murder of John Lennon) and John Hinckley (who was acquitted under the insanity defense for the attempted assassination of Ronald Reagan). According to Black, the figure of the criminal is "all that remains in the modern age of the sacred and demonic characters of the age of myth" (p. 30), and the ways in which individuals react to artistic representations of aggression and violence need to be studied and accounted for to learn what specific cultural conditions help to bring about media-related murder. Using Chapman and Hinckley as examples, he contends that the boundaries between the figurative and literal criminal have become blurred in contemporary society.[16] The following passage from Black's book is provoking and particularly pertinent to the relationship between psychopathy, crime, and the projection of evil:

> Is the individual in these cases really a psycho- or sociopath who mistakes fantasy for reality, fiction for fact, art for action? Or should we regard him rather as an artistic illiterate who is unable to recognize the figural and fictive suspension from the real that art entails? Might such an individual even be a rigorous idealist or supreme literalist who detects a deeper reality hidden beneath the veil of art, and who responds iconoclastically tearing away those media-mediated appearances that bear no relation to the real? In the postindustrial, postmodern society of the late twentieth century, where violence is routinely sublimated into art and where almost every aspect of reality has been thoroughly aestheticized by advertising and the mass media, the criminal sociopath may be the individual who desperately tries to see the world as it "really" is, in all its unsublimated, sublime violence. Artistic representations of slayings provide fictional displacements for or simulacra of the act of murder for everyone except the artistically illiterate. Such persons are unable to recognize art as art, not simply because they live in a private world of make-believe fantasy, or because they have not received the proper "aesthetic education," but because they are absolute Realists who find no truth or

---

[16] Other examples include Ted Kaczynski ("The Unabomber") who was influenced by John Conrad's novel *The Secret Agent;* Barry Loukaitis, a 15-year-old who killed a teacher and two classmates with a high-powered rifle in a junior high school algebra class in Moses Lake, Washington, in 1996 who, according to the prosecutor in the case, got ideas to plan and carry out the murders from Stephen King's book *Rage* (written under a pseudonym) and the film *Natural Born Killers* (Seattle Post-Intelligencer, September 24, 1996); and two teenage girls who went on a crime spree and are said to have emulated the characters in the film *Thelma and Louise* (Seattle Post-Intelligencer, October 3, 1996).

> meaning whatsoever either in their own private fantasies (the Imaginary) or in the collective fantasies of art and the media (the Symbolic). (p. 25)[17]

Recalling Cleckley's contention that the psychopath does not have the passion to produce art, that such a person would be unable to recognize art as art is not surprising. But, does the routine sublimation of violence into art in contemporary culture play a role in the development of primary psychopathy, or in the extent to which the use of mental mechanisms of psychopathy are learned and tolerated in society at large? Can some primary psychopaths *learn* to sublimate through art if unable to procure objects of aggression? Does the cultural fascination with media violence reflect a cultural sublimation and projection (both of which are considered to be higher-level or functional defenses) or a more primitive (and dysfunctional) unconscious defense against experiencing the characteristics we share with psychopaths and/or the socio-functional nature of psychopathy?

One function of the projection of the psychopathic image in literature, film, TV, and music is that the image of the psychopath symbolizes the human ability to survive and succeed at all costs. This function is supported by historical examples of mythical characters such as the golem and the Nordic warrior (Hickey, 2006) and by theories on subclinical psychopathy (e.g., Babiak & Hare, 2006; Cleckley, 1941, 1988; Harrington, 1972; Rieber & Green, 1989; Smith, 1978) that view psychopathy as an adaptive survival strategy. From this perspective, many personality and behavioral features classically associated with psychopathy, such as superficial charm, conning and manipulative nature, and lack of empathy and remorse, promote high functioning despite underlying personality psychopathology (Hall & Benning, 2006).

Mythical characters like the golem have appeared across cultures throughout history—the Nordic warrior, the Roman God Saturn, the vampire, the werewolf, the zombie, the witch—all represent the devilish ability to destroy the innocent without conscience. For example, the medieval Jewish mythical figure, the golem, a clay figure supernaturally brought to life by a rabbi's whisper in times of trouble is said to have shown the Jewish people the value of aggressive response during violent threat. Hickey (2006) describes the golem as a type of "historical monster" who was a "robot" or "artificial person" who occasionally ran amok and had to be destroyed. According to Hickey, the "person who can orchestrate the destruction of another human being and have no remorse, no feeling for his or her victim or external need to defend his or

[17] The term "sublimation" used in this passage is a Freudian term referring to a higher-level defense mechanism that directs or transforms negative urges into a more acceptable form of outlet. Freud believed that artistic creation was a manifestation of sublimation. The term is often used loosely in reference to any redirection of socially unacceptable impulses into acceptable channels.

her actions exemplifies the term *golem*" (p. 47). *Are today's psychopaths a modernized, scientifically sterilized, empirically identifiable version of these ancient human monsters? Have ancient monster archetypes morphed into the clinical psychopaths of today? Have theories and empirical research on psychopathy evolved to the point where the phenomenon can now be scientifically explained and understood as a clinical entity that is conceptually and empirically distinct from the historical archetypes of the human monster?*

In contemporary culture, the psychopath appears in the movies, on TV, in computer games, and in real-life news media in the form of a human being as physically normal and more often than not charming and attractive. The American media glorification and dramatization of the psychopath differs from the legend of the golem in that the urge to destroy is not "successfully" projected onto a lump of clay. The legend of the golem reminded the Jewish people of the need to detach from other human beings at times when survival is at stake. However, in the story of the golem, the Jews recognize the horror of the golem and recognize that once destroyed the golem can never again be brought to life and that if it is looked upon the looker will die. This suggests a willing and deliberate projection of the evil the golem represents with the recognition that the golem is intrinsic to human nature. A more appropriate term for what could be occurring in American culture may be what psychodynamic theorists call *projective identification*—a primitive defense mechanism (used by the psychopath and the psychotic) that differs from *projection* in that an unwanted feeling is not successfully projected. In other words, as "bad, evil, criminal, aggressive, destructive" drives are *projected* onto the image of psychopath, the image is simultaneously identified with.

This projection of evil onto a particular group is a tactic historically used during times of political upheaval and social instability. According to Faith (1993), "From a functionalist point of view, community solidarity is strengthened when authorities (of the state, church, universities, medicine, law) can covertly or overtly identify a single consensual enemy, against which 'the people' can rally" (p. 13). Mythical projections of evil like the golem, the vampire, and the werewolf are "safe" in the sense that anxiety about evil (and the guilt over its recognition in ourselves) is alleviated through imagination and art. In our minds, these "others" are "containers" of evil that provide relief in the safety of a book or a film (Zweig & Abrahms, 1991). The projection of evil becomes problematic, however, when the object of the projection looks too much like an ordinary human being. As individuals are educated less through religion and myth and more through science and politics, new conceptions of evil develop. Women are evil by nature, Jews wear the tail of the devil, communists are villains, homosexuals are infectious, blacks are violent criminals. Without the mythical monster, we must defend ourselves by scientifically or politically identifying an evil "other," or else we will be terrorized or destroyed by the violence, aggression, and chaos within ourselves.

The result of this defensive process is the collective inability to articulate, and to integrate, ego identity. The salience of media violence coupled with the seductive power of fiction appears to have exacerbated individual and cultural displays of the psychopathic mechanism in 20th-century America and perhaps all of Western culture. Citing cases of John Hinckley and Mark David Chapman, Black (1991) contends that "the social norm in postindustrial society and in postmodern culture is no longer the ethical world of the real, but the aesthetic realm of the hyperreal" (pp. 138–139). The 20th-century American monster is projected onto the movie screen and the TV news—as Hannibal Lecter, Ted Bundy, Mickey and Mallory, and Richard Allen Davis—and sometimes the boundary between media images and real life are blurred to the point where the projection bounces back and becomes the unsuspecting viewer (or voyeur). The modern projection of evil is a long shot away from the stilled, cobweb-covered, (probably) gray clay figure of the medieval Jews that can only be awakened by a rabbi's secret whisper.

Juxtaposition of the clinical-categorical and cultural-dimensional models of psychopathy offers a framework with which to approach the phenomenon from four avenues: (1) psychopathy is a clinical personality disorder that is categorically distinguished by an inability to bond and a unique relationship between psychodynamic, cognitive, and behavioral levels of personality; (2) behavioral manifestations of psychopathy are inhibited, disinhibited, and generally shaped by cultural forces that, in turn, shape cultural definitions of psychopathy and perceptions about who is and who is not a psychopath; (3) psychopathy is a personality mechanism used by all human beings, individually and collectively, to a greater or lesser degree, as a means to break away (cut off, dissociate, split) from guilt feelings and human attachment when the need arises; and (4) psychopathy is a modern cultural projection of evil that is "unsuccessful" relative to the mythical and biblical projections of earlier times. The central question remains, when scientific and popular conceptions of psychopathy are intertwined with conceptions of criminality, what role does psychopathy (the construct, the clinical condition, and the personality dynamic) play in the criminal justice process?

The Remorse Factor: Fact, Fiction, and Media Depictions of Criminals, Psychopaths, and All Other Evildoers

The Psychopath's Inability to Feel

Many authors consider the fundamental feature of psychopathy to be a lack of attachment to other human beings. This feature has been referred to as a "defect in affect" (Cleckley, 1941), "lack of empathy" (Hare, 1991, 2003), absence of conscience (Hare, 1993), "failure to put oneself in another's position" (Yochelson & Samenow, 1976), and "fundamental disidentification with humanity" (Meloy, 1988). This inability to experience human emotion is what makes psychopaths more prone to criminal behavior than individuals who do not possess the disorder. Attachment is a fundamental human need. A person who is not attached to others is not constrained by guilt or remorse and consequently can harm others with no experience of emotion.

The emotional experience of the psychopath has been the focus of much research attention (Blair, Mitchell, & Blair, 2005; Demetrioff, Porter, & Baker, 2017; Kosson, Vitacco, Swagger, & Steuerwald, 2016; Patrick, 2018c; Steuerwald & Kosson, 2000; Sutton, Vitale, & Newman, 2002; Van Honk & Schutter, 2006). Many scholars, forensic practitioners, and laypersons share the view that psychopaths are emotionless. However, broad generalizations about the emotional experiences of psychopaths are contradicted by the disorder's complexity and are inconsistent with research suggesting that psychopaths are capable of experiencing some emotional states (Kosson, Vitacco, Swagger, & Steuerwald, 2016; Steuerwald & Kosson, 2000) including momentary anxiety, sadness (Reid, 1978), anger, exhilaration, and contemptuous delight (Meloy, 1988). Although there is no direct test of whether a person feels a particular emotion, researchers have measured emotion in psychopaths indirectly by examining the attribution of emotion to others (Blair, Mitchell, & Blair, 1995), emotional reactivity to positive or negative mood induction (Habel et al., 2002), startle reactivity (Patrick, 2001; Patrick, 2018a; Vaidyanathan, et al., 2011), physiological arousal to aversive stimuli (Kosson, Vitacco, Swagger, & Steuerwald, 2016; Steuerwald & Kosson, 2000), and amygdala dysfunction[18] (Blair, Mitchell, & Blair, 2005; DeLisi, Umphress, & Vaughn, 2009).

This growing body of research on the emotional experience of the psychopath suggests that the core emotional detachment factor of psychopathy is related to a weak defensive activation system (low avoidance) and to traits of high dominance and low anxiousness (Patrick, 2001). Psychopaths exhibit externalizing behavior accompanied by dispositional fearlessness (boldness) or callous unemotionality (meanness) or some combination of the two (Patrick, 2018c). Psychopaths are able to extrude painful elements from conscious self-experience (Lafarge, 1989), have a reduced sensitivity to emotion (particularly fear and anxiety) mediated by attentional differences and coping mechanisms, and that emotional impairment may be specific to situations in which the psychopath is not experiencing strong emotion (Steuerwald & Kosson, 2000). Patrick (2007) suggests that emotional processing in the psychopath can be viewed as a dual process whereby different affective processing

---

[18] The amygdala is an almond-shaped structure located in the middle of the brain. The amygdala regulates behavioral expression of emotional reactions (see Blair, Mitchell, & Blair, 2005, for discussion of amygdale dysfunction in the psychopath).

deviations are associated with the different facets of psychopathy. High Factor 1 scores are associated with "diminished defensive reactivity to aversive cues and a temperament profile involving agency and stress resistance," and high Factor 2 scores are associated with "a range of externalizing syndromes that are marked by traits of low constraint and heightened NEM [negative emotionality]" (pp. 240–242).

As a result of this incapacity for human emotion and attachment to others, the psychopath learns early on how to read other people and to manipulate them to meet personal needs. The psychopath is able to mimic—or unconsciously simulate and consciously imitate human emotion (Meloy, 1988). Yochelson and Samenow (1976) refer to the psychopath's imitation of emotional expression as "sentimentality," a cognitive thinking error unique to the "criminal personality" (a term they use synonymously with psychopathy). This view is supported by Cleckley (1941) who contended that, absent true affect, the psychopath is a "subtly constructed reflex machine that can mimic the human personality perfectly" (Cleckley, 1976, p. 228). Blair, Mitchell, and Blair (2005) suggest that the amygdala dysfunction in the psychopath contributes to impaired aversive conditioning, processing of fear and sad expressions, and instrumental learning.

This inability to feel makes it possible for the psychopath to harm other people without guilt and makes it impossible for the psychopath to experience empathy and remorse.

Why do they always say, He (or occasionally she) "showed no remorse"?

"A sinister, abhorrent and entitled sexual deviant has been jailed for 16 years for the prolonged sexual abuse of two children. . . . *The defendant shows* ***no remorse*** . . . *he continues to deny the offending*" (Leask, May 10, 2018).

"[A]ccording to court documents, *he showed* ***no remorse***, only cared about 'not being in the newspaper.'" (Man charged with paying high school students for sex acts) (Runevitch, May 8, 2018).

"*For that* ***lack of remorse***, *for his racially charged motive, for the impact it had on families, Roof deserves the death penalty,* Nathan Williams, an assistant U.S. attorney." (In response to mass shooter Dylann Roof's jail writings—"I would like to make it crystal clear I do not regret what I did. I am not sorry. I have not shed a tear for the innocent people I killed," he wrote, and later continued, "I have shed a tear of self-pity for myself. I feel pity that I had to do what I did in the first place") (Maxwell, January 4, 2017).

"He showed ***no sign of remorse*** or concern for the victims of his reckless driving, three of whom were still lying on the ground" (Hosen, October 16, 2015).

"Bride *showed* ***no remorse*** in husband's death" (Associated Press, March 26, 2014).

> *"I looked at him a lot—***no remorse***. . . . The evidence showed it was all about him."* (Juror after sentencing of a father convicted of abusing his infant son who was found with 42 fractures—including to each finger and toe—bite marks, severe bruising and at least one of his fingernails was torn off) (Emily, April 1, 2011).
>
> *"Grant is a perverted, callous and violent individual. He is a sexual predator who preyed on the most vulnerable section of our society. He has said nothing to us about his offending and has not as far as we know shown* ***any sign of remorse****."* (Scotland Yard commander in reference to Delroy Grant, a gerontofile suspected of up to 1,000 rapes of elderly women, sex attacks, and burglaries) (Dixon & Twomey, March 25, 2011).
>
> *"The Florida pastor whose burning of a Koran last month set off a deadly protest in Afghanistan today called the deaths "very tragic" but expressed* ***no remorse*** *about his stunt."* (Regarding the pastor of a small nondenominational church in Florida who publicly burned the Koran, which incited a deadly riot in Afghanistan in which a dozen people were killed, two of whom were beheaded) (Johnson, April 1, 2011).
>
> *"She has demonstrated* ***no remorse*** *and no respect for the court."* (Jury consultant commenting on the nude colored leather dress actress Lindsay Lohan wore to her grand theft hearing) ("Lindsay Lohan shows no remorse with tight court outfit," March 11, 2011).

The phrase he or she "showed no remorse" has practically become official court and media dictum as the final reference to the convicted as they are escorted out of the courtroom. This statement is directed at individuals who appear to show no emotion after having committed a horrific crime or in defiance of societal norms. Why is its absence in the expressions of the convicted so noteworthy?

The absence of remorse in individuals convicted of crimes is remarkable because emotional experience, empathy, and remorse are human indicators of public safety, community ties, and respect for the social contract. Individuals who blatantly defy this courtroom expectation are in danger of being perceived as cold, callous, remorseless, and by extension, psychopathic. Certainly not all convicted offenders are psychopathic, but the association between lack of remorse and psychopathy and the connotations of the absence of the expression of remorse in the aftermath of crime have broad implications and consequences.

Psychopathy, Criminality, and Evil

Ruffles (2004) argues that the law's avoidance of the concept of evil has resulted in a reliance on the mental health profession to explain evil in expert terms through diagnoses of antisocial personality disorder and psychopathy.

Psychopaths are often referred to as "snakes" or "reptiles" in both popular culture and the academic literature. Meloy (1988) proposes the reptilian-state theory suggesting that the emotional state of the psychopath is more similar to that of reptiles than humans. The reptilian cerebrotype (brain structure) is the first evolutionary step in the development of the human brain. The common denominator between mammals is the structure of the limbic system in the brain that is responsible for the experience and expression of emotion supporting behaviors such as parental response to offspring, hoarding, and sociability. The brain structure of the reptile supports certain behaviors such as establishment and defense of territories, hunting, feeding, mating, dominance, competition, aggression, and imitation. Like reptiles, psychopaths are missing behaviors that are products of the limbic system including hoarding (to protect the future) and social behavior. Unlike most mammals, the primary psychopath does not become attached to others, express emotion, or engage in hoarding behavior (i.e., saving for a rainy day). Like the reptile, the primary psychopath is defensive, predatory, aggressive, competitive, and imitative (superficial). Clinical observations support the idea that psychopaths engage in acts of visual predation or a "reptilian stare." According to Meloy (1988), the psychopath's reptilian state is a psychobiological state that can be momentary or long-lasting, and the conceptual parallels between psychopathic behavior and the "functional prevalence of the reptilian cerebrotype" are striking (p. 69). There is no neurophysiological or neuroanatomical research to support the association between the brain structures and behaviors of psychopaths and reptiles. However, the psychopath-reptile analogy, discussed in the research literature and more widely in popular culture, may provide additional insight into the distinctive emotional life of the psychopath.

Psychopathy, Crime, and Criminal Justice Policy and Practice

Study of psychopathy is crucial to the understanding of criminal behavior and criminal justice policy and practice. Psychopathy explains human predatory aggression and violence (Porter, Woodworth, & Black, 2018). The emotional dysfunction in the psychopath and associated traits are empirically associated with aggressive behavior, particularly instrumental, cold-blooded, predatory behavior. However, the condition calls to question fundamental premises upon which the criminal justice system is based. To understand psychopathy is to doubt the basic notions of free will, determinism, insanity, criminality, personality, and the human person. Psychopaths choose to commit immoral and criminal acts freely (Yochelson & Samenow, 1976), although their choices may be determined in early infancy (Meloy, 1988). Psychopaths are not legally insane, yet they are personality disordered and more dangerous and difficult to explain than those who are (Cleckley, 1941, 1988). Most psychopaths are criminals, but most criminals are not psychopaths (Hare,

1993). Psychopaths are not attached to others (Meloy, 1988), but attachment is universal to humans and mammals (Ainsworth, 1989). Psychopaths lack moral sense, though morality distinguishes person from animal (Murphy, 1972). Psychopathy can be considered categorically or dimensionally, but where the line is drawn is often arbitrary or based on psychometric tests that do not measure a homogeneous condition.

The Influence of the Concept of Psychopathy at Each Stage of the Criminal Justice System: An Overview

Psychopaths are criminally versatile. Those who break the law "run the gamut from petty theft and fraud to cold-blooded violence" (Hare, 1998, p. 195). Cleckley (1941, 1988) distinguishes the psychopath from the typical criminal who has passion, purpose, and loyalty to a particular group or code of conduct. The criminal works consistently for a goal that can be understood by the average person, sparing himself or herself as much shame and discomfort as possible at the expense of another. The typical murderer does so in the heat of passion or for a particular purpose such as money or fame, or as the result of psychosis, neurotic compulsion, or some other psychopathological condition. Unlike the typical criminal, the psychopath is not purposive at all, engaging in acts that make no sense to the average observer without the slightest attention to consequences and with absolutely no sense of loyalty to anything or anyone. And unlike the psychotic criminal, who is exempt from legal responsibility, the psychopath does not "have the common decency to go crazy" (Rieber & Green, 1989, p. 48).

Sociologists and criminologists have addressed the relationship between emotional attachment, cognition, and behavior using different terminology and a more general application than have psychologists. In sociological terms, crime is associated with weak or broken social bonds (Hirschi, 1969), defensive techniques (Sykes & Matza, 1957), and linguistic accounts that justify and excuse behavior (Gabor, 1994; Scully & Marolla, 1984). Direct parallels can be drawn between Hirschi's (1969) social bond theory and Meloy's (1992) theory of violent attachments, between Sykes and Matza's (1957) techniques of neutralization and Kernberg's (1987) primitive borderline defenses, and between Scully and Marolla's (1984) findings on the vocabulary of rapists, Gabor's (1994) study of crime by the public, and Rieber and Vetter's (1995) research on the deceptive aberration of language in the psychopath. The similarities across disciplines in the explanations of antisocial behavior reflect an important theoretical link that is necessary to examine the congruence between the psychopathy as a categorical versus a dimensional concept.

Because nonpsychopaths have formed attachment in infancy, it makes sense to analyze the ways in which they detach from a sociological, rather than psychological, perspective. The techniques used in ordinary life to detach from others in order to engage in an antisocial act are superficial in the sense that they are not deeply rooted in the psyche and are primarily learned through culture. According to Blackburn (1993):

> Deviant acts may or may not be a consequence of personality characteristics, but they are not in themselves traits, and belong in a different conceptual domain of *social deviance*. . . . Socially deviant behaviors, then are neither necessary nor sufficient criteria of a disorder of personality, and there is no *a priori* reason for expecting those who are homogeneous in terms of social deviance to belong to a single category of personality deviation. (pp. 84–85)

It is important to remember that crime is a *behavioral manifestation*, while psychopathy is an *internal psychological condition* that produces a particular set of traits and behaviors. In some cases psychopathy may produce crime. However, all criminals are not psychopaths. Clinically and categorically, psychopathy is a personality disorder possessed by an individual that is shaped through environmental, situational, and biological factors. Culturally and dimensionally, psychopathy can be conceptualized as a continuum of traits and behaviors that are possessed by all human beings to a lesser or greater degree. Criminal behavior may be produced by an individual who is clinically and categorically psychopathic or by nonpsychopaths (who may possess any one of a number of internal conditions) who possess psychopathic traits that relieve the guilt associated with committing a particular act.

Ethical Issues Intrinsic to the Conceptualization of Psychopathy and Application of the Construct to Criminal Justice Policy and Practice

The label "psychopath" has such a negative connotation that the potential for harm when the label is used has to be a central part of any discussion of the application of the concept on an individual and practical level. *When individuals are given a score on a forensic assessment test like the PCL-R that indicates they are a primary or secondary psychopath, what are the consequences of this diagnosis? Should inmates who are administered the PCL-R be asked to give consent prior to administration? If research shows that when jurors are presented information indicating that a defendant is psychopathic, and they are more likely to vote in favor of a sentence of death, should such testimony be allowed in capital sentencing decisions? If research shows that there is a potential to alter developmental pathways of psychopathy in adolescent years or earlier, is it acceptable to forensically assess psychopathy in a child to determine if he or she is a budding psychopath? If research shows that psychopaths are less amenable to treatment, is it acceptable to screen out psychopaths in correctional treatment programs? What if a parent in a divorce proceeding is called a psychopath by an angry spouse and scores higher than average on measures of psychopathy in a child-custody evaluation? What are the ethical implications of these and other applications of the psychopathy construct in the criminal and civil justice systems?*

In the years since publication of the PCL-R, the construct of psychopathy has made its way into a broad range of decision points in the criminal and civil justice systems. Expert testimony on psychopathy has been presented in civil and criminal cases including witness credibility, child custody, juvenile transfers to adult court, insanity, competency to stand trial, civil torts, and civil commitment. Review of cases show that psychopathy is a "powerful diagnostic label that can exert profound influence over the legal decisions rendered by the courts" (Lyon & Ogloff, 2000, p. 139). Although the PCL-R does better than other instruments in predicting general and violent recidivism (Hemphill & Hare, 2004), there is a high false-positive rate when the PCL-R is used in the prediction of dangerousness (Freedman, 2001), and some authors have gone so far as to say that there should be an ethical ban on psychiatric and psychological predictions of dangerousness in capital sentencing proceedings and "Death to the Psychopath" (Cavadino, 1998, p. 5). There is evidence that PCL-R testimony has been misused and misinterpreted in legal settings (Edens, 2001), that the PCL-R's ability to measure offender risk may not be as unparalleled as the research literature suggests (Gendreau, Goggin, & Smith, 2002; Walters, 2012), that psychopathic defendants are more likely to be perceived as dangerous and sentenced to death (Edens & Petrila, 2006; Edens, Petrila, & Kelley, 2018), that the term "psychopath" is "moralism masquerading as medical science" (Cavadino, 1998, p. 6) that carries "considerable emotional baggage and may lead to harmful stigmatization or processing of offenders by poorly informed criminal justice authorities who often perceive psychopathy as a discrete entity or taxon" (Gendreau, Goggin, & Smith, 2002, p. 413). Ultimately, "for most of those labeled as psychopathic it is a real stroke of bad luck" (Cavadino, 1998, p. 8).

In the 1996 article "Psychopathy: A Clinical Construct Whose Time Has Come," published in *Criminal Justice & Behavior,* Robert Hare predicted:

> Even those opposed to the very idea of psychopathy cannot ignore its potent and explanatory and predictive power, if not as a formal construct then as a static risk factor. In the next few years, indices of psychopathy almost certainly will become a routine part of the assessment batteries used to make decisions about competency, sentencing, diversion, placement, suitability for treatment, and risk for recidivism and violence. (Hare, 1996a, p. 49)

True to his prediction, over 20 years later, the PCL-R has become the single most widely used measure of psychopathy in clinical and research settings on an international scale, and the psychopathy construct has made its way into a broad range of forensic, legal, civil, and criminal justice settings (Babiak et al., 2012). But Walters (2004, p. 137) cautions, "for the majority of individuals who respond to and act on the psychopathic label—judges, prosecutors, correctional workers, parole boards, probation officers—do not appreciate the intricacies and limitations of psychological testing and may misuse the results to the detriment of the individual and society." In light of the extent to which the psychopathy construct has been utilized in the criminal justice systems around the world and the considerable ethical ramifications of its misuse, comprehensive examination of the role of the construct of psychopathy for criminal justice is timely and critical.

CHAPTER TWO

Theory and Research on Psychopathy

[T]raditionally confused with a fairly heterogeneous group under a loose and variously understood term, a type of patient exists who could, without exaggeration, still be called the forgotten man of psychiatry. If this patient can be presented as he has appeared so clearly during years of observation, if some idea can be given of his ubiquity, and, above all, if interest can be promoted in further study of his particular status among other human beings, I shall be abundantly satisfied.

—Hervey Cleckley (1941, 1988, p. 17)

Moralizing about psychopathy is an ever-present potential contaminant of scientific research on psychopathy, especially since the principle impairment in psychopaths is one of empathic judgment. Can we think objectively about a clinical problem that by its very nature is partially defined by community morals?

—J. Reid Meloy (2001, p. 171)

The historical evolution of the concept of psychopathy is a fascinating journey through the intersection of religion, science, law, and criminological and psychological theory. The metaphor of the hydra has been used to describe the historically fused but contemporarily separate and antagonistic relationship between religion, law, and science. The "transition from ancient sorcery to modern science . . . was not as smooth or complete as we like to believe" (Faigman, 1999, p. 7). The history of the concept of psychopathy from early references to contemporary research is a case example of this bumpy intersection of religion, science, and law.

Early references to biblical and mythological monsters that possessed characteristics very similar to the psychopath of today have evolved into complex dialogue on the nature of human depravity and its societal response, diagnostic consensus and classification, the development and standardization of psychometric measurement, links between psychopathy to criminal behavior and recidivism, and to sophisticated theoretical perspectives and empirical research on different components of the condition. The terms "evil" and "wicked" are outside the paradigms of science, yet historical, clinical, and contemporary popular cultural references to psychopaths (Meloy, 2001) suggest that it is very difficult to untangle moral judgment from clinical diagnosis, especially when we are talking about a psychopathological condition characterized by chronic emotional detachment that predisposes a person to engage in aggressive, predatory human behavior that harms other people, threatens public safety, and violates criminal law. *Can a human condition so intimately connected to the metaphysical concept of evil be understood and explained scientifically, treated fairly and ethically, and managed effectively in the mental health and criminal justice systems? Where does clinical diagnosis end and moral judgment begin? Will identification, assessment, and understanding of the fundamental feature of psychopathy that produces the cold, remorseless, defect in affect and human disidentification in the psychopath take us any further in terms of determining how do deal with and manage these individuals in our communities?*

Historical Evolution of the Concept of Psychopathy

Early Development of the Concept[1]

The year 1801 marks the first description of the condition now recognized as psychopathy. Pinel was the first to describe a condition he called "manie sans delire" (mania without delusions), based on the case of a wealthy aristocrat "unmoved by passion." Prior to Pinel's discovery it was universally believed that the intellect was involved in insanity. Pinel's mania without delusions was a condition of mania existing with no apparent loss of cognitive ability. Pinel's findings spurred several decades of discourse over the issue of whether insanity was moral or intellectual. Prior to this, conceptions of insanity were based on demon influences and inherent derangement. The discovery of a form of madness that did not include delusion or delirium shook long-standing beliefs about how insanity could be identified and what in fact it actually was (Maughs, 1941).

These questions appeared almost a half century after what has been marked as the beginning of modern criminology. In 1764 Cesare Beccaria's *Trattato dei delitti e elle pena* was published in Italy, and in 1767 republished in London, under its English title, *Essay on Crimes and Punishments*. Beccaria, and other idealists, such as Montesquieu and Voltaire, held the values of intellectual

---

[1] Maughs offers an extensive account of the evolution and historical development of the concept of psychopathy from the 18th century through the 1930s. Much of the review presented here on the development of the concept of psychopathy from the late 1700s through the 1930s is adapted from Maughs.

and artistic romanticism and the objective of rejecting the abuses and powers of the state that had resulted from abuses encountered through the social philosophy of "classical realism" that had embodied the views of the church (Jones, 1986). The theological beliefs that demonic evil was at the root of deviance had caused hundreds of years of abuse and power imbalance, and the classical idealists wanted change.

This change was realized toward the end of the 18th century and the beginning of the 19th century. Technological advance and the Industrial Revolution caused towns to grow and prosper, crime to flourish, and the ideas of maximization of production with minimal effort to rule social interaction as well as economics. Jeremy Bentham adapted these economic principles to criminology and led the utilitarian movement that took hold during the first three decades of the 1800s. Utilitarianism offered practical implementation of the idealist philosophy directing concern toward prevention of crime through policing and the advent of "functional" prisons designed as workhouses and carefully planned prison programs. With Bentham's ideas came a century of development in corrections and policing, and throughout the criminal justice system a new, humane, and "functional" way to deal with criminals and other social undesirables was under way (Barnes, 1972; Foucault, 1977, 1995; Jones, 1986).

The birth of modern criminology and changes in the concept of insanity spawned new beliefs about the origins of deviance and raised difficult questions. Pinel's discovery that a mental disorder existed that could not be identified through intellectual impairment intruded on the control that Beccaria's ideas and Bentham's actions had placed on the criminal justice system. *If a person could be insane and continue to have all of his or her mental faculties intact, who would be included in this new and broader definition? If insanity is the result of moral defect as well as intellectual, how could free will and responsibility be determined in the eyes of the law?*

In 1837 Prichard was the first to popularize the term "moral insanity," separating insanity into the two forms of intellectual and moral. Prichard believed the prognosis of moral insanity was more unfavorable than the intellectual. Prichard's description encountered problems because during his time the etiology of mental disease was unknown and classification was based on symptomatology and behavior. Prichard's description was based on behavioral features that included individuals experiencing a wide variety of different conditions sharing only outstanding symptoms. Soon after, the association between psychopathy and criminality became of concern. In 1838 Woodward suggested that more attention needed to be paid to claims of moral insanity in criminal cases distinguishing moral insanity from moral turpitude and the moral depravity associated with crime by the diseased function of organs and nerves connected with the brain. Woodward supported the concept of moral insanity and saw its roots as physical disease but was not comfortable with the automatic connections his colleagues were making between moral insanity and criminal behavior.

In 1846, Connolly, the first to maintain that there is always some degree of cognitive defect in moral insanity, suggested that imbecility and idiocy could affect moral faculties and believed the condition to be congenital or possibly a result of permanent disease or temporary illness causing defect in some portion of the brain. A decade later the discussion of the relationship of psychopathy and criminality continued with the 1857 article called "Moral Insanity" published in the *American Journal of Insanity*. The article dealt with the importance of the doctrine of moral insanity in criminal cases, the prelude to the half-century-long controversy over whether the concept of insanity should be based on moral or intellectual defect, or both. In this article, the author considers moral insanity the usual condition of "bad men," says, "The law does not care whether insanity is intellectual or moral," and rejects the doctrine of moral insanity on the grounds that it is "elastic enough to cover every possible shade of criminality" (Maughs, 1941, p. 335).

Not surprisingly, this article appeared a decade after the M'Naghten case (1843), which held that an individual was not guilty by reason of insanity if their actions were the result of mental defect or disease, cognitive impairment (strictly the ability to "know"), and the understanding of the "nature of the criminal act" and of "right" from "wrong." Modern formulations of the insanity defense have been derived from this case. Thus, much of the post-1843 discussion regarding mental conditions (particularly psychopathy) that were historically linked with insanity involved scrutiny of the components of the new legal definition of the concept.

From 1840s through the 1870s emphasis was placed on clarification of the question of intellectual defect in moral insanity (Jones, 2017). Kitching wrote that moral and intellectual faculties differed across people and that there is no relation between the development or strengths of the two faculties. A person could possess great intellectual development with major deficiencies in moral abilities, or high moral development and low intellectual ability. Kitching separated moral insanity into two forms: (1) idiocy and imbecility existing from birth affecting the moral faculties and (2) developmental arrest of moral faculties in early life whereby free action was perverted or impeded. This separation of moral insanity into two forms was the first separation of the disorder into the types now known as primary and secondary. Kitching's basis for this separation may not be identical to the criteria that many others used after Kitching; however, this idea that the disorder exists in two types has remained in the discourse. Kitching's claim that intellectual and moral faculties are unrelated is also still a major component of the concept of psychopathy, since it is now a common belief that psychopathy is not associated with low IQ (Hare, 1970; McCord & McCord, 1964; Wilson & Herrnstein, 1985), and although some have associated the disorder with high IQ (Cleckley, 1982; Yochelson &

Samenow, 1976), it is generally believed that IQ influences the manifestation of the disorder but is not associated with the underlying disorder.

Excitement over scientific positivism and its application to the social sciences was likely the impetus for Kitching's and other distinctions between the two types of psychopathy. Darwin's (1859) *Origin of Species* inspired researchers to try to identify traits that could predict criminal behavior, many of whom chose to go beyond the traditional disease model. Thus, the disease model was extended to the idea that developmental arrest could also cause moral insanity (and other deviant conditions), and therefore there had to be two forms of the disorder (Jones, 1986).

In 1866 Falret suggested that physicians abandon examining the act or conduct of the patient and look at the individual as a whole through his or her physical and moral condition and past, present, and future. Falret raised issue with the broad categories of Pinel and Prichard and suggested taking several varieties of mental disease out of the classification of moral insanity. Falret also discussed the question of confinement and the difficulties in determining insanity in cases of moral insanity. He believed that there should be no absolute rule, that sometimes confinement would be necessary for medical reasons and other times for security objectives, and that determining insanity in such cases would be a difficult task given legal issues regarding partial and total responsibility. Falret's views were, like Kitching's, consistent with the newfound positivist philosophies. Falret introduced issues that were important with respect to the overlapping concerns of the mental health and criminal justice systems. These issues (specifically, whether to treat or to punish, who should decide this, and who should receive which sanction) are still very much a part of the relationship between the criminal justice and mental health systems.

In 1873 there was brief return to the linking of moral insanity with sin. Ordronaux believed that it is the moral superiority of humans that places him or her above the animals, and with no evidence of physical pathology it could only be concluded that moral insanity was not a mental condition or disease but that the condition was moral depravity, in other words, conscious sin. The presentation of this seemingly backward notion following the century-long discussion (in the psychological fields) appearing to lead away from this view was not the only one of its kind during this time. Several years later the positivist movement in criminology began with Cesare Lombroso's search for the "criminal man." Although Lombroso did not directly equate criminality with sin as Dr. Ordronaux did, he associated criminality with moral inferiority and encouraged other researchers to search for tangible ways in which deviants differed from "normal" human beings. Between 1878 and 1897 Lombroso wrote *L'Uomo delinquente*. Lombroso's work consisted of five editions, three volumes, and 1,900 pages of items and elements related to criminality. Lombroso is most known for his focus on "atavistic" traits related to criminality consisting of physical features akin to those of prehistoric man, but his work points to numerous other types of causative agents as well (Vold, 1958).

Lombroso and his followers Enrico Ferri and Raffaele Garafolo represent the beginning of positivist criminology. Ferri and Garafolo were interested in both constitutional and developmental criminality and extended Lombroso's theory that physical anomalies cause criminality to the idea that "psychic anomalies" and psychological attributes that could be inherited or learned in early stages of infant development also cause crime (Jones, 1986). These ideas, published mainly in the criminological literature, were consistent with those of Kitching that led to the two-typed classification of moral insanity. Thus, in both the mental health and criminal justice fields, deviance was being separated into two types.

Between 1877 and 1900 two schools of thought existed regarding the concept of moral insanity. The first denied the existence of the concept based on the philosophical grounds of the ideas such as those of Falret and Ordronaux and the 1957 "Moral Insanity" article. The second referred the condition to physical deficiencies and proceeded study in the Lombrosian direction in search of objective etiological features. Many writers denied the existence of insanity without involvement of intellectual faculties and were considered to be of the first group. Several writers, such as Savage in 1882, tried to find a middle ground suggesting that in cases of moral insanity there could be intellectual impairment so slight that it is unnoticed (consistent with what Kitching had proposed in 1857). He (also) divided moral insanity into two groups, distinguishing those whose insanity was the result of mental disease from those whose condition was the result of social effects of early development. Other writers, such as Gasquet, furthered Savage's view suggesting that the difficulties in conceiving of moral insanity as distinct from intellectual insanity arose because the complexities of mental processes were being ignored, and that freedom of choice was dependent on the integrity of the brain. Others, such as Tuke in 1885 continued this thought offering a developmental twist suggesting that since moral feelings were the latest to develop, it was possible that the condition of moral insanity may be the natural outcome of mental evolution and dissolution.

Although several writers attempted to resolve the conflict through the linking of slight intellectual impairment with moral defect, most who believed in the unity of the mind insisted that moral insanity was sin and that there was no such will that was "free" from intellectual direction unless there was evidence of physical disease or defect causing the intellectual as well as the moral faculties to be impaired. These writers considered Pinel's mania without delirium and Prichard's moral lunatics to be cases of early stages of insanity that would eventually exhibit delirium. These writers resisted turning away from the idea that deviance is rooted in biology and that this disturbed constitution leaves no mental component untouched.

In 1888 there was a meeting of the Italian Phreniatric Society that was dominated by discussion of moral insanity. Throughout the days of discussion in this meeting all of the prominent arguments were addressed. Moral insanity was called a metaphysical concept because morality was based on degrees of civilization. This idea of moral insanity as an uncivilized nature was attacked for reverting to nonpsychological Lombrosian theories of "atavism." Lombroso attacked theories of others, calling them metaphysical, and discussion about all different degrees of defect, contributory factors, and etiological explanation from the biological to the developmental to the sociological to the philosophical abounded. The issues presented in this meeting set the stage for the many studies that would investigate the existence of the separate concepts of psychopathy and criminality and the awareness that each may be rooted in constitutional or developmental etiologies.

The first quarter of the 20th century marked a switch to what Maughs (1941) calls the "period of psychopathy." Prior to 1900 discussions of moral insanity were limited to the conflicts between the philosophical and the anthropological schools over the unity of the mind versus the separation of moral and intellectual spheres. During this time emphasis moved from theoretical discourse to productive research on the causes and problems of psychopathy. In 1888 Koch had coined the term "psychopathic inferiority" referring to defects preventing the individual from adjusting to the environment. Koch included both congenital and acquired conditions. There was some resistance to the use of the term "psychopathic" because the term had been used as a synonym for insanity. Gradually distinctions were made between the term "psychic constitutional inferiority" introduced by Meyer referring to definite physical inferiority and "psychopathic personality" referring to conditions lacking apparent physical defect. With this, psychopathy became linked with the developmental rather than the constitutional form of moral insanity, and study of the disorder expanded to environmental influences.

The Period of Psychodynamics

During the first decades of the 1900s study of the relationship between the moral and intellectual components of the psychopathy continued, in addition to research investigating the relationships between constitutional inferiors and dementia precox, and between epilepsy and psychopathy. In 1913 the British Mental Deficiency Act was passed legally distinguishing "true mental defectives" as those displaying mental defect from an early age coupled with criminal propensity on which punishment has no effect. These "defectives" were, in other words, stupid criminals (a classification hardly consistent with most of the historical or contemporary definitions of psychopaths).

In 1914 Birnbaum published *The Psychopathic Criminal*. His work represents a major contribution in the history of the study of psychopathy. His ideas, over 100 years old, most resemble those of the contemporary researchers and uncannily coincide with contemporary theories. Birnbaum believed that psychometric tests were responsible for misclassifying psychopathy with other disorders. He emphasized the emotional component of psychopathy that could not be measured and held that the distinguishing feature of the disorder was pathological affectivity and that individual personality was the important determinant of psychopathy rather than individual character traits. He saw no parallelism between criminality and psychopathy and did not believe that criminal behavior was necessarily the predominant manifestation of psychopathy (Maughs, 1941; McCord & McCord, 1964). Birnbaum believed that psychopaths could possess high or low intelligence and that intelligent psychopaths were able to neutralize antisocial tendencies, while high intelligence could not sufficiently mediate tendencies motivated by emotional factors (Maughs, 1941). He found that criminality was not the most frequent manifestation of psychopathy and that criminal behavior usually depended on traits that made adaptation to general social life difficult. Thus, psychopathy was based on endogenous factors, while criminality was based on external influences and could not be considered a stigma of degeneracy.

Interesting distinctions were also made between types of psychopaths during this time. In 1917 Tredgold recognized primary psychopaths as those with an absence of moral sense, and secondary psychopaths as those whose moral sense is defective as a result of an absence of training. The first group was considered by Tredgold to consist of primarily females, largely prostitutes, who, as a result of their general weakness of will, were unable to resist ordinary temptations of everyday life. This belief was common at this time as a result of Victorian attitudes about women, hysteria, and the inherent defect in morality of the female nature (Chesler, 1971). Interestingly, however, regardless of how women were described and segregated, they were included in the study of psychopathy in these early years. Tredgold's placement of females in the primary category is directly opposite of Karpman's (1941, 1946) placement of females in the secondary category. These arbitrary gender classifications are likely based on changes in social attitude rather than on actual psychological phenomena. Tredgold's placement of women in the primary group is one of the few deviations from the historical tendency to classify women as mentally ill (Allen, 1987), rather than associate them with any form of criminality. Perhaps, in Tredgold's time, because psychopathy was not thought of as distinct from insanity as it is today, there was more of a tendency to classify females as such.

In 1918 Glueck (one of the few researchers mentioned in both the psychological and criminology literatures) turned attention to the relationship between psychopathy and crime. His work marks the beginning of the objective study of the etiology of psychopathic criminality, and his findings supported Birnbaum's hypotheses. In a study of 608 prisoners he found 91

(15 percent) could be classified as "native-born" psychopaths. Thus, the majority, although they were legally defined as criminals, were not psychopaths based on the psychological definition of the term. Glueck observed various features of this group of psychopaths, such as number of sentences; indulgence in alcohol, drugs, and/or gambling; deviations from normal behaviors in childhood; school and work career; and conceptions about sex. Glueck found the majority of this group had numerous prison sentences, deviated from normal behaviors in childhood, had irregular and inefficient school and work careers, and held low morals with respect to sexual behavior (Maughs, 1941). However, because all of Glueck's subjects were offenders, his study did not help to resolve the issue Birnbaum raised regarding lack of parallelism between psychopathy and criminality, and oddly, this particular issue was not raised again for many years.

The 1920s are marked by studies of the histories and characteristics of psychopaths in an attempt to find a legitimate line of demarcation. In 1920 Froukel wrote that the concept of psychopathy lacked objective criteria, just as others had said of the old concept of moral insanity. Froukel said that the line of demarcation between psychopathy and normality was arbitrary and gradual, that the stigma of the designation of psychopathy based on this arbitrariness was valueless, and that judgment of the individual had to be based on past history alone. Many of the subjects of the 1920s studies were drawn from highly selective groups. Army hospitals were a fertile ground for male subject selection because it was a common belief that psychopaths were attracted to the military life (Maughs, 1941). Female subjects were drawn from courthouses and from groups of delinquents. Although these studies may have provided interesting information about the individual subjects and groups, they offer little to help distinguish features of psychopathy because of the highly selective groups from which they were drawn. Results from the studies of female psychopaths in particular may be especially problematic because the groups studied are not well defined and the presentations of the results appear to be unrelated to the usual features assessed in other studies.

Theories of adjustment and attachment also appeared during the 1920s. Johnson (1923) wrote that chronic psychopathic inferiors suffered from either too little or too much fear reaction, and as a result there were opposite bases for failure in adjustment. Johnson believed personality was the primary determinant of psychopathic behavior and that fear was the basic emotion of the individual. Her groups consisted of individuals who were either too weak or too strong in "moral impressionability." The weakly impressioned became bad-natured when frustrated by desire, and low levels of fear enhanced this bad nature. She called these individuals psychopaths. Johnson called the strongly impressioned "psychoneurotics" who were drawn to acting out in flight from high levels of fear. Johnson argued that the two groups were only superficially similar, that diagnosis could not be made based on symptoms alone, and that only deep study into causation of behavior would reveal the differences between the groups. Johnson also believed that the psychopathic defect was inborn and that the psychopath could not be cured. Her distinction of fearful and fearless groups marks the first distinction of psychopathy based on opposite fear reactions. The idea that primary psychopaths are fearless and anxiety-free while secondary psychopaths are fearful and highly anxious is found in other major works (e.g., Karpman, 1941), and it has since been empirically established that traditional measures of psychopathy encompass both anxious and nonanxious types (Lykken, 1957).

Theories of attachment also consistent with contemporary perspectives appeared during the 1920s as well. Clark believed the behavior of psychopaths was the result of a lack in the development of "sentiments." Suttie explained psychopathy in terms of lacking "social rapport" and suggested that intellectual impairment existed in these individuals, not as the cause of moral defect, but as the result of the absence of personal attachments necessary in the proper fostering of intellectual development. Other writers described the psychopath as lacking in "moral wisdom," characterizing the psychopath as intellectually capable of acquiring school knowledge, while devoid of all altruistic and moral feeling and possessing strong antisocial tendencies.

Psychodynamic perspectives entered in the mid-1920s. Maughs (1941) calls the emphasis on psychodynamic processes that began in the 1920s the "period of psychodynamics" in the history of the concept of psychopathy, and his account of the evolution of the concept ends during the height of this period. Smith, in 1926, wrote that the definition of moral insanity was misleading and superfluous. Smith saw no absolute system of morality, believed that all people were born with no moral sense, that this sense developed through psychodynamic processes, and that minor degrees of regression resulted in psychopathic behavior (Maughs, 1941). Maughs cites Karpman, Partridge, and Henderson as the primary writers in the beginnings of the psychodynamic approach toward understanding psychopathy. The ideas of these authors spurred a return to theoretical study of the etiology of the disorder. This period of study provided a powerful foundation for contemporary applied research.

In 1924, Karpman, who later produced major works on the subject of psychopathy, conducted a lecture at St. Elizabeth's Hospital. He discussed the emotional component of the disorder and emphasized that psychopathy was only one of the different types of conditions found in criminal populations. Karpman believed that property crimes were the psychopath's usual offense. This emphasis on emotional issues changed the direction of the study of the etiology of the disorder. Attention was directed to psychodynamic, developmental, and social processes. Many writers supported Karpman's position, and new emphasis was placed on theories of phenogenic etiology rather than on theories espousing congenital factors or demonic possession (Maughs, 1941).

Partridge (1930) added to Karpman's perspective believing that psychopathy is characterized by feelings of inadequacy, insecurity, and inferiority accompanied by strong demands met by the individual through a variety of reaction patterns, generally in the form of tantrums, sulking, and/or running away. Partridge saw psychopaths as having failed to pass through normal childhood phases that would allow them to properly adjust to reality. These individuals retain childish ways of dealing with environmental demands and thus end up being social problems. Partridge did not find a lack of moral sense in his subjects, but he did note a tendency to ignore the interests of others because of their own desires, restlessness, and demands. Partridge believed in "relative psychopathy," that the most logical approach to studying mental disorder was to observe all mental development from the standpoint of psychopathy. He saw the attempt to classify and subdivide psychopathy as hopeless, and proposed the term "sociopathic" to stand for the condition of pathological social relations. Partridge believed that if deviation in social relations were the primary criteria of the disorder that a whole class could be considered in terms of socialized behavior. Henderson, like Partridge, saw the factors operating in psychopathy as no different than the factors involved in other disorders and regards psychic immaturity as the basic feature of the disorder as it also is in cases of the neurotic and the psychotic (Maughs, 1941).

The contradictory forces that shaped understanding of moral insanity in the 1800s (Jones, 2017) and discussions of psychopathy in the early 1900s were particularly significant in the evolution of criminological thought. These forces moved criminology from a focus on biology to the mental state of the offender and normalized criminal behavior at a time when biological theories had been dominant for 50 years and provided a new (mental-emotional) explanatory framework. It was a catalyst for the takeover of psychiatric decision making in criminal justice, which led to the treatment approach that dominated the literature for the next 50 years. It helped open new chapters in deviance theory and sexuality with a focus on heterosexual masculinity as a standard for normality (when previously masculinity itself was used), which paved the way for the next generation's preoccupation with sexual psychopaths, although the distinction between psychopathy and sexual psychopathy was not made during this time (Rafter, 1997).

In criminology at this time, the study of criminality focused on social rather than psychological forces. Clifford Shaw's Chicago Area Project that ran from 1932 to 1957 had a major influence on views concerning the causes of crime. Shaw's study focused on situational forces of inner-city life. Criminologists such as Sutherland, Lemert, and Merton examined social imbalance and relationship of crime with social interaction exacting powerful theories including Sutherland's theory of differential association and Merton's theory of anomie. The sociological emphasis during this time may have contributed to the widespread use of Partridge's term "sociopathy." However, the term was not used as he had originally defined it. Partridge defined sociopathy as an impairment in social relations, not, as the term is now often defined, as a form of deviance that is the result of environmental or social (rather than psychological) causes. Partridge's original definition of sociopathy is more akin to traditional definitions of psychopathy that explain the disorder as a defect in the ability to attach to others.

In later writing Karpman (1941) attempted to narrow the definition of psychopathy based on symptomatic versus personality features. He justified this distinction stating:

> There is not even unanimity as to the definition of the term psychopathy. To some psychiatrists the presence of a delinquency is sufficient to label the reaction as psychopathic so that psychopathy becomes synonymous with delinquency, we find that this in itself has been allowed a large latitude and what some psychiatrists will define as delinquency, other psychiatrists would regard merely as being a peculiar behavior trait. (Karpman, 1941, p. 112)

Karpman used the terms "symptomatic" and "idiopathic" to describe the two types that were traditionally classified under the heading of psychopathy. He saw the symptomatic psychopaths as bearing superficial resemblance to the idiopathics through their behavior but maintained that this condition was the result of a completely different psychogenesis. Karpman called idiopathic psychopaths "anethopaths" and considered these individuals to be the only true or primary psychopathic types. Karpman argued for the narrowing of the concept of psychopathy to include only the group he called anethopaths and offered case study examples where he distinguishes the symptomatic type from the anethopathy.[2]

The "period of psychodynamics" can be seen as lasting well into the 1960s. However, its heyday was primarily in the 1940s and 1950s when psychiatrists such as Karpman (1941), Henderson (1947), Lindner (1945, 1946, in Selinger, Lucas, & Lindner, 1952), Cleckley (1941, 1946, in Selinger, Lucas, & Lindner, 1959), Glueck and Glueck (1950), McCord and McCord (1959), and

[2] Karpman offers an example of a male patient and a female patient. He diagnoses the female as a symptomatic type and the male as an anethopath. His diagnoses are based on the identification of psychogenic factors in the patients' early development. The female patient's case history includes evidence of early abuse, while the male patient's does not. Karpman bases his conclusions on this case history content. Although his theoretical distinctions are valuable and consistent with contemporary directions, his diagnoses can be seen as sex-biased. As discussed in Chapter 3, studies have shown that clinicians (particularly those of Karpman's time) tend to record information regarding inner dynamics and past abuses in case records of females more often than they do while recording information on male patients. In addition, they attribute psychodynamic explanations to female patients more often than they do to male patients. See Allen (1987).

Frankenstein (1959) dominated the literature. Most of these writers considered psychopathy a result of disturbed or disrupted psychodynamic development, primarily the result of underdevelopment of the superego, a concept initially proposed by Aichorn (1935). However, each writer brought his or her own twist to the subject (such as Lindner's proposal of "hypnoanalysis" in the treatment of psychopathy, McCord and McCord's "milieu therapy," and Cleckley's study of noncriminal psychopathy). Together these works remain valuable not only as stepping-stones in the evolution of the concept but as guidebooks to be used in contemporary research and theory development.

Cleckley's (1941, 1988) book *The Mask of Sanity* is considered the foremost classic work on psychopathy and continues to be the subject of research and discourse about psychopathy today (Crego & Widiger, 2016; DeShong, Helle, & Mullins-Sweatt, 2016; Ramsland, 2013; Scott, 2014). In addition to offering intensive case histories, rich theoretical perspective, and treatment recommendations, Cleckley introduced the notion of noncriminal psychopathy. Cleckley's suggestion that psychopaths exist in every element of society launched a movement that viewed psychopathy as a political issue. Thus, Cleckley's work marks the return to issues Birnbaum raised regarding the separateness of the conditions of criminality and psychopathy. According to Cleckley, psychopathy is a condition that can only be recognized in the context of full social intercourse (through interactions with family, coworkers, friends, etc.), and many psychopaths do not engage in criminal behavior, although they do possess many antisocial, manipulative, and irresponsible traits that are the result of a "defect in affect." He distinguishes the criminal from the psychopath by stating, "The criminal, in short, is usually trying to get something we all want, although he uses methods we shun" (Cleckley, 1982, p. 149). Thus, like Birnbaum, Cleckley associates criminality with utilitarian motives based on external influences while also associating psychopathy with obscure motives based on defective affectivity.

After publication of the *Mask of Sanity,* concern arose regarding the attention toward criminal psychopaths while (according to Cleckley) so many noncriminal psychopaths existed. This perspective of psychopathy as a political issue coincided with the beginnings of analytical criminology, which presented crime causation as political and economic. In 1958 publications by Dahrendorf ("Out of Utopia," published in the *American Journal of Sociology*) and Vold (*Theoretical Criminology*) fostered the "new criminology" that, with and without reference to Karl Marx, explained crime based on political factors. Others, such as Quinney (1970) wrote on how crime is a product of the social manipulation of the politically powerful. Writers such as Mailer (1959), Duff (1977), Smith (1978), and Ray and Ray (1982) introduced this analytical perspective to discussions of psychopathy, suggesting that psychopathy, as an explanation for criminality, is politically constructed and sanctioned. Recent authors have revived this focus on the ways in which political contexts nurture, validate, and provide a home for individuals with psychopathic traits (Babiak & Hare, 2006; Lilienfeld et al., 2012).

Cleckley's work, although clinically and psychodynamically oriented, also inspired study in other directions. The 1960s and 1970s were dominated by psychobiological studies focusing on physiological aspects of psychopathy. Research took the biological approach using measurements of electroencephalogram (EEG) activity, autonomic activity, nervous system, verbal learning, instrumental conditioning, and genetic correlates. Psychometric tests were also being used and developed during this time. Intelligence tests, self-report inventories, and projective tests were used heavily in research of all kinds. Much of this study was dominated by Hare (1965a, 1965b, 1965c, 1966a, 1966b, 1968a, 1968b, 1969, 1970, 1980, 1982, 1985a, 1985b), who later incorporated Cleckley's psychopathic criteria into the *Psychopathy Checklist–Revised* (Hare, 1991, 2003) and popularized the scientific conception of psychopathy in his book written for the lay audience, *Without Conscience: The Disturbing World of Psychopaths among Us* (Hare, 1993).

The DSM and the Clinical (Mis)diagnosis of Psychopathy

The American Psychiatric Association (APA) has never included psychopathy as a personality disorder in the *Diagnostic and Statistical Manual of Mental Disorders* (DSM). In 1952 the condition most closely associated with psychopathy was "sociopathic personality" with several different reactions (antisocial, dyssocial, sexual deviation, and addiction to alcohol or drugs) listed under the main heading. Individuals could be classified in this category if they were:

> ill primarily in terms of society and of conformity with the prevailing cultural milieu, and not only in terms of personal discomfort and relations with other individuals. However, sociopathic reactions are very often symptomatic of severe underlying personality disorder, neurosis, or psychosis, or occur as the result of organic brain injury or disease. Before a definitive diagnosis in this group is employed, strict attention must be paid to the possibility of a more primary problem where such underlying disturbance will be diagnosed when recognized. Reactions will be differentiated as defined below. (American Psychiatric Association, 1952, p. 38)

The second edition of the DSM (DSM-II) published in 1968 removed the different reaction types, relabeled the disorder "antisocial personality," and stated that the term be reserved for individuals who are:

> basically unsocialized and whose behavior pattern brings them repeatedly into conflict with society. They are incapable of significant loyalty to

> individuals, groups, or social values. They are grossly selfish, callous, irresponsible, impulsive, and unable to feel guilt or to learn from experience and punishment. Frustration tolerance is low. They tend to blame others or offer rationalizations for their behavior. A mere history of repeated legal or social offenses is not sufficient to justify this diagnosis. (American Psychiatric Association, 1968, p. 43)

The revisions following the DSM and DSM-II were published in 1980 (DSM-III), 1987 (DSM-III-Revised), DSM-IV (1994), DSM-IV-TR (2000), and DSM-5 (2013), all using the term "antisocial personality disorder" with movement toward greater objectivity and reliability, less adherence to the personality focus, and narrowing of the concept proposed by Karpman, Birnbuam, Cleckley, and numerous other writers of every decade from the late 18th century to the present.

Over the past 40 years there has been criticism of the antisocial personality disorder (APD) classification directed at the strict behavioral definition that appears to blur the line between personality disorder and social deviance. Although APD has been beneficial in the sense that its descriptive features provide clinicians with objective criteria and a reliable diagnostic tool, APD does separate antisocial syndromes having sociological, neurotic, traumatic, depressive, and political bases from the characterological bases of psychopathy (Reid, 1985). Research has revealed that the classification of APD originally adopted to replace psychopathic classification is inconsistent with distinguishing characteristics of primary psychopathy, and recent research continues to support a distinction between psychopathy and APD (Ogloff et al., 2016; Shepherd, Campbell, & Ogloff, 2016; Wall, Wygant, & Sellbom, 2015; Walsh & Wu, 2008). Some people who are called psychopaths do not have APD, not all individuals meeting the criteria for APD are psychopaths, and some individuals who do not meet APD criteria may be psychopathic through a combination of cognitive-behavioral and psychodynamic criteria (Gacono & Meloy, 1988). The inconsistency between criteria defining APD and those that have traditionally defined psychopathy lies in the change from the trait-based definition of psychopathy to the behavioral-based definition of APD. Because APD diagnosis is based on behavioral criteria, the definition is said to pay too little attention to personality traits underlying the disorder (Harpur, Hakstian, & Hare, 1988).

Most psychopathic offenders meet the criteria for APD, but most offenders diagnosed with APD are not psychopaths (Hare, 2003). APD classification over-includes features of antisocial and criminal behavior and under-includes personality features that may be more indicative of psychopathy. APD is too liberal on behavioral dimensions and too narrow on dimensions of personality, including individuals who are not characterologically psychopathic but rather those with symptomatic psychopathy who suffer from underlying emotional disturbance (Hare, 1980; Hare & Schalling, 1978). These "secondary psychopaths" represent approximately 70 percent of APD diagnosis, while only 30 percent can be considered psychopathic in the strict clinical sense (Hare, 1980). It has been suggested that classification that is more consistent with traditional definitions of psychopathy consist of multiple diagnosis across differential DSM-III-R axes (Wulach, 1988), and that psychopathy and APD are antisocial manifestations of borderline personality structure that also underlies the other Cluster B personality disorders in DSM-II-R (borderline personality disorder, histrionic personality disorder, and narcissistic personality disorder) (Gacono & Meloy, 1988; Jordan et al., 1989; Meloy, 1988). In recent years a sophisticated understanding of secondary psychopathy has developed conceptualizing the condition along a continuum of severity consisting of heterogeneous subtypes differentiated by biosociopychological etiology (Yildirim, 2016; Yildirim & Derksen, 2016).

Blackburn (1988) points out that throughout the history of the concept of psychopathy attempts to clarify the concept have been made by Karpman (1948), Cleckley (1982), Hare (1980), and others; official criteria have changed in the DSM-I, DSM-II, DSM-III, and DSM-III-R; and definitions have varied in specificity and content. However, no one has provided a definition that constitutes a homogeneous group. Although personality traits are central to the DSM-III, DSM-III-R, DSM-IV, and DSM-IV-TR, and DSM-5 concepts of personality disorder, the behavioral classification of APD does not describe the disorder in terms of personal deviance and is based on a definition of social deviance that does not distinguish or differentiate individuals in terms of personality. From Blackburn's (1988) perspective, the traits constituting APD criteria belong to the domain of social deviance, not personal deviance, and individuals exhibiting APD criteria may possess a variety of personality styles. "Employing such criteria in the definition of a disorder of personality raises the same issues for the identification of a homogeneous class as would classifying democrats by reference to eye colour" (Blackburn, 1988, p. 506). This perspective has been empirically validated over time with the recognition that APD largely reflects secondary psychopathy, which is a heterogeneous construct (Yildirim, 2016; Yildirim & Derksen, 2015).

Blackburn considers other attempts to clarify the concept of psychopathy as hybrid concepts that simply narrow the criteria in ways that still contain elements of both social and personal deviance domains. Karpman's (1948) introduction of the distinction of "idiopathic" (also called anethopathic) and "symptomatic" psychopathy as antisocial individuals who either lack conscience ("idiopathic," or primary) or whose antisocial behavior is a symptom of underlying neurosis ("symptomatic," or secondary) are examples of such a hybrid concept. From Blackburn's perspective, Karpman's distinction is confused, and although it is logically correct to say that antisocial individuals are psychodynamically heterogeneous, the primary-secondary distinction is

Karpman's refusal to recognize personality disorders as a separate group.[3] Attempts to conceptualize psychopathy by Cleckley and Hare are also hybrid concepts that combine the discourses of social and personal deviance. From this perspective, the diagnostic categories that have emerged confound different universes of discourse resulting in classification schemes that contain a variety of deviant personalities, and until we have an adequate system for describing the universe of personality deviation, we cannot understand how personal attributes contribute to socially deviant behavior (Blackburn, 1988).

The nomenclature, descriptions, nature of social condemnation, and treatment prognosis of psychopathy have changed over time throughout the more than 200-year discourse. Arrigo and Shipley (2001a, 2001b) identify 13 transitions that have impacted understanding of psychopathy (see Table 2.1, Historical Context of Psychopathy).

The foci in the 1800s primarily involved discussion on the nature of psychopathy, its relationship to legal concepts of criminality and insanity, and debate over whether or not it was possible to hold someone responsible for criminal behavior if morally depraved but cognitively intact. The 1900s was characterized by a shift in focus to differentiation between primary and secondary types, identifying different manifestations of the condition, and in the later years, on development and standardization of assessment tools to measure psychopathy. Early conceptualizations focused on personality features of the disorder. The rise of sociology and criminology and the shift in the criminal justice system to more of a "just deserts" model of justice gave way to alternative terms such as "sociopathy" and discussion on the role of environmental factors in shaping the disorder. Movement to the APD classifications in the different editions of the DSM moved the conceptualization away from the focus on personality to focus on the behavioral features of the condition.

The PCL-R: Recapturing the Personality in Personality Disorder

There is a single thread joining the differing explanations of the disorder throughout the history of the study of psychopathy. Every theory, researcher, and clinician has addressed the psychopath's inability to connect emotionally with others. This feature has been called "lack of empathy," "lack of remorse," "absence of conscience" (Hare, 2003), "defect in affect" (Cleckley, 1941, 1982), "failure to put oneself in another's position" (Yochelson & Samenow, 1976), "human disidentification," and a "reptilian nature that is void of

---

[3] Although Karpman does separate psychopathy into the two groups, a review of his writings (1941, 1946) reflect his personal desire to abandon the notion that those in the symptomatic group are psychopaths. In fact, he proposed that the concept be narrowed to include only the idiopathic group.

Table 2.1 Historical Context of Psychopathy

Date	Theorist	Terminology	Description	Social Condemnation	Prognosis
1801	Pinel	Manie sans delire	Insanity without delirium	Morally neutral	Moral treatment
1812	Rush	Moral alienation of the mind	Total perversion of moral faculties	Social condemnation	Medical treatment
1835	Prichard	Moral insanity	Personality defect	Intensification of social condemnation	Legal defense
1891	Koch	Psychopathic inferiority	Congenital personality types	Attempts to shed social condemnation	Depends on type: chronic or temporary
1897	Maudsley	Moral imbecility	Cognitive deficits affecting criminal behavior	Criminal class	Useless to punish those who can't control behavior
1904	Krafft-Ebing	Morally depraved	Savages in society	Severe condemnation	Indefinite commitment to asylums
1915	Kraepelin	Psychopathic personalities	Vicious/wicked, born criminals, liars, swindlers	Moral judgment/ social condemnation	Poor

1941	Cleckley	Psychopath	Detached/narcissistic interpersonal style	Pejorative	Poor
1952	APA's DSM	Sociopathic personality; antisocial/dyssocial sociopath	Social perspective; Cleckley features with some criminal behaviors	Pejorative	Poor
1968	DSM-II	Antisocial personality disorder	Personality traits of psychopaths and antisocial behaviors	Pejorative	Poor
1980/1987	DSM-III/DSM-III-R	Antisocial personality disorder	Chronic violation of social norms/antisocial behaviors	Pejorative/association with offenders and criminal behavior	Poor but symptoms diminish with age
1985/1991	Hare's PCL/PCL-R	Psychopathy	Personality/antisocial behavior two-factor model; reliable and valid	Pejorative	Poor/can become worse with treatment
1994/2000	DSM-IV/DSM-IV-TR	Antisocial personality disorder	Focused on behavioral criteria/antisocial behaviors	Pejorative/association with offenders and criminal behavior	Poor but symptoms diminish with age
2013	DSM-5	Antisocial Personality Disorder	Focused on behavioral criteria/antisocial behaviors	Pejorative/ Association with offenders and criminal behavior	Poor but symptoms diminish with age

Adapted from Arrigo and Shipley (2001a, 2001b).

human affect" (Meloy, 1988). Debate regarding the centrality of personality versus antisocial and criminal behavior features of the disorder has persisted for decades. Researchers continue to suggest that the criminal behavior component of psychopathy is a correlate rather than a fundamental component of the disorder (Skeem & Cooke, 2010). Recent empirical research confirms that callousness/lack of empathy is the central feature of psychopathy (Verschuere et al., 2018).

Despite the consistency in the literature on psychopathy regarding the personality component of the psychopathy construct and the fundamental feature of the emotional absence in the psychopath, current and previous DSM classifications of APD have not directly addressed this feature and continue to confuse the distinction between psychopathy and APD. The current DSM-5 APD classification (APA, DSM-5, 2013) continues to weigh classification heavily on behavioral characteristics attempting to capture the lack of empathy feature through "Lack of remorse, as indicated by being indifferent to or rationalizing having hurt, mistreated, or stolen from another," one of seven indicators that can be used to meet the criteria of three items for the criterion "A pervasive pattern of disregard for and violation of the rights of others" (APA, 2013, p. 659). The DSM-5 description of APD reads, "This pattern has also been referred to as psychopathy, sociopathy, and dyssocial personality disorder" (p. 659), and under the "Associated Features Supporting Diagnosis" section notes that "individuals with antisocial personality disorders lack empathy and tend to be callous, cynical, and contemptuous of the feelings, rights, and suffering of others" (p. 660). This suggestion that lack of empathy and remorse that have commonly been included in traditional conceptions of psychopathy indirectly implies that personality traits associated with emotional absence are important for assessment purposes for APD classification. Lykken (2018) summarizes the enduring issues with the APD classification:

> The cookbook-like, relatively objective character of the diagnostic criteria for ASPD[4] is obvious; what is not so apparent is the fact that there is no theoretical or empirical basis for supposing that this scheme carves Nature at her joints. Because there may be a variety of psychological causes for a given action, classifying people by their actions rather than their psychological dispositions or traits, although natural for the purposes of criminal law, is less useful for the purposes of psychiatry or science. (p. 23)

[4] As previously noted, authors use both ASPD and APD as an acronym for antisocial personality disorder. APD is used throughout this text for brevity.

Thus, the diagnostic confusion in DSM APD classifications noted many years ago (Hare, 1996b) persists in the current DSM-5 APD classification in its current form. This diagnostic confusion is particularly problematic because while most cases of psychopathy diagnosed in prison and forensic settings would meet the diagnostic criteria for APD, only about half of APD cases meet criteria for psychopathy (Widiger & Crego, 2018).

The *Psychopathy Checklist–Revised* (PCL-R) was developed by Robert Hare (1991, 2003) to meet the need for reliable and valid assessment of psychopathy. Unsatisfied with the lack of consensus in definitions of psychopathy at the time (late 1970s), Hare set out to develop a psychometrically sound and standardized assessment tool so that meaningful and systematic research could be conducted on the clinical construct of psychopathy. Hare and his students and colleagues first developed a global clinical procedure using a seven-point rating scale rating prison inmates along the scale based on the degree to which their personality and behavior were deemed consistent with the Cleckley (1941, 1988) conception of the psychopath. This procedure generated reliable ratings but involved integrating extensive interview and case history data into a single score, which proved to be difficult for others to determine what went into the rating. This seven-point rating scale was the forerunner to the *Psychopathy Checklist* (PCL) (1980) originally referred to as the *Research Scale for the Assessment of Psychopathy*. The PCL was an attempt to quantify the Cleckley conceptualization of psychopathy and to operationalize assessment procedures used by Hare and colleagues so that researchers could be on the same page when conducting studies on psychopathy. The PCL was a 22-item scale developed through statistical determination of which more than 100 personality and behavioral items had the best psychometric properties that were used in an earlier study involving rating the 16 Cleckley characteristics on a 0–2 point scale. Subsequent research rating the PCL with prison inmates confirmed the reliability and validity of the 22 items (Hare, 1991, 2003). The PCL met a great need in the 1980s when most studies and published research articles on psychopathy utilized wildly disparate definitions and measurement procedures and was well received by researchers.

The revised version of the PCL, the *Psychopathy Checklist–Revised* (PCL-R), was developed after experience using the PCL and feedback from other researchers. Two of the 22 items were removed ("Drug or alcohol abuse not direct cause of antisocial behavior" and "Previous diagnosis as a psychopath") because of difficulties in scoring and reliability and titles of some of the items were changed. The first edition of the PCL-R was published by Multi-Health Systems and made available commercially in 1991, and the second edition was published in 2003. Derivatives of the PCL-R were subsequently published including the *Psychopathy Checklist: Screening Version* (PCL:SV) (Hart, Cox, & Hare, 1995), the *Psychopathy Checklist: Youth Version* (PCL:YV) (Forth, Kosson,

& Hare, 2003), the *Hare P-Scan* (Hare & Hervé, 1999), and the *Self-Report Psychopathy Scale* (SRP 4) (Paulhus, Neumann, & Hare, 2017).

The PCL-R is comprised of two factors (Factor 1: interpersonal/affective and Factor 2: social deviance) and four facets (interpersonal, affective, lifestyle, and antisocial) consisting of features that distinguish personality features (Factor 1) and behavioral (Factor 2) features of the disorder. Factor 1 items are comprised of interpersonal and affective personality characteristics derived from Cleckley (1941, 1988) and reflect the personality (interpersonal/affective) component of the disorder. Factor 2 items reflect the antisocial behavior (social deviance) component of the disorder including antisocial behaviors similar to those included in the APD classification in the *Diagnostic and Statistical Manual for Mental Disorders* (APA, DSM-5, 2013). Research has provided support for three-factor (Cooke & Michie, 2001) and four-factor models of psychopathy with specific PCL-R items associated with interpersonal, affective, and lifestyle (three-factor model) and interpersonal, affective, lifestyle, and antisocial factors (four-factor model) (Hare, 2016; Hare & Neumann, 2006; Hare, Neumann, & Mokros, 2018; Neumann, Kosson, & Salekin, 2007). This four-factor model, based on an earlier version of the model described by Hare (2003) that included the four facets within the original two-factor model, offers a more complex understanding of the fundamental facets of the personality and behavioral components of the disorder.

The PCL-R's incorporation of personality features of the Cleckley conceptualization of psychopathy and behavioral features included in the APD criteria was a step forward from the historically loose association between psychopathy and the DSM APD classifications. The PCL-R emphasizes the personality component of the disorder. Of the 20 items in the PCL-R, 13 represent standard personality descriptors (glibness, grandiosity, manipulativeness, pathological lying, shallow affect, absence of guilt, callousness, poor behavioral controls, impulsivity, irresponsibility, callousness, lack of planning, failure to accept responsibility) and at least four of the remaining seven reference enduring behavioral patterns reflective of personality (promiscuous sexual behavior, parasitic lifestyle, many short-term marital relationships, criminal versatility) (Lynam & Derefinko, 2006). However, the ongoing debate in the literature over whether or not the Factor 2 social deviance component of psychopathy is critical to the psychopathy construct continues to cloud consensual understanding of the disorder. Researchers have suggested that the PCL-R has become so heavily used in clinical and research settings that the predictive utility of the PCL-R cannot substitute for construct validity and "the field is in danger of equating the PCL-R with the theoretical construct of psychopathy" (Skeem & Cooke, 2010, p. 433). Others have emphasized the need to situate the psychopathy construct within the broader literature on personality to examine the association between psychopathy and structural models of personality including the five-factor model (FFM); Eysenck psychoticism, extroversion, and neuroticism (PEN) model; and other commonly used models prominent in personality science (Lynam, Miller, & Derefinko, 2018).

Researchers have suggested alternative constructs and means of assessing psychopathy beyond the PCL-R that may better capture the personality features of the condition. Patrick, Fowles, and Krueger (2009) and Patrick (2018) offer a triarchic conceptualization of psychopathy that encompasses historical themes of disinhibition, boldness, and meanness that make up the syndrome of psychopathy and suggest that other measures such as the Psychopathic Personality Inventory (PPI) (Lilienfeld & Andrews, 1996) may better capture these personality features of the disorder. Lynam and Derefinko (2006) and Lynam, Miller, and Derefinko (2018) suggest that psychopathy is a particular constellation of basic personality traits that exist within structural models of personality such as the five-factor model (FFM), Eysenck's psychoticism, extraversion, and neuroticism (PEN) model, Tellegen's three-factor model, and the Consensus Big Four. Gacono and Meloy (1988) propose the "levels hypothesis" emphasizing the psychodynamic, cognitive, and behavioral components of psychopathy and suggest that unconscious defensive processes can be inferred from conscious cognitive style that has empirical support (Helfgott, 1997, 2004). Kosson, Gacono, and Bodholdt (2000) and Kosson, Gacolo, Klipfel, and Bodholdt (2016) emphasize the interpersonal dynamics and internalized defensive operations of psychopathy that manifest in particular interpersonal cues and suggest that PCL-R assessment of psychopathy be augmented with the *Interpersonal Measure of Psychopathy (IM-P),* an experimental assessment tool developed and designed to measure interpersonal aspects of the psychopathic personality not adequately captured by the PCL-R.

Contemporary Research: What Causes Psychopathy?

In *The Psychopathic Mind*, Meloy (1988) explains the underlying dynamics involved in the development of psychopathy, offering what he considers to be the most fundamental feature of the condition. He defines psychopathy as a:

> deviant developmental disturbance characterized by an inordinate amount of instinctual aggression and the absence of the object relational capacity to bond. Psychopathy is a process: a continuous interplay of factors and operations that are implicitly progressing or regressing toward a particular end point . . . a fundamental disidentification with humanity. (Meloy, 1988, p. 5)

Meloy's definition reflects a synthesis of theories from a variety of disciplines (e.g., biology, psychology, sociology) and perspectives (psychodynamic, behavioral, cognitive), emphasizing the developmental context in which the disorder emerges. This attention to developmental issues illustrates the particular dynamics involved in the etiology of the disorder. From this perspective, psychopathy is not necessarily inherent but deeply rooted in complex psychodynamic processes. Psychopathy is neither the product of an unchangeable inborn defect or purely environmental factors.

Biological Predisposition

A large body of research has accumulated on the biological factors that predispose an individual to psychopathy. Biological factors do not "cause" the disorder, however, research supports a link between psychopathy and a number of biological deficits and anomalies including genetic predisposition, neurotransmitter imbalance, low autonomic arousal, and brain damage (Glenn & Raine, 2014; Kiehl, 2014; Loomans, Joke, & van Marle, 2013; Marshall et al., 2017; Ortega-Escobar, Alcázar-Córcoles, Puente-Rodríguez, & Peñaranda-Ramos, 2017; Raine, 1993; Raine, 2013; Raine & Sanmartin, 2001; Stratton, Kiehl, & Hanlon, 2015; Tamatea, 2015; Van Honk & Schutter, 2006; Waldman, Rhee, LoParo, & Park, 2018), dysfunction in the amygdala, and part of the limbic system associated with fear and other emotions (Blair, Jones, Clark, & Smith, 1997; Blair, Mitchell, & Blair, 2005; DeLisi, Umphress, & Vaughn, 2009). Much of the research on the biological factors associated with psychopathy applies also to criminality and antisocial behavior and violence. Anatomical research focusing specifically on psychopathy is "nearly nonexistent" (Raine & Yang, 2006, p. 290). Research has focused more generally on antisocial conditions utilizing heterogeneous samples (including psychopathic and nonpsychopathic offenders), so it is difficult to sort out whether or not the findings apply to psychopaths or offenders more generally.

For example, Raine (2001) found that violent offenders are more likely to have preshrunken prefrontal cortexes, though this anomaly is found more often in offenders who engage in affectively motivated violence rather than predatory violence (most often committed by psychopaths). Similarly, research on neurochemical basis of psychopathy has targeted the antisocial behavior component of the condition (Factor 2) but says little with respect to the affective-interpersonal component (Factor 1). It appears that there is a relationship between impaired central serotonergic activity and impulsive and aggressive behavior, but like other findings, this says little about the neurotransmitter role in instrumental predatory aggression and the defect in affect component of psychopathy (Minzenberg & Siever, 2006). With respect to the relationship between genetics and criminal behavior more generally, it is unlikely that there is a genetic contribution to specific antisocial or criminal behaviors. Rather, genetics likely play a role in determining the probability that a person will learn an antisocial rather than a prosocial strategy to get his or her needs met. Thus, the emotional dysfunction in the psychopath that makes it so easy to harm and take advantage of others may have a genetic contribution (Blair,

Mitchell, & Blair, 2005). There is some research suggesting that environmental stressors such as birth complications in pregnancy are associated with conduct disorder, delinquency, and violence in adulthood. However, these stressors appear to be associated with reactive aggression rather than instrumental and predatory aggression (Blair, Mitchell, & Blair, 2005).

One of the most consistent findings is that psychopaths experience low anxiety and low-fear reactions to aversive stimuli. Both the "low-fear hypothesis" (Lykken, 1957) and the "behavioral inhibition system (BIS) deficit" in psychopaths have been consistently supported in a range of studies that have measured the psychopath's avoidance to punishment and aversive conditions and autonomic arousal and startle reflex. Fowles and Dindo (2006) propose a dual-deficit model of psychopathy suggesting that the deficit in psychopathy is a combined deficit of low-fear and low-anxiety hypothesizing that low fear makes anxiety less likely in the psychopath. However, both low fear and low anxiety, while rooted in temperament, are highly dependent on environmental influences producing a developmental failure that is associated with deficits in anxiety and fear reactions shaped by parent-child interactions and other environmental contributors. This temperamentally based fearlessness has been empirically associated with Factor 1 of the PCL-R, and externalizing disinhibition and reward-seeking behavior, a manifestation of low anxiety, is associated with Factor 2 of the PCL-R (Fowles, 2018).

Environmental Influences

Biological influences do not alone "cause" psychopathy. Environmental forces such as attachment in infancy, family factors, and culture play a critical role in the development and manifestation of psychopathy and may actually be responsible for many of the differences found in neuroanatomy and neurochemistry research (Farrington & Bergstrom, 2018; Fowles, 2018; Glenn & Raine, 2014; Raine, 2013). Like the biological research, much of what is known about psychopathy and environmental factors comes from the more general research on environmental causes of antisocial and criminal behavior, although there has been increasing focus specifically on the epigenetics specific to psychopathy and the implications for criminal justice decision making (Tamatea, 2015).

From a psychodynamic and developmental perspective, psychopathy is the product of genotypic-phenotypic interaction—a biologically predisposed condition exacerbated by environmental forces that develops in infancy prior to 36 months. Infants who are biologically predisposed develop psychopathy as a result of an interactive process between the individual and environment. According to Meloy (1988), all infants experience "hard" and "soft" sensations. Hard sensations can be anything that the infant experiences as harshness (e.g., parental abuse, neglect, loud noises, cold expressions). Soft sensations are perceived by the infant as comforting, soothing, and facilitate human bonding. Psychopaths experience a preponderance of hard sensations and as a result turn inward, attach to the narcissistic core of their personality, and build an impenetrable wall of primitive defenses that impede human bonding. Beyond infancy and into adulthood environmental forces can shape the manifestation of psychopathy. Hare (1996c) suggests that differential environmental circumstances can lead a psychopath raised in a privileged environment to engage in phony stock trading or manipulative power politics, while those reared in disadvantaged situations may engage in violent crime.

Research on the influence of family factors on psychopathy and longitudinal studies examining psychopathy across the life course is sparse to nonexistent (Farrington & Bergstrom, 2018). Although early work in the 1950s, 1960s, and 1970s suggested that maternal deprivation, parental rejection, erratic discipline, an antisocial parent, and poor parental supervision could have negative effects resulting in delinquent and antisocial behavior, few studies have examined the influence of these factors on psychopathy. Virtually all of the findings on family contributors to psychopathy are extrapolated from longitudinal studies of criminal behavior that have focused on career criminality with the idea that the group that life-course researchers consider "chronic offenders" is equivalent to the group that personality researchers have called "primary psychopaths."[5] This is highly problematic in making sense of the role of family influences in psychopathy because the constructs overlap but are not identical. For example, a study utilizing a sample of 75 institutionalized juvenile male offenders found that self-reported memories of ineffective parenting practices including poor monitoring/supervision and inconsistent discipline were significantly associated with increased levels of psychopathic traits as measured through the PCL:YV; however, the association was significant only for Factor 2 (social deviance) lifestyle and antisocial facets (Molinuevo, Pardo, González, & Torrubia, 2014).

The only longitudinal study including childhood risk factors that has measured psychopathy is the *Cambridge Study in Delinquent Development*, a 40-year longitudinal survey of development of offending and antisocial behavior that followed 411 London boys from age 8 to age 48. The PCL:SV was administered, and a subset of "most psychopathic" males who scored 10 or more were identified. Although none of these men met the threshold for psychopathy (a high score in a community sample is considered 16 or above) and

[5] Farrington notes that the reason for the scarcity of longitudinal research focusing on psychopathy is the low prevalence of psychopathy in community samples, and the PCL-R was designed for use with prison samples. The development of the PCL Screening Version (PCL:SV) has enabled researchers to use the tool in community samples in longitudinal research treating psychopathy as a dimension rather than a category.

cannot be considered in the same category as individuals who would score about 30 on the PCL-R (primary psychopaths), the study found that the best predictor of the higher scoring males were having a convicted father or mother, physical neglect, low family income, low involvement of the father with the boy, and coming from a disrupted family (Farrington, 2006; Farrington & Bergstrom, 2018).

What about the influence of cultural factors? Can cultural influences cause psychopathy? Researchers have only just begun to explore these questions, recognizing that the more we know about the differences and similarities across culture, the more we may understand the etiology of psychopathy. Most researchers acknowledge that the manifestation of psychopathy may be shaped by environmental and cultural influences such as gender-role socialization, ethnic background, and culture. However, the PCL-R was developed and normed almost exclusively on European American males in the United States and Canada, so results from studies employing the PCL-R with other samples have to be interpreted with caution (Hare, 2003). Results to date suggest that international prison populations have lower mean scores on the PCL-R and lower base rates of psychopathy in comparison with North American prison populations, that sociocultural variables may contribute to behavioral differences in psychopathy across ethnicity (Fanti, Lordos, Sullivan, & Kosson, 2018; Sullivan & Kosson, 2006), and that lower rates of psychopathy are found in female samples (Cunliffe, Gacono, Meloy, & Taylor, 2013; Cunliffe et al., 2016; Jackson & Richards, 2007; Verona & Vitale, 2006, 2018). The two conclusions warranted at this point in the research on ethnic and cultural differences in psychopathy is that (1) there is evidence for reliability and at least partial construct validity of psychopathy across ethnicities, and (2) ethnic differences in the mechanisms underlying psychopathy and the manifestation of psychopathy may exist and need to be further explored (Fanti, Lordos, Sullivan, & Kosson, 2018).

Cognition and Information Processing

The historical link between psychopathy and criminality rests on the psychopath's absence of cognitive defect. Unlike psychotics who are out of touch with reality and can be considered legally insane, psychopaths have the capacity for sound judgment, know the difference between right and wrong, and cannot be considered under the insanity defense. However, despite the recognition of the psychopath as cognitively intact for legal purposes and culpable for criminal behavior, research suggests that the psychopath's information-processing abilities and mechanisms are intact, but dysfunctional. Recent research suggests that the assumption that psychopaths are not cognitively impaired may stem from oversimplified models of cognitive functions, and psychopaths may be impaired in more subtle aspects of cognition not captured by standard measures of intelligence or executive ability (Hamilton & Newman, 2018; Hiatt & Newman, 2006; Vitale et al., 2016).

The literature on cognitive and language processing of psychopaths shows a broad array of deficits. Psychopaths appear to perform well on explicit tasks performed in isolation but not as well on complex dual-task paradigms and show poor performance in response modulation. In processing language, psychopaths use fewer cohesive ties and elaborate associations. Hiatt and Newman (2006) identify two emergent themes from the cognition and information-processing research: (1) difficulty in accommodating unintended secondary cues and cerebral-processing abnormalities and (2) the hypothesis that these two components of cognitive deficits may stem from a common mechanism.

Central to arguments regarding distinguishing psychopathy from APN is the distinction between *cognitive deficiencies* and *cognitive distortions* (Wallace, Schmitt, Vitale, & Neman, 2000; Vitale et al., 2016). Cognitive deficiencies involve some type of deficit in information-processing abilities of memory, learning, or attention. Cognitive distortions involve a negative pattern and style of thinking; however, information processing abilities are intact. Psychopaths engage in a particular style and pattern of thinking and expression that involve communication of deceit and deception and facilitate antisocial behavior. This is a cognitive distortion. However, recent findings support the notion that psychopaths experience cognitive deficiencies in addition to using distorted cognitive schema that support antisocial behavior.

Wallace, Schmitt, Vitale, and Neman (2000) hypothesized that the psychopath's diminished capacity to learn from experience and change their behavior in anticipation of adverse consequences results from cognitive deficiencies rather than distortions, and that the core feature of psychopathy is a deficit in attention resulting from impairment of the response modulation process and self-regulation. This response modulation hypothesis (RMH) has been the focus on a great deal of research in recent years (Hamilton & Newman, 2018; Vitale et al., 2016). The RMH states that psychopaths have a cognitive deficit that makes them unable to shift attention from carrying out a behavior to evaluating behavior, and once fixated on a goal are unable to stop or change their behavior in response to nonsalient stimuli (e.g., recognition of long-term consequences). Antisocial personality disordered offenders (who are not necessarily psychopaths) use maladaptive cognitive schemas (e.g., "weak people get what they deserve"), but such schemas are cognitive distortions, not deficits, and are not in themselves indicative of psychopathy. However, deficit in response modulation paired with cognitive distortions and antisocial personality style is a compelling explanation for psychopathic behavior. Wallace, Schmitt, Vitale, and Neman (2000) suggests that the PCL-R can be viewed along a continuum whereby scores < 30 reflect the degree of cognitive distortion used, while a score of ≥ 30 reflects evidence of cognitive deficit seen only in psychopaths (and not antisocial personality disordered offenders).

Yochelson and Samenow's (1976) criminal personality theory, based on an intensive study and treatment program conducted in Saint Elizabeth's Hospital from 1961 until 1976, offers illustration of the cognitive distortions of the psychopath. In their three-volume work, *The Criminal Personality*, the authors offer detailed description of the thinking errors and patterns of the psychopath (Samenow, 2013). At the core of the psychopath's cognitive style are mechanisms Yochelson and Samenow term "corrosion" and "cutoff." These mechanisms enable the psychopath to gradually eliminate any thoughts that would deter the commission of a particular act and ultimately to abruptly cut off such thoughts in order to complete the act with no remorse or feelings of guilt and are supported by a cognitive style that shapes the psychopath's every attitude, value, and belief. The psychopath's behavior is dictated by cognitive-thinking errors that facilitate chronic criminal and manipulative behavior.

Yochelson and Samenow abandoned sociological, psychodynamic, and mental illness models traditionally applied to the understanding and treatment of criminal behavior after many years of working with offenders who they believed possessed a "criminal personality." They found that the individuals in their study possessing the criminal personality came from a variety of backgrounds and the usual conditions upon which criminal behavior was blamed (e.g., low socioeconomic conditions, parental neglect, family dysfunction) did not appear to be connected to criminal thought. Yochelson and Samenow coined the term "criminal personality" for therapeutic purposes for the subpopulation of offenders they worked with who, when confronted with the standard psychodynamic approach, tended to create excuses for their own behaviors. Their concept of the criminal personality is consistent with historical and contemporary conceptualizations of psychopathy[6] (Samenow, 2013).

The authors identified three types of thinking errors—general thinking patterns, automatic errors in thinking, and thinking errors that manifest in criminal behavior. Examples of thinking errors include a sense of uniqueness, thrust for power, fragmented thinking, lying, victim stance, failure to put oneself in another's position, lack of trust, pretentiousness, ownership, a lack of interesting responsible performance, and superoptimism. Central to the criminal personality model is the "continuum of responsibility," which views criminality along a continuum of "responsibility" to "irresponsibility," with "nonarrestable," "arrestable," and "extreme" criminals included under the heading of "irresponsibility." The "criminal personality" (and the psychopath)

---

[6] Samenow noted that the psychopath is "in most ways indistinguishable from the criminal" (Samenow, 1984, p. 107).

fall at the "extreme criminal" along this continuum. The thinking errors that exemplify the "criminal" style of thought maintain the extremely irresponsible lifestyle.

Recent research and discourse have rooted deficits in cognitive thinking and decision making in the psychopath's emotional deficiency, suggesting that the malfunction in emotional affective processing in psychopathy has the effect of damaging moral judgment resulting in an inability to apply abstract concepts (Maiese, 2014). Others highlight the importance of understanding the disconnection between the ability to make moral judgment (the result of a cognitive process) and the ability to feel and experience emotion, which calls for understanding of cognitive and emotional processes in psychopathy with recognition that cognition and emotion are intertwined in terms of cognitive processing, but that emotion in itself is not the driving force behind moral judgment (Zhong, 2013).

Psychopathy and Emotion

Cleckley (1941, 1988) suggested that the psychopath suffers from "semantic dementia"—discordance between language and emotion and the attempt to mimic emotion and manipulate meaning through language. "Words provide a window into the minds of criminals, helping to determine whether they fit any particular personality profile, such as psychopathy" (Woodworth et al., 2012, p. 31). The psychopath's language is seen as a tangible and analyzable trait through which to identify the processes by which psychopaths "cut off"feelings of guilt about their antisocial behavior (Helfgott, 2004; Rieber & Vetter, 1995). A number of studies support Cleckley's concept of semantic dementia. The language of psychopaths is less emotionally intense than the language of nonpsychopaths and appears to be an adaptive reflex of psychopathy rather than a direct cause to manipulate (Brites et al., 2016). Psychopaths use fewer cohesive ties while telling stories (Brinkley et al., 1999) and extract less information from affective words (Williamson, Harpur, & Hare, 1991). When psychopaths recount their crimes, they are more likely to use explanatory cause-and-effect descriptors such as "because" and "since," use a higher frequency of disfluencies such as "um" and "uh," use more past tense and less present tense, and those with higher PCL-R Factor 1 scores give less emotionally intense descriptions of their crimes and use more emotionally negative language, suggesting that psychopaths operate on a rational but primitive level, and this is reflected in the language they use when describing their crimes (Hancock, Woodworth, & Porter, 2013).

Although the absence of emotion is seen as the core feature of psychopathy, there is some disagreement regarding whether or not and/or how psychopaths experience emotion. Recent research has begun to explore the psychopath's experience of emotion, types of emotion, the presentation of emotion, and whether or not it exists at all. In general this research has found that psychopaths experience attenuated fear and anxiety responses, diminished intensity in anger experiences and difference in the types of situations that lead to anger in comparison with nonpsychopaths (e.g., surface/superficial anger reaction at being put down or one-upped), the absence of genuine grief and despair, experience of pleasure through "contemptuous delight" (Meloy, 1988), and the absence of boredom or sadness or depression with the "zero state" (Yochelson & Samenow, 1976), the closest experience to these emotions (Kosson, Vitacco, Swagger, & Steuerwald, 2016; Steuerwald & Kosson, 2000). An interesting study by Durand, Plata, and Arbone (2017) found that individuals with high levels of psychopathic traits are less likely to stigmatize other psychopaths. In other words, one's own psychopathy level is inversely related to negative attitudes toward psychopaths.

An interesting area of research focusing on the emotional processing in psychopaths has focused on the violence inhibition mechanism (VIM), a cognitive mechanism that reduces the likelihood of aggressive attack when the aggressor is faced with distress cues. The VIM hypothesizes that distress cues inhibit aggression and violent attack. In other words, when one human being is faced with distress cues in another (such as behavioral and facial expression of fear and distress), these behavioral/facial displays will operate as a mechanism to inhibit aggression and subsequent violent attack. Blair, Jones, Clark, and Smith (1997) suggest that psychopathy may be the result of early dysfunction in the VIM. Research has empirically supported the inverse association between the distress processing involved in the VIM and callous and unemotional traits associated with psychopathy (Fido et al., 2017). Related research has found that individuals who possess callous and unemotional psychopathic traits exhibit a deficit in neural processing of emotional stimuli (Contreras-Rodríguez et al., 2014), and that psychopathy is associated with deficits in the recognition of emotional expression of sad, happy, and fearful faces (Pera-Guardiola et al., 2016) and reduced recognition of fear in others (Stanković et al., 2015).

Psychodynamic Theory and Borderline Personality Organization

The developmental origins of psychopathy are perhaps best conceptualized within the range of borderline personality organization and explained by psychodynamic theory (Meloy, 1988, 2001). Although much of the research that has accumulated on psychopathy has come from neuroscience, personality theory, and cognitive psychology, and it is widely understood that psychoanalytic treatment is not appropriate for violent individuals, in particular those who possess psychopathic traits, psychodynamic theory has much to offer in understanding violence (Yakeley & Meloy, 2012) and in terms of its explanatory power to describe how psychopathy develops. In *The*

Psychopathic Mind, Meloy (1988, p. 59) describes the early development of psychopathy:

> The developmental origins of psychopathy are characterized by a precocious separation from the primary parent during the symbiotic phase of maturation; failures of internalization that begin with an organismic distrust of the sensory-perceptual environment; a predominate, archetypal identification with the stranger selfobject that is central to the conceptual self and object fusions within the grandiose self-structure during the period of separation-individuation; a failure of object constancy and a primary narcissistic attachment to the grandiose self; and states of relatedness (separate from the *traits* of primary narcissistic attachment) that are aggressively and sadomasochistically pursued with actual objects.

These five developmental themes—separation from the primary parent, internalization failures, identification with the stranger selfobject,[7] failure in object constancy and narcissistic attachment to the grandiose self, and aggressively and sadomasochistically pursued states of relatedness—are what distinguish the psychopath from the narcissist and other personality disorders.

Psychopathy and other personality disorders develop by 36 months of age. The developmental process in infancy involves the phenomenological interaction between genotypic and phenotypic forces. Psychopathy develops when the infant experiences harsh sensory experience with the primary caregiver, an experience of twoness too harshly, an atavistic fear of predation, and an organismic distrust of the environment. If the infant experiences "precocious separation" accompanied by a predominance of "hard sensations" (unpleasant and uncomfortable) rather than "soft sensations" (pleasurable and comfortable) in the external environment, a "narcissistic shell" forms to ward off malevolent predators (Meloy, 1988).

Kernberg's theory of borderline personality organization (BPO) views personality along a continuum from psychotic to borderline to neurotic (see Figure 2.1, Kernberg's Theory of Borderline Personality Organization). Kernberg's BPO offers a theoretical framework with which to better understand psychopathy and its relationship with other disorders.

Psychotics are characterized by the use of primitive defenses and being out of touch with reality, borderlines are characterized by the use of primitive defenses and being in touch with reality, and neurotics are characterized higher level defenses and being in touch with reality. Kernberg (1985a) places

---

[7] A psychoanalytic term describing an infant's internal preconceived fantasy that helps the infant anticipate a predator in the external world (Meloy, 1988, p. 46).

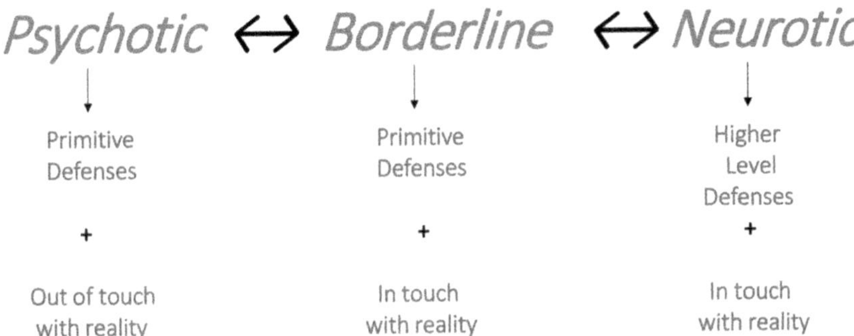

Figure 2.1 Kernberg's Theory of Borderline Personality Organization

borderline organization in between the neurotic and the psychotic, and considers the fixation and/or regression of the borderline individual as representing an intermediary stage between psychosis and neurosis. The common defensive structure underlying the borderline disorders of APD, NPD, HPD, and BPD confuses attempts to conceptualize psychopathy as a homogeneous disorder. Although conceptualizing psychopathy psychodynamically appears to alleviate the problem of definition based on social deviance, it does not distinguish psychopathy from the other borderline disorders. Within the framework of borderline personality organization, psychopathy sits within the borderline level of personality with the DSM-5 Cluster B personality disorders. All of these personality disorders share the common features of the use of primitive defenses and intact cognition.

The relationship between psychopathy and the Cluster B personality disorders (APD, NPD, BPD, and HPD) in the DSM has been discussed by a number of authors (Blackburn, 2007; McGlashan & Heinssen, 1989; Wulach, 1988). Others have examined the relationships between APD and HPD (Cale, 2002; Fernbach, Winstead, & Derlega, 1989; Ford & Widiger, 1989; Kass, Spitzer, & Williams, 1983; Lilienfeld et al., 1986; Morrison, 1989; Spalt, 1980; Warner, 1978; Williams & Spitzer, 1983); APD and NPD (Centifanti et al., 2013; Gacono & Meloy, 1988; Gacono, Meloy, & Heaven, 1990; Kernberg, 1989; Meloy, 1988; Mouilso & Calhoun, 2012); and APD, NPD, and BPD (Centifanti et al., 2016; Cunliffe, Johnson, & Weiss, 2013; Gacono, Meloy, & Berg, 1992; Howard, Khalifa, & Duggan, 2014; Lishner et al., 2015; Lowenstein, Purvis, & Rose, 2016; Matusiewicz et al., 2018; Miller et al., 2010; Sprague et al., 2012; Verona & Vitale, 2018; Viljoen et al., 2015; Wulach, 1988). The Cluster B personality disorders are organized around borderline level of personality organization (Kernberg, 1989) and share common behavioral features such as impulsive acting out, unpredictable behavior, and dramatic presentation, as well as a common intrapsychic structure centered around lower lever defensive organization that utilizes primitive defenses.

The primitive defenses that characterize the defensive process used by the psychotic and borderline personalities in the BPO continuum have been identified in Rorschach protocol responses (Cooper & Arnow, 1986) and illustrate how the primitive defenses cognitively manifest.

Splitting

Splitting is a fundamental defense that regulates the internal dynamics of psychopaths and others with severe personality disorders (Kernberg, 1984). Splitting refers to the division of self and internal objects into "all good" and "all bad" resulting in sudden and complete reversals of all feelings and conceptualizations about one's self or one's views about a particular person—a primitive dissociation of good and bad aspects of the self and of internal representations of others (Kernberg et al., 1989). Cooper and Arnow (1986) offer an example of splitting from the Rorschach (response to Card III) of a young adult male borderline reflecting the radically polarized self and object representations of splitting (alternating themes of love and rage and birth and death):

> Those are two hip Boston Women at an all-female disco, still carrying their bags (laughter), wearing high heels and in love with each other because they're so identical. Uh, between their breasts is not white, it's red, so that would mean they're not capable of giving milk to each other, but their hearts have only rage or something. But they have reproduction on their mind, because this is somewhat of a fetus, sort of gangling, hanging fetus with an umbilical cord. And then of course you have the sticky road ahead of them which lies between them which would be this grayish design between them. But they're bitches, because their hands are sort of knife-like pointing daggerlike at themselves. This is also like the dancing, this is sort of like a guitar. (p. 151)

This verbal response to the Rorschach offers illustration of the cognitions attached to the splitting mechanism showing how primitive defenses can be identified in projective tests through cognitive representation.

Primitive Idealization

Primitive idealization exaggerates the tendency to see external objects as good. The qualities of goodness in others are exaggerated pathologically to the exclusion of commonplace human defects with no toleration for imperfection. The counterpart to this idealization is the complete devaluation of others, or the perception of others as persecutory or dangerous (Kernberg et al., 1989). Primitive idealization is characterized by the borderline individual's creation of all-good and powerful images so that they may be insulated and protected against bad objects or their own anger (Kernberg, 1976).

Drawing again from Cooper and Arnow's (1986) Rorschach analysis, an example of primitive idealization in a Rorschach response would be human figure percepts described in blatantly positive terms such as objects of fame or strength, or enhancement of human form by describing forms as angels, idols, or famous figures. The authors suggest that primitive idealization may be evident in a patient's reference to the examiner through comments such as, "You really know how to listen," or "These tests were really amazing—you must have learned so much about me. I know you could help me" (p. 160). Through such verbalizations it can be inferred that the examiner is aggrandized and made so powerful that he or she cannot be destroyed by the individual's aggression.

Projective Identification

In contrast to projection (a higher level defense), projective identification is characterized by the tendency to continue to experience the impulse while it is at the same time projected onto the other person, fear of the other person, and the need to control that person (often done in a way that elicits behavior in the person that seemingly validates the projection). A distinction between projection and projective identification is that projection is centered around repression, whereas projective identification is centered around splitting (Kernberg, 1985b, 1992). Projective identification is an unsuccessful kind of projection that leads the individual to "continue to experience the impulse as well as the fear of that impulse while the projection is alive" (Kernberg, 1976, p. 31). This leads to a "fearful empathy" with the target of the aggression and a need to control the object to avoid counterattack. The individual simultaneously fears attack from the object (due to projection of all-bad, all-aggressive images), and yet feels a bond with the object as a result of experiencing the same feelings as those that have been projected onto the object. The relationship between the self and the object is defined by an aggressive need to control and to ward off attack (Kernberg, 1976).

Devaluation

Devaluation is a derivative of splitting represented by the activation of ego states that reflect a highly grandiose, omnipotent self that relates to depreciated and devaluated representations of others, including the devalued aspects of the self (Kernberg et al., 1989). This mechanism serves to mitigate both unfulfilled longings for objects as well as the fear of persecutory action by others. Kernberg (1976) suggests one of the motives involved in denial is revenge—the individual is frustrated by the withholding aspects of objects and seeks retaliatory destruction. Cooper and Arnow (1986) propose that during Rorschach administration, derogatory remarks toward the examiner, the treating enterprise, the construction of the blot, or the self are suggestive of devaluation. In addition, responses containing human or animal percepts pejoratively described as "an ugly looking face" or "a bird without wings" in which injuries or flaws signify anger (p. 163) are also considered indicative of devaluation.

Omnipotence

Like devaluation, omnipotence is also a derivative of splitting represented by ego states reflective of grandiosity and omnipotence that relate to depreciated representations of others and projection of devalued aspects of the self. Omnipotence is an idealization of the self in which there is an unconscious conviction that one deserves to be praised by others and treated as privileged. The mechanism may also involve the inner conviction that objects (often idealized) can be manipulated to deter aggression or project aggression (Kernberg, 1976). On the Rorschach, omnipotence can be seen in direct descriptions of self in blatantly positive terms. For example, as in the form of remarks by the individual of special personal abilities such as, "I think you're going to hear some very distinctive responses. My vocabulary is incredible" (Cooper & Arnow, 1986, p. 165).

Denial

Denial is exemplified by the presence of emotionally independent areas of consciousness. Borderline individuals using this mechanism are aware that their perceptions, thoughts, and feelings about the self or others are completely opposite those perceptions, thoughts, and feelings of other times. This recognition has no emotional relevance and does not influence present mind-set (Kernberg et al., 1989). Denial may also manifest itself as simple disregard for a portion of subjective experience or a portion of the external world. The individual utilizing denial in this form will acknowledge intellectual awareness of the portion that has been denied but does not integrate it with the rest of his or her emotional experience. Kernberg (1985a) stresses that the portion denied in the present is something that, in other areas of the person's consciousness, the person is aware. Emotions are denied that have been experienced (and remembered), and awareness of the emotional relevance of particular situations is denied.

Denial of internal aggression and of bad aspects of needed objects implies denial of reality aspects of the ego and of the external world as well, so that denial and splitting reinforce each other, leading to impoverishment in reality testing (Kernberg, 1985b). This particular "lower level" denial is different from higher level forms of denial linked with repression. In such forms the emotional relevance of what is denied has never been present in consciousness and remains repressed. Thus, denial is a broad group of defensive operations, within which the lower level type related to splitting is representative of the denial most prominent in borderline organization (Kernberg, 1985a).

Kernberg's borderline personality theory is a useful framework with which to situate psychopathy along the continuum of human psychopathology. The recognition of psychopathy as a condition that falls under the borderline level of personality distinguishes psychopathy as a condition characterized by intact reality testing and the use of primitive borderline defenses. The use of unconscious primitive defenses and the capacity to know the difference between right and wrong are a critical piece in understanding the mental mechanisms of psychopathy and how unconscious defensive process and conscious cognitive style produce interpersonally harmful behaviors that appear to be rooted in and/or associated with lack of remorse.

Theory and research on psychopathy has come a long way in the years since Pinel first identified the psychopath. Even though psychopathy is "one of the oldest and most enduring of all criminological ideas" (Rafter, 1997, p. 235), few scholars have examined its impact on criminological and criminal justice theory. The historical role that psychopathy has played in the development of criminological theory, the developing research that has contributed to the development of reliable and valid psychometric assessment tools to measure psychopathy, and the state of the research suggest that psychopathy is central to criminological thought and criminal justice decision making with many questions still left unanswered.

CHAPTER THREE

The Mental Mechanisms of Psychopathy: Unconscious Defensive Process and Conscious Cognitive Style

If I was there and stopped the rape she would be so grateful at some later date she might make love to me. . . . I wonder if rape victims would pay me to kill the guy here that raped them.

—High PCL-R-rated prisoner (PCL-R = 33) response to being asked what he would do if he were in the bar during the rape scene depicted in the film *The Accused*

The PCL-R is a critical tool in research and assessment of psychopathy and a much improved measure of psychopathy in comparison with the DSM APD classification, a number of authors note the importance of using other measures in conjunction with the PCL-R to assess components of personality that may not be identified through the PCL-R (Blackburn, 1998; Brinkley, Bernstein, & Newman, 1999; Brinkley, Newman, Harpur, & Johnson, 1999; Cunliffe, Gacono, Meloy, & Taylor, 2013; Gacono & Meloy, 1994; Gacono, Loving, Evans, & Jumes, 2002; Gacono & Meloy, 2002; Helfgott, 1997, 2004; Meloy & Gacono, 2016), and there has been growing consensus on the need for assessment of psychopathy through instruments beyond the PCL-R (Patrick, 2018b). A critical question is whether or not the PCL-R and other measures such as the Rorschach and MMPI assess what many authors consider to be the fundamental feature of psychopathy referred to as a "defect in affect" (Cleckley, 1976), "lack of empathy" (Hare, 1991), absence of conscience (Hare, 1993), "failure to put oneself in another's position" (Yochelson & Samenow, 1976), and "fundamental disidentification with humanity" (Meloy, 1988). Although there is no direct test of whether a person feels a particular emotion, researchers have measured emotion indirectly by examining the attribution of emotion to others (Blair, Jones, Clark, & Smith, 1997), emotional reactivity to positive or negative mood induction (Habel et al., 2002), and physiological arousal to aversive stimuli (Steuerwald & Kosson, 2000).

The Relationship between Unconscious Defensive Process and Conscious Cognitive Style

A feature of psychopathy not fully captured by the PCL-R is the relationship between defensive process and cognitive style and the existence of primitive borderline defenses inextricably linked to the psychopath's inability to feel (Meloy, 1988). Gacono and Meloy (1988, 1994) suggest that a particular relationship between unconscious defensive process and conscious cognitive style distinguishes psychopathy. The authors propose the "levels hypothesis"—that unconscious defenses are manifest in and can be inferred from assessment of the psychopath's cognitive style, including the psychopath's verbalizations (Gacono & Meloy, 1994). Other authors (Eichler, 1966; Rieber & Vetter, 1995; Kosson, Gacono, & Bodholdt, 2000; Kosson, Gacono, Klipfel, & Bodholdt, 2016) have explored the manifestation of defense mechanisms in psychopaths' speech patterns and verbalizations suggesting that the language of the psychopath is a "tangible and analyzable trait" showing core personality features of psychopathy (Rieber & Vetter, 1995, p. 79). Verbal expressions and interpersonal style of the psychopath can be used as a "map" to guide forensic practitioners in the assessment, treatment, and management of psychopathic patients (Kosson, Gacono, & Bodholdt, 2000; Kosson, Gacono, Klipfel, & Bodholdt, 2016).

Human disidentification is a core feature of psychopathy that involves different components of personality. A more developed understanding of the human disidentification of the psychopath is crucial to development of assessment measures that fully capture the psychopath's affectless core. Gacono and Meloy (1988) integrate Yochelson and Samenow's (1976) cognitive concepts with Kernberg's (1975, 1985a, 1985b) psychodynamic concept of borderline primitive defenses to explain the mental mechanisms of the psychopath and the simultaneous use of unconscious primitive defenses and conscious cognitive style during the commission of a violent crime. This unconscious defensive process/conscious cognitive style (UDP/CCS) relationship offers understanding of psychopathy in terms of levels of personality.

Gacono and Meloy (1988) view splitting and other primitive defenses (primitive idealization, devaluation, projective identification, omnipotent control, denial) as unconscious defensive processes that are manifest in the psychopath's cognitive-behavioral style. The "zero state" is a cognitive thinking error described by Yochelson and Samenow (1976) that is the psychopath's greatest fear. This fear has been described by Cleckley (1941, 1946) as an inner emptiness, and by Wishnie (1977) as an inner state of anxiety, and as an experience of self-perception containing three beliefs: The individual is worthless; everyone else thinks so too; and this state of being a "nothing" will last forever. The extreme fear of this inner state is protected by the psychopath's grandiose self-structure (a central part of the CCS), and facilitated by the primitive defenses that make up the UDP. Through the UDP/CCS, the psychopath maintains an overvalued sense of grandiosity that protects an undervalued representation of self. Kernberg's (1975, 1985a, 1985b) primitive defense constitute the UDP of the psychopath that works together with the CCS to protect the psychopath from experiencing the "zero state." Through this process, the psychopathic individual is psychically free to commit acts of violence that require an incredible amount of human detachment. It is through the lifelong use of this process that the psychopath experiences complete human disidentification. The conceptualization of the UDP/CCS relationship is based on key elements of the primary psychopath's personality structure that defend against feelings of emptiness and worthlessness (i.e., zero state), and maintain the psychopath's grandiose self-structure.

Through the use of primitive defenses and cognitive thinking errors the psychopath simultaneously holds highly unrealistic, overvalued (grandiose), and undervalued (inner emptiness) representations of self. Both splitting and shutoff are very much a part of the mental process used by the psychopath to commit a violent act. The psychopath can only relate to others as a conceptual extension of himself or herself (Meloy, 1988), and thus others are also viewed as all good or all bad, and this view provides the psychopath the mental picture necessary to commit a violent act. The commission of the violent act is used by the psychopath to maintain self-esteem and a grandiose self-structure. The levels hypothesis attempts to understand and explain the psychopath's affectless core through this UDP/CCS relationship. The UDP/CCS relationship reflects the mental mechanisms involved in human disidentification. The defensive processes of the personality support the psychopath's ability to disconnect emotionally with others through a cognitive style that perpetuates this disconnection. When the psychopath commits a violent or otherwise harmful act, these mental mechanisms protect the psychopath from experiencing empathy for the victim or other feelings that would interfere with the commission of the act. Unconscious defenses are maintained by and can be inferred through conscious cognitive thinking errors that enter the mind of the psychopath at different stages throughout the commission of an act.

The Levels Hypothesis

Gacono and Meloy (1988, 1994) propose the levels hypothesis to explain the relationship between defensive process, cognitive style, and psychopathic behavior and suggest that the psychopath's defensive process can be inferred from cognitive style (see Figure 3.1).

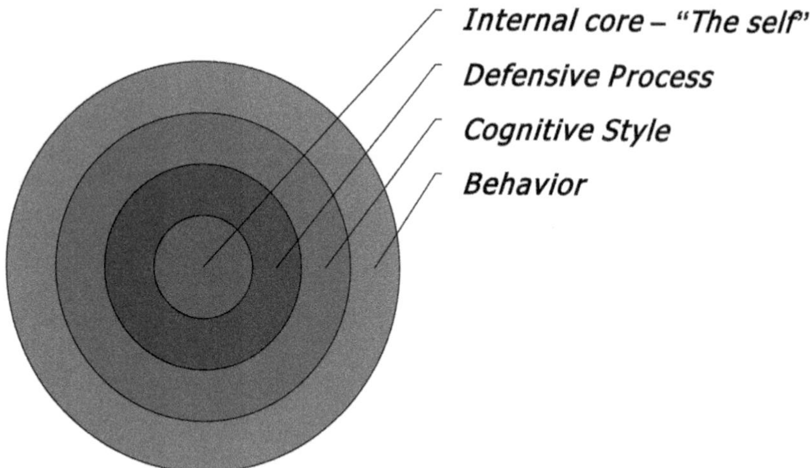

Figure 3.1 The Levels Hypothesis

The psychopath's defensive process is made up of primitive defenses that make up borderline personality organization (Kernberg, 1966, 1967, 1984, 1985a, 1985b, 1992), and the conscious cognitive style of the psychopath involves the use of cognitive thinking errors that Yochelson and Samenow (1976) suggest are distinctive to the "criminal personality."

To illustrate the unconscious defensive process (UDP)/conscious cognitive style (CCS) relationship, Gacono and Meloy (1988) offer a hypothetical scenario of the mental mechanisms of a psychopath before, during, and after the commission of a violent rape, consisting of pairings of particular unconscious defenses and conscious cognitive thinking errors. The hypothetical rape scenario shows how particular thinking errors and defenses are associated with each other during the commission of a violent act. The following is an adaptation of this hypothetical rape scenario showing the unconscious defenses used by the psychopath in the commission of this act:

> A male psychopath (P) walks into a crowded bar. He looks across the room and sees a woman/victim (V). He identifies and selects V through the process of *primitive idealization* whereby V meets P's "goodness of fit" stereotype (rooted in his early childhood development). P watches V for awhile employing *projective identification* whereby he projects onto V his own feelings of interest saying to himself, "She wants me, she wants me bad." P walks over to speak with V, and V says, "Get lost buddy." Reality invades. In order to maintain the all-good/all-bad view of himself and others (*splitting*), P transforms V into a monster through the process of *devaluation* by calling her a "no good bitch/whore." Because P has transformed V into the monster, he is now the victim and engages in *omnipotent control*, which

entitles him to attack and rape V. P tells himself, "She deserved it and asked for it" and *denies* that he has caused V harm.

The hypothetical rape scenario presented by Gacono and Meloy (1988) suggests that particular thinking errors and defenses are associated with each other during the commission of a violent act. Pairings of defense mechanisms and cognitive thinking errors represent different stages of the mental mechanisms of a psychopath prior to, during, and after the commission of a violent crime. Examples of associations within the stages are splitting/cutoff, shutoff; primitive idealization/grandiosity; projective identification/anger; omnipotent control/power thrust; devaluation/sexuality; and denial/entitlement. Each of the pairs consists of a primitive defense and a "criminal personality thinking error" (Yochelson & Samenow, 1976) representing successions of the mental process involved in the psychopath's ability to commit a violent act. For example, in the first stage, idealization/grandiosity, the psychopath idealizes the object (victim) based on a "goodness-of-fit" stereotype derived from previous experience with persons symbolized by the victim. The conscious component of this stage takes the form of a grandiose identification of the object whereby the psychopath convinces himself that the object is attracted to him in some way. The subsequent stages continue the mental process through various defensive techniques and cognitive distortions that enable the psychopath to commit a violent act while maintaining a grandiose self-image and preventing the zero state (see Table 3.1 for UDP/CCS associations).

Gacono and Meloy's (1988) model offers an integrative explanation of psychopathy that moves beyond traditional personality versus behavioral explanations. Their "levels" hypothesis explains psychopathy in terms of the relationship between conscious cognitive style (CCS) and unconscious defensive processes (UDP), and presupposes the idea that the psyche can be accessed at different levels determined by the tool of access, context, and conscious state of the subject (Stone & Dellis, 1960). Gacono and Meloy (1988) propose that the unconscious defensive process can be inferred from and is manifest in the conscious cognitive style of the psychopath. Their hypothetical example of the mental mechanisms of a psychopath, before, during, and after the commission of a violent crime, offers an integrative theoretical perspective of the psychopathic personality inclusive of psychodynamic, cognitive, and behavioral components of the disorder.

Most criminal offenders who manifest psychopathic symptoms cognitively and behaviorally (in terms of APD criteria) do not exhibit deficiency in affect. In fact, they are considered to suffer from underlying emotional disturbance (Hare & Schalling, 1978) that is the antithesis of psychopathy. These individuals have been included in groups of psychopaths because tests such as the MMPI have failed to distinguish these anxious psychopaths from their

Table 3.1 Unconscious Defensive Process (UDP)/ Conscious Cognitive Style (CCS) Associations

PRIMITIVE DEFENSE	THINKING ERROR
1. Splitting	Cutoff/shutoff
2. Primitive idealization	Criminal pride
	Uniqueness
	Pretentiousness
	Perfectionism
	Sentimentality
	Sexuality
3. Projective identification	Victim stance
	Refusal to be dependent
	Power thrust
	Anger
	Sexuality
4. Omnipotent control	Criminal pride
	Uniqueness
	Pretentiousness
	Perfectionism
	Ownership/entitlement
	Failure in empathy
	Refusal to be dependent
	Lying
	Power thrust
	Anger
	Sexuality
5. Devaluation	Criminal pride
	Uniqueness
	Pretentiousness
	Perfectionism
	Failure in empathy
	Sexuality
6. Denial	Criminal pride
	Uniqueness
	Lying
	Anger

nonanxious counterparts (Lykken, 1957). The historical assumption of an affectless core underlying APD criteria has been the crux of much of the misunderstanding, misdiagnosis, and confusion regarding the relationship between psychopathy and criminality. The isolation of a homogeneous element of psychopathy is dependent on the acknowledgment and identification of psychodynamic structure. On the other hand, identification of psychodynamic processes alone without attention to antisocial behavior excludes the antisocial lifestyle (social deviance) component of the disorder and may also fail to identify the homogeneous element within the concept. Viewed psychodynamically, the psychopath possesses an abnormal personality that can be distinguished from neurosis and psychosis. However, this distinction does not capture a defining feature that sets psychopathy apart from other borderline personality disorders such as narcissistic personality (NPD), histrionic personality (HPD), and borderline personality (BPD).

In the scenario hypothesized by Gacono and Meloy (1988, 1994), the borderline primitive defenses are linked with Yochelson and Samenow's (1976) cognitive thinking errors to illustrate the mental mechanisms of a psychopath before, during, and after the commission of a violent rape. According to the authors, splitting enables the psychopath to simultaneously possess overvalued and undervalued representations of self. These polar self-representations must be kept separate to enable avoidance of the "zero state" (undervalued self-representation) through grandiose overvaluation that facilitates acting out behavior. The psychopath uses primitive idealization and projective idealization to idealize the potential victim who meets a "goodness-of-fit" stereotype. Projective identification provides a vehicle to externalize and control the victim. The initial stalking of the victim is an example of the thinking error "power thrust" that influences most of the psychopath's cognitive-behavioral style. Power thrust and omnipotent control are accompanied by exhilaration, and the "corrosion" and "cutoff" mechanisms prevent deterrents that would interfere with the psychopath's grandiose fantasies. Projective identification and omnipotent control maintain the grandiose self-structure preventing the "zero state." "Lack of empathy," "ownership," and "entitlement" are supported by the grandiose self-structure through projective identification. When the victim becomes angry or frightened, this interferes with the psychopath's grandiose fantasies, and he "takes back" the projective identification. The victim is then devalued, transformed into a "monster," and the psychopath is entitled to victimize her, denying the reality of the victim as deserving of empathy and the monstrosity of his own actions. Denial and dissociation occur on an unconscious level enabling the grandiose self-structure, while corrosion and cutoff exclude and eliminate interfering cognitions. The defensive processes disallow any conscious feelings of empathy (Gacono & Meloy, 1988, 1994).

Empirical Study of the Defensive Process/Cognitive Style Relationship in Psychopaths

Two studies conducted in 1991–1992 provided empirical support for Gacono and Meloy's levels hypothesis (Helfgott, 1991, 1992, 1997, 2004). The studies compared scores on the PCL-R and two experimental measures—a "Cognitive Checklist" designed to measure Yochelson and Samenow's cognitive thinking errors and a "Defense Checklist" designed to measure borderline primitive defenses. The 1992 study involved a subsample of the earlier study including 39 DSM-III-R ASPD (APA, 1987) inmates and 18 undergraduate students. Subjects were classified as primary, secondary, or nonpsychopaths using the *Psychopathy Checklist–Revised* (PCL-R) (Hare, 1991) and the two experimental measures. Results showed that cognitive style increased by psychopathy level and that scores on measures of defensive process and cognitive style were significantly correlated for the primary psychopaths (≥ 12 on Factor 2 of the PCL-R) (Helfgott, 1992, 1997).

Qualitative data from the second study (Gacono & Meloy, 1994; Helfgott, 1992) offer illustration of the unique ways in which primitive defenses are exhibited by psychopaths. The "Defense Checklist" used in the study was a six-item checklist scored on a 0–2 point scale—the six items representing the primitive defenses (splitting, primitive idealization, projective identification, omnipotence, devaluation, denial) present in borderline personality organization (Gacono & Meloy, 1988; Meloy, 1988; Kernberg, 1966). The checklist was scored based on self-report responses to a questionnaire designed to elicit verbal manifestation of the individual defenses. The questionnaire included unstructured and structured questions regarding the subject's thoughts and feelings before, during, and after viewing a 13-minute segment of the film *The Accused* (Kaplan, Jaffe, & Lansing, 1988) depicting a violent rape scene.

Narrative responses to the questionnaire following viewing the film segment were examined in relation to Kernberg's theory of borderline personality organization and Gacono and Meloy's hypothesis through the hypothetical rape scenario. The Defense Checklist was scored based on responses to the questionnaire. Primitive defenses were assessed based on whether responses matched Kernberg's definition of each defense.

To illustrate the expression of primitive defenses in the language of the psychopath, Helfgott (2004) presents narrative responses of three primary psychopaths (PCL-R > 30) who received the highest scores on all three measures (PCL-R, Cognitive Checklist, Defense Checklist) in the 1992 study. Their PCL-R scores were 33, 36, and 38. Their offenses were murder/armed robbery involving setting the victim on fire, murder by multiple stabbing, and double murder/torture. Their sentences ranged from 13 years to life. One was black, two were white, and their ages ranged from 28 to 32 at the time of the study. The narrative responses of these subjects contain striking examples of borderline primitive defenses. Although defensive organization did not appear to differ significantly across nonpsychopath, secondary psychopath, and primary psychopath groups in the quantitative analysis (and a curvilinear relationship was observed) (Helfgott, 1997), the responses of the highest scoring subjects contain statements that powerfully illustrate the unique use of borderline defenses not observable through quantitative analysis. The following are segments of the subjects' responses to Defense Questionnaire with explanation of how statements were scored for splitting, omnipotence, primitive idealization, projective identification, devaluation, and denial.

Psychopath 1

This subject's responses contained numerous examples of splitting and omnipotence. Many of his statements blatantly contradicted each other. For example, the subject appeared to intellectually understand what the victim in the scene had experienced through comments such as:

> As the men were cheering and chanting I thought she must really feel bad, not just being raped and gang raped, but cheered on by other patrons to go further with it. As each was on top of her I thought she is going to remember each one of them and see to it that she gets them one way or another.

However, when asked to put himself in the place of the victim, his answers were superficial. For example, when asked what he thought the woman was feeling during the rapes he responded:

> I just know I'll catch AIDS, herpes, and shit, get knocked up and all that, and why is no one stopping this?

These seemingly sympathetic and understanding statements were contradicted by their superficial tone, and the intermixing of contradictory comments expressing enjoyment while viewing the activities in the scene. The predominance of splitting and omnipotence in this subject's narrative present a striking picture of the fragmentation and dissociation involved in the psychopathic mental process. The following are examples of particular defenses found in this subject's responses:

Splitting

> Since it is a true story I didn't like seeing it. I really like seeing tits and ass, it turns me on (while in jail where I can't have sex except with myself). But,

rape scenes always make me think of what if it was my family and friends being raped.

Primitive Idealization

She had nice tits. She had just the right amount of cheapness and class in her clothes and attitude . . . she sure can dance.

Projective Identification, Omnipotence

If I was there and stopped the rape she would be so grateful at some later date she might make love to me. . . . I wonder if rape victims would pay me to kill the guy here that raped them. . . . I wish I could see the whole video again.

Devaluation

I thought she was a sleaze looking for a hot time.

Denial

I don't like rape or people that rape. However, being in jail for life and seeing females walk around me makes me wonder if some day I might just say fuck it and grab one for myself (but, I won't because everyone would know I'm a scum-bag rapist and I couldn't live with that). . . . I guess if I ever was to rape anyone I would just have to kill them too so they could not tell and to ensure that I would never have to face them. For some reason I think about raping women a lot lately and never did before. I don't think it has anything to do with hurting or humiliating them, more along the line of control or kinky sex.

Psychopath 2

This subject's responses contained violent comments with vulgar references. The violence appeared to be primarily directed toward the rapists in the scene; however, the subject directed the strongest violent statement toward the college student who testified against the rapists. The subject said he identified the least with this character and stated that if he were there he would "break both his legs at the knees where it's most painful" (scored for omnipotence). This individual was the only subject to pick the college student as the character he least identified with.

Another theme reflected in this subject's responses was the presentation of himself as the victim's savior. Although the subject made many violent references to virtually everyone in the film segment, he did not direct expressions of physical violence toward the victim. However, in several places in the questionnaire he expressed enjoyment with comments such as, "it excited me a little to watch."

The following statements are examples of particular primitive defenses found in this subject's narrative:

Splitting, Omnipotence, Devaluation, Denial

> She was getting what she deserved. It excited me a little to watch. But also at the same time I thought I'd like to take a couple of the guys in the scene and beat them half to death with ball-bats then take them into a black faggot neighborhood and let the homo niggers rape them. . . . I would have punched the guy in the throat and as he lay on the ground in pain attempting to get his breath I would have escorted the lady out.

Psychopath 3

This subject's responses contained statements about how the world "should" be. Throughout the questionnaire, he refers to himself as "a devout Christian," "highly emotional" when a "wounded person or animal calls out for help," and, generally, as a person who absolutely cannot tolerate anger, hate, or violence directed toward women, children, or animals. He appeared concerned with making himself look especially good. He wrote a long essay in the freewriting section on the "beauty" and "true bliss" of "two people with the common goal of joy" (apparently referring to consensual sex, contrasting this activity with the rape that occurred in the film). He continued with, "I just can't see how anyone could beat, force, or hog-tie a woman and have sex—and really believe they're enjoying it." The subject also expressed protective feelings for his sisters and other women in his life; however, he called the victim in the film a "floozie" and a "tramp" and said he would never be interested in her (this statement was scored for devaluation). Following this statement he said he wouldn't rape the woman but would "find her weakness and load up on it," but added that this is what he would have done in the past, not now.

A distinct feature of this subject's responses was the frequent and haphazard placement of song lyrics (including Guns N' Roses—"Sweet Child O' Mine," Guns N' Roses, 1987) amidst his responses, both logically and illogically connected to the content of his answers. Several of these lyrics were scored for splitting because they contained polar themes in the same sentence and represented a sharp redirection from what he had been discussing immediately before.

The following statements are examples of primitive defenses in this subject's narrative:

Omnipotence

I can't begin to fathom the destruction I would inflict if I would ever get my hands on the assailant(s). . . . I am big enough to kick and shake holes in the ground *(in reference to what he would do if anyone tried to rape one of his sisters).*

Splitting

I am a connoisseur of love songs and ask that if people can be gentle why can there be so much violence. . . . "Only true love can conquer hate. . . ." I may be in prison and I may remain so for the duration of my life—but the only punishment would be that I spent my life all alone. "Your hair reminds me of a warm soft place—that when I was a child I would hide—to wait and pray till the rain and thunder quietly passed me by . . ."

(The quotation marks are the subject's, apparently to distinguish song from comment.)

Psychopath 1's responses to being asked to identify with the initial rapist in the scene are particularly illustrative of Gacono and Meloy's (1988, 1994) hypothetical example of the psychopathic mental mechanisms involved in the commission of a violent rape. The subject's responses to questions regarding the character's thoughts at different stages in the film segment exactly matched the mental mechanisms the authors propose are involved in the psychopath's commission of a violent rape. The following are this subject's successive responses (and the defenses they were scored for) to his being asked to identify with the leading male character in the scene at different points throughout the rape:

Primitive Idealization, Devaluation

Now this is one hot little bitch.

Omnipotence

Oh yeah, I can't wait to slam the big guy in her.

Projective Identification

She is just playing hard to get.

Omnipotence

Fuck this. I'm taking this cunt and I will make her love it.

Omnipotence, Denial, Devaluation

> Oh well, I can't stop now. I have gone this far. Oh yeah, this is real guy kind of shit. We sure will show this cunt a good time.

Quantitative results from the 1992 study showed that Cognitive Checklist scores increased by psychopathy level, scores on the Cognitive and Defense Checklists were significantly correlated for the primary psychopaths (≥ 12 on PCL-R Factor 2), and nonsignificant trends for correlations for the primary psychopaths (PCL-R ≥ 27 and Factor 1 ≥ 11) (Helfgott, 1992, 1997). Although Defense Checklist scores did not differ significantly across the nonpsychopath, secondary psychopath, and primary psychopath groups, analysis of mean scores on the three measures revealed a curvilinear relationship between psychopathy level and borderline primitive defenses (Helfgott, 1992). The findings suggest that it may be the particular relationship between cognitive style and defensive process that marks psychopathy underscoring the need for exploration of expression of primitive defenses in the language of psychopaths. These narrative responses illustrate the personality mechanisms that regulate the psychopath's interpersonal style and offer rich illustration of the unique unconscious defensive process/conscious cognitive style relationship consistent with Gacono and Meloy's (1988, 1994) "levels hypothesis."

Consistent with the levels hypothesis, the narrative responses of psychopaths illustrate the manifestation of defensive process through cognitive style and specific thinking errors. Analysis of primitive defenses in psychopathic narratives can provide important insights for criminal justice and forensic practitioners including enhanced understanding of the psychopath's experience of emotion, as a guide for forensic practitioners in assessment, treatment, and management of psychopaths, and as an assessment tool that can supplement other methods and measures at different stages of the criminal justice process (e.g., correctional management and treatment, parole supervision, prediction of dangerousness, criminal profiling).

The Psychopath's Experience of Emotion

Many scholars, forensic practitioners, and laypersons share the view that psychopaths are emotionless. However, broad generalizations about the emotional experiences of psychopaths are contradicted by the complexity of the disorder and inconsistent with research suggesting that psychopaths are capable of experiencing some emotional states (Kosson, Vitacco, Swagger, & Steuerwald, 2016; Steuerwald & Kosson, 2000) including anger, exhilaration, and contemptuous delight (Meloy, 1988). Current research suggests that psychopaths have a reduced sensitivity to emotion (particularly fear and anxiety) that is mediated by attentional differences and coping mechanisms.

Furthermore, emotional impairment may be specific to situations in which the psychopath does not experience strong emotion (Kosson, Vitacco, Swagger, & Steuerwald, 2016; Steuerwald & Kosson, 2000).

The manifestation of defensive process through cognitive style in psychopaths' narratives shed light on the unique process through which the psychopath is able to mimic human emotion, and/or (depending on one's view) the different level of emotion experienced by the psychopath relative to nonpsychopaths. The narratives presented contain a preponderance of "sentimentality," a thinking error identified by Yochelson and Samenow (1976) and mentioned in early writings on psychopathy (Maughs, 1941). According to Yochelson and Samenow (1976), the "criminal personality" (a term they use synonymously with psychopathy) can only express feelings for others through sentimentality. This view is supported by Cleckley (1941, 1976) who contended that, absent true affect, the psychopath is a "subtly constructed reflex machine that can mimic the human personality perfectly" (Cleckley, 1976, p. 228). The "mimicking" of empathy through sentimentality is evident in the narratives of the psychopaths presented. The subjects' responses contained references to women, children, animals, and/or other living beings seen as defenseless. At times, the subjects appeared to be protective of the rape victim, relating her to women and children in their own lives. On the other hand, their comments were superficial in tone, and they expressed considerable anger and violence toward others in the film segment (and at times toward the victim as well). In the case of Psychopath 2, anger was expressed toward the only person in the scene who appeared to be disturbed by the gang rape. Furthermore, all three subjects presented themselves as the victim's savior, saw themselves as rescuing her through violence, and appeared to think that through this sort of expression they were presenting themselves as powerful and worthy of the victim's attention (as was the case in Psychopath 1's response that the woman would be so grateful to him for having rescued her that she would offer to make love to him).

These expressions of sentimentality were intermixed with those of enjoyment and are evident in many of the statements scored for multiple primitive defenses. The subjects referred to the victim as a "sleaze," a "cunt," or a "tramp," at some point in their narratives, and made other derogatory remarks toward the victim and others in the film segment. While these individuals, at times, present themselves as sentimental about what is happening to the victim and expressed concerned about particular people in their own lives (people who they viewed as defenseless), the preponderance of grandiose and omnipotent thinking, contradictory statements, violent and derogatory references, and the superficial tone of their responses illustrate what Cleckley (1976) meant by the term "reflex machine." Though "sentimentality" was not a thinking error particularly emphasized in Gacono and Meloy's (1988) hypothetical rape scenario, this cognitive error is salient in the narratives suggesting that "sentimentality" is a conscious tool fueled by the unconscious use of borderline primitive defenses used by psychopaths to mimic or mediate human emotion.

Defenses expressed in the narratives are consistent with the findings of recent cognitive/information-processing studies that have attempted to empirically explore Cleckley's (1976) "semantic dementia"—the psychopath's attempt to mimic emotion and manipulate meaning through language. Rieber and Vetter (1995) suggest that the language of the psychopath reflects underlying personality mechanisms, in particular the ability to dissociate feelings of guilt. The inflated presence of splitting in the narratives can be more fully understood in conjunction with Brinkley et al.'s (1999) finding that psychopaths use fewer cohesive ties when telling stories. The salience of denial, devaluation, omnipotence, sentimentality, and superficial apathy is consistent with results presented by Williamson, Harpur, and Hare (1991), showing that psychopaths extract less information from affective words than nonpsychopaths, and Blair, Jones, Clark, and Smith's (1997) and others' findings (e.g., Contreras-Rodríguez et al., 2014; Fido et al., 2017; Pera-Guardiola et al., 2016; Stanković et al., 2015) that psychopathy is the result of early dysfunction within the violence inhibition mechanism (VIM), a cognitive mechanism that reduces the likelihood of aggressive attack when the aggressor is faced with the display of distress cues. Consistent with the narratives presented here, Blair and colleagues (1997) found that when psychopaths are asked to identify with protagonists in stories where someone is harmed, their dominant attribution to story protagonists is indifference and happiness in striking contrast to the guilt and regret attributed by the controls. Integration of psychodynamic and cognitive/information-processing models is a necessary step to more fully understand the relationship between defensive process and cognitive style in the psychopath, and whether or not psychopathic language is the result of conscious deceptive manipulation of meaning or cognitive deficit developmentally rooted in borderline personality organization. Analysis of psychopaths' verbal expressions offers rich contextual information that has the potential to enhance understanding of the psychodynamic and cognitive mechanisms that mediate emotional expression in psychopaths.

Why Understanding the Mental Mechanisms of Psychopathy—Unconscious Defensive Process/Conscious Cognitive Style—Matters

Attention to the unique ways in which the emotional experience of psychopaths is expressed through (and mediated by) primitive defenses offers a deeper understanding of the emotional states of individual psychopathic clients to guide clinician-patient interactions. Steuerwald and Kosson (2000) caution clinicians to be careful not to assume that the apparent absence of one emotional state implies the absence on another. The authors suggest that it may be inappropriate to conclude that the psychopath is emotionless and that “the psychopath’s ability to experience emotions may be richer than is commonly believed” (p. 114). The psychopath’s use of primitive defenses reveals the unique ways in which emotion is mediated by defensive process.

Cognitive manifestation of defensive process in the language of the psychopath reflecting particular defenses (e.g., primitive idealization, devaluation) and their cognitive counterparts (e.g., sentimentality, anger) provides necessary qualitative information to further explore the emotional capacity of psychopaths. In other words, *is the sentimentality expressed by psychopaths a mimicry of human emotion or a unique emotional response mediated by defensive process? Is the anger expressed by psychopaths a superficial emotionless pseudo-anger, as suggested by Yochelson and Samenow (1976), or is it rooted in a complex emotional state influenced by interpersonal factors and moral development* (Kosson, Vitacco, Swagger, & Steuerwald, 2016; Steuerwald & Kosson, 2000)? Given that psychopaths may not express emotion in usual ways, analysis of defensive process in psychopaths’ self-reports and verbal expressions can supplement knowledge of the individual’s history, behavioral observations, and clinical judgment to better understand the psychopath’s emotional state. Attention to interpersonally expressed primitive defenses can aid clinicians in interactions with psychopathic patients in interviewing, developing treatment plans, and dealing with countertransference reactions (Kosson, Gacono, & Bodholdt, 2000; Kosson, Gacono, Klipfel, & Bodholdt, 2016).

Gacono and Meloy (2002) and Gacono (2013) stress the importance of understanding psychopathy as a taxon (PCL-R ≥ 30) for research purposes and as a dimensional construct along a continuum of severity in clinical/forensic settings. They recommend that other tests (including assessment of defensive process) be used in conjunction with the PCL-R to further delineate the dimensional aspects (behavioral and intrapsychic characteristics) of antisocial and psychopathic subjects. While the PCL-R (Factor 1) measures personality features distinguishing psychopathic from nonpsychopathic APDs, Factor 1 ratings depend on clinician inferences about the motives and accuracy of patient self-reports and interpersonal style (Kosson, Gacono, & Bodholdt, 2000; Kosson, Gacono, Klipfel, & Bodholdt, 2016). With the subjective nature of Factor 1 ratings, aspects of the interpersonal style of the psychopath can be lost. With this in mind, the Interpersonal Measure of Psychopathy (IM-P) was developed as a supplement to the PCL-R to assess the core personality of the psychopath by identifying and coding interpersonal behaviors (Kosson, Gacono, & Bodholdt, 2000; Kosson, Gacono, Klipfel, & Bodholdt, 2016).

The IM-P was designed to quantify verbal and nonverbal behaviors observed in interactions with antisocial individuals. Recent research on the validity of IM-P suggests that IM-P scores correlate significantly with interviewer emotional reactions, with PCL-1 Factor 1 ratings, and violent interpersonal behavior (Kosson, Gacono, & Bodholdt, 2000; Kosson, Gacono, Klipfel, &

Bodholdt, 2016). The IM-P consists of 21 items reflecting interpersonal behaviors rated based on observation of behaviors, including verbal expressions. The 21 IM-P items are listed in Table 3.2.

IM-P items were designed to capture the interpersonal style of the psychopath, in particular the borderline primitive defenses and their expression through cognitive and behavioral style. The measure is founded on research and clinician experience suggesting that understanding defensive process and cognitive style is crucial to the assessment, treatment, and management of psychopaths. For example, Kosson, Gacono, & Bodholdt (2000) and Kosson, Gacono, Klipfel, & Bodholdt (2016) suggest that whenever splitting and projective identification are common, clinicians should pay attention to patients' inferences about interviewers' motives and their own uncharacteristic emotional reactions, and that emotional reactions should guide safety considerations, course of treatment, and dangerousness management.

Identification of primitive defenses in the language of the psychopath offers concrete information with which to score IM-P items. For example, statements such as *"If I was there and stopped the rape she would be so grateful at some later date she might make love to me. . . . I wonder if rape victims would pay me to kill the guy here that raped them."* in Psychopath 1's responses to the video segment (scored for splitting, omnipotence, and projective identification) provide information to support and score IM-P items 13 (ethical superiority), 14 (expressed narcissism), 17 (showmanship), 18 (angry), and 20 (expressed toughness). Identification of primitive defenses in the language of the psychopath can be used in conjunction with, or as a foundation for, scoring items on the IM-P to assess the degree of psychopathic disturbance and to guide clinicians in their interactions with psychopathic patients. Second, assessment of primitive defenses through written and verbal narratives offers a method through which subclinical psychopathy may be empirically investigated.

Understanding the UDP/CCS relationship and how unconscious defensive process and conscious cognitive style drive the mental mechanisms of psychopathy and produce behaviors that appear to be remorseless is important for theoretical understanding and empirical research and has direct implications for criminal justice practice. The unconscious process of psychopathy, the cognitive distortions used in conjunction with primitive defenses, and the way these processes operate at different levels of personality have implications for understanding how unconscious processes produce cognitive thinking errors that drive behaviors that appear to be rooted in lack of remorse, empathy, and human attachment. Research on the psychopath's ability to feel and the ways in which cognitive deficits and distortions influence behavior require understanding the different levels of personality. Instruments that have the ability to capture unconscious defensive process and conscious cognitive style and the relationship between the mental mechanisms of psychopathy and their behavioral manifestation provide an important supplement to the PCL-R

Table 3.2 Description of Items from the Interpersonal Measure of Psychopathy (IM-P)

1. *Interrupts:* Doesn't allow interviewer to finish sentences and behaves as if entitled to speak at any time.	11. *Frustration with argument avoidance:* Expresses frustration when conversation is redirected away from argument/conflict. Appears to want to engage in argumentative discourse.
2. *Refuses to tolerate interruption:* Expresses anger or dissatisfaction when interrupted.	12. *Perseveration:* Persistence with line of conversation, behavior, etc., despite clinician discouragement/contradiction/rebuke.
3. *Ignores professional boundaries:* Ignores established rules of conduct. Attempts to cross the line by making inappropriate requests/comments.	13. *Ethical superiority:* Makes comments to suggest he/she is superior to clinician.
4. *Ignores personal boundaries:* Ignores customary social boundaries. Attempts to engage clinician in personal conversation.	14. *Expressed narcissism:* Builds self up by embellishing achievements, status, and uniqueness.
5. *Tests interviewer:* Asks targeted questions/makes requests with purpose of determining who interviewer is and how far he/she is willing to go (e.g., whether or not will overlook certain rules/regulations).	15. *Incorporation of interviewer into personal stories:* Interviewer is given a hypothetical role (usually an antisocial role or lower position than interviewee) in personal stories.
6. *Makes personal comments:* Makes reference to interviewer's appearance, personal life, etc.	16. *Seeking of alliance:* Attempts to identify commonalities with interviewer/to establish a partnership/camaraderie.
7. *Makes requests of interviewer:* Asks interviewer for favors, special consideration, items, etc.	17. *Showmanship:* Embellishes accomplishments/attempts to "one-up" interviewer and others.
8. *Tends to be tangential:* Avoids direct response. Discusses peripherally related subjects while refusing to focus on topic at hand.	18. *Angry:* Expressions of anger at inappropriate times and in response to generally benign conversation.
9. *Fills in dead space:* Talks during moments of silence. Appears unable to tolerate quiet-empty space.	19. *Impulsive answers:* Responds to interviewer questions quickly, without thought.
10. *Unusual calmness or ease:* Low anxiety and calmness in interactions with interviewer.	

Table 3.2 (*continued*)

20. *Expressed toughness:* Makes comments/engages in body language to convey power, toughness, strength.	21. *Intense eye contact:* Makes a point to maintain direct eye contact with interviewer.

Adapted from Kosson, Gacono, & Bodholdt, 2000, p. 221, in Helfgott (2004).

and risk assessment instruments because they have the capacity to do a deeper dive into the unconscious roots and cognitive distortions that behaviorally express as remorseless and lacking in emotion.

Understanding the mental mechanisms of psychopathy can aid criminal justice and mental health professionals in interpersonal interactions with individuals with high levels of psychopathy to improve workplace safety. One of the most critical areas in which understanding the mental mechanisms of psychopathy is important is in situations where expert testimony is offered to understand the mitigating and aggravating factors in a criminal adjudication and sentencing. Understanding the unconscious defensive process, conscious cognitive style, and levels of personality involved in psychopathy and the harmful behaviors produced by the mental mechanisms of psychopathy is critical to understanding an individual's potential for harm, determining criminal culpability, and in assessing the presence or absence of remorse.

CHAPTER FOUR

Psychopathy from an Interdisciplinary Perspective

Criminology benefits from borrowing from a wide array of disciplines, but frequently the borrowing is from one stream of thought within a discipline, with competing perspectives ignored. The psychological perspective . . . has been largely ignored in criminology.

—Julie Horney, American Society of Criminology 2005 presidential address (Horney, 2006, p. 2)

The Social Sciences on Psychopathy: Will There Ever Be a Place for a Psychological Construct in Criminological Theory?

At the 2011 Western Society of Criminology annual meeting in Vancouver, British Columbia, Robert Hare was awarded the Paul Tappan Award for Outstanding Contributions to the Field of Criminology. This was a pivotal moment in the history of the intersection of the fields of psychology and criminology. Of the many awards Dr. Hare has received for his work in developing the PCL-R, including awards from the American Psychological Association, the American Academy of Forensic Psychology, the American Psychiatric Association, the Canadian Psychological Association, the Queen Sophia Center for the Study of Violence in Valencia Spain, the National Commission of Correctional Health Care, and the governor general of Canada who awarded him the Order of Canada, the Western Society of Criminology award is the only one granted by a professional organization comprised of criminologists.

Thirty years ago one would be hard-pressed to find more than one or two panels at a criminology conference that focused on the topic of psychopathy or personality and criminal behavior. In fact, conversations in criminological circles in the 1960s, 1970s, 1980s, and early 1990s were suspicious of biological and psychological theories supplanted by sociological theories of crime that have provided the framework for contemporary criminology and criminal justice.[1,2] In the discipline of psychology there has similarly been an absence of focus on and interest in criminology. In the 1990s, Gendreau (1996) noted that he had heard psychologists express puzzlement as to why anyone would want to read sociological journals, completely disregarding major sociological contributions to criminology. Criminology has been criticized for accentuating social-environmental factors contributing to crime, and conversely the psychopathy model has been criticized for overemphasizing internal dispositions over situational influences (Walters, 2004). This theoreticism, the tendency of researchers to accept or reject knowledge on the basis of personal values and experiences and the inclination to ignore and/or disparage knowledge bases and entire disciplines outside of one's own affiliation or framework, is nowhere more pronounced than in the study of criminal behavior. This historical gap between psychologists and sociologists has characterized much of the academic discourse and divide in criminological theory over nearly a century (Helfgott, 2008).

The paradigm shift in criminology and criminal justice from the rehabilitation to the just deserts/due process era raised issues regarding offender rights and the injustices uncovered with indeterminate sentence release decisions in the hands of psychologists and psychiatrists. The extensive amount of empirical research on psychopathy and its assessment in the fields of psychology, psychiatry, and neuroscience and the empirical link that has been established between psychopathy, criminal behavior, and recidivism has compelled a return (and new appreciation of) psychological and biological theory and research in criminology/criminal justice. This recognition of the importance of the psychopathy construct to criminology had made way for exciting interdisciplinary research and a forward-looking and integrative approach to the study of criminal behavior.

One of the most academically exciting results of the renewed interest in psychological and biological research in criminology and criminal justice is the integration of theoretical perspectives that have long existed in theoretical

[1] In 1992 I completed my doctoral dissertation entitled "The Unconscious Defensive Process/Conscious Cognitive Style Relationship: An Empirical Study of Psychopathic Dynamics in Criminal and Noncriminal Groups." One of my most vivid memories after completing the dissertation was the reaction I received from a faculty member in my department (a sociologically trained criminal justice scholar who was not a member of my doctoral committee). After he congratulated me on completing the dissertation, he added, "I wish you would have chosen a different topic." Knowing his views, I knew he was referring to the topic of the assessment of psychopathy. He and other faculty members and crime scholars at the time were concerned about the location of criminal behavior in static personality and biological factors that could not be changed, and thus could be used in a dangerous and potentially unethical manner as a formal mechanism of social control.

[2] For purpose of clarity and brevity I include sociological theories of crime under the umbrella of "criminology/criminal justice" given the historical sociological underpinnings of the discipline of criminology/criminal justice.

vacuums. Parallel theories have existed for years in psychology and criminology/criminal justice. Recently, some of these theoretical perspectives have merged to inform empirical research (e.g., DeLisi, 2009; DeLisi et al., 2018; Vaughn & DeLisi, 2008). For example, it has long been held that a small group of chronic offenders commit the majority of all crime. In sociological circles, this is referred to as the "six-percent solution" based on the 1970s Wolfgang cohort study that found that six percent of the longitudinal sample was responsible for more than 50 percent of crime. In psychological circles, scholars generally speak about the five percent of chronic offenders who are likely to score high on measures of psychopathy who are responsible for more than 50 percent of all crime. Until recently these areas of inquiry existed in parallel but were largely independent (Vaughn & DeLisi, 2008). Although there has been some scholarly integration in recent years, many theories and research findings continue to be isolated within disciplinary boundaries. Integrative theoretical frameworks offer great promise in developing a more sophisticated understanding of the relationship between psychopathy and criminal behavior and the sanctioning, management, and treatment of psychopaths in the criminal justice system.

Theory Integration, Interdisciplinary Criminology, and the Contribution of Psychopathy to Criminology/Criminal Justice

The lack of complex integrated theory construction (largely rooted in historical competition between macrolevel sociological theories and microlevel psychological theories) and the inability to come up with a general theory to explain criminal behavior has called question to how much criminologists really know about crime. There has been recent recognition among criminologists that comprehensive and accurate understanding and prediction of criminal behavior requires theoretical and disciplinary integration. Many disciplines and knowledge bases are necessary to fully understand criminal behavior. Theory and research from diverse fields—criminology/criminal justice, sociology, psychology, psychiatry, neuroscience, biology, philosophy, public health, social work, law, anthropology, political science, economics, cultural and media studies, women's studies, and others—have contributed to the study of crime.

Although no unified theory or model of crime yet exists that can be considered truly integrative (Fishbein, 2001; Schmalleger, 2004), promising integrative models have emerged that offer insight into the developmental pathways and manifestations of criminal behavior (e.g., Barak, 1998; Gottfredson & Hirschi, 1990; Moffit, 1993; Robinson, 2004; Robinson & Beaver, 2009). Criminologists are challenged to develop a comprehensive and coherent explanation of criminal behavior that takes into account the diverse and sometimes conflicting theories, frameworks, and perspectives across the broad range of disciplines from which criminal behavior has been historically approached (Helfgott, 2008). Theory integration across disciplines is critical in making sense of the relationship between psychopathy and crime and in sorting out the criminal justice implications of the psychopathy construct.

The Importance of Psychopathy in Criminology and Criminal Justice

What is the contribution of the construct of psychopathy to criminology/criminal justice? Psychopathy is "one of the most durable, resilient and influential of all criminological ideas" (Rafter, 1997, p. 236). The extensive and growing body of research on the empirical association between psychopathy and general and violent recidivism suggests that psychopathy can be seen as at least a partial theory of crime. A number of scholars have attempted to integrate psychopathy into theories of crime (DeLisi, 2009; DeLisi et al., 2018; Fox, Jennings, & Farrington, 2015; Weibe, 2012), integrative frameworks to explain types of crime (Hickey, 2015; Meloy, 2000; Pardue, Robinson, & Arrigo, 2013, 2014), and into disciplines where theory and research on psychopathy has been historically absent (Reidy et al., 2015). However, there is still much to be done to bridge what are in some cases large disciplinary gaps. For example, while the term "psychopathy" is the term used in neuroscience and psychology and has long been the scientific term used by psychopathy scholars, there are still scholars in criminology and other fields who use the terms "sociopath" and "psychopath" interchangeably (Pemment, 2013).

On the other hand, there are scholars who challenge the centrality of psychopathy to theories of crime. For example, Walters (2004) suggests that a flaw of the conceptualization of psychopathy as a theory of crime is the low base rate of psychopaths in the general prison population. Walters contends that while psychopathy does not meet the criteria for a good general theory of crime, the concept has a role to play in criminological theory because a psychopathic minority commit the majority of crime. Walters argues that the link between psychopathy and extreme crime is an illusory correlation because the concept is tautological with no clear demarcation between criterion (Factor 2 items on the PCL-R) and outcome (antisocial and criminal behavior)[3] and

[3] Further research is needed to sort out the issue of tautology and whether this empirical link is illusory (i.e., PCL-R items associated with criminal behavior predict criminal behavior). Factor 2 items on the PCL-R include need for stimulation/proneness to boredom, parasitic lifestyle, poor behavioral controls, early behavior problems, lack of realistic, long-term goals, impulsivity, irresponsibility, juvenile delinquency, revocation of conditional release, and criminal versatility. Of these items, only juvenile delinquency and criminal versatility directly involve behaviors that violate the law.

that the construct is limited as a theory of crime by its own limitations and omissions.[4]

Walters's critique of the utility of psychopathy for criminology/criminal justice notwithstanding, the large body of research linking the construct with general and violent recidivism, the worldwide use of the PCL-R in criminal justice decision making, and the growing body of work integrating psychopathy into dominant theories of crime such as developmental and life course criminology (e.g., Corrado, DeLisi, Hart, & McCuish, 2015; Flexon & Meldrum, 2013; Fox, Jennings, & Farrington, 2015; McCuish, Corrado, Hart, & DeLisi, 2015; McCuish & Lussier, 2018), the general theory of crime (e.g., DeLisi et al., 2018), and biosocial criminology (DeLisi & Vaughn, 2015; Raine, 2013) make it impossible to overlook in terms of its role in the criminal justice system. Hare and colleagues relentlessly maintain that "no other clinical construct . . . comes close to psychopathy in terms of its general usefulness for the criminal justice system" (Hemphill & Hare, 2004, p. 205) and that "psychopathy is such a robust and important risk factor for violence that failure to consider it may constitute professional negligence" (Hart, 1998, p. 133).

Crime, Personality, and Social Deviance

One of the most central and longstanding debates in the history of the evolution of the concept of psychopathy has revolved around the importance of personality (personality deviance) versus antisocial behavior (social deviance) features of the condition. The primary reason that the construct of psychopathy has become the "single most important clinical construct in the criminal justice system" (Hare, 1998, p. 189) is because psychopathy is comprised of both personality antisocial behavior features. Psychopathy is a disorder of personality that manifests in antisocial behavior. Psychopathy is a *psychological* construct. The psychopathology of the psychopath can be explained and understood from the perspective of psychology and psychiatry—its developmental origins, biological predisposition, genotypic-phenotypic interaction, cognition and information processing, emotional experience, forensic assessment, and so on can be explained by theory and research from the fields of psychology, psychiatry, neuropsychology, and psychobiology. However, criminal behavior is a *social* construct that requires theoretical perspectives and

[4] These limitations include attributional error (labeling the individual rather than the pattern of behavior), failing to recognize human capacity for choice over deterministic traps/ genetics/biology attribution to psychopathy, a preference for dichotomization and reductionism over dimensional constructs, exclusive person-based rather than stressing interactive principles that consider individual and situational factors, isolationism without consideration of contextual factors, and lack of recognition that change is a natural developmental process even for those with a seemingly entrenched criminal lifestyle under proper circumstances.

research outside of the disciplines of psychology and psychiatry. Understanding crime means asking questions such as: *Who decides what behaviors are to be deemed antisocial, deviant, and criminal? What economic, political, and cultural forces influence changes over time in psychological constructs and diagnostic categories and criteria and how they are used in the criminal justice system? How do environmental and cultural context shape antisocial, deviant, delinquent, and criminal behavior? What factors influence the effectiveness of criminal justice sanctions on different types of offenders? How do images of the psychopath in popular culture influence criminal justice policy, practice, and decision making?* These and other questions require theory and research beyond psychology and psychiatry, from criminology/criminal justice, sociology, cultural studies, economics, political science, and other fields. Given the nature of psychopathy, integrative theories and interdisciplinary perspectives are necessary for full understanding of psychopathy. More importantly, the societal response to psychopathy—the way the construct is being used in the criminal justice system for risk assessment, correctional management, to make decisions about sentencing and treatment amenability and other criminal justice decisions—depends on integration, linkages, information sharing, and mutual respect between the disciplines of psychology and criminology/criminal justice and the mental health and criminal justice systems.

Conflicting Objectives of the Criminal Justice and Mental Health Systems

Psychopathy presents a condition that explains criminality in terms of psychopathology. This creates a number of dilemmas because the criminal law is based on the notion that individuals rationally choose to commit crime. By definition, psychopaths are not psychotic. They know right from wrong, are responsible for their actions, and with their lack of conscience are inclined to commit criminal behavior. These dilemmas are dealt with in social policy through the dichotomizing of the concepts of criminality and insanity and the separation of criminal justice and mental health into two distinct systems with conflicting objectives. Criminal justice and mental health systems have different goals and require different backgrounds and expertise (Harte, 2015). The goals of the criminal justice system are due process, punishment, and public protection. The goals of the mental health system are individual functioning and psychological change. Individuals who do not function properly (with respect to their cognitive capacities) are not held responsible and are dealt with in the mental health system.

Throughout history psychopathy has been studied in both the fields of criminology[5] and psychology. However, most of this study has been contained

[5] I am speaking here of traditional criminology, which has historically been a subfield of sociology. The term "criminology" means the study of crime, which can be, and has been, approached through

within separate circles of academicians, split by their choice of disciplines. Many criminologists believe psychology is not an exact science, what psychologists choose to study is not measurable, that psychological assessment tools invade due process rights and seriously conflict with objectives of the legal system, and that criminality is best explained by sociological factors (Pfohl, 1985; Vold & Bernard, 1986). Many psychologists and psychiatrists, on the other hand, believe that criminologists do not take into consideration the importance of individual psychological factors in the development of criminality and psychopathy and that much of the criminological research has been "anti-psychological" (Andrews & Bonta, 1994, 2006). These clinicians and researchers maintain that a purely environmental, biological, political, or economic explanation of crime is simplistic, archaic, and not conducive to the development of appropriate measures of dealing with the social and individual problems associated with both psychopathy and criminality. These writers also suggest that many legal policies designed to protect due process rights seriously conflict with the *practices* of psychology and psychiatry but are not theoretically inconsistent with the *objectives* of psychology and psychiatry (McCord & McCord, 1964; Menninger, 1968; Walters, 1990).

Historically, few authors have written in both the criminology and psychology literature. Among them early writers are Robert Lindner, Joan and William McCord, Bernard, Eleanor, and Sheldon Glueck, Samuel Yochelson, and Stanton Samenow. More recently, Andrews and Bonta (1994, 2003, 2006, 2010), Bartol (1995, 2010), Helfgott (2008, 2013a), Walters (1990), Moffit (1993), Palermo (2011), Arrigo (2000), Rafter (1997), DeLisi (2009), and others have intersected the fields, though disciplinary conflict continues to exist (Gendreau, 1996; Walters, 2004). According to Menninger (1968), in theory, the fields of psychiatry, criminology, penology, and jurisprudence are intimately connected, but in practice the gulf between these disciplines is very wide. Almost 50 years later, the disconnection between the mental health and criminal justice systems (and the disciplines on which they are founded) continues to present problems in dealing with individuals who represent a threat to social order.

Ongoing disagreement between the fields of psychology and criminology/criminal justice and the lack of academic crossover have been a major obstacle in the study of psychopathy. Because the concept involves the complex interplay of individual personality and socially deviant behavior, study of the condition, by definition, calls upon both fields. Understanding psychopathy demands integration of psychological and sociological/criminological explanations of human behavior and reconciliation of the opposing objectives of the criminal justice and mental health systems. An initial step toward this

a variety of disciplines. As multiple perspectives and approaches to the study of crime have become integrated, the idea that criminology "belongs" to sociology is subject to debate.

reconciliation is the recognition of primary psychopathy as a mental illness and secondary psychopathy as a form of social deviance. In other words, if primary psychopathy were seen (and could be assessed) as distinct from secondary psychopathy, then the mental health and criminal justice systems might work together to deal with each condition accordingly.

Mention of psychopathy can be found in criminology, criminal justice, and abnormal psychology textbooks. Although individual researchers do not often participate in the discourse of both fields, psychopathy as a phenomenon is rarely discussed in either discipline without reference to the other. In the history of criminology, psychopathy is often described as a mental disorder or mental illness and has been associated with sexual deviation (Radzinowicz & Wolfgang, 1971).[6] It has been described as "by all odds the prime criminogenic personality trait" (Wilson & Herrnstein, 1985, p. 198). In Desola's (1982) *Crime Dictionary*, a "psychopath" is defined as a:

> person suffering from mental aberrations and disorders, especially one who perceives reality clearly except for his or her own social or moral obligations and seeks instant gratification in criminal or otherwise abnormal behavior.

"Psychopathic personality" is defined as "(penological parlance) criminal, especially a criminal psychopath." "Psychopathic hospital" is defined as "insane asylum" (Desola, 1982, p. 121). The related terms "sociopathic personality" and "antisocial personality" are defined respectively as "antisocial character disorder marked by moral deviation and often total involvement in crime" (Desola, 1982, p. 143).

These definitions represent notions of psychopathy that most psychologists and psychiatrists would disagree with, or, at most, would find to be very confused. For example, in the various definitions relating to psychopathy, the disorder has been consistently portrayed in texts as if it were synonymous with insanity and criminality. Although it is easy to understand the overemphasized association with criminality in these definitions (because of the behavioral component of the disorder), the association of psychopathy with insanity is completely inconsistent with the fact that psychopathy cannot be considered under the insanity defense (Cleckley, 1941, 1988). In fact, the

---

[6] This association of sexual deviation and psychopathy has worked its way into the legal system. The term "sexual psychopath" is an early precursor to the sexually violent predator designation used in court to impose civil commitment. The definition of the term has differed over time state by state, and although its adoption may have been a result of the historical connection between psychopathy and sexual deviance, its definition (in any state) is not the same as traditional or contemporary psychological definitions of psychopathy. See S. R. Smith & R. G. Meyer (1987). *Law, behavior, and mental health policy and practice.* New York: New York University Press.

American Law Institute's (ALI) revision of the insanity defense contains a clause that specifically excludes conditions of abnormality manifested by repeated criminal or antisocial conduct. Goldstein (1967) suggests that this clause represents a purposeful effort to bar psychopathy from the defense.

Psychopathy is barred from the other defenses because the condition does not entail cognitive defect that would render an individual with the disorder incapable of understanding right from wrong. The M'Naghten and control tests have been criticized because they do not recognize that mental processes are interrelated and interdependent (Goldstein, 1967), and Glueck (1927) suggests that the insanity tests "unscientifically abstract out of the mental make-up but one phase or element of mental life, the cognitive, which, in this era of dynamic psychology, is beginning to be regarded as not the most important factor in conduct and its disorders" (McCord & McCord, 1964, p. 178). Thus, while there is considerable debate over the bases for the insanity defenses, in the history of the law of insanity, psychopathy represents the antithesis of insanity rather than its synonym. Because of the way in which criminal law is applied through the fundamental concept of "mens rea" (evil mind) and "actus reus" (the actual, voluntary performance of a criminal act), individuals who do not exhibit lack of cognitive defect must be held responsible for their acts. Thus, while former chief justice Cordozo believes that "Everyone recognizes that the present [legal] definition of insanity has little relation to the truths of mental life" (Cordozo, 1930), it has been, and remains, extremely difficult to resolve the issues involved in the opposing objectives of the criminal justice system's demand for responsibility in the law, and the mental health system's desire to treat mental illnesses that manifest in criminal behavior.[7] The late editor of the *International Journal of Offender Therapy and Comparative Criminology* and clinical professor of psychiatry George Palermo notes, "in spite of the numerous psychiatric and forensic observations, the law continues to assess psychopaths only from a behavioral point of view, disregarding years of clinical observation" (Palermo, 2011, p. 3). According to Palermo (2011),

> Ultimately, the question is, will present law regarding psychopaths change according to these recent findings and begin to look at psychopaths as mentally disordered individuals who not only have diminished criminal responsibility but above all have a need for psychiatric treatment, treatment that, because of their illness, they reject? (p. 4)

---

[7] For a recent review of the insanity defenses and discussion of the incompatibility of the criminal justice and mental health systems regarding the issue of insanity, see Low, Jeffries, and Bonnie (1986).

This is a question that has long been raised in discourse on psychopathy and how the condition should be dealt with in the criminal law and continues to be a conundrum at the intersection of psychology and law.

Despite the necessary tendency in criminal justice to garble "the truths" of mental life (particularly with respect to psychopathy), the field of psychology, prior to 1980, made a careful attempt to separate psychopathic character traits from symptomatic behaviors. In Chaplin's (1975) *Dictionary of Psychology*, psychopathy is defined as:

1. An individual suffering from a mental disorder.
2. An individual with a personality disorder which is not psychotic in nature, which is lacking in manifest anxiety, and which involves inadequate social adjustment. The term is so all-inclusive that it is gone out of use in favor of more specific diagnostic categories. (Chaplin, 1975, p. 430)

A "more specific diagnostic category" was (at the time of Chaplin's writing) "sociopathic personality," defined as:

> a personality whose disturbance is in the area of social relations, particular one with sexual anomalies or antisocial behavior, or whose attitude could be described as asocial. (Chaplin, 1975, p. 502)

Prior to 1980, the American Psychiatric Association used the terms "sociopathic personality disorder" (American Psychiatric Association, DSM, 1952) and "antisocial personality disorder" (American Psychiatric Association, 1968). Both of these conditions were defined as personality disorders marked by social maladjustment and were similar to Chaplin's definitions of psychopathy and sociopathy in that the definitions did not exclude or overwhelm personality trait criteria with criteria based on behavioral symptoms. As previously discussed, the DSM-III (1980), DSM-II-R (1987), DSM-IV (1994), DSM-IV-TR (2000), and DSM-5 (2013) criteria for antisocial personality disorder are strictly behavioral.

The discrimination of primary from secondary psychopathy would mean that many individuals presently thought to be psychopathic and incapable of change could be viewed as hopeful candidates for good citizenry. This distinction is likely to impact general perceptions of inmates within institutions and of other offenders processed through the criminal justice and correctional systems. An awareness that the majority of offenders within institutions are not primary psychopaths, and that secondary psychopathy does not represent an unchangeable condition or a deeply ingrained characterological defect, is likely to diminish confusion regarding the association of psychopathy and criminality and reduce casual misapplications of the label of psychopathy within correctional institutions,[8] and in the public domain as well. On the other hand, the ongoing shifts in conceptualization of psychopathy as a dimensional rather than categorical construct (Bresin, Boyd, Ode, & Robinson, 2013; Edens, Lilienfeld, Marcus, & Polythress, 2006; Edens, Marcus, & Vaughn, 2011; Feihauer et al., 2012; Moreira, Almeida, Pinto, & Fávero, 2014; Patrick, 2018b; Walters, 2008, 2013; Wright, 2009) has the potential to continue to cloud the issue. It is possible that acknowledgment that the majority of offenders are more similar than different from the "normal" population would redirect correctional objectives and allocation of resources. It is a commonly held belief that offenders are hopeless, and treatment does not work in correctional settings. This belief persists despite research findings that have suggested otherwise (Gendreau & Ross, 1987; McCord & McCord, 1964; Meloy, 1988; Samenow, 2013; Walters, 1990; Yochelson & Samenow, 1976;). Although clinicians believe that primary psychopathy can be treated (Cleckley, 1941; Hare, 1993; McCord & McCord, 1964; Meloy, 1988; Yochelson & Samenow, 1976), most agree that individuals who have been traditionally considered secondary psychopaths (the bulk of inmate populations) are more amenable to treatment than are individuals who meet the criteria for primary psychopathy. Thus, the awareness that most offenders are not primary psychopaths, in conjunction with the abandonment of the term "secondary psychopathy," may foster increased implementation of treatment programs within correctional institutions.

The identification of primary psychopaths within correctional institutions may, however, impose negative consequences on those diagnosed as such. These individuals may be segregated from the general population, treated more negatively than others, and, for utilitarian reasons, are likely to receive the least amount of treatment resources. On the other hand, it is equally likely that the identification of primary psychopaths may have positive consequences. Detailed treatment programs have been developed specifically for primary psychopaths and for individuals with high levels of psychopathic traits, requiring strict behavioral controls and a therapeutic approach distinct from those geared toward the personality styles of other individuals (Cleckley, 1941; de Boer, Whyte, & Maden, 2008; de Ruiter, Chakhssi, & Bernstein, 2016; Meloy, 1988; Polaschek & Skeem, 2018; Samenow, 2013; Wilson & Tamatea, 2013; Wong & Hare, 2004; Yochelson & Samenow, 1976). Thus, the ability to distinguish primary psychopathy may facilitate the placement of

[8] In my own experiences within correctional institutions I have overheard correctional staff and prisoners themselves jokingly refer to prisoners as psychopaths. Although these references were in jest, the daily use of the term suggests that many who live and work within correctional institutions believe, as Wilson and Herrnstein (1985) maintain, that psychopathy is the dominant personality style of inmate populations.

those so diagnosed into either segregated units within institutions or specialized treatment programs both designed to address the particular security, management, and rehabilitative needs of these inmates.[9] The lack of success in correctional treatment programs of the past has been attributed to the treatment of heterogeneous groups with the same methods (Gendreau & Ross, 1987). Correctional treatment where specific methods are applied to individuals assessed with high levels of psychopathic traits aligned with the risk-need-responsivity principle (Wong & Hare, 2004) is a promising direction for future programs, and there is a growing body of research that offers hope for treatment success for individuals who possess high levels of psychopathic traits, in particular juveniles (Polaschek & Skeem, 2018). However, it is important that studies examining the effectiveness of treatment for psychopathy incorporate opportunities to examine the amenability of treatment of primary psychopathy utilizing dimensional and categorical models in methodological frameworks.

The use of the concept of psychopathy in the criminal justice context threatens due process of justice-involved individuals. In the field of psychology, it has been difficult to abandon the concept because the disorder has been clinically evident in the historical discourse for so many years (Cleckley, 1941; Frankenstein, 1959; Karpman, 1946; Lindner, 1945, 1946; Meloy, 1988; Yochelson & Samenow, 1976), and research has literally exploded in the last 30 years highlighting empirical findings, areas of consensus, and continued debate (Gacono, 2016; Patrick, 2018b). The conflicting objectives of criminal justice and psychology are compounded by the fact that psychopathy has been defined as a disorder that does not exist independent of criminal behavior. In the criminal justice system it is practically dangerous from a due process perspective to identify individuals based on elusive criteria such as personality. The idea of such identification raises serious legal issues involving violations

[9] The increasing amount of research supporting the dimensional model of psychopathy and studies evaluating treatment programs that include individuals who score below 30 on the PCL-R continue to make it difficult to determine the treatment amenability of primary psychopathy. Some of the early discussions of specialized treatment programs for psychopaths (e.g., Cleckley, 1941; Yochelson & Samenow, 1976) addressed primary psychopathy in the sense that the program recommendations were designed to address the unique features of the categorically distinct subset of personality disordered individuals. The growing support for the dimensional model, while avoiding the problematic arbitrary line drawn by the PCL-R cutoff of 30 and recognizing that human personality may be more dimensional than categorical in reality than a scientific taxon suggests, creates a methodologically difficult framework to examine the effectiveness of treatment for primary psychopaths who score 30+ on the PCL-R from the categorical perspective. Although recent findings (e.g., de Ruiter, Chakhssi, & Bernstein, 2016; Polaschek & Skeem, 2018) offer some hope with respect to the effectiveness of treatment for psychopaths, it is unclear as to whether or not this hope extends to individuals who would be considered to be PCL-R 30+ primary psychopaths.

of constitutional and civil rights.[10] However, individuals also have the right to be treated (Smith & Meyer, 1987). On the other hand, the psychological community is not comfortable with descriptions of mental disorder based on behavioral criteria alone, particularly with respect to personality disorders. Often, similar behaviors stem from different origins, and behavioral reactions and symptoms can vary depending on environmental and situational factors (Millon, 1980). This issue of personal versus social deviance has complicated the development of a consensual concept of psychopathy and has reinforced the division between the criminal justice and mental health systems.

Distinguishing Primary from Secondary Psychopathy

At what point on the continuum of PCL-R scores can an individual be deemed psychopathic? What factors enable the condition to progress from a few traits and behaviors to the full-blown clinical condition? Central to these questions is the long-standing idea that psychopathy exists in primary and secondary forms. This distinction between primary and secondary psychopathy dates back to the mid-1800s–mid-1900s when Kitching (mid-1800s) separated moral insanity into two forms—a defect existing from birth and a developmental arrest in early life. Koch (late 1800s) introduced the notion of congenital and acquired "psychopathic inferiors," Tredgold (early 1900s) recognized primary psychopaths as individuals with an absence of moral sense and secondary psychopaths as individuals whose moral sense is defective as a result of the absence of training (Maughs, 1941), and Karpman (1941, 1946, 1948) distinguished symptomatic from idiopathic psychopaths and called the idiopathic types "anethopaths" who he believe were the only true or primary psychopaths.

Fast forward 200 years and the discourse continues with a historically rich and empirically based understanding of the distinction between primary and secondary psychopathy (Hicks & Drislane, 2018) with primary psychopathy rooted in emotional deficit and secondary psychopathy in emotional disturbance (Yildirim, 2016; Yildirim & Derksen, 2015):

> [A] basic differentiation might be made between two continua of possible psychopathic phenotypes, namely the primary and secondary psychopathic continuum—with the core pathology in primary psychopathy being a deficiency of emotion, caused largely by genetic factors, and the core pathology in secondary psychopathy being a disturbance of emotion,

---

[10] For example, personality assessment can be considered a violation of privacy rights, and psychological treatment can be considered cruel and unusual punishment. Furthermore, differential application of psychological labels across gender and problems associated with applying culture-bound psychological tests across races and culture can easily be questioned on civil rights grounds. For detailed discussion of these historical issues, see Smith and Meyer, 1987.

> caused mainly by destructive environmental influences on emotional and moral development. (Yildirim, 2016, p. 166)

It is quite remarkable that in the span of 200 years the theoretical differentiation between primary and secondary psychopathy has changed very little, and it is worth reviewing the historical precursors to the current efforts to empirically examine the heterogeneity of the psychopathy construct and the homogeneity of the primary and secondary subtypes.

Throughout history, primary psychopathy has been thought of as inherent and untreatable (a discrete clinical condition), while secondary psychopathy has been described as a more superficial condition caused by environmental factors (a dimensional perspective). The inclusion of secondary psychopathy in the general definition of the concept has been the crux of the historical struggle to identify the condition as a homogeneous entity. The criteria for primary psychopathy have been based on characterological defect, while criteria for secondary psychopathy have been based on behavioral symptoms. Many writers have suggested that primary and secondary psychopaths share the common bond of antisocial, manipulating, or immoral behavior, but that they are divided by the etiology of this behavior.

The following definition synthesizes the many ways in which primary and secondary psychopathy has been presented in the literature:

> The primary psychopath engages in antisocial behavior as a result of a genetic or biological predisposition directed by particular psychodynamic forces that occur in infancy. The secondary psychopath's antisocial behavior, on the other hand, is the result of strictly environmental forces (such as membership in a deviant group) that occur at developmental stages beyond infancy. The fundamental distinction between the two types is the ability to attach emotionally to others and to experience the natural anxiety associated with human attachment. The primary psychopath forms no attachments as a result of early developmental obstruction, and thus is capable of harming others with little or no anxiety. The secondary psychopath forms human attachments, possibly to deviant subgroups, or possibly not. However, whether or not the secondary psychopath appears to be attached to others, emotional connection to other human beings is present. (Helfgott, 1992)

Psychologically, the distinction between the types is dependent on particular developmental phenomena. The primary psychopath, consistent with Meloy's (1988) definition, does not successfully pass through the developmental stages necessary for an individual to form human attachment, to develop one's own identity, and to experience other human beings as separate from oneself. With this psychic awareness comes the ability to empathize, to know that others are not unfeeling objects, but that they are, like oneself, human beings who feel pleasure and pain. The secondary psychopath successfully passes through the developmental stages considered necessary to form human attachment and thus is not deeply void of anxiety associated with harming others. The secondary psychopath may separate from already formed attachments later in life (e.g., a teenager who joins a gang, a young adult who becomes a member of a cult) but is likely to separate and attach to other individuals for emotional reasons. The secondary psychopath's antisocial behavior may be the result of a variety of forces—high anxiety or some other uncomfortable mental condition, attachment to a deviant subculture, or basic need. Secondary psychopaths are a heterogeneous group in the sense that the etiology of their antisocial behavior cannot be explained through the identification of one single psychological phenomenon, while primary psychopaths are a homogeneous group in the sense that they are deficient in the ability to emotionally attach to other human beings.

Secondary psychopathy is not a categorical psychopathological condition (though both the scientific and popular definitions of psychopathy are often expanded to include this group). Although there is currently a great deal of theoretical and empirical activity focused around reviving the notion of secondary psychopathy aligned with the dimensional model of psychopathy (Hicks & Drislane, 2018; Kimonis, Fanti, Goulter, & Hall, 2017; Yildirim, 2016; Yildirim & Derksen, 2015), it is worth considering how or and whether the separation of psychopathy into the two types clouds the relationship between personality deviance (primary) and social deviance (secondary). Blackburn (1988) and Brinkley et al. (2004) emphasize the problem of conceptualizing psychopathy based on heterogeneous elements. According to Blackburn (1988), the concept of psychopathy has historically contained the domains of personal deviance and social deviance, which renders psychopathy a mythical disorder based on cultural norms that is a "moral judgment masquerading as a clinical diagnosis" (p. 511). These two distinct concepts have been used to explain the disorder in different terms dependent on place and time. Social deviance has been emphasized in North American concepts of psychopathy, while personal deviance has been associated with European conceptualizations (Blackburn, 1988, 2003, 2007). There has been minimal commonality psychometrically across the two concepts, and the concepts may be etiologically as well as conceptually distinct (Barbour-McMullen, Coid, & Howard, 1988; Dinwiddie, 2015). These issues have made the psychopathic disturbance difficult to distinguish independent of sociocultural influence.

Despite the ambiguity in clinical descriptions over time, conceptual frameworks have been remarkably consistent. Pinel's recognition of psychopathy in 1801 is not far from contemporary definitions distinguishing the disorder. Every author on the subject has addressed the element of human detachment in some way. Descriptions and explanations of this element of human detachment have become more articulate and sophisticated over time as theories become more integrated with the acknowledgment of cognitive, behavioral, and psychodynamic explanations. Meloy's (1988) integrative definition of psychopathy is an example of such a theory. From this perspective, psychopathy is psychobiologically predisposed, but there are deficient and conflictual object experiences that determine its phenotypic expression. In other words, there may be a genetic or biological contribution to the formation of psychopathy in an individual; however, this predisposition must be set off by obstruction at a particular stage of psychodynamic development. Furthermore, expression of psychopathy may be affected by environmental and situational forces.

Meloy's emphasis on the "interplay of factors" involved in the formation of a "fundamental disidentification with humanity" raises the key issue of the importance of distinguishing between personal and social deviance in discussions of psychopathy. This distinction requires separate analyses of characterological personality traits and socially influenced behavioral symptoms and reactions and the relationships between them. The development of a meaningful concept of psychopathy and the important distinction between its primary and secondary forms is dependent on the resolution of this issue of personal versus social deviance.

A visual representation of the psychopathy construct and the distinctions between the domains of personal deviance and social deviance is provided in Figure 4.1.

The intersection of the two domains consists of the human disidentification component of Meloy's definition of psychopathy that distinguishes the primary form of the disorder from its secondary counterparts. The elements in this intersection include the developmental failure to achieve object constancy, identification of/attachment to grandiose self-structure during separation-individuation, and fundamental disidentification with humanity. The elements within the personal and social deviance domains (that are not necessarily included in their intersection) are items drawn from the PCL-R representing the personality/Factor 1 and the behavioral/Factor 2 features of psychopathy.

The purpose of the diagram is to show that there are separate types of deviance involved in the condition of psychopathy. Primary psychopathy is present only if the elements of the personal and social deviance domains coexist with the elements that are contained within their intersection. In other words, the feature of human disidentification contained within the intersection of the personal and social deviance domains is the distinguishing feature of primary psychopathy. Thus, the elements in both the personal and social deviance domains that are not included in their intersection represent manifestations of the disorder that may not necessarily remain constant across culture, socioeconomic status, gender, and race/ethnicity.

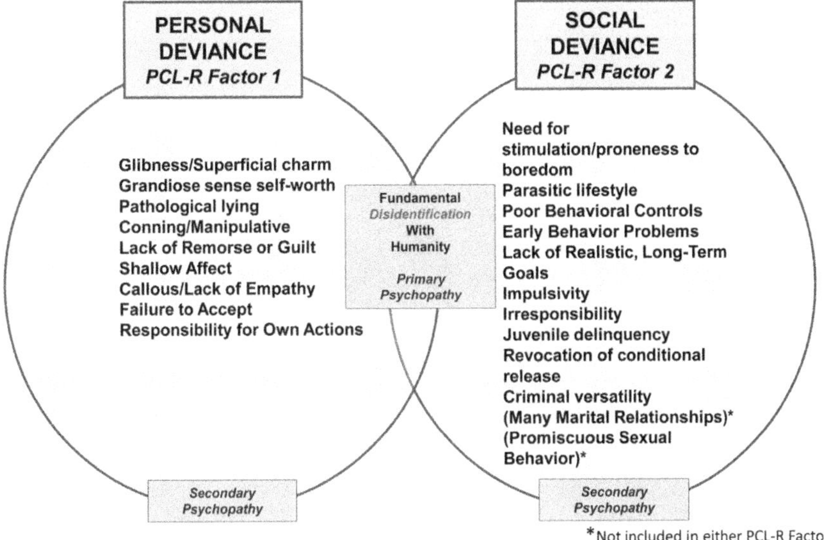

Figure 4.1 Personal/Social Deviance

Psychopathy across Culture, Gender, Socioeconomic Status, and Race/Ethnicity

Psychopathy and Culture

How do sociocultural influences influence the manifestation of psychopathy? Are certain cultures breeding grounds for psychopaths? What is the relationship between masculinity, masculine stereotypes, and psychopathy? How does race/ethnicity and socioeconomic status influence both the presentation and assessment of psychopathy? These and other questions regarding sociocultural influences on the development and manifestation of psychopathy are only beginning to be understood. Research on the relationship between psychopathy and culture has taken a backseat to the surge of research published in recent years in the areas of violence risk assessment and psychopathy and neurobiological studies. The increasing acceptance of psychopathy in Western culture, the use of the PCL-R internationally, and research showing that the PCL-R has considerable cross-cultural generalizeability (Hare, 2001) have created renewed interest in the cross-cultural validity of psychopathy (Cooke & Michie, 1999; Neumann et al., 2012; Wilson et al., 2014) as well as interest in cultural and ethnic differences in its manifestation (Fanti, Lordos, Sullivan, & Kosson, 2018; Sullivan & Kosson, 2006; Tütüncu et al., 2015).

An interesting body of literature exists that has examined psychopathy as a disturbance of culture (Harrington, 1974; Mailer, 1959; Rieber & Green,

1989; Smith, 1978).[11] Several authors portray the psychopath as an existentialist antihero who is "the man of the future" (Harrington, 1972), at once admired and condemned for his rational rebellion (Mailer, 1958) and "extrasocial" ways (Smith, 1978). From this perspective, psychopathy is a way to get ahead in America (and other individualist cultures)—a societal value that embodies a toleration for lawlessness, conning, and cheating that is "as American as apple pie" (Rieber & Green, 1989, p. 85). According to Rieber and Green (1989), the conflict between rugged individualism and community values in the larger urban landscape has resulted in a tendency "to wink at successful invasions of the moral code" (p. 85), creating what the authors call the "psychopathy of everyday life." Meloy (1988) cites the rise in stranger homicides and serial murder as evidence that psychopathy is a growing clinical and sociocultural phenomenon in the United States and other cultures, and Rieber and Green (1989) suggest that the public tolerance of the actions of political and governmental figures reflects a type of "bystander intervention" whereby the psychopathy of everyday life is tolerated and admired.

This notion of the psychopathic culture raises a fundamental issue relevant to the distinction between primary and secondary psychopathy. Cultural values may inhibit, disinhibit, and generally shape psychopathic expression and the ways in which psychopathy is defined in the larger social context. This does not necessarily mean that particular cultures will produce a greater number of primary psychopaths. However, a culture that glorifies, condones, and/or accepts the characteristics of the psychopath (e.g., superficial charm, a grandiose sense of self-worth, conning, lying, need for stimulation, impulsivity, many marital relationships, sexual promiscuity, and failure to take responsibility for actions) may inadvertently support the existence of the secondary psychopath whose behavior may be deemed psychopathic but is not likely to produce a significantly greater number of primary psychopaths who have not developed a sense of attachment in the early years of psychodynamic development. For example, Schimmenti, Capri, La Barbera, and Caretti (2014) studied the levels of psychopathy in Mafia culture in Italy and found that while the presence of psychopathic traits was high in convicted Mafia members, the Mafia members maintained a capacity for emotional connection and showed evidence of treatment amenability.

This raises the question—*how many psychopaths are roaming about in free society, the workplace, the college classroom, or the school playground who have*

---

[11] Academic discourse on the relationship between psychopathy and culture appeared to peak in the 1970s and 1980s (and began with Cleckley's attention to noncriminal psychopaths in the *Mask of Sanity* in 1941). Much of this early attention did not involve empirical research but represents an important synthesis of theory and research in psychology, criminology, sociology, anthropology, and philosophy that offers a theoretically rich foundation for future and much needed research in this area.

escaped the attention of the criminal justice system? Is it easier to hide if you are a psychopath in certain cultures or subcultures where psychopathic values are glorified and validated? Cleckley (1941, 1988) was the first to popularize the notion of the successful, noncriminal psychopath with case study examples of psychopaths (a "businessman," "gentleman," "man about the world," "scientist," "physician," and "psychiatrist") able to maintain a facade of normality—a "mask of sanity" followed by other researchers who discussed the "extrasocial psychopath" (Smith, 1978), "subclinical psychopath" (Ray & Ray, 1982), the "adaptive psychopath" (Rieber & Green, 1989), "white-collar psychopaths" (Hare, 1993), "successful psychopath" (Hall & Benning, 2006), and the "industrial psychopath" (Babiak & Hare, 2006).

Hall and Benning (2006) describe the "successful psychopath" as "one who embodies the essential personality characteristics of psychopathy but who refrains from serious antisocial behavior" (p. 459) and raise the notion of an adaptive or subclinical variant of the more maladaptive clinical condition. Benning, Venables, and Hall (2018) suggest that successful psychopathy be conceptualized as achievement in one or more spheres of activity without salient debilitating problems and externalizing outcomes in individuals who score high on psychopathic traits. Babiak and Hare (2006) describe the "industrial psychopath" who seeks power through money and fame. Rieber and Green (1989) use the term "adaptive psychopaths" to refer to individuals whose day-to-day functioning is not characterized by the impulsivity, hostility, and chaos associated with the clinical condition but who exhibit certain hallmarks of psychopathy such as thrill seeking through dangerous behavior, omnipotence expressed in the feeling that they will never get caught, and an innate dissociative capacity that enables them to demarcate periods of antisocial behavior from their "normal" periods. According to Hare (1993), "white-collar psychopaths" are lawyers, doctors, politicians, teachers, counselors, or those who hold any high status or respected position. These upper-level psychopaths "are aided by the common expectation that certain classes of people are presumably trustworthy because of their social or professional credentials" (p. 107).

The notion of successful, industrial, or "corporate" psychopaths has been fully described in Babiak and Hare's (2006) *Snakes in Suits: When Psychopaths Go to Work*:

> [P]sychopaths do work in modern organizations; they often are successful by most standard measures of career success; and their destructive personality characteristics are invisible to most people with whom they interact. They are able to circumvent and sometimes hijack succession planning and performance management systems in order to give legitimacy to their behaviors. They take advantage of communication weaknesses, organizational systems and processes, interpersonal conflicts, and

> general stressors that plague all companies. They abuse coworkers and, by lowering morale and stirring up conflict, the company itself. Some may even steal and defraud. (Babiak & Hare, 2006, p. xiv)

Understanding the nature of noncriminal psychopathy is an important piece in sorting out the relationship between psychopathy and criminal behavior. Recent research suggests that similar etiological processes underlie criminal and noncriminal psychopathy. However, criminal and noncriminal psychopaths are differentiated by the latter's ability to evade the law, higher socioeconomic status, higher levels of executive function, elevated physiological reactivity, and a greater push toward psychopathic behavior by environmental circumstances. Studies to date suggest that high levels of fearless dominance but not impulsive antisociality may characterize the noncriminal psychopath (Benning, Venables, & Hall, 2018; Hall & Benning, 2006).

The phenomenon of the noncriminal psychopath raises a number of important questions. *Are noncriminal psychopaths less extreme versions of criminal psychopaths, or do they represent a more adaptive variant of the personality that perhaps should not be considered disordered? How does noncriminal psychopathy overlap with its criminal expression? If the psychopathic behavior of noncriminal psychopaths appears to be more influenced by environmental forces, then are certain cultures, subcultures, career paths/workplaces, etc., more or less likely to breed psychopathy?* Recent findings suggesting that psychopathic traits may have both positive benefits and negative consequences in some occupations such as law enforcement (Falkenbach, McKinley, & Larson, 2017) raise new questions and avenues in need of further exploration.

Psychopathy and Gender

Psychopathy, antisocial personality disorder (APD), and crime are overwhelmingly male phenomena. Part of this sex difference can be attributed to sex-role socialization and the socialization of aggression. Sex-role socialization shapes the ways aggression manifests across gender. Boys are encouraged to play rough, to contain emotion, and to fight for what they believe in. Female aggression is often expressive rather than instrumental and directed toward family members and friends rather than strangers (Letendre, 2007). The most remarkable thing about the socialization of aggression in girls is its absence (Campbell, 1993). As a case in point, consider a young girl who possesses aggressive narcissism (the personality component of psychopathy) and is taught, throughout her childhood, that she will receive attention when she cries but not when she hits. She learns that little girls do not misbehave. Little girls are pretty, patient, and quiet. They should not expect too much. And when they grow up, they will be valued more highly if they find a man. But she is filled with aggression, coupled with the narcissistic need for attention and admiration. What does she do? As she grows up, she masks her aggression with tears, passivity, and physical attractiveness, finding that she gets what she wants this way. Because her aggressive narcissism renders her more forceful and in need of attention than those without this interpersonal style, she is excessively emotional, overly attentive to her physical appearance, and adept at getting whatever she wants. Her behavior does not appear to be antisocial at all. Rather, as a woman she emerges a dramatically flamboyant social butterfly.

This hypothetical example illustrates the complexity of the relationship between traits and symptoms in the manifestation of psychopathy (and other conditions). The woman possesses the internal personality trait of aggressive narcissism. However, as a result of the ways in which she has been socialized, she does not display the antisocial behaviors commonly associated with the psychopathic disorder. In fact, her behavior appears quite the opposite—as pathologically prosocial. Research shows that women tend to experience internalizing symptomatology such as depression and anxiety, whereas men tend to experience externalizing psychopathology such as antisocial behavior, aggression, and substance abuse (Verona & Vitale, 2006, 2018). When women do act "out," anger and aggression are often (re)directed inward and manifest in the form of eating disorders, self-mutilation, or psychiatric or physical illness. Even when women engage in extreme forms of criminal behavior, this behavior is often directed toward their own children or family members who they are more likely to see as extensions of themselves than strangers or nonfamily members.[12]

Although there was some attention to female psychopathy in the early 1900s (Spaulding, 1923),[13] researchers did not begin to empirically explore female

[12] Diane Downs, subject of Ann Rule's (1987) book *Small Sacrifices,* is an example of a female manifestation of psychopathy. Downs was said in court to have a histrionic personality disorder and was also referred to as an antisocial personality and a psychopath. Downs shot her three children, one of whom died, one paralyzed, and the other seriously wounded because she believed her lover didn't like kids. Downs saw one of her talents as being able to bear children and believed she could replace her children by getting pregnant again. She was a charming, seductive, dramatic person who held a job and did not have a criminal history until the day she shot her children.

[13] Edith Spaulding wrote *An Experimental Study of Psychopathic and Delinquent Women* in 1923, reporting results from a rehabilitation program for women at New York State Reformatory for Women at Bedford Hills. However, given the lack of consensus on the definition of psychopathy at the time and the loose use of the term "psychopath" in the early 1900s, it is unknown how many women in the facility would be considered psychopaths today, although 7 of the 20 women in the study were recorded as "Psychopathic Personalities." The book includes a pullout with details on the women with crimes including "Bigamy," "Keeping Disorderly House," "Endangering the Morals of Children," "Prostitution," "Petit Larceny," and "Grand Larceny" and notes that "The women in this group have been misfits in our entire social scheme, both outside and inside institutions. From the main population of the institution, no matter what its fundamental nature may be, they stand out as a distinct, although as yet inadequately classified, group" (p. xiv).

psychopathy until the 1970s and 1980s. This early work suggested that the female manifestation of psychopathy is not APD but histrionic personality disorder (HPD) (Ford & Widiger, 1989; Horowitz, 1977; Lilienfeld et al., 1986; Spalt, 1980; Warner, 1978), that APD and HPD represent sex-typed categories of a single disorder with psychopathy manifests differently across the sexes as APD in males and HPD in females (Warner, 1978), that HPD is most often diagnosed in women while APD is most often diagnosed in men (Coolidge, Marle, Van Horn, & Segal, 2011; Spalt, 1980), that clinicians are influenced by the labels given to the disorders (Ford & Widiger, 1989), and that the DSM in general, and personality disorder classifications in particular, embody sexist concepts and values with an androcentric bias that pathologizes stereotypically feminine behaviors (Brown & Ballou, 1992).

Histrionic personality disorder is characterized by excessive emotionality, attention-seeking, self-centeredness, shallow expression of emotion, superficial charm, flirtatiousness, dramaticization, sexual provocativeness, seductiveness, use of physical appearance to attract attention, inappropriate and excessive reactions, and theatricality (DSM-5, 2013). Studies have shown that the APD criteria reflect stereotypically masculine behaviors while the HPD criteria reflect stereotypically feminine behaviors (Horowitz, 1977), that manifestations of the hysterical personality are learned, have symbolic meanings, and are culturally defined (Horowitz, 1991), and that sex bias in clinician expectations account for the sex differentiation between APD and HPD (Ford & Widiger, 1989). And, in fact, Cleckley (1941) used characters from the film *Gone with the Wind* (Fleming & Selznick, 1939) to illustrate gendered manifestations of psychopathy, noting that it was Scarlett O'Hara rather than Rhett Butler who displayed histrionic characteristics more closely resembling psychopathy than did the antisocial characteristics Butler displayed.

Research conducted on female psychopathy over the last 20 years has focused on sex bias in forensic assessment, validity of the PCL-R with female samples, differential gender manifestations of psychopathy, and recommendations for modification of PCL-R items in forensic assessment of psychopathy with women (Anton et al., 2012; Cunliffe, Gacono, Meloy, & Taylor, 2013; Cunliffe et al., 2016; Eisenbath, Osterheider, Nedopil, & Stadtland, 2012; Forth, Brown, Hart, & Hare, 1996; Forouzan & Cooke, 2005; Jackson, Rogers, Neumann, & Lambert, 2002; Kreis & Cooke, 2011; Logan, 2011; Sadeh, Javdani, Finy, & Verona, 2011; Sprague et al., 2012; Verona & Vitale, 2006, 2018) as well as findings on the male and female brain that suggest that biological characteristics of the male brain are said to make it more susceptible to antisocial traits than the female brain (Pemment, 2015). In their review of the literature on psychopathy in women, Verona and Vitale (2006, 2018) conclude that while there is evidence to suggest that there is sex bias in diagnosis of psychopathy, data from a range of studies suggest that men and women manifest antisociality and psychopathy differently. PCL-R scores are lower in female prison populations than they are in male prison populations with lower Factor 2 scores in women. Women are less likely than men to show aggressive symptoms and early behavioral problems and more likely to exhibit higher rates of HPD, BPD, and somatization and prostitution and sexual misbehavior. Furthermore, the PCL-R does not do a good job predicting violence in women, and some researchers have suggested that the PCL-R items need to be modified to adequately discriminate between psychopathic and nonpsychopathic women.

The differential manifestation of psychopathy in women is an area of great importance in the forensic assessment of psychopathy. Based on findings on differential gender manifestations psychopathy, researchers have made specific suggestions for changes to PCL-R items or special consideration in rating items on the PCL-R. For example, Cunliffe et al. (2016) identify 11 PCL-R items that require special consideration when scoring females, recognizing that the female manifestation of PCL-R items may present differently. For example, on PCL-R items such as Item 2, "grandiose sense of self-worth," men generally present with an inflated ego and remarkable exaggerated regard for their own abilities, while women tend to present with a sense of self as damaged accompanied by interpersonal dependency portraying herself as a victim, dependent on others, and unable to take care of herself. On Item 8, "callous lack of empathy," unlike men, women are not likely to present themselves with "callous disregard," only concerned with "Number 1."[14] Rather they may present in a gentle and friendly manner and give the impression they are concerned for their family, children, and victims, requiring additional file review information be considered in forensic assessment (Cunliffe et al., 2016). In general, while male psychopaths view themselves with self-admiration and grandiosity, female psychopaths present as distressed while engaging in the same process (elevated ego with lack of self-awareness). Thus, female psychopaths experience chronic self-criticism and shame that are unrelated to remorse or guilt. Rather, long-standing frustration over unmet needs culminates in a self-critical, unhappy, dissatisfied presentation of a negative self-image (Cunliffe, Gacono, Meloy, & Taylor, 2013).

The two-factor structure of the PCL-R better integrates traits with symptoms than does the behaviorally weighted classification of APD and may be able to identify psychopathy independently of cultural influences. It is likely that a female psychopath or a noncriminal psychopath would score high on Factor 1 of the PCL-R, and perhaps on Items 11 (promiscuous sexual

---

[14] From Hare (2003) PCL-R Rating Booklet.

behavior)[15] and 17 (many marital relationships), and there has been some suggestion that the way females present may result in elevated Factor 1 scores in women such as manipulation in the context of intimate relationships (Verona & Vitale, 2018). However, such a score may not be high enough to warrant a diagnosis of psychopathy as a result of lower ratings on Factor 2 resulting from differential manifestation of antisocial traits. The PCL-R was developed through study of male criminals. Although there is some evidence to suggest that use of the PCL-R may be warranted in minority populations (Kosson, Newman, & Smith, 1990) and noncriminal groups (Babiak & Hare, 2006; Hare, 1993), these applications are only beginning to be explored. Use of the PCL-R to assess psychopathy in females may be more problematic given the gender differences that have been found in the manifestation of psychopathy (Hare, 1991; Peaslee, 1993; Raine & Dunkin, 1990; Warner, 1978) and the ways in which gender stereotypes have influenced psychological classifications (Hamilton, Rothbart, & Dawes, 1986; Verona & Vitale, 2006, 2018), criminal law (Faith, 1993; Naffine, 1997), criminal justice and mental health policy (Allen, 1987; Brown & Ballou, 1992; Daly, 1994), and definitions of antisocial behavior and aggression (Bjorkqvist & Niemela, 1992; Campbell, 1993; Gilbert, 2002; Kirsta, 1994; Letendre, 2007).

Research on psychopathy that is cognizant of feminist, multicultural, and socioeconomic perspectives calls for a new definition of antisocial behavior that better applies to individuals whose aggressive narcissism has been shaped, through cultural forces, into behavior that appears to be prosocial when it is nothing of the kind. Jackson and Richards (2007) suggest generation of new models with female psychopaths in mind that attend to gender differences in the role of childhood physical and sexual abuse in promoting the development of psychopathy and modification of laboratory techniques used in measuring cognitive affective correlates that are more oriented toward women,[16] and examination of noncriminal female psychopaths. Recent laboratory findings suggest that PCL-R Factor 1 traits may be related to emotional dysregulation and suicidality in women who score high on the PCL-R when accompanied by Factor 2 antisocial traits, which is not found in men who score high on the PCL-R (Sprague et al., 2012). Furthermore, Factor 2 traits may be less pronounced in women because Factor 2 traits are likely to be expressed by female psychopaths in self-directed violence and emotional reactivity rather than violence directed toward others (Sadeh, Javdani, Finy, &

[15] High scores on this item may be the result of sex bias in assessment or gendered behavioral expression of antisocial traits.

[16] For example, when using rewards in experimental studies, women may respond more positively to use of visitation privileges than to small monetary rewards that are often used in studies involving incarcerated male psychopaths.

Verona, 2011). In their review of the literature on psychopathy in women, Verona and Vitale (2018) conclude:

> [A]lthough high-psychopathy men and women have similar underlying deficits in emotional and attentional processing, these deficits are either manifested differently across the genders or the measures currently used to assess impulsive-disinhibitory tendencies in the laboratory are inadequate for indexing real-life expressions of these tendencies in women. (p. 522)

In this new and important area of research on psychopathy, gender, and criminal behavior, more theory development, testing, and refinement are needed to accommodate what is known about gender differences in developmental processes, temperament, biology, and socialization using mixed-gender samples to test directly for gender equivalence and modification (Verona & Vitale, 2006, 2018). This is particularly important in light of recent focus in the risk assessment literature and practice around the need for gender responsive risk assessment instruments (Boppre & Salisbury, 2016; Van Voorhis, Wright, Salisbury, & Bauman, 2010).

Psychopathy, Socioeconomic Status, and Race/Ethnicity

Socioeconomic status and racial/ethnic background may also affect the ways in which antisocial behavior is manifest and defined. Cleckley (1941, 1988) has said that many psychopaths "mask" their condition and exist quite successfully without coming into contact with the criminal justice system and without ever receiving a diagnosis of psychopathy. The phenomenon of successful psychopathy is likely a developmental pathway of the condition shaped by socioeconomic status or other environmental or cultural variables. Cooke and Michie (1999) found differences in the prevalence of psychopathy between Scotland and North America; Kosson, Smith, and Newman (1990) found significantly higher PCL-R scores in African American samples; and lower mean PCL-R scores have been reported in international samples (Fanti, Lordos, Sullivan, & Kosson, 2018; Sullivan & Kosson, 2006). The predictive utility of the PCL-R has been demonstrated with African American (Kosson, Smith, & Newman, 1990; Vachon, Lynam, Loeber, & Stouthamer-Loeber, 2012) and Latino samples (Sullivan, Abramowitz, Lopez, & Kosson, 2006); however, findings examining the relationship between race/ethnicity and socioeconomic status suggest that the predictive power of the PCL-R is contingent on SES in European Americans but not African Americans (Walsh & Kosson, 2007). There is much to unravel regarding the role of culture, ethnicity, socioeconomic status, and psychopathy. Although review of the historical and cultural literature suggests that psychopathy transcends time and culture, there is evidence to suggest that there may be ethnic differences in the manifestation of psychopathy. Sociocultural factors and biases may influence scoring of the PCL-R and diagnoses of psychopathy and the label of psychopathy may be over applied to ethnic groups such as African Americans who come into greater contact with the criminal justice system as a result of selective enforcement (Fanti, Lordos, Sullivan, & Kosson, 2018; Sullivan & Kosson, 2006).

Returning to the PCL-R, Factor 2 items (which are closely associated with APD criteria) such as early behavioral problems, juvenile delinquency, lack of realistic long-term goals, irresponsibility, and revocation of conditional release are likely to be rated higher in individuals who, as a result of socioeconomic conditions, are forced into situations in which they behave in these ways for survival. These criteria are designed with the image of the common criminal in mind, who is prototypically a young, economically disadvantaged male who is a member of a minority group. The criteria may be completely inapplicable to women whose aggressive narcissism is tempered and/or rerouted in response to social pressures to behave in a prosocial rather than antisocial manner, except in the case of girls and women who are forced to shed stereotypically female behavior in order to survive.[17]

A Theoretical Model of Primary-Secondary Psychopathy

Smith (1978, 1985) associates psychopathy with individualist culture describing the psychopath as "extrasociety" rather than antisociety. From this perspective, the psychopath represents the logical and psychological extreme within American society—a caricature that goes beyond societal limits. This understanding of personality based on cultural analysis (rather than, e.g., psychoanalysis) is superficial and simplistic and useful to illustrate the differences between primary and secondary psychopathy and the categorical and dimensional models of the psychopathy construct. The features of Smith's (1985) "extrasocial" psychopath lie within both the personal and social deviance domains. However, they do not include the components of Meloy's definition that lie in their intersection. In other words, a person can possess some or all of both the personality and behavioral characteristics of psychopathy but not possess the fundamental human disidentification element. Smith's extrasocial psychopath is the individual who engages in cultural extremes. For Smith, the features in both the personal and social domains represent both successful and unsuccessful extremes in American culture. The extrasocial

[17] See Campbell (1993) for a discussion of the socialization of aggression in girls who must behave in such a way to survive (e.g., runaways, female gang members, girls who have never fit the social stereotype of femininity).

psychopath can be either the grandiose, conning, remorseless, superficial charmer and/or the irresponsible, criminally versatile, impulsive, liar.

The expression of psychopathy based on cultural "extremes" does not encompass features that are culturally universal. In other words, if it is argued that a particular culture is more likely to reinforce and validate values that align with psychopathic character traits, this suggests that culture influences either the development or manifestation of psychopathy. However, since cultural values are relative, any suggestion that psychopathy is influenced or shaped by culture, contradicts the notion of the universality of psychopathy. In addition, factors such as cross-cultural differences in legal systems and criminal justice processes impact knowledge about psychopathy across cultures given that much of the research on psychopathy is conducted in prison systems and incarceration policies in different cultures affect the percentage of psychopaths incarcerated in prison systems (Wernke & Huss, 2008). Smith's culture-based definition of the extrasocial psychopath is valuable in the sense that it points out that psychopathy is not necessarily a condition that can be identified through behaviors that are culturally defined as criminal. However, the definition does not help distinguish the psychopathic personality independent of cultural influence, nor does it lend itself to cross-cultural analysis.

The establishment of homogeneity within the concept of psychopathy runs parallel to the establishment of the universality of psychopathology in general. The ultimate goal is the understanding of the functional relationship between cultural characteristics and psychopathology (Draguns, 1980). According to Draguns (1989, p. 269), "Once such a relationship is specified, it should be possible to predict manifestations of abnormal behavior from cultural characteristics and to infer cultural characteristics from manifestations of psychopathology." With respect to psychopathy, an understanding of this functional relationship will allow conceptualization of psychopathy that distinguishes sociocultural manifestations from characterological disorder as the condition continues to be studied at a fast pace on a global level (Bolt, Hare, & Neumann, 2007; Cooke, Michie, Hart, & Clark, 2005; Cooke & Michie, 1999; Hare et al., 2000; Hoppenbrouwers, Neumann, & Lewis, 2015; Issa et al., 2017; Jonason et al., 2017; McCuish, Mathesius, Lussier, & Corrado, 2018; Mokros et al., 2011; Neumann et al., 2012; Rosan, Frick, Gottlieb, & Fasicaru, 2015; Shariat et al., 2010; Shou et al., 2017; Somma, Borroni, Drislane, & Fossati, 2016; Veen, 2011; Verschuere et al., 2018; Wernke & Huss, 2008; Wilson et al., 2014).

The establishment of a homogeneous and universally applicable concept of psychopathy requires an understanding of the disturbance as both a characterological and a cultural phenomenon. A look at the personal-social/trait-symptom issue in relation to cross-cultural perspectives of universalism-relativism and dimensions of individualism-collectivism and masculinity-femininity

(Hofstede, 1980, 1988) provides an expositive framework on which the relational nature of the personal-social domains may be understood. The point of drawing these analogies is to show how culture and gender mold both personal and social manifestations of psychopathy. However, despite the superficial effects and affects of these factors, a universal feature of human nature (specifically, the human need to attach to others) distinguishes the presence or absence of primary psychopathy.

This analysis may be approached against the backdrop of the universalist-relativist discourse in the cross-cultural psychology literature. From the universalist perspective, clinically, cultural differences can be thought of as accents of a common language. However, the differences between individuals in any culture are greater than the differences between cultures (Berman, 1989). Thus, psychopathology is a universal phenomenon with symptomologies dependent on cultural distinction. In contrast, the relativist stance supports the infinite social plasticity of psychopathology. Representative of this viewpoint, culture will increase and intensify particular psychopathological symptoms according to its major preoccupations, at the same time relying socially in a greater degree upon these very individuals. These two perspectives are not necessarily incompatible but may represent differences based on seriousness of disorders and have received both support and criticism in empirical studies (Draguns, 1989).

Meloy's (1988) definition of psychopathy as a genotypic-phenotypic process resulting in "fundamental disidentification with humanity" represents the universalist view. In contrast, Smith's (1978, 1985) culture-specific definition of psychopathy represents the relativist view. In support of the compatibility of both perspectives, Meloy believes that psychopathic disturbance is a growing clinical and sociocultural phenomenon and cites statistics of increasing frequencies of stranger homicides and serial murder in the United States as evidence of this and research suggesting that kids reared in an "image-based, nonlinear, multimedia, briefly attentive society" may not develop deeper levels of identity and meaning (Meloy, 1988, p. 7), thus are more likely to develop psychopathy.

This suggestion that children growing up in such societies are more likely to become psychopaths, again, represents a superficial conceptualization of psychopathy. This is precisely Smith's contention—that the psychopathic personality, as it has been defined (in English meaning), represents a caricature of societal values. In societies that place a premium on competition and material success, the psychopath is not antisocial at all but is seen as a logical psychological extreme who goes beyond the limits. This behaviorally defined psychopath possesses many of the traits necessary for success within the marketplace of capitalistic society (Smith, 1978). In fact, studies have suggested that entrepreneurs are similar and exhibit behaviors more comparable to psychopaths than to "normal" populations, and entrepreneurs are mildly psychopathic and can be objectively viewed in terms of psychopathic characteristics (Winslow & Solomon, 1989).[18]

Such entrepreneurial behavior is praised and admired in capitalistic cultures to the point where psychopathy may be less disturbing, more expected, and more acceptable to society as a whole. Therefore, only extreme psychopaths and those of minimal social value will be noticed and/or sanctioned as psychopathic. However, these findings suggest a curvilinear relationship between psychopathy and entrepreneurism. An equally strong case can be made that the psychopath lacks traits necessary for success in the marketplace. Psychopathic traits such as "lack of realistic long-term goals," "irresponsibility," and "poor behavioral controls" would likely interfere with a successful entrepreneurial career. Thus, the linking of psychopathy with the traits of the successful entrepreneur does not help to define psychopathy in a homogeneous manner.

Psychopathy has also been connected to existentialism. Like the psychopath, the existentialist often appears in literature as separated from others, guiltless, rational, unconcerned with time, and as seen by others as possessing an inner sense of power. Camus's "Mersault" in *The Stranger* (1942) has been called a psychopath (Duff, 1977) for being unable to understand or take part in the values, interests, and emotions of those around him. Smith (1978) suggests that Mersault's inability to understand others also means he is unable to exploit them as the psychopath does. However, there is another, more fundamental difference between Mersault and the psychopath. Duff's suggestion that Mersault is a psychopath is based on an oversimplified reading of *The Stranger* and of the fundamental tenets of existentialism. Although Mersault exhibits classically psychopathic behavioral traits (such as not crying when his mother dies and appearing remorseless after he commits murder), his acceptance of responsibility for his actions and intense personal realization of his experience would not be in the conscious repertoire of the psychopath. Furthermore, Camus does not present enough information about Mersault to be able to diagnose him with a personality disorder and/or rate him on the PCL-R.

Thus, despite the superficial features tying together existentialism and psychopathy, there is a fundamental difference between the two. Existentialism embodies ultimate responsibility, and the existentialist is intimately responsible for his or her decisions and experiences (Camus, 1942, 1955).

[18] In this study five measures (of mental adjustment, career success, interpersonal behavior, problem solving, and values) were used to assess psychopathic characteristics. Of these tests, only one (the MMPI) has been extensively used in research on psychopathy. Furthermore, research has shown that the MMPI does not discriminate between nonanxious (primary) and anxious (secondary) psychopaths (Lykken, 1957). Thus, the measures used in the study may not reliably reflect the presence or absence of psychopathic style as the authors appear to presume.

Conversely, psychopathy is marked by flight from responsibility. The psychopath is responsible to no one, including himself or herself (Samenow, 2013; Yochelson & Samenow, 1976). The psychopath is individual only in the sense of raw ego, of blatantly placing himself or herself in front of everyone else, and stands behind none of his or her decisions, fleeing into inauthenticity as a protection against fundamental being (Smith, 1978). The psychopath is completely estranged from existential conception (Yochelson & Samenow, 1976), is fixated on the object world (Meloy, 1988), and is maximally dependent on others (Yochelson & Samenow, 1976). The psychopath is "the antithesis of the existential man" (Smith, 1978). In sum, it could be said that the existentialist has a powerfully integrated identity based on ultimate personal responsibility, while the psychopath lacks an integrated identity as a result of constant flight from the self. This identity issue is central to Meloy's (1988) definition of psychopathy presented in the introduction. The superficiality of the analogy between the existentialist and the psychopath offers illustration of the problem of assessing psychopathy through personality and/or behavioral characteristics that do not fully capture the "human disidentification" component. Assessment of psychopathy has to go beyond a superficial level of analysis if we do not want existentialists to be misdiagnosed as psychopaths.

The association of criminality with psychopathy illustrates the other extreme, linking psychopathy with unsuccessful societal roles. The DSM-5's use of APD's behavioral criteria detects a disturbance based solely on behavior deemed undesirable, irresponsible, and antisocial by Western society. To return to Blackburn's statement, based on behavioral criteria alone, surely APD can be thought of as a "moral judgment masquerading as a clinical diagnosis." Given Smith's argument, APD can be viewed as the diagnostic selection of psychopathy based on social status. APD criteria are too descriptive, inclusive, criminally biased, and socioeconomically skewed to be clinically useful (Meloy, 1988), and are not representative of psychopathy in the clinical sense, but only of general criminal populations (Hare & Schalling, 1978). APD is a "dump-all" for society's undesirables, with 80 percent of criminal populations qualifying diagnostically (Wells, 1988). These findings suggest that in behavioral terms, these individuals are considered clinically antisocial; however, this determination is one of criminality, not of psychopathy. Thus, APD diagnosis appears to be biased in the direction of lower socioeconomic status and minority groups and is consistent with Smith's thesis that psychopaths who are of minimal social value are identified while psychopaths of higher social status are not. Characteristics included in APD diagnosis can be viewed as culturally based symptoms that are possibly, though not necessarily, connected to the psychopathic disturbance. As was the case with the analogy between existentialism and psychopathy, the association between individualism and psychopathy is also oversimplified and superficial.

The possible association of individualism with competition (Draguns, 1990; Triandis, 1990) and with psychopathy (Smith, 1978) raises the issue of the linking of particular personality styles and disorder with the cross-cultural dimensions of individualism-collectivism. Individualist cultures appear to be prototypical of psychopathic style, involving an inner-directed self-concept, while collectivist cultures involve tradition-directed self-concept. Other features shared between psychopathy and individualism are lack of time perspective and lack of attachment. Goals are closer in time among individualists, while distant goals are more common among collectivists. The time frame of individualists is bound by their birth, while the time frame of collectivists includes many generations (Triandis, 1990). This same immediate time reference is characteristic of social psychopathy (Smith, 1985). With respect to attachment, individualists have excellent skills in interacting superficially with many in-groups (such as social and professional networks) but have fewer skills in interacting intimately with others (Triandis, 1990), which is also a feature of psychopathy (Cleckley, 1984; Hare, 1985a; Hare & Schalling, 1978).

Western societies are traditionally thought of as individualistic, and content analyses have found more individualistic themes in Western autobiographies (Triandis, 1990). In the United States a person characterized as not unique or "similar to the average person" would be offended. This desire to be unique has been found in psychopathic personalities, exaggerated to the point of extreme inner fear of being usual (Cleckley, 1941; Gacono & Meloy, 1988; Samenow, 2013; Yochelson & Samenow, 1976). In general, individualist cultures can be characterized by inner-directedness, resentment of conformity, independence, and narcissism (all features of psychopathy), while collectivist cultures are characterized by "concern," a sense of oneness with others, a perception of complexities and relationships, and a tendency to keep others in mind (Hui & Triandis, 1986) (all features absent in the psychopathic personality).

The analogy drawn between individualism and psychopathy falls through upon deeper analysis. To begin, the parallel between inner-directed self-concept is weak. Although psychopaths may appear self-serving, their motivation to behave in such a way is the result of never having developed an integrated identity as a result of failure to pass through the developmental stage of separation-individuation (Meloy, 1988). Thus, the motivation behind the self-directed behavior of the psychopath is actually (when viewed psychodynamically rather than behaviorally) the antithesis of the self-directed motivations of an individual who possesses an "inner-directed" self-concept. As was the case with the existentialist, the inner-directed individual is likely to have a well-integrated identity to be so directed. The psychopath, on the other hand, because of his or her lack of identity integration, is directed away from other human beings, and this includes the self.

Figure 4.2 illustrates the inadequacy of the analogy between individualism and psychopathy.

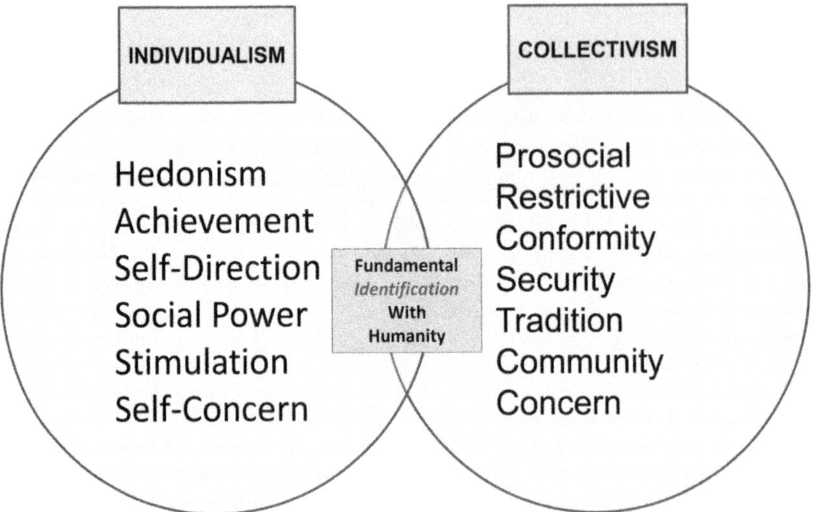

Figure 4.2 Individualism/Collectivism

The individualism/collectivism and subclinical/antisocial psychopathy domains presented below the personal/social deviance domains will be used to discuss the complex interplay of individual and culture in the formation of primary psychopathy and its secondary manifestations. Analysis of the relationships between each of these domains illustrates the particular problems involved in defining psychopathy based on the traditional criteria included in the nonintersecting portions of the personal and social deviance domains.

As can be seen in the diagram of the individualism/collectivism domains (Figure 4.2), while individualist cultures share surface values with psychopathy, these cultures, and the general concept of individualism, do not share the psychopath's virtual absence of human attachment. Critics of the individualist-collectivist dichotomy share questions with critics of the concept of psychopathy. Both discourses involve the conflict between personal interest and group interest, and are needy of finer distinction. Schwartz (1990) suggests the individualist-collectivist dichotomy is insufficient for three reasons:

1. The dichotomy leads us to overlook values that inherently serve both individual and collective interests (maturity values).
2. The dichotomy ignores values that foster the goals of collectives other than the in-group (e.g., universal prosocial values).
3. The dichotomy promotes the mistaken assumption that individualist and collectivist values each form coherent syndromes that are opposed to one another. (Schwartz, 1990, p. 151)

A crucial point in Schwartz's criticism is that collectivists often show less consideration than individualists for the welfare of strangers, and individualists may be more universally collective. In addition, Schwartz proposes that individualist and collectivist goals need not conflict. One's values could consist of hedonism, achievement, self-direction, social power, and self-stimulation—all serving self-interest but at the same time not at the expense of any collectivity. These same values may be promoted by leaders of collectives for their group. To illustrate, Schwartz cites an interesting study comparing the values of priests to service station dealers. Service station dealers gave higher priority overall to individualist values, conforming to the image of priesthood as an occupation forgoing selfish concerns, and of service station dealers as individualistic entrepreneurs. Interestingly, while the service station dealers gave higher priority to enjoyment and achievement values, it was priests who considered independent thought, choice, action, and creativity more important (Schwartz 1990).

Comparison of the values in the individualist-collectivist domains in Figure 4.2 can be compared with those in the personal–social deviance domains in Figure 4.1 to illustrate the distinguishing the homogeneous elements of the universes in both constructs. Schwartz's contention is that "maturity values"—expressing understanding and appreciation for different ideas and behaviors—are shared by both individualism and collectivism (these values can also be seen as the humanism distinguishing existential individualism and psychopathic individualism). In fact, studies show that extreme individualists exhibit higher levels of these values than do collectivists (Schwartz, 1990). Thus, the "lack of concern" (Hui & Triandis, 1986) that appears to differentiate individualism from collectivism is not applicable upon analysis on the individual level. The dimensions may be useful for "broad-brush analyses," but there are crucial distinctions if the construct is to be used to explain or understand underlying levels of the construct (Schwartz, 1990).

An interesting parallel between the psychopathy and individualism-collectivism constructs illustrates the different conclusions that could be reached when using the "broad-brush" analyses of these concepts. Schwartz reported that in his study the subtypes of individualist and collectivist values held together two-thirds of the time. This is an interesting finding when compared to the personal–social deviance dichotomy. When the psychopath is diagnosed with a "broad brush," by way of superficial, behavioral features, such as those making up APD criteria, approximately two-thirds of (criminal) populations tested will fit the profile (Hare & Schalling, 1978; Wells, 1988). Thus, the personal-social dichotomy and the majority of values contained within each domain holds together two-thirds of the time as does the individualist-collectivist construct. This theoretical parallel suggests that APD classification that does not acknowledge a deeper level of analysis, or the shared feature of both domains, may be useful in some sense, possibly in detecting psychopathy of a symptomatic nature.

However, the validity of the culturally circumscribed psychopath does not require or suggest stopping at this phenotypic level (Smith, 1978). The "myth of family independence" and the reality of interdependence found in studies of the American family highlight what is missed by "broad-brush analysis" of both the individualist-collectivist and personal–social deviance dichotomies. These studies show that there is not an ambivalence of basic values within the American family. While on one hand commitment to individualism is prevalent, on the other, a great deal of interdependence exists within families (Kagitcibasi, 1989). In fact, families in individualist cultures are much more interdependent than are collectivist families who rely on extended families and are affected by more people. Thus, the traditional individualist-collectivist dichotomy (Hofstede, 1980, 1988) is not meaningful when considering marital relationships and familiar groups (Hui & Triandis, 1986).

Figure 4.2 presents Schwartz's "maturity values" as representative of homogeneous elements within the individualist and collectivist domains. Although the domains contain distinct features, they share the common element of "maturity values," defined as "appreciation, understanding, and acceptance of oneself, of others, and the surrounding world (broad-minded, world of beauty, wisdom, mature love)" (Schwartz, 1990). Interestingly, these values are the same as those involved in the humanism differentiating existentialist from the psychopath. Thus, Hofstede's (1980, 1988) cultural dimensions of individualism-collectivism share these features of "maturity values" or humanism that can be translated to a shared attachment to humanity that exists independently of differential cultural manifestations. There is homogeneity in the condition these cultural dimensions are describing. The condition is humanity, its homogeneity is found in the shared features of both domains—primarily, the ability to attach, in some way, to some form and portion of humanity.

Distinguishing primary from secondary psychopathy is especially important to clarify confusion regarding the existence of psychopathy across subcultural groups. For example, there has been much discussion and research concerning the different manifestations psychopathy may take in criminal versus noncriminal populations and across males and females. Since secondary psychopathy can be seen as synonymous with APD, the secondary form of the disorder (general criminality) is not a condition applied to noncriminals, is infrequently applied to women (Herson & Turner, 1991), and is further complicated because women tend to be rated lower on the PCL-R Factor 2 antisocial traits (Verona & Vitale, 2006, 2018).

Ray and Ray's (1982) "subclinical psychopaths" and Babiak and Hare's (2006) "industrial psychopaths" represent the "doctors, lawyers, and judges" who are just as psychopathic, if not more so, than criminal psychopaths in prison (Cleckley, 1941, 1988). Widom's (in Hare & Schalling, 1978) "unsuccessful psychopaths," are likely to fit APD criteria and represent the social undesirables who are identified as criminal psychopaths. The difference between these two groups—the "subclinical" and "unsuccessful"—is not necessarily their level of primary psychopathy (which we would need deeper analysis to identify) but their social effectiveness and the particular manifestations (of either primary or secondary psychopathy) that are associated with the different social situations of the "successful" and the "unsuccessful" individual.

Figure 4.3 shows the subclinical/antisocial domains below those of the personal/social deviance domains. The subclinical psychopath may possess all of the elements within the personal deviance domain but none of those included in the social deviance domain. Conversely, the antisocial psychopath may possess the elements of both or just the social deviance domain. The fact that APD criteria are included only in the social deviance domain illustrates how subclinical psychopaths are excluded from identification. The absence of acknowledgment of the elements contained in the intersection of the subclinical/clinical-antisocial domains also illustrates how criminals can be incorrectly identified as psychopaths (e.g., by exhibiting features included in both the personal and social deviance domains but not those within their intersection). Noncriminal individuals, however, are excluded from this practice as well.

The PCL-R differentiates primary and secondary psychopathy based on scores related to clinical-behavioral criteria. Individuals who score above 30

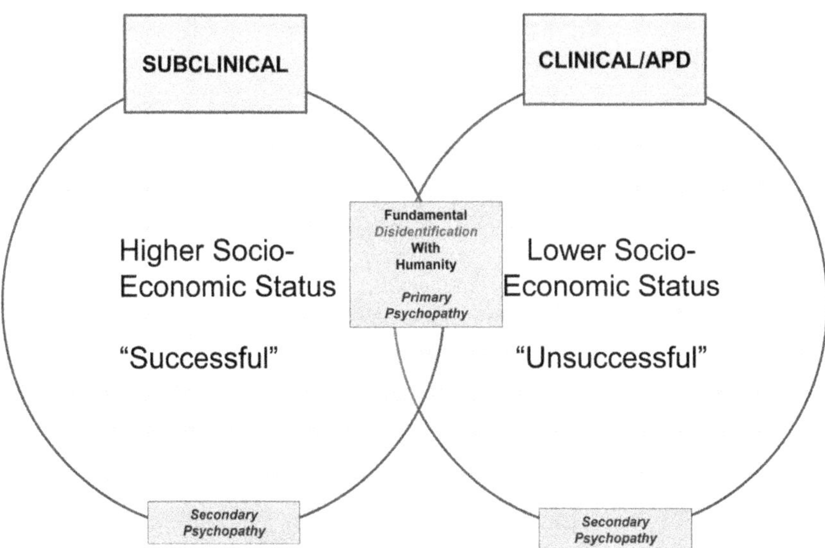

Figure 4.3 Subclinical/Clinical-Antisocial Psychopath

are considered primary psychopaths, 20–29 secondary psychopaths, and 0–19 nonpsychopaths (Hare, 2003). However, the arbitrary cutoff of 30 based on scoring of the PCL-R 20 items does not ensure that the fundamental core of psychopathy is captured. *What is the difference between an individual who scores 29 and someone who scores 31? The person with the 29 is a secondary psychopath, and the person who receives 31 is a primary psychopath? Do those two points capture the fundamental disidentification with humanity?*

Thus, if "human disidentification" is the homogeneous element within the concept of psychopathy, to properly assess the disorder this feature needs to be identified. Primary psychopathy can be found within the shared area of the personal–social deviance domains. The primary psychopath may exhibit various manifestations contained within both domains but will possess the feature of human disidentification. The secondary psychopath may exhibit identical clinical-behavioral manifestations but possesses some element of human identification. The subclinical and the unsuccessful psychopath may possess primary *or* secondary disturbance. However, it is likely that the majority of both groups would fit the secondary criteria, since studies have shown that only 33 percent of those considered APD (a behavioral indicator of both primary and secondary) are psychopaths in the clinical sense (Hare & Schalling, 1978), and others suggest even lower figures (Yochelson & Samenow, 1976). This primary-secondary distinction is crucial to the understanding of the issue of personal versus social deviance. The distinction has been addressed throughout the history of the concept (Arrigo & Shipley, 2001a, 2001b; Dinwiddie, 2015; Hare & Schalling, 1978; Jones, 2017; Maughs, 1941; McCord & McCord, 1964; Rafter, 1997) and represents the line of demarcation that separates the personality disorder of psychopathy from its symptomatic counterparts (most notably criminality).

The differential manifestations between the two groups, regardless of primary or secondary distinction, are based on sociocultural characteristics. The psychopath with high socioeconomic status in American culture will behave differently than the psychopath with low socioeconomic status in American culture. Based on research findings to date, this may be particularly true for European American psychopaths (Walsh & Kosson, 2007). Although success is likely to be hindered by particular traditionally psychopathic features such as "irresponsibility," these features are socioculturally based, may not be a core feature of the condition, and regardless of their presence or absence would not necessarily impede the appearance of success. Although it is likely that an upper-class psychopath will not be extremely successful (relative to his or her situation), it is also likely that he or she will have more opportunities for success than the lower-class psychopath and may therefore appear relatively successful. Thus, the high-SES psychopath may be a morally vacant (but successful) businessperson, a prominent psychologist, or the president (Babiak & Hare, 2006; Lilienfeld et al., 2012; Wallis, 2016).

On the surface high-SES psychopaths are not likely to appear antisocial. They appear to be "extrasocial" and socially desirable. Yet, a deeper look into their lives may reveal illegal or simply immoral behavior, with or without the element of human detachment. The low-SES psychopath may be a thief, a rapist, a killer, or just a liar. However, the low-SES psychopath, especially of secondary nature,[19] is most likely to be imprisoned at some point in his or her lifetime, while the high-SES psychopath of primary or secondary nature has slim chance of legal sanction.

This position is hypothetical at this point. However, the growing body of research examining psychopathy in noncriminal populations has begun to shed light on the adaptive qualities of psychopathy (Babiak & Hare, 2006; Benning, Venables, & Hall, 2018; Falkenbach, McKinley, & Larson, 2017; Hall & Benning, 2006; Moriera et al., 2014) with hope for a more sophisticated understanding of the phenomenon of successful psychopathy. Given the problems in the development of the concept of psychopathy in general, and the inability to identify the condition in nonpsychopaths, there is no empirical evidence to support this claim. However, Sutherland's (1949) criminological theory of "differential association" provides a theoretical framework on which the theory can be empirically tested. Both primary and secondary manifestations of psychopathy are socially conceived and socially sanctioned. Differential responses may be a matter of differential association. According to this theory, criminal behavior can be explained as "learned in association with those who define such behavior favorably and in isolation from those who define it unfavorably" (Sutherland, 1949, p. 234). From this perspective, those with higher socioeconomic status will be exposed to an entirely different set of values and circumstances than will those with lower socioeconomic status. The criminality (and "normality") spawned from each will be qualitatively different as a result of the fundamental situational differences. If the upper-class psychopath wants something, his or her challenge may be a matter of business transaction, and his or her wants will be dependent on upper-class values and circumstance. If a lower-class psychopath wants something, his or her challenge is more likely to be a matter of violence, and his or her wants will reflect the values and circumstance of the lower-class structure. While differential association theory is a general criminological explanation of

---

[19] Smith considers the secondary psychopath more likely to be imprisoned because he or she usually engages in a more haphazard type of criminal behavior than the primary psychopath. It is a common belief that primary psychopaths are more skilled than others at manipulation and deceit, and Smith suggests that only extreme psychopaths and those who are socially undesirable are caught. It is likely that the psychopaths who are caught are either severely unlucky or at the end of their psychopathic careers (see Hare, McPherson, & Forth, 1988, for a study on psychopathic burnout).

"white-collar" versus "street" crime, the theory makes sense with respect to noncriminal and psychopathic behavior as well.

Differential manifestations along intracultural dimensions can be extended to cross-cultural dimensions. Differences in secondary psychopathy and the manifestations of primary psychopathy are likely to vary greatly across cultures. The psychopath in the individualist culture will behave differently than the psychopath in the collectivist culture. In fact, the entire criteria upon which secondary psychopathy (or APD) would change across cultures since what is antisocial (and sanctioned) in one culture may not be in another. Given that the secondary disturbance is a matter of symptom, and is defined in behavioral terms (APD), such a diagnosis would be dependent on particular social rules. The APD diagnosis derived from Western-based criteria would be meaningless in cultures with different rules and values, since "antisocial" classification is dependent on knowing what "social" is.

Specific examples of intracultural sex differences in psychopathic manifestations may offer generalizable illustrations of the manifestations and perceptions of psychopathy across different cultures. Hofstede (1980, 1988) views masculinity-femininity as a meaningful cross-cultural dimension, although he defines the concept rather idiosyncratically (Draguns, 1989). Thus, a look at how psychopathy manifests differently across gender within American society may illustrate how psychopathic manifestations can differ across cultures as well. Other subcultural groups such as race or ethnicity could be used to illustrate this point as well. It is likely that socialization differences within and societal attitudes toward particular minority groups would affect manifestations of psychopathy. Furthermore, intracultural attitudes toward and socialization practices of particular racial or ethnic groups are likely to vary across cultures as well (depending on the social value placed on group within the culture). However, at present, there is an abundance of literature regarding sex differences in psychopathic manifestation, while little has been published regarding the validity of the psychopathy construct in different racial and ethnic groups.[20] Thus, a look at the gender issues in the psychopathy literature provides excellent examples to illustrate the point that manifestations of psychopathy are dependent on socialization practices and societal perceptions. Just as psychopathy is misunderstood through analogies with individualist culture, and differentially manifested and sanctioned depending on social structure, so is the case across gender.

---

[20] There appears to be only one published study addressing the validity of the psychopathy construct in black inmates (see Kosson, Smith, & Newman, 1990). Other studies have focused on specific ethnic subpopulations including Mexican gang members (Valdez, Kaplan, & Codina, 2000) and psychopathy in Iran, which is the first study involving psychopathy in a non-Western country (Shariat et al., 2010).

Studies have shown that psychopathy is manifested differently across the sexes and have suggested that APD and histrionic personality disorder (HPD) refer to the same condition shaped into different forms in males and females by the same cultural forces that determine sex stereotypes. Figure 4.4 shows the APD and HPD domains (consisting of the DSM-III-IV-TR criteria for each disorder) compared with the masculinity and femininity domains in Figure 4.5, consisting of features drawn from Hofstede's (1980, 1988) construct.

The shared feature in the intersection of the APD/HPD domains represents "fundamental disidentification with humanity," as was the case in the intersection of the personal and social deviance domains of Figures 4.1 and 4.3. The element contained within the intersection of the masculinity and femininity domains includes the feature "identification with humanity" similar to the individualist/collectivist construct in Figure 4.2, which is a universal experience in both masculine and feminine cultures independent of the culture's gender.

As is the case in individualism-collectivism and subclinical-antisocial constructs, gender differences in manifestations of psychopathy (represented by APD and HPD) are superficial and confusing, and do not include features that can adequately represent or identify psychopathy. Many aspects of HPD are a result of greater emphasis on emotional expressiveness and responsiveness in female children. Girls are encouraged to base their identity and worth on their ability to elicit emotional responses from others. Conversely, APD is based on criteria that represent exaggeration of stereotypically masculine traits. Both diagnoses have registered high on scales detecting their relationship to cultural sex stereotypes (Warner, 1978).

To illustrate the influence of stereotyped values in these classification schemes are the following excerpts taken from DSM-III-R definitions of HPD and APD:

HPD

> The essential feature of Histrionic Personality Disorder is pervasive and excessive emotionality and attention-seeking behavior. . . . Individuals with Histrionic Personality Disorder are uncomfortable or feel unappreciated when they are not the center of attention. Often lively and dramatic, they tend to draw attention to themselves and may initially charm new acquaintances by their enthusiasm, apparent openness, or flirtatiousness. These qualities wear thin, however, as these individuals continually demand to be the center of attention. . . . The appearance of behavior of individuals with this disorder are often inappropriately sexually provocative or seductive. This behavior is directed not only toward people in whom the individual has a sexual or romantic interest, but occurs in a wide variety of social, occupational, and professional relationships beyond what is appropriate for the social context. Emotional expression may be shallow and rapidly shifting. . . . Individuals with this disorder are

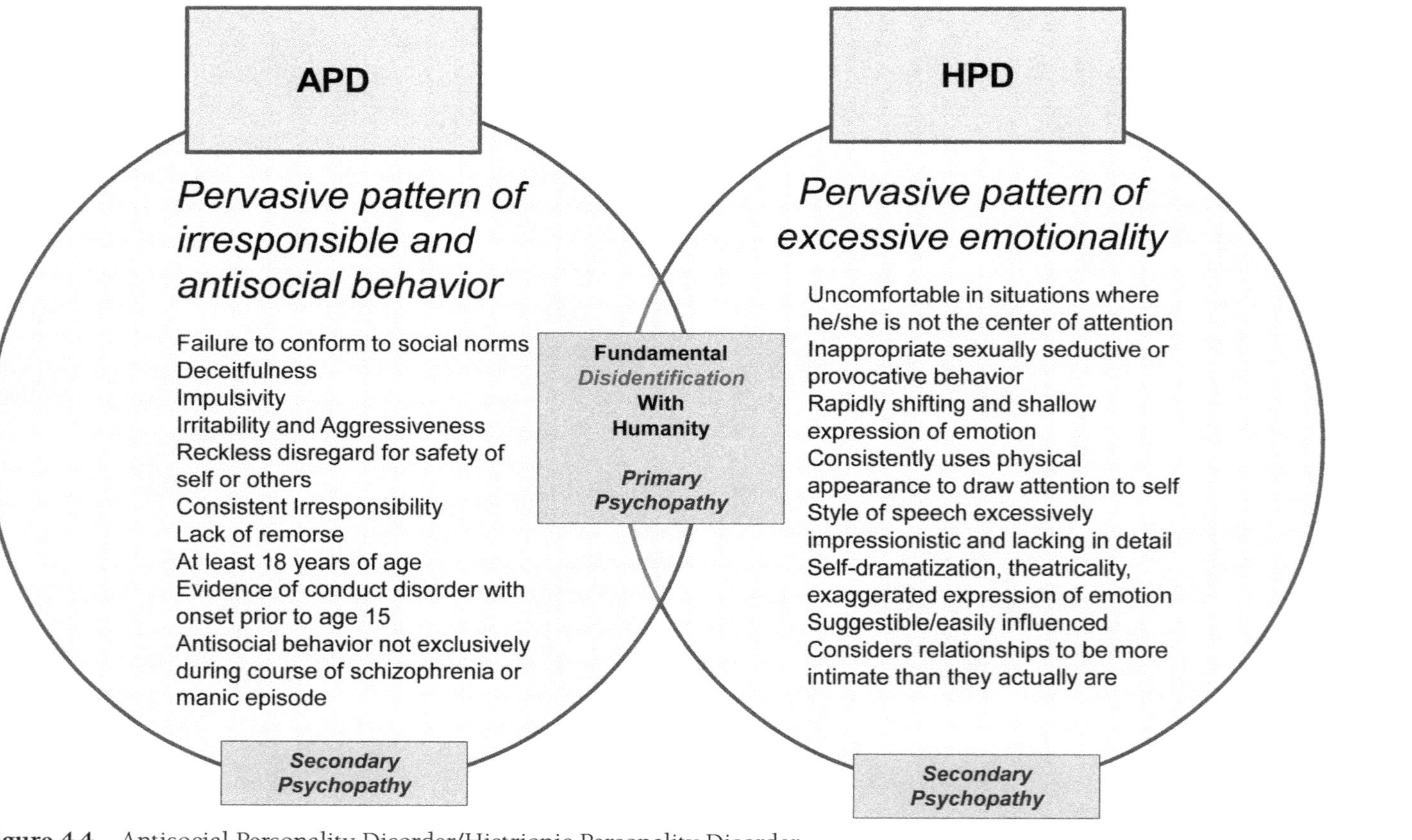

Figure 4.4 Antisocial Personality Disorder/Histrionic Personality Disorder

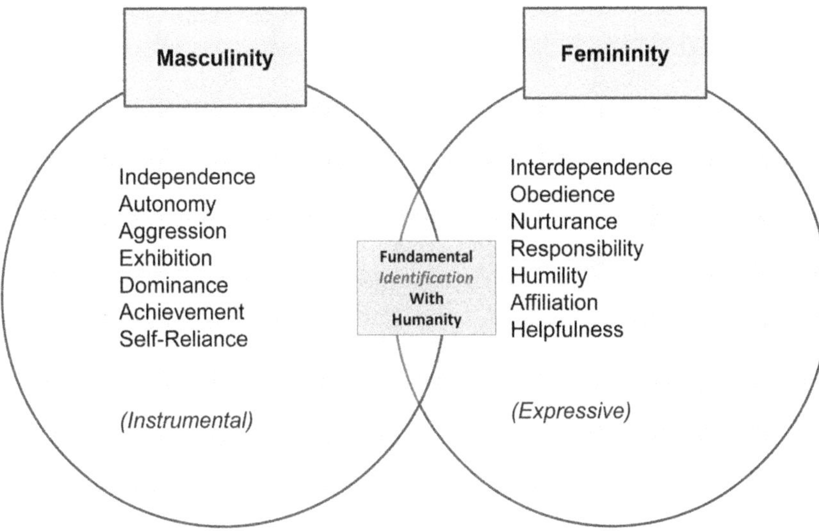

Figure 4.5 Masculinity/Femininity

characterized by self-dramatization, theatricality, and exaggerated expression of emotion. . . . However their emotions often seem to be turned on and off too quickly to be deeply felt, which may lead others to accuse the individual of faking these feelings. (American Psychiatric Association, DSM-5, 2013, pp. 667–668)

APD

The essential feature of Antisocial Personality Disorder is a pervasive pattern of disregard for, and violation of the rights of others that begins in childhood or early adolescence and continues into adulthood. This pattern has also been referred to as *psychopathy, sociopathy, or dyssocial personality disorder*. . . . Individuals with antisocial personality disorder fail to conform to social norms with respect to lawful behavior. They may repeatedly perform acts that are grounds for arrest . . . such as destroying property, harassing others, stealing, or pursuing illegal occupations. Persons with this disorder disregard the wishes, rights, or feelings of others. They are frequently deceitful and manipulative in order to gain personal profit or pleasure . . . tend to be irritable and aggressive and may repeatedly get into physical fights or commit acts of physical assault. . . . Individuals with antisocial personality disorder also tend to be consistently and extremely irresponsible. . . . Individuals with antisocial personality disorder show little remorse for the consequences of their acts. (American Psychiatric Association, DSM-5, 2013, pp. 659–660)

The crux of the description of HPD is exhibition of excessive emotionality. The crux of the description of APD is irresponsible and aggressive behavior. Both disorders represent people with shallow affect and the inability to bond with others to the point of extreme self-centeredness and lack of empathy. The major difference between the two is that HPDs generally do not harm others. This association between the disorders has been discussed by many researchers (e.g., Gacono & Meloy, 1994; Gacono, Meloy, & Heaven, 1990; Spalt, 1980; Verona & Vitale, 2006; Warner, 1978). However, the major similarity between the two could be (as suggested by the inability to bond and lack of empathy included in both descriptions) the "fundamental disidentification with humanity." However, APD and HPD are assessed through behaviors (although this is less the case with HPD); thus again the primary feature of psychopathy is not entirely captured by these diagnoses.

Despite the gender-based labels and classification criteria of APD and HPD, eight of Cleckley's 16 features characterizing psychopathy are shared by both disorders, and the others could be shown to be common to both or related to sex-differentiated expression of anxiety (Warner, 1978). Warner (1978) suggested early on that the lower levels of expressed anxiety in APD compared to the expression of excessive emotionality in HPD is a result of the unique defensive technique utilized by these individuals and that both the fugue states and amnesiac episodes of HPD and the APD's antisocial behavior serve the purpose of evasion of social responsibility. Studies show that hysterics and psychopaths tend to marry each other and produce hyperactive children who later demonstrate APD or HPD depending on their sex (Spalt, 1980). Genetic links have also been found between APD, HPD, and somatization disorder (SD). APD and SD may constitute sex-typed alternative pathways for the expression of HPD, with each of the disorders considered as stages or endpoints of a shared pathogenesis (Lilienfeld et al., 1986).

These sex-typed expressions are the result of differential social practices that teach males to express certain emotions (such as anxiety, anger, and need for attention) outwardly and females to express inwardly (Verona & Vitale, 2018). Tavris and Wade (1984) suggest that, historically, males have been presented as more likely than females to experience anxiety associated with Oedipal fears and sexuality and that both sexes experience anger equally often. However, males are more inclined than females to act on emotions aggressively. Studies have shown that sex differences in aggression are most apparent in childhood and that males exhibit more aggression in action, fantasy, communication, and play than do females (Maccoby & Jacklin, 1974), that this sex difference appears at the age of two or three, when children first begin to play with each other (Tavris & Wade, 1984), and may be biologically based (Baron-Cohen, 2003; Pemment, 2015; Svedholm-Hakkinen, Ojala, & Lindemann, 2018). Sex differences in attention-seeking behavior also appear to affect psychopathic manifestations. In addition to the differences in angry and anxious acting out, the need for attention is also expressed more aggressively in males. Studies have shown that APD and HPD individuals are led to make contact with others through the attention-seeking behavior appropriate to his or her sex and that these stereotypic patterns become reinforced, giving a false impression of diverging disorders in the two sexes (Warner, 1978). These findings have been supported in more recent research on female psychopaths (Cunliffe, Gacono, Meloy, & Taylor, 2013, Cunliffe et al., 2016; Verona & Vitale, 2006, 2018)

Further compounding these culturally directed differences in actual manifestations, DSM-5 criteria reflect difference between the sexes through the nature of the criteria and the ways in which the disorders are perceived and diagnosed by clinicians. Some have suggested that APD and HPD represent sex-typed categories of a single disorder (Spalt, 1980; Warner, 1978). Sex bias in clinician expectations and diagnoses has been substantiated. There is a clear tendency for clinicians to diagnose women with HPD and not APD even when presented with cases containing more APD than HPD criteria. There is also a tendency for men not to be diagnosed with HPD. Thus, a significant part of sex differentiation between APD and HPD is a function of bias in clinician judgment, rather than in actual disorder base rates. Clinicians may also be influenced by the labels given to the disorders (Ford & Widiger, 1989), which are historically linked to Freudian theories concerning hysteria and masochism. In addition, the traits that describe the disorders may be sex-linked, suggesting that women are diagnosed with HPD and men with APD because APD is behaviorally anchored while HPD classification is trait-dominated (Hamilton, Rothbart, & Dawes, 1986), and in Western society women are most often described clinically and casually in terms of traits, while men are described through behavior (Allen, 1987).

This filtering of the sexes into different classifications has existed since (and likely before) Karpman's writings in his diagnoses of female psychopaths as symptomatics (Karpman, 1941). Even in his inclusion of females in his group of anethopaths,[21] he specified the females as the "passive type" and the males as "aggressive." Karpman and his colleagues acknowledged "the problem of psychopathic women," although little is said aside from a short quote by one of Karpman's colleagues, Lucille Dooley. She comments, "Attempts at psychoanalysis of the psychopathic woman have met with little success. . . . After spending much time and labor, the analyst finds the patient mentally and emotionally just as she was when she started" (Karpman, 1946, p. 287). More than 60 years later there is even greater distinction between the sexes, through the completely separate diagnoses of HPD and APD; the issue is a profound illustration of the difficulty in studying psychopathy as a form of

[21] Karpman's term for the primary psychopath.

personal deviance while its manifestations have been historically identified by social designation compounded with differential manifestations resulting from socialized sex differences.

The issue of control is a key factor in understanding sex-differentiated expressions, especially when pertaining to psychopathy, since the primary drive of the male or female psychopath is for power and control (Cleckley, 1941; Meloy, 1988; Samenow, 2013; Yochelson & Samenow, 1976). The internal and external responses of both sexes are attempts to gain control over what appears to the individual to be an unmanageable situation or state of being. In Western culture females are taught they may gain control through emotion, while men are taught to gain control through action (Allen, 1987).

Real-life historical examples of different expressions of male and female psychopathy may help illustrate. Kevin Coe and Diane Downs are prototypical examples of individuals who fit the core disorder of APD and HPD but whose expressions of deviance depart with their sex. Both Coe and Downs, while convicted of their crimes in the 1980s, are still incarcerated (Downs in prison in Chowchilla, California, and Coe in the Special Commitment Center at McNeil Island in Washington State) and continue to be featured in the news (Mischke, 2014; Terry, 2010). Kevin Coe was convicted of multiple rapes in the early 1980s in Spokane, Washington. He is considered to be a classic psychopath (Olsen, 1983). Diane Downs was convicted of the murder of one of her children and the attempted murder of her other two children in Springfield, Oregon, also in the early 1980s (Rule, 1987). The stories of these two individuals reveal similarities in attempts to control others and the search for power. Coe attempted control through the manipulation of others and achieved power through rape and abuse of women. Downs also attempted control through manipulation of others, and her thought processes and statements throughout her trial were strikingly similar to those of Coe's (Olsen, 1983; Rule, 1987). However, her power was not gained through the abuse of others in the usual sense. Although she did murder one of her children and seriously wounded the two others, Downs believed her children were part of her and that she could kill them and reproduce them with her own body. The story of Downs's life preceding the crime showed how she manipulated her world with her body through pregnancy and various sexual means (Rule, 1987). Thus, her attempt to kill her children was phenomenologically directed internally, while Coe's rape and abuse of complete strangers displays a more external manifestation.

The various domains were used to illustrate the many ways in which expressions of psychopathy may differ across and within cultures. The personal and social deviance features traditionally associated with psychopathy were shown to exist independently of the primary component of "fundamental disidentification with humanity." This illustration shows the different ways in which psychopathy may manifest across cultural and subcultural groups and returns the discussion to the following question: If the society within which one lives and the group to which one belongs determines how both primary and secondary psychopathy manifest, then is psychopathy a "relative" or a "universal" disturbance?

The relativist conceptualization of the disorder, as Smith (1978, 1985) has proposed, is useful in explaining and understanding the dynamics of secondary psychopathy; however, this perspective does not explain the primary disturbance. The understanding and conceptualization of primary psychopathy is dependent on a universalist perspective, such as that proposed by Meloy (1988). However, both frameworks are meaningful in the conceptualization of psychopathy. Given the value of both relativist and universalist conceptions, and the awareness that the two are complementary rather than conflicting, it may be possible (although confusing) to consider the disturbance as both a legitimate personality disorder, and a collection of normative personality traits that may manifest behaviorally, independent of the primary characterological disturbance. Smith (1978) has said that the full range of approaches to the psychopath, along cross-cultural, physiological, and behavioral perspectives, has not yet been brought under one cover for comparative consideration. Attention to the relationships between these perspectives is an attempt to find such cover.

This discussion answers the relativist versus universalist question by suggesting that primary psychopathy is a universal condition distinguished by a "fundamental disidentification with humanity" that is the result of an individual's failure to achieve object constancy and to pass through the developmental stage of separation-individuation. Secondary psychopathy may also exist universally, but the criteria by which it may be identified is culturally and subculturally relative. Secondary psychopathy is a synonym for culturally deviant behavior that is not the result of a deeply ingrained personality disorder, and therefore it is wrongly termed psychopathy. Figure 4.6 shows the primary and secondary pathways psychopathy may take, from etiology to symptomatology to classification.

Figure 4.6 uses gender as an example to show the different manifestations and social response to psychopathy. However, again, other cultural or subcultural groups (such as race or socioeconomic status) could be substituted for gender, or perhaps, added to the chart since membership in any particular group could produce differential psychopathic manifestations.

Parallel Theories and Interdisciplinary Connections That Enhance the Understanding of Psychopathy

Attachment and Control Theories

The idea of human disidentification as the universal feature of psychopathy rests on the fact that human attachment is universal (Ainsworth, 1989). The attachment behavioral system is biologically rooted and characteristic of human beings and primates (Harlow, 1961). This implies that attachment is a basic process of functioning that is universal in human nature and

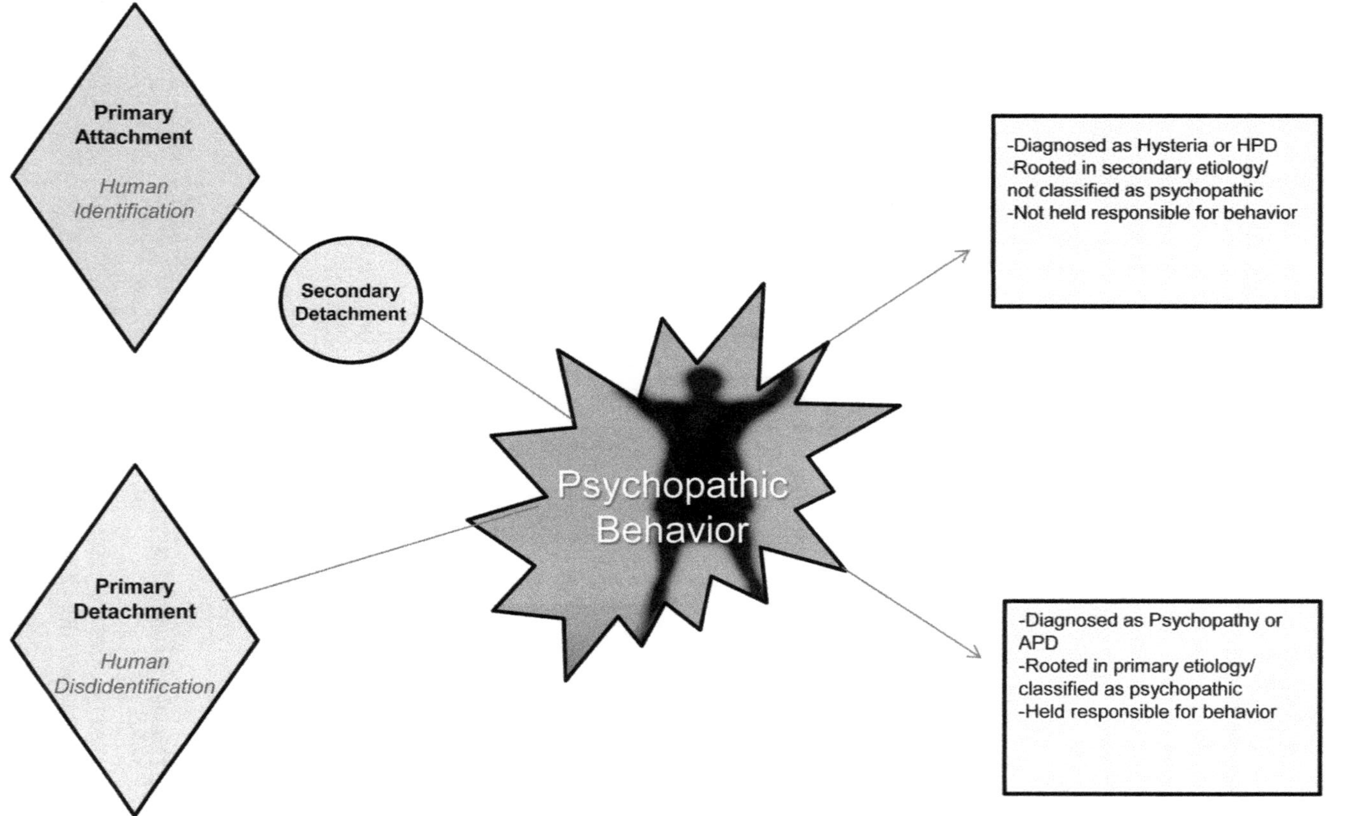

Figure 4.6 Psychopathy Pathways

independent of genetic constitution, cultural influence, and individual experience. Attachment behavior evolved through natural selection because of its survival advantage, through increasing chances of the infant being protected by those in close proximity. The universal processes involved in infant attachment are well substantiated, and research supports the universality of attachment beyond infancy as well (Ainsworth, 1989).

Beyond primary attachments to parents and surrogate figures, additional types of affectional bonds are represented in all cultures. Affectional bonds are secondary attachments that are long-lasting, are characteristic of the individual (not the dyadic), and entail representation of the internal organization of the individual. An attachment is an affectional bond. Hence, an attachment figure is never wholly interchangeable or replaceable by another. The attachment behavioral system as not only its outward manifestations, but also inner organization rooted in neurophysiological processes. This inner organization is subject to developmental change through the interaction of genetic guidance and environmental influence. Outwardly observable behavioral manifestations and situations in which they are evoked change with the inner organization (Ainsworth, 1989).

The absence of attachment in the psychopath is a result of a defensive structure built in early childhood to ward off attachment to an abusive, unpredictable, overindulging, or overbearing primary caregiver. The lack of attachment is not the actual absence of connection, as is the case with schizoid types, but is a defensive structure that denies feeling in order to protect. This denial is not necessarily a response to rejection, as may be the case with schizoid states, but to confusion. In the psychopathic response feelings are not cut off, they are shut off. Unlike the schizoid state, where there is disconnection of feeling, the psychopath's absence of connection is a matter of denial, rather than true disconnection (Institute for Bioenergetic Analysis, 1975). It is important to emphasize that the psychic confusion at the root of psychopathy is not necessarily a confused response to neglect or abuse. Psychopathy may develop in an indeterminate variety of situations and is not simply the product of family dysfunction (Meloy, 1988; Samenow, 2013; Yochelson & Samenow, 1976).

Object constancy is the psychodynamic marker of normative attachment. It is the capacity to feel and to use the psychological presence of the primary love object even when he or she is not present or is disapproving. Object constancy is the "bedrock of socialization," which implies an affective investment in the object, is dependent on object permanency, and allows for differentiation of actual objects from the manipulation of them. Object constancy is the intrapsychic paragon of safety for the child. The psychopathic child fails to achieve object constancy, does not complete passage through separation-individuation with an emotionally supportive caregiver, and subsequently relates in an objective fashion, living detached from humanity. The process of human attachment is reciprocal (Ainsworth, 1989; Meloy, 1988).

In psychopathic detachment both child and parent play a role. The psychopathic response to confusion during primary attachment is dependent on an individual process of genotypic-phenotypic interaction. Given this explanation, psychopathy could be found in any parent-child situation, within any group, and across every culture.

Attachment theory has also been used to explain criminal behavior (Grady & Shields, 2018; Hirschi, 1969; Lindberg, Fugett, & Adkins, 2015). According to Hirschi's social bond theory (Hirschi, 1969), lack of belief and involvement in, and attachment, investment, and commitment to the values of society lead an individual to engage in criminal and antisocial activity. Social bond theory, however, may best be applied to secondary psychopaths. Individuals who feel rejected by society or do not have a personal investment in societal values will search for acceptance in another arena, perhaps within a deviant subgroup or through a rebellious identity. Although the principle behind social bond theory is that individuals' lack of attachment to society presents them with a situation where they have nothing to lose by engaging in criminal activity, the theory is too general to distinguish primary psychopathy. Certainly, the primary psychopath is free to commit crime because he or she is not attached to humanity; however, the lack of belief, involvement, investment, commitment, and attachment of the primary psychopath is much more ingrained than that of the secondary psychopath. Thus, social bond theory encompasses the different degrees of detachment experienced by both primary and secondary psychopaths.

The way in which Hirschi's (1969) theory explains criminality as the result of weak social bonds can be applied to the dynamics involved in the development of secondary psychopathy, while Ainsworth's (1989) theory of infant attachment best explains the dynamics involved in the development of primary psychopathy. Social control theory can be thought of as pertaining to detachment occurring later in life, for example, in adolescence. Detachment and alienation experienced during the teenage or adult years may certainly be helpful in explaining criminal behavior; however, this sort of detachment is qualitatively different from the human disidentification experienced by the primary psychopath. The primary psychopath does not attach to humanity in the first place, while the secondary psychopath (or, more accurately put, the nonpsychopathic criminal) becomes detached later in life. Simply, the primary psychopath does not attach in infancy, while the secondary psychopath does. This is the fundamental difference between the two. Thus, theories that do not identify this key difference are unable to distinguish primary psychopathy.

Primitive Defenses and Techniques of Neutralization

Parallel theories in criminology/criminal justice and psychology offer some insight into the subtle differences between the primary and secondary psychopath that may shed light on how nonpsychopaths and secondary psychopaths are able to use similar cognitive mechanisms in order to keep themselves from experiencing guilt and remorse that comes from primary identification and attachment. Primary psychopaths employ primitive defenses to unconsciously protect themselves from experiencing the zero state. Secondary and nonpsychopaths employ cognitive strategies on a more conscious level that has the effect of eliminating internal and external deterrents very similar to what psychopaths do when they use unconscious defense mechanisms and cognitive thinking errors to "cut off" any thoughts that may interfere with their commission of a criminal or antisocial act.

Techniques of Neutralization

In criminology/criminal justice, Sykes and Matza's (1957) techniques of neutralization theory is a widely known and explains the cognitive process by which people come up with ways to rationalize or "neutralize" their guilt over engaging in behaviors they know are wrong. Sykes and Matza contended that delinquents were more or less committed to conventional beliefs and that in order to engage in delinquent acts they had to develop specific justifications by defining it as acceptable given the particular circumstances to rationalize their behavior and maintain a positive self-image. The neutralization techniques include condemnation of the condemners ("They're making it hard for me"), appeal to higher loyalties ("I have to do it to support my family), denial of injury ("No one got hurt"), denial of victim ("They had it coming to them"), and denial of responsibility ("I didn't mean to do it") (Sykes & Matza, 1957). Neutralization theory has been applied to noncriminal groups to explain the cheating behavior of college students (McCabe, 1992), property offenses such as auto theft (Copes, 2003), sex offenses (Stermac, Segal, & Gillis, 1989), and violent offenses (Agnew, 1994). For example, Stermac, Segal, and Gillis (1989) found that rape is the product of traditional male sex-role stereotypes and that rapists (seen as having an excess of stereotypical maleness) express more positive attitudes toward women and less endorsement of rape myths than controls. Rapists excuse or deny their behavior by employing distinct excuses and justifications that reflect cognitive schemas and neutralization techniques that allow them to rationalize their behaviors. Rape "excusers" maintain a positive image of themselves by attributing their behavior to alcohol and drug use, emotional problems, or compartmentalizing their rape behavior by presenting themselves as "good guys" in other areas of their lives. Rape "deniers" utilize cognitive schema such as "nice girls don't get raped," "women mean yes when they say no," "women are seductresses," etc. (Scully & Marolla, 1984). These cognitive distortions allow rapists to neutralize (and continue) their behavior.

In a study of societal attachments, offending frequency, and techniques of neutralization among auto thieves, Copes (2003) found that socially attached offenders are more likely to use neutralizations than less attached offenders and that when low attached offenders did use neutralizations, they used different ones than the high attached offenders did. High attached offenders used more techniques of neutralization, and the most popular technique was "appeal to higher loyalties." Most said they stole cars to fit into peer groups or to support their families. The second most common technique was "denial of victim," and victims were perceived as careless. Offenders with low attachments were less likely to use techniques of neutralization, and when they did the most common technique was "denial of victim." They saw their act as justified as an act of revenge against a victim. The second most common technique was "denial of responsibility"—they believed they were owed something from society. Additionally, when high attached offenders used "denial of victim," they did so in a different way. They saw the victims as careless, while the low attached offenders saw the victim as deserving as a result of actions directed at the offender:

> [T]here may be a sequential order to neutralization techniques. Young offenders who are still attached to conventional society rely on those techniques that can protect them from developing a negative self-identity. As they grow less attached to society and engage in more criminal offenses they either no longer experience internal guilt or have learned to effectively cope with it. Offenders then rely on neutralizations that give them the ability to manage social identities. (Copes, 2003, p. 122)

Thus, level of attachment was associated with both the extent and nature of the use of the techniques of neutralization. Given that human attachment is the demarcation between primary and secondary psychopathy, this has important implications for understanding the similarities and differences in the ways in which primary, secondary, and nonpsychopaths neutralize guilt to manage self and social identities.

Kernberg's Theory of Borderline Personality Organization and Primitive Defenses

Kernberg's theory of borderline personality organization (BPO) is particularly helpful in terms of understanding how internal conditions across the continuum of personality produce a tendency toward criminal behavior. According to Kernberg (1966, 1967, 1984, 1985a, 1985b, 1992), personality is organized along a continuum from "psychotic" to "borderline" to "neurotic" and defined by capacity for reality testing and unconscious defensive process. Psychotic personality organization is characterized by absence of reality testing and the use of primitive defenses, borderline personality organization by capacity for reality testing and use of primitive defenses, and neurotic by capacity for reality testing and use of higher level defenses.

Kernberg's "primitive defenses" center around the lower level mechanism of *splitting* and the related mechanisms of *primitive idealization, projective identification, denial, omnipotence, and devaluation*. Splitting is a genotypic defensive operation that is expressed through the phenotypic defensive process of dissociation. This defensive operation is pathognomonic of general borderline ego functioning, particularly in the psychopath (Meloy, 1988). Kernberg (1976) views splitting as alternating ego states, each consisting of completely separate complex psychic manifestations, a fundamental feature of the borderline ego functioning experienced by the narcissistic, histrionic, borderline, and psychopathic personalities. Splitting is a defensive process exemplified by lack of personality integration and the continual existence of cohesive personality attitudes with different aims, goals, and moral and aesthetic values (Kohut, 1971). Put simply, splitting is the view of oneself and others as all good or all bad with an inability to reconcile the two identities.

The subsidiary defenses of primitive idealization, projective identification, omnipotence, devaluation, and denial protect the ego from conflict by dissociating or actively separating contradictory experiences of the self and of others. As a result, the contradictory ego states (e.g., good/bad) are alternatively activated, and as long as they are kept apart, anxiety related to these conflicts is controlled or prevented. Although these defenses protect the individual from intrapsychic conflict, they do so at a cost of weakening the person's ego functioning, reducing adaptive effectiveness and flexibility (Kernberg, 1985b). This "lower level" of the borderline personality organization differs from "higher level" functioning that centers around repression and other higher level operations such as reaction formation, intellectualization, rationalization, and isolation, all of which protect the ego from intrapsychic conflict. The lower level defenses are shared by the psychotic and the borderline personality, while the neurotic utilizes higher level operations. Borderline disorders are set apart from the psychotic by their capacity for reality testing, which is not present in psychotic organization (Kernberg, 1985b).

Kernberg (1985a) views borderline personality organization as an intermediary stage between psychosis and neurosis. Primitive defenses facilitate criminal behavior because they enable an individual to objectify and harm other human beings while maintaining an image of themselves as all-good. By definition, crime requires mens rea (a guilty mind); thus individuals who are psychotic may commit criminal behavior but if they are determined to be out of touch with reality they are not legally responsible for their behavior. On the continuum from psychotic to borderline to neurotic, individuals with personalities organized at the borderline level of functioning are most susceptible to criminal behavior by the very nature of their defensive structure.

Primitive (and higher level) defenses operate at an unconscious level, while techniques of neutralization operate at a more conscious level (Helfgott, 2008). However, the parallels between techniques of neutralizations and primitive defenses are that both are mechanisms used to defend against feelings of anxiety, guilt, and remorse. Copes's (2003) findings that low and high attached offenders use different neutralization techniques and the same techniques in different ways suggest that there are similar but different processes at work when low attached (primary psychopaths) and high attached (nonpsychopaths or secondary psychopaths) attempt to neutralize guilt and manage their identities. Low attached individuals do not need to neutralize guilt on a conscious level because they are so well defended via primitive defenses at an unconscious level. The use of primitive defenses shapes the manifestation of the neutralization techniques; for example, victim blaming is supported by the unconscious defensive process of devaluation and omnipotent control. However, high attached people use similar processes on a conscious level to ward off feelings that may get in the way of feeling good about themselves before, during, or after the commission of antisocial or criminal behavior. The parallels between these two theories and the ways in which they can be applied to understand the nuances between the neutralizing and defensive techniques of psychopaths as compared to nonpsychopaths and primary psychopaths offer an integrative understanding of the sometimes subtle differences and similarities between primary and secondary psychopathy that may contribute to clarifying the distinction and resolving aspects of the long-standing confusion and confounding of the domains of personal and social deviance.

CHAPTER FIVE

The Psychopath in Popular Culture

A census taker once tried to test me. I ate his liver with some fava beans and a nice Chianti.

—Hannibal Lecter, *The Silence of the Lambs*

I have all the characteristics of a human being: blood, flesh, skin, hair; but not a single, clear, identifiable emotion, except for greed and disgust.

—Patrick Bateman, *American Psycho*

People fake a lot of human interactions, but I feel like I fake them all, and I fake them very well. That's my burden, I guess.

—Dexter Morgan, *Dexter*

What comes to mind when you hear the word "psychopath"? Most people can probably come up with a relatively quick answer to this question. The term "psychopath" is ingrained in the popular imagination. Even those with little or no education in the field of forensic psychology and criminology seem to have a pretty good understanding of who and what a psychopath is. In an era when the proliferation of scientific research on psychopathy has been enormous and criminal justice decisions are being made utilizing forensic assessment of psychopathy, it is important to understand the relationship between the scientific and popular conception of psychopathy. *When citizens vote for legislation like three-strikes laws or sexually violent predator laws or when expert testimony is presented on psychopathy in a jury trial, do jurors have scientific studies and real-life psychopaths in mind or a conglomeration of fictional psychopaths like Hannibal Lecter, Patrick Bateman, and Dexter Morgan?*

There has been very little research on the popular conception of psychopathy. What has been written includes analyses of psychopaths in film (Gregory, 2002; Jermyn, 1996; Knight, 2013; Leistedt & Linkowski, 2014; Pettitt, 2016; Sargeant, 1996; Simpson, 2000; Wahid et al., 2016; Wilson, 1999), crime films (Rafter, 2006), serial killers in popular culture (Epstein, 1995; Jenkins, 1994), or more general discussions of the public attraction to violent entertainment

(Fowles, 1999; Goldstein, 1998; Lloyd, 2002; Sparks & Sparks, 2002). The popular association of psychopathy with serial murder and criminal violence and aggression clouds the issue given the enormous amount of media coverage on serial killers with what some have called a "Hannibal Lecter Culture" (Campbell, 2002) with serial killers plastered on magazine covers, film screens, board games, trading cards, and even outlets for serial killer art. Some suggest that the serial killer film has replaced the Western in American genre fiction and that the serial killer has become the "new mythic monster." This popular view of the serial killer as a mythical figure has elevated the status of the serial killer to a supernatural being and blurred the boundaries between fantasy and reality for the general public, policy makers, and criminal justice professionals. Even police have been known to release offenders because they did not fit the media stereotype of a serial killer (Epstein, 1995).

The fascination with and overrepresentation of crime, psychopathy, violence, and extreme forms of criminal behavior such as serial murder in literature and popular culture (Black, 1991; Jenkins, 1994) has led scholars to examine the reflexive relationship between popular culture depictions of crime, scientific conceptions, and criminal justice practice. Considerable theoretical attention has been directed to the relationship between crime and popular culture. Scholars now argue that film and other representations of crime and violence run parallel to academic criminology and are of equal social significance, calling for theoretical discourse of "cultural criminology" (Ferrell, 1995; Ferrell & Hamm, 1998; Ferrell, Hayward, & Young, 2008, 2015; Ferrell & Sanders, 1995), "popular criminology" (Rafter, 2007), and "gothic criminology" (Picart & Greek, 2003) that recognizes late modern cultural looping, "in which the gritty, on the ground reality of crime, violence, and everyday criminal justice is dangerously confounded with its own representation" (Ferrell, Hayward, & Young, 2008, p. 130). Cultural criminology, popular criminology, and gothic criminology offer a framework for understanding the complementary and reflexive relationship between academic/scientific and aesthetic/popular accounts of crime, violence, and psychopathy.

So, just how important are popular culture depictions of psychopaths to criminological theory and criminal justice practice? The notion that aesthetic representations of psychopathy run parallel to, and are just as important as, academic/scientific explanations generates a long list of questions that have yet to be answered. *Where do people get their ideas about psychopathy? Are psychopaths in popular culture accurate portrayals of real-life psychopaths? Is there a discrepancy between popular and scientific conceptions of psychopathy? Do artistic depictions of psychopaths capture the complexity of the personality of the psychopath more completely than scientific explanations of the condition? In this era of prolific research on psychopathy, how much has the scientific conception of the condition made its way into the popular consciousness? Do popular culture representations of psychopathy influence criminal justice professional views of the offenders they work with and decisions they make? How do popular images of psychopaths make their way into real-life crime and criminal justice practice? And why are people so fascinated with psychopaths in popular culture?* Sorting out the relationship between the popular and scientific conceptions of psychopathy is critical for understanding the role psychopathy plays in real-world criminal justice and forensic policy and practice.

The Psychopath in Myth, Literature, Film, and Popular Culture

From the beginning of recorded history, there have been depictions of characters that researchers now identify as psychopaths in art, biblical text, folklore and myth, literature, and popular culture. In biblical times, the perception of Cain as the original evil (Hammer, 1990; Meloy, 2001) and the "stubborn and rebellious son" is one of the earliest notions of psychopathy (Rotenberg & Diamond, 1971). The founding texts of Judeo-Christian and Greco-Roman culture deal with violations of the law, and literature from its beginnings has contained larger- than-life characters who have committed cold-blooded acts of crime and violence (Black, 1991), and the biblical notion of Lucifer and Satan is filled with references to callous, remorseless, and inhumane aspects similar to those found in the condition of psychopathy (Zimbardo, 2007). Aspects of the Greek god Odysseus have been characterized as "primitive, cold-blooded, psychopathic levels of the primitive mind/brain" (Leader, 2009, p. 515), and mythical figures in different cultures over time such as the Nordic warrior, the Roman god Saturn, the vampire, the werewolf, the zombie, the witch, and the golem possess features very similar to the psychopath that give them the ability to destroy the innocent without conscience.

In 1941 Cleckley wrote in *The Mask of Sanity* about "fictional characters of psychiatric interest." Cleckley suggested that while many fictional characters regarded as evil may appear to possess characteristics of psychopathy, most of these characters are nothing like true clinical psychopaths. According to Cleckley, psychopaths "show no consistent pursuit of what might be called evil; their exploits are fitful, buffoonish, and unsustained by any obvious purpose. Consistent hatred of others is not a guiding line in their life scheme" (pp. 317–318). Fictional psychopaths that Cleckley identifies who might be loosely called psychopaths in his time include Heathcliffe in Brontë's *Wuthering Heights,* Prince Myshkin in Dostoevski's (1869) *The Idiot,* Svidrigailov in Dostoevski's (1951) *Crime and Punishment,* and Scarlett O'Hara in *Gone with the Wind.* However, Cleckley argues that most of these fictional depictions fall short in conveying in total the portrait of the true psychopath:

> [W]e seldom find in imaginative writing anyone who could fit the picture that emerges as we consider the histories in this book. Often, however, we find characters who in some aspect or some phase of their activities suggests what we have seen in the psychopath, and we find others no less abnormal whose qualities may be used in contrast. (Cleckley, 1941, 1988, p. 318)

In contrast with fictional characters who miss the mark in their portrayal of the true psychopath, Cleckley cites compelling depictions: Dostoevski's (1880) senior Karamazov in *The Brothers Karamazov*, Mildred in Maugham's (1915) *Of Human Bondage*, Rags in Scott's (1947) *The Story of Mrs. Murphy*, and the character Sandra Deare in the comic strip *Judge Parker.* According to Cleckley, the most successful of all portrayals of the psychopath is Charlie Carewe in Mary Astor's (1963) *The Incredible Charlie Carewe* who, in Cleckley's words is "an exquisite example of the psychopath" and the best to be found in any work of fiction.

In the years since the original publication of the *Mask of Sanity*, fictional psychopaths have become increasingly ingrained in popular consciousness. Popular culture is saturated with references to the "psychopath." Television shows, movies, and commercials use the term in passing conversation to refer to callous affectless individuals who appear to have no qualms about harming other people and show no signs of empathy or remorse.[1] Advertisements refer to the "dashing psychopath" (in FX series *Justified,* Egner, 2012), and the popular Emmy-nominated Showtime series *Dexter* (Johannessen, 2006–2013), which averaged 5.12 million weekly viewers and was renewed for eight seasons. New films emerge daily with all-star casts.

If one were to try to compile a list of fictional psychopaths in literature, television, film, computer and video games, comic strips, cartoons, commercials, and other cultural artifacts, the list would be endless. The monster narrative is an essential feature of storytelling. "Tales of evil, aggressive, selfish humans give powerful structure to the narratives of events. Telling the story of a crime, the emergence of a dictatorship, a failed marriage, or a failed business in terms of a single evil individual gives the storytelling a great line" (Hesse, 2009, p. 208). Fictional psychopaths depicted in books and films[2] include Rhoda

---

[1] I have heard reference to the term "psychopath" on television sitcoms, musicals, and films that have little to nothing to do with psychopaths—for example, in the film *Idiot Brother*, a comedy starring Paul Rudd and Zooey Deschanel, Deschanel's character makes reference to someone in a passing joke as a psychopath. As my daughter was growing up, I often worked at my computer while she was watching TV after school and have heard numerous passing references to psychopaths on the sitcoms she was she was watching. I am also often working while my daughter is watching shows on ABC Family, and I have heard numerous references to psychopaths on sitcoms involving high school students. There are so many of these references in daily life it would be virtually impossible to catalog them all.

[2] It is difficult to "assess" and catalog fictional psychopaths, even just using the criterion "lack of remorse" or PCL-R items associated with interpersonal, affective, lifestyle, and antisocial behavior, because many characters exhibit these characteristics but then appear to exhibit some type of

Penmark in *The Bad Seed* (1956), Henry Evans in *The Good Son* (Ruben, Page, & Ruben, 1993), *The Silence of the Lambs*' Hannibal (Utt, Bozman, & Demme,1991), *American Psycho*'s Patrick Bateman (Solomon et al., 2000), *Cape Fear*'s (1991) Max Cady (Bartlett & Thompson, 1962; DeFina & Scorsese, 1991), *Taxi Driver*'s Travis Bickle (Phillips, Phillips, & Scorsese, 1976), Blair Sullivan and Bobby Earl Ferguson in *Just Cause* (Glimcher et al., 1995), Aaron in *Primal Fear* (Lucchesi, Koch, & Holbit, 1996), Mickey and Mallory Knox in *Natural Born Killers* (Hamsher et al., 1994), Mr. Ripley in *The Talented Mr. Ripley* (Horberg, Sternberg, & Minghella, 1999), Tracy Safian in *Malice* (Becker, Pfeffer, & Becker, 1993), Catherine Tramell of *Basic Instinct* (Marshall, Kassar, & Verhoeven, 1992), Bridget Gregory in *The Last Seduction* (Shestack & Dahl, 1994), John Doe in *Se7en* (Kopelson & Fincher, 1995), Anton Chigurh in *No Country for Old Men* (Rudin et al., 2007), and Billy Bickle and Charlie Costello in *Seven Psychopaths*[3] (Broadbent et al., 2012). These are among the many contemporary fictional characters who exhibit features of the psychopath (see Table 5.1 for a list of contemporary psychopaths in film).

A number of authors have offered analyses of psychopaths in film, literature, art, and popular culture (Black, 1991; Jermyn, 1996; Neroni, 2005; Rafter, 2007; Rafter & Brown, 2001; Sargeant, 1996; Simpson, 2000; Thompson, 2007; Wilson, 1999). However, there is definitional confusion about what exactly constitutes a psychopath film, and some of these studies include films in which the characters are psychotic or nonpsychopathic serial killers or other types of depraved or criminal individuals.[4] Although Cleckley suggested many years ago that many depictions of evil characters were far from true psychopaths,

---

feeling for an individual (e.g., Mickey and Mallory in *Natural Born Killers*, Dexter in the TV series *Dexter*) or some level of anxiety (Patrick Bateman in *American Psycho*), or display behaviors that are indicative of possible psychosis of more complicated Axis I diagnosis (e.g., John Doe in *Se7en*, Henry in *Henry: Portrait of a Serial Killer*). Also, some characters who play a minor role appear to be clearly psychopathic; however, there is not enough attention to their character to be able to understand the individual "when he is connected to the circuits of full social life" (Cleckley, 1941, 1988, p. 22).

[3] There is also a comic book titled *7 Psychopaths* by Vehlmann and Phillips (2010) with a description of the book that reads, "7 men, 1 impossible mission—assassinate Hitler! With World War II in full swing, there's only one-way to draw the war to a quick end: kill Hitler. But who would be insane enough to try? Joshua Goldschmidt knows just the men to do it. Insane? Psychotic? Mad? Call them what you will, but the SEVEN PSYCHOPATHS are now the only hope the world has." (See http://www.amazon.com/7-Psychopaths-Fabien-Vehlmann/dp/1608860329#_)

[4] For example, some authors and Internet lists of psychopathic films include films such as *Henry: Portrait of a Serial Killer* (1990) (Rafter, 2006; Wilson, 1999). However, the title character in *Henry*, based on the real-life story of Henry Lee Lucas and Otis Toole, presented with psychotic symptoms and may not be clearly defined as a psychopath. Similarly, although many would consider *Taxi Driver* (1976) a film about a psychopath, the character Travis Bickle might be better described as a secondary psychopath who based on cultural forces found himself behaving for a time period as a psychopath in pursuit of a higher cause. The film *Natural Born Killers* (1994) is another complicated film to categorize because the characters Mickey and Mallory appear to love each other but no one else. They too may be more appropriately classified as secondary psychopaths.

Table 5.1 Psychopaths in Film*

Date	Title	Character	Actor(s)	Director/Producer	Production Co.
1931	*"M"*	Hans Beckert	Peter Lorre	Fritz Lang/Seymour Nebenzal	Paramount Pictures
1939	*Gone with the Wind*	Scarlet O'Hara	Vivien Leigh	Victor Fleming/David O. Selznick	MGM
1944	*Double Indemnity*	Phyllis Dietrichson	Barbara Stanwyck	Billy Wilder/Buddy DeSylva	Paramount
1946	*Gilda*	Gilda Mundson	Rita Hayworth	Charles Vidor/Virginia Van Upp	Columbia
1947	*Out of the Past*	Kathie Moffat	Jane Greer	Jacques Tourneur/Warren Duff	RKO
1947	*Scarlet Street*	Kitty March	Joan Bennett	Fritz Lang/Walter Wanger	Universal
1948	*Lady from Shanghai*	Elsa Bannister	Rita Hayworth	Orson Welles/Orson Welles	Columbia
1950	*Sunset Boulevard*	Norma Desmond	Gloria Swanson	Billy Wilder/Charles Brackett	Paramount
1950	*Gun Crazy*	Bart Tare/Annie Laurie Starr	John Dall/Peggy Cummins	Joseph H. Lewis/Frank and Maurice King	United Artists
1953	*The Asphalt Jungle*	Alonzo D. Emmerich	Louis Calhern	John Huston/Arthur Hornblow Jr.	MGM
1954	*Niagra*	George Loomis	Joseph Cotton	Henry Hathaway/Charles Brackett	20th Century Fox
1955	*East of Eden*	Cal Trask	James Dean	Elia Kazan/Elia Kazan	Warner Bros.
1955	*Rebel without a Cause*	Jim Stark	James Dean	Nicholas Ray/David Weisbart	Warner Bros.
1956	*Kiss Me Deadly*	Gabrielle	Gaby Rogers	Robert Aldrich/Robert Aldrich	United Artists
1956	*The Bad Seed*	Rhoda Penmark	Patty McCormack	Mervyn LeRoy/Mervyn LeRoy	Warner Bros.

1957	*In Cold Blood*	Perry Smith/Dick Hickock	Robert Blake/Scott Wilson	Richard Brooks/Richard Brooks	Columbia
1960	*3:10 to Yuma*	Ben Wade	Glenn Ford	Delmer Daves/David Heilweil	Columbia
1961	*Peeping Tom*	Mark Lewis	Carl Boehm	Michael Powell/Nat Cohen	Anglo-Amalgamated
1962	*Cape Fear* (original)	Max Cady	Robert Mitchum	J. Lee Thompson/Sy Bartlett	Universal
1963	*Whatever Happened to Baby Jane?*	Jane Hudson	Bette Davis	Robert Aldrich/Robert Aldrich	Warner Bros.
1966	*The Sadist*	Charles A. Tibbs	Arch Hall Jr.	James Landis/L. Steven Snyder	Fairway International
1969	*Who's Afraid of Virginia Woolf?*	George/Martha	Richard Burton/Elizabeth Taylor	Mike Nichols/Ernest Lehman	Warner Bros.
1969	*The Honeymoon Killers*	Martha Beck/Raymond Fernandez	Shirley Stoler/Tony Lo Bianco	Warren Steibel/Leonard Kastle	Cinerama Releasing
1971	*Whatever Happened to Aunt Alice?*	Claire Marrable	Geraldine Page	Leo Katzin/Robert Aldrich	ABC
1971	*Clockwork Orange*	Alex DeLarge	Malcolm McDowell	Stanley Kubrick/Stanley Kubrick	Warner Bros. Pictures
1971	*Play Misty for Me*	Evelyn Draper	Jessica Walter	Clint Eastwood/Robert Daly	Universal and Malpaso

(continued)

Table 5.1 *(continued)*

Date	Title	Character	Actor(s)	Director/Producer	Production Co.
1971	*The Sugarland Express*	Lou Jean and Clovis Michael Poplin	Goldie Hawn and William Atherton	Steven Spielberg/David Brown and Richard Zanuck	Universal
1971	*What's the Matter with Helen?*	Helen Hill	Shelley Winters	Curtis Harrington/George Edwards and Edward Feldman	United Artists
1972	*Straw Dogs*	Charlie Venner and Norman Scutt	Del Henney and Ken Hutchison	Sam Peckinpah/Daniel Melnick	Cinerama
1967	*Bonnie and Clyde*	Bonnie Parker and Clyde Barrow	Faye Dunaway and Warren Beatty	Arthur Penn/Warren Beatty	Warner Bros.
1973	*The Godfather*	Vito and Michael Corleone	Marlon Brando and Al Pacino	Francis Ford Coppola/Albert Ruddy	Paramount Pictures
1974	*Badlands*	Kit Carruthers	Martin Sheen	Terrence Malick/Terrence Malick	Warner Bros.
1976	*The Godfather: Part II*	Michael Corleone	Al Pacino	Francis Ford Coppola/Francis Ford Coppola	Paramount Pictures
1976	*Taxi Driver*	Travis Bickle	Robert De Niro	Martin Scorsese/Julia and Michael Phillips	Columbia Pictures
1979	*Carrie*	Carrie White	Sissy Spacek	Brian De Palma/Brian De Palma and Paul Monash	United Artists
1980	*The Onion Field*	Greg Powell and Jimmy Smith	James Wood/ Franklyn Seales	Harold Becker/Walter Coblenz	Avco Embassy

1981	*Body Heat*	Mary Ann Simpson (alias Matty Tyler)	Kathleen Turner	Lawrence Kasdan/Fred Gallo	Warner Bros.
1983	*Mommie Dearest*	Joan Crawford	Faye Dunaway	Frank Perry/Frank Yablans	Paramount Pictures
1986	*The Hitcher*	John Ryder	Rutger Hauer	Robert Harmon/David Bombyk and Kip Ohman	TriStar Pictures
1983	*Scarface*	Tony Montana	Al Pacino	Brian De Palma/Martin Bregman	Universal Pictures
1986	*Manhunter*	Francis Dollarhyde and Hannibal Lecter	Tom Noonan and Brian Cox	Michael Mann/Richard Roth	De Laurentiis and Red Dragon
1987	*Blue Velvet*	Frank Booth	Dennis Hopper	David Lynch/Fred Caruso	De Laurentiis and Paramount
1987	*Black Widow*	Catherine	Theresa Russell	Bob Rafelson/Lawrence Mark and Harold Schneider	20th Century Fox
1987	*Fatal Attraction*	Alexandra Forrest	Glenn Close	Adrian Lyne/Stanley Jaffe and Sherry Lansing	Paramount
1988	*Wall Street*	Gordon Gekko	Michael Douglas	Oliver Stone/Edward Pressman	20th Century Fox
1990	*The Vanishing* (original)	Raymond Lemorne	Bernard-Pierre Donnadieu	George Sluzier/Anne Lorden and George Sluzier	Argos Films

(continued)

Table 5.1 *(continued)*

Date	Title	Character	Actor(s)	Director/Producer	Production Co.
1990	*The Silence of the Lambs*	Hannibal Lecter	Anthony Hopkins	Jonathan Demme/Kenneth Utt and Edward Saxon	Orion Pictures
1990	*The Godfather: Part III*	Michael Corleone	Al Pacino	Francis Ford Coppola/Francis Ford Coppola	Paramount Pictures
1991	*Cape Fear (remake)*	Max Cady	Robert De Niro	Martin Scorsese/Barbara De Fina, Steven Spielberg, Robert De Niro, etc.	Amblin Entertainment and Universal Pictures
1991	*Goodfellas*	Henry Hill	Ray Liotta	Martin Scorsese/Irwin Winkler	Warner Bros.
1991	*Misery*	Annie Wilkes	Kathy Bates	Rob Reiner/Rob Reiner and Andrew Scheinman	Metro-Goldwyn-Mayer and Columbia
1992	*Scissors*	Angela Anderson	Sharon Stone	Frank de Felitta/Don Levin and Mel Pearle	DDM Film Corp.
1992	*Basic Instinct*	Catherine Tramell	Sharon Stone	Paul Verhoeven/Mario Kassar and Alan Marshall	TriStar Pictures
1992	*Single White Female*	Hedra "Hedy" Carlson	Jennifer Jason Leigh	Barbet Schroeder/Barbet Schroeder	Columbia Pictures
1992	*The Crying Game*	Jude	Miranda Richardson	Neil Jordan/Stephen Woolley	Palace Pictures
1992	*The Hand That Rocks the Cradle*	Mrs. Mott "Peyton Flanders"	Rebecca DeMornay	Curtis Hanson/David Madden	Hollywood Pictures

1992	*Reservoir Dogs*	Mr. Blonde/Blue/Brown/Orange/Pink/White	Harvey Keitel/Tim Roth/Michael Madsen/Chris Penn/Steve Buscemi/Eddie Bunker	Quentin Tarantino/Lawrence Bender	Miramax Films
1993	*Gun Crazy* (remake)	Anita Minteer	Drew Barrymore	Tamra Davis/Matthew Bright	First Look International
1993	*The Vanishing* (remake)	Barney Cousins	Jeff Bridges	George Sluizer/Larry Brezner and Pieter Jan Brugge	20th Century Fox
1993	*The Good Son* (remake)	Henry	Macauley Culkin	Joseph Ruben/Joseph Ruben	20th Century Fox
1993	*Malice*	Tracy	Nicole Kidman	Harold Becker/Harold Becker and Charles Mulvehill	New Line, Castle Rock, Nelvana
1993	*The Point of No Return*	Maggie Hayward	Bridget Fonda	John Badham/Art Linson	Warner Bros.
1993	*The Crush*	Adrienne	Alicia Silverstone	Alan Shapiro/James Robinson	Morgan Creek and Warner Bros.
1994	*Kalifornia*	Early Grace	Brad Pitt	Dominic Sena/Jonathan Demme and Peter Saraf	Polygram, Viacom, Propaganda
1994	*Mother's Boys*	Jude Madigan	Jamie Lee Curtis	Yves Simoneau/Jack Freedman and Patricia Herskovic	Dimension Films

(continued)

Table 5.1 *(continued)*

Date	Title	Character	Actor(s)	Director/Producer	Production Co.
1995	*Natural Born Killers*	Mickey and Mallory Knox	Woody Harrelson and Juliette Lewis	Oliver Stone/Arnon Milchan and Jane Hamsher	Regency, Alcor, Ixtlan
1995	*Copycat*	Peter Foley and Daryll Lee Cullum	William McNamara and Harry Connick Jr.	Jon Amiel/Arnon Milchan and Mark Tarlov	Regency Enterprises
1995	*Just Cause*	Bobby Earl Ferguson	Blair Underwood	Arne Glimcher/Arne Glimcher, Steve Perry, and Lee Rich	Warner Bros.
1995	*The Last Seduction*	Bridget Gregory	Linda Fiorentino	John Dahl/Jonathan Shestack	October Films
1996	*Se7en*	John Doe	Kevin Spacey	David Fincher/Arnold Kopelson and Phyllis Carlisle	New Line Cinema
1995	*Slingblade*	Karl Childers	Billy Bob Thornton	Billy Bob Thornton/Larry Meistrich and David Bushell	Miramax Films
1995	*The Usual Suspects*	Roger "Verbal" Kint	Kevin Spacey	Bryan Singer/Kenneth Kokin, Michael McDonnell, and Bryan Singer	Gramercy Pictures
1995	*Citizen X*	Andrei Chikatilo	Jeffrey DeMunn	Chris Gerolmo/Timothy Marx, Robert Stone, and Webster Stone	Asylum Films and Citadel
1995	*Casino*	Sam "Ace" Rothstein	Robert De Niro	Martin Scorsese/Barbara De Fina	Universal Pictures

1995	*Assassins*	Robert Rath and Miguel Bain	Sylvester Stallone and Antonio Banderas	Richard Donner/Richard Donner, Joel Silver, Bruce Evans, etc.	Silver Pictures, Canal
1996	*Primal Fear*	Aaron Stampler, aka "Roy"	Edward Norton	Gregory Hoblit/Gary Lucchesi and Howard Koch Jr.	Paramount Pictures
1996	*Fargo*	Carl Showalter and Gaear Grimsrud	Steve Buscemi and Peter Stormare	Joel and Ethan Coen (both)	Polygram, Working Title, Gramercy
1996	*A Thin Line between Love and Hate*	Brandi	Lynn Whitfield	Martin Lawrence/George Jackson and Doug McHenry	You Go Boy!, Jackson-McHenry Productions, and New Line
1997	*Freeway*	Bob Wolverton	Kiefer Sutherland	Matthew Bright/Chris Hanley and Brian Wyman	The Kushner-Locke Company
1987	*Full Metal Jacket*	Animal Mother	Adam Baldwin	Stanley Kubrick/Stanley Kubrick and Jan Harlan	Harrier Films and Natant
1999	*Kiss the Girls*	Casanova/Nick Ruskin	Cary Elwes	Gary Fleder/David Brown and Joe Wizan	Paramount
1999	*Cruel Intentions*	Kathryn Merteuil and Sebastian Valmont	Sarah Michelle Gellar and Ryan Phillippe	Roger Kumble/Neal Moritz	Original Film, New Market Capital Group, Columbia

(continued)

Table 5.1 *(continued)*

Date	Title	Character	Actor(s)	Director/Producer	Production Co.
1999	*The Bone Collector*	Richard Thompson	Leland Orser	Phillip Noyce/Martin and Michael Bregman	Universal and Sony Pictures
2000	*Double Jeopardy*	Nick Parsons	Bruce Greenwood	Bruce Beresford/Leonard Goldberg	Paramount
2000	*American Psycho*	Patrick Bateman	Christian Bale	Mary Harron/Christian Solomon, Chris Hanley, and Edward Pressman	Edward R. Pressman Film Corp. and Lions Gate
2001	*The Cell*	Carl Stargher	Vincent D'Onofrio	Tarsem Singh/Julio Caro and Eric McLeod	Radical Media and New Line
2001	*Hannibal*	Hannibal Lecter	Anthony Hopkins	Ridley Scott/Ridley Scott and Dino De Laurentiis	Universal, Scott Free, Metro-Goldwyn-Mayer
2001	*Don't Say a Word*	Patrick Koster	Sean Bean	Gary Fleder/Arnon Milchan, Arnold and Anne Kopelson	Regency, Village Roadshow, New Regency, etc.
2002	*Along Came a Spider*	Gary Soneji and Jezzie Flannigan	Michael Wincott and Monica Potter	Lee Tamahori/David Brown, Joe Wizan, Morgan Freeman, and Marty Hornstein	Rhythm and Hues, Revelations, and Paramount

2003	*Red Dragon*	Hannibal Lecter	Anthony Hopkins	Brett Ratner/Dino De Laurentiis	Metro-Goldwyn-Mayer, Scott Free, and Universal
2004	*Monster*	Aileen Wuornos	Charlize Theron	Patty Jenkins/Charlize Theron, Mark Damon, Clark Peterson, Donald Kushner, and Bryan Wyman	DEJ Productions, Media 8, Newmarket
2004	*Highwaymen*	James Cray and Fargo	James Caviezel and Colm Feore	Robert Harmon/Bradley Jenkel, Carroll Kemp, and Mike Marcus	New Line, Millennium, and Cornice
2005	*Collateral*	Vincent	Tom Cruise	Michael Mann/Michael Mann and Julie Richardson	DreamWorks
2006	*V for Vendetta*	V	Hugo Weaving	James McTeigue, Joel Silver, Larry and Andy Wachowski, and Grant Hill	Vertigo Comics, Virtual Studios, Silver Pictures, and Warner Bros.
2007	*No Country for Old Men*	Anton Chigurh	Javier Bardem	Joel and Ethan Coen (both)	Miramax and Paramount

(*continued*)

Table 5.1 *(continued)*

Date	Title	Character	Actor(s)	Director/Producer	Production Co.
2007	*Funny Games*	Peter and Paul	Brady Corbet and Michael Pitt	Michael Haneke/Hamish McAlpine, Christian Baute, Chris Coen, etc.	Celluloid, Tartan, Film4, and Warner
2002	*Enough*	Mitch Hiller	Billy Campbell	Michael Apted/Rob Cowan and Irwin Winkler	Columbia
2007	*3:10 to Yuma* (remake)	Ben Wade	Russell Crowe	James Mangold/Cathy Konrad	Relativity Media and Lionsgate
2008	*Fracture*	Ted Crawford	Anthony Hopkins	Gregory Hoblit/Charles Weinstock	Castle Rock and New Line
2009	*The Dark Knight*	Joker	Heath Ledger	Christopher Nolan/Christopher Nolan, Emma Thomas, and Charles Roven	Legendary, DC Comics, Syncopy, and Warner Bros.
2009	*Inglorious Basterds*	Hans Landa and Aldo Raine	Christopher Waltz and Brad Pitt	Quentin Tarantino/Lawrence Bender	A Band Apart, Studio Babelsberg, Weinstein Company, and Universal
2009	*The Orphan*	Esther	Isabelle Fuhrman	Jaume Collet-Serra/Jennifer Davisson, Killoran, Leonardo DiCaprio, and Susan Downey	Dark Castle Entertainment

2011	*Gamer*	Ken Castle	Michael C. Hall	Neveldine and Tyler/Tom Rosenberg, Gary Lucchesi, Richard Wright, and Skip Williamson	Lakeshore and Lionsgate
2011	*Straw Dogs* (remake)	Charlie Venner	Alexander Skarsgaard	Rod Lurie/Rod Lurie and Marc Frydman	Battleplan and Screen Gems
2011	*Lincoln Lawyer*	Louis Roulet	Ryan Phillippe	Brad Furman/Sidney Kimmel, Tom Rosenberg, Gary Lucchesi, Richard Wright, and Scott Steindorff	Lionsgate, Lakeshore, SKE, and Stone Village
2012	*We Need to Talk about Kevin*	Kevin Katchadourin	Ezra Miller	Lynne Ramsay/Jennifer Fox, Luc Roeg, and Bob Salerno	BBC, Forward, Artificial Eye
2012	*Rampart*	Dave Brown	Woody Harrelson	Oren Moverman/Ben Foster, Lawrence Inglee, Ken Kao, and Clark Peterson	Amalgam and Millennium
2012	*Seven Psychopaths*	Charlie	Woody Harrelson	Martin McDonagh/Martin McDonagh, Graham Broadbent, and Peter Czernin	Blueprint, CBS
2013	*Wolf of Wall Street*	Jordan Belfort	Leonardo DiCaprio	Martin Scorsese/Riza Aziz, Leonardo DiCaprio, Joey McFarland, and Emma Tillinger	Red Granite Pictures

(*continued*)

Table 5.1 *(continued)*

Date	Title	Character	Actor(s)	Director/Producer	Production Co.
2014	*Gone Girl*	Amy Dunne and Nick Dunne	Rosamund Pike and Ben Affleck	David Fincher/ Ceán Chaffin, Joshua Donen, and Arnon Milchan	Twentieth Century Fox
2014	*Night Crawler*	Louis Bloom	Jake Gyllenhaal	Dan Gilroy/Jennifer Fox, Tony Gilroy, Jake Gyllenhaal, David Lancaster, and Michel Litvak	Bold Films
2015	*The Visit*	Nana and Pop Pop	Deanna Dunagan and Peter McRobbie	M. Night Shyamalan/Marc Bienstock	Blinding Edge Pictures, Blumhouse Productions
2016	*The Girl on a Train*	Tom	Justin Theroux	Tate Taylor/ Jared LeBoff and Marc Platt	Amblin Partners/Dream Works
2017	*Dismissed*	Lucas Ward	Dylan Sprouse	Benjamin J. D. Arfman/Lifshitz, Raphael Margules, and Sev Ohanian	Boulderlight Pictures
2017	*Get Out*	Armitage family members	Catherine Keener, Bradley Whitford, and Caleb Landry Jones	Jordan Peele/Jason Blume and Edward Hamm	Universal Pictures

2017	*It*	Pennywise the Dancing Clown	Bill Skarsgård	Andy Muschietti/Seth Grahame-Smith, and David Katzenberg	New Line Cinema
2017	*Baby Driver*	Doc	Kevin Spacey	Edgar Wright/Tim Bevan, Eric Fellner, and Rachael Prior	TriStar Pictures
2017	*Psychopaths*	Multiple characters	Larry Fessenden, James Landry Hébert, Jeremy Gardner, Sam Zimmerman, Angela Trimbur, and Ashley Bell	Mickey Keating/ William Day Frank, Al Lewison, Cam McLellan, and Jenn Wexler	Glass Eye Pix
2018	*Acrimony*	Melinda Moore-Gayle	Taraji Penda Henson	Tyler Perry/Mark E. Smith, Will Areu, and Ozzie Areu	Tyler Perry Studios

*This list offers examples of films that show characters with psychopathic traits and is by no means exhaustive. Some of the characters in these films may not be primary psychopaths; however, they are included here because their traits and behaviors as reflected in the films are largely consistent with the scientific conception of psychopathy and the central feature of lack of conscience, affect, and empathy, or they are characters that have been referred to in popular culture as psychopaths. Some of the characters in these films may be more accurately classified as secondary psychopaths who show callous disregard for others in one scene in the film, but they then exhibit behaviors inconsistent with psychopathy in other scenes (e.g., *Natural Born Killers*), they exhibit psychopathic characteristics throughout most of the film but also show symptoms of psychosis (e.g., *The Shining, American Psycho*), are part of a primary/secondary duo (*In Cold Blood, The Onion Field*), and/or are difficult to evaluate given information left out and innuendos in the final scenes of the film (e.g., *Gone Girl*).

Wilson (1999) argues that it is "the exuberance for evil that most vividly defines the cinematic psychopath (p. 84), and Rafter (2006) suggests that the PCL-R and the scientific conception of psychopathy offer a definitional framework to classify psychopath films as those in which the main character lacks conscience and exhibits symptoms of psychopathy (Rafter, 2006, p. 94). There is currently no consensus on what constitutes a "psychopath film," and much of what has been written about the cinematic psychopath has drawn from "a confusion of psycho movies with slashers and serial killer films" (Rafter, 2006, p. 94). Given this definitional confusion in the film studies literature, the popular conception of psychopathy is likely to be much less clear than the current scientific conception.

Parallel to the explosion of scholarly journal articles on psychopathy in the scientific literature and film and television characters in popular culture, there has also been an influx of trade publications on psychopathy written for more general audiences. Robert Hare's (1993) *Without Conscience* was one of the first trade publications written by a scientific scholar on psychopathy that introduced the scientific research on psychopathy to the general public. *Without Conscience* was followed by other books on related topics such as *Snakes in Suits* (Babiak & Hare, 2006), *The Sociopath Next Door* (Stout, 2005), *In Sheep's Clothing* (Simon, 2010), *Women Who Love Psychopaths* (Brown, 2009), *Emotional Vampires* (Bernstein, 2002, 2014), and *The Psychopath Test* (Ronson, 2011). There has also been a proliferation of mass market publications on psychopathy written by lay authors from lesser known publishers including books such as *The Psychopath's Bible* (Hyatt, 2010), *Surviving a Sociopath* (Perkins, 2010), and *Danger Has a Face* (Pike, 2011). The self-publishing industry has led to an increase in the number of publications on psychopathy that have made their way into the market through outlets such as Amazon.com's *CreateSpace*. Books such as *Pass the PCL-R: Your Guide to Passing the Hare Psychopathy Checklist–Revised* (Gentry, 2011) and *Laughter Effects: Humor and Inspiration for Victims of Sociopaths* (Martin, 2011) now populate the popular discourse. This is an interesting new arena that bridges the scientific and popular realms—a sort of infotainment that straddles academic and popular discourse.[5]

[5] These books are interesting additions to the popular market. They are self-published, poorly written, and sloppily organized. However, they are readily available through Amazon.com for anyone doing a search using the term "psychopath." When the books come in the mail, they are as polished and glossy on the outside as a book published from a major publisher. Thus, for anyone who does not know the names of reputable publishers or the difference between a self-published and a published book, the material in these sources may be seen as just as legitimate and accurate as a book that has been peer reviewed and published through a major publishing house. The increase in the number of these sorts of publications on psychopathy reflects a merging (or perhaps morphing is a

Of particular note is the cultural awareness of forensic assessment measures available to assess psychopathy. Jon Ronson's book *The Psychopath Test* is a mass market trade book that questions the industry of risk assessment and prediction of dangerousness with focus on the PCL-R. When this book came out, it was wildly popular, became a *New York Times* Best Seller, and was featured in a *Ted Talk* and on *This American Life* and other TV and radio outlets. Ronson, a documentary filmmaker, writer, and author of the internationally best-selling books *Them: Adventures of Extremists* and *The Men Who Stare at Goats* is an engaging speaker from London who was able to make the usually dry (from a popular culture perspective) world of forensic assessment something of an entertaining freak show that got everyone talking.[6] Gentry's (2011) *Pass the PCL-R* is another example of the mainstreaming of conversation on the forensic assessment of psychopathy, which is a relatively new phenomenon in the history of the evolution of the construct of psychopathy and the popular conception of psychopathy.

Pass the PCL-R is particularly interesting as a cultural artifact reflecting the state of the contemporary popular conception of psychopathy. It is a self-published book written without any information about the author's background and misspellings and errors[7] for the purpose of instructing people who may have been labeled as psychopaths on how to score low on the PCL-R.[8] The book contains the disclaimer, "The authors are not lawyers and none of the information contained constitutes legal advice. You are responsible for your actions and behavior. If you have any legal questions consult your attorney" (Gentry, 2011, p. 4). *Pass the PCL-R* systematically goes through all 20 items of the PCL-R with detailed instructions about how to properly answer as if one were not in fact a psychopath (or to advise nonpsychopathic individuals who find themselves in the unfortunate position of being the subject of a PCL-R administration to be careful to not inadvertently respond to interviewer

---

better word) of the scientific and popular realms. The effect this will have on the popular conception of psychopathy remains to be seen.

[6] I have studied psychopathy for almost 30 years. Many people know this but rarely have much to say to me about it at social events on campus or elsewhere. The first edition of the PCL-R was published in 1990, more than 22 years ago. However, for about six months after publication of Jon Ronson's book *The Psychopath Test* in 2011, almost everywhere I went someone asked me if I had read the book or heard Ronson speak, and wanted to know more about "this psychopath test."

[7] For example, "shallow affect" is spelled "shallow effect" (Gentry, 2011, pp. 5, 38), and the PCL-R and readers are warned, "It's not about if you are a psychopath or not, you just need to do well on a standardized test" (p. 10).

[8] *Pass the PCL-R*, a 124-page 5½ × 8½-inch paperback book, originally became available as an expensive self-published book with a price tag of $72.53. A few months later it was republished under Amazon.com's *CreateSpace* with the lower price of $26.73.

questions as a psychopath would). For example, the following advice is offered on how to score low on Item 6, "lack of remorse or guilt":

> This is a big one. You may have committed this crime a long, long time ago and have talked about it enough that you have come to terms with it and can speak frankly about it. Some people you speak with in prison might brag about the crimes they have committed and talk about them in a very cavalier way. This is not what you want to do. Not only do you need to get the words right, but you need to show that the power of what they mean affects you. The remorse that you feel needs to be toward the victims of your crimes and not the self-pity for the situation you are in. . . . An example of what would be appropriate to say years later if you really hurt or killed someone in the past:
>
> > "I feel a great deal of remorse for (use her name) I mean. . . . I was very mad at the time, but . . . that didn't justify what I did. I got really carried away and now I can't take it back . . . there is nothing I can do . . . I wish I could take it back. . . . He didn't deserve that. . . . But there is nothing I can do now" (p. 35).

In response to a psychologist's interview question, "What does it feel like?" to solicit information to score Item 6, "lack of remorse or guilt," interviewees are instructed to say:

> "It feels painful inside, it's like my conscience is carrying a big weight around and I want to drop it . . . but when I think about it . . . it just gets heavier" (p. 36).

Further instructions pertaining to the "lack of remorse" item and the above suggested response include:

> Don't give this answer while staring right back at the psychologist. You have to look bothered and upset. Most people would look down and they would be slow at answering follow-up questions. Some would also take a deep breath and exhale slowly. It should take awhile to get back to answering questions normally. Remember, you can't use exactly what I have written here, you need to come up with your own similar thing to say that is meaningful to you. There is a possibility that the psychologist has read this document and is listening for quotes out of here as an indication of deception (p. 36). . . . You will score well on this trait if you say you don't think that you shouldn't be let out of prison because you don't think you deserve it. This would be very hard to convince him of unless you truly believe it and can give an academy award winning performance. Things you should NOT say:

"I had a reason at the time, that is why it was done. Can't turn the world back now."

"I stole the stuff, but they were well insured so it doesn't matter."

"Yeah, quite unfortunate that things led to that."

"What, he is fine. I have my own problems."

"I should have buried their bodies in the desert, I wouldn't be here right now" (p. 38).

Pass the PCL-R also has a section on the Rorschach in which all 10 inkblots are presented. The author states:

> This test came out in the 1920s and consists of the psychologist showing you 10 pictures of inkblots and asking you what they look like and why you think so. . . . Your answers are only half of what he is grading. The other half is how you answer. Lucky for you, the Rorschach has been around so long the copyright has expired. So, I can show you all the inkblot pictures right here. . . . I intended to publish these in color, but the printer was going to charge me 4 times the price. . . . You can view these in full color online for free, PassthePCLR.com. (Gentry, 2011, p. 98)

Clearly this and other self-publications show that there appears to be an understanding in culture of what or who psychopaths are that has a life of its own beyond how the condition is understood in the academic and research sphere. The psychopath is the bad guy of bad guys, the human monster who can do anything to anyone without even a flicker of remorse. Every psychological thriller, crime drama, soap opera, and even some comedies and musicals, has one. The psychopath is distinguished from other conditions as one in which individuals so afflicted consciously choose to engage in harmful acts with negative empathy (Baron-Cohen, 2011) and without remorse. These individuals are considered by many to be the epitome of human evil (Richman, Mercer, & Mason, 1999). But, what explains the cultural fascination with psychopaths? *Do images of psychopaths in myth, literature, and popular culture fulfill some cultural need? Does the popular conception of psychopathy serve some function in culture?*

Why the Fascination with Psychopaths in Film and Pop Culture?

The psychopath is simultaneously glorified and despised in American pop culture. Popularity of films portraying psychopaths such as *The Silence of the Lambs, Natural Born Killers, Se7en),* television series like *Dexter* and *Criminal*

Minds, novels such as Capote's (1965) *In Cold Blood* and Dostoyevsky's (1951) *Crime and Punishment*, writers such as Jack Olsen and Ann Rule (among others) whose numerous true-crime accounts of psychopaths are best sellers sold at every bookstore and grocery outlet, and film noir and neo-noir genres attest to the cultural fascination with the psychopath. In an era where science has supplanted religious and metaphysical views of evil, the figure of the psychopathic criminal is "all that remains in the modern age of the sacred and demonic characters of the age of myth" (Black, 1991, p. 30).

A number of authors have addressed the roots of the cultural fascination with psychopathy (e.g., Cleckley, 1988; Hare, 1993; Harrington, 1972; Hesse, 2009; Rieber & Green, 1989; Smith, 1978), crime and violence more generally (Black, 1991; Bok, 1998; Duncan, 1996; Goldstein, 1998; Lesser, 1993), and the relevance of aesthetic representations of psychopathology, violence, and crime in popular culture to academic and general understanding (Black, 1991; Ferrell, 1995; Ferrell, Hayward, & Young, 2008; Ferrell & Sanders, 1995; Picart & Greek, 2003; Rafter, 2006; Rafter, 2007). However, much is left unanswered regarding the psychological and sociocultural dynamics of this fascination and of the function of the psychopathic image.

Jungian psychologists have explored the cultural function of the relationship between psychopathy, shadow, and evil. This body of work offers a deeper understanding as to why human beings are so fascinated with evil and the symbols with which it is associated across time and culture (e.g., vampires, werewolves, witches, communists, whales, sharks, serial murderers, space aliens, criminals, psychopaths). Stories reflecting a human obsession with the light and the dark sides of nature have circulated since the beginning of time in all cultures. Many cultures find ways to make anomalous human behavior associated with deviance, crime, and evil evident to the group. In primitive civilizations, jesters were assigned to engage in behaviors that conflicted with group rules—to laugh when everyone else cried and to cry when everyone else laughed. Some North American tribes hold "shadow catharsis festivals" whereby a member of the tribe was elected to perform, ritualistically, shocking acts contrary to group standards (Franz, 1995). From this perspective, evil is imagined and "contained" in "others" through the arts, media, and political propaganda. Unconscious impulses to behave in ways that are considered "evil" are projected onto another person, a movie screen, or a character in a novel for the purpose of stimulation and release (Zweig & Abrahms, 1991).

Media effects research has focused on a number of key theoretical areas in the research literature to explain what people get from viewing images of violence and human depravity. Sparks and Sparks (2002) identify six theoretical mechanisms in the media violence literature that have our understanding of the influence of violent media:

1. ***Catharsis:*** Media violence provides a cathartic outlet that allows viewers to engage in fantasy aggression that reduces the need to carry out aggressive behavior.
2. ***Social learning:*** Media characters serve as role models. If people see aggressive characters being rewarded rather than punished for the behavior, they will be more likely to imitate the behavior.
3. ***Priming:*** Exposure to violent media images plants aggressive and violent cues in people's minds, making them easily cognitively accessible. These cues interact with the viewers' emotional state and can increase the likelihood of aggressive behavior.
4. ***Arousal:*** People become physiologically aroused when they view media violence in a way that intensifies the emotional state of the viewer.
5. ***Desensitization:*** The more violent media a person consumes, the more dulled a person's sensitivity to violence will become. This can contribute to aggressive behavior by reducing the recognition that aggression and violence are behaviors that should be curtailed.
6. ***Cultivation and fear:*** Viewing violent media cultivates a particular social reality and induces high levels of fear that can persist for days, months, or years after initial exposure.

All six of these theoretical areas have been explored at length in the media effects literature. All but the catharsis theory have received empirical support.[9]

In his book *Why We Watch*, Goldstein (1998) suggests that the appeal of violent entertainment is not widespread and the premise that portrayals of violence are inherently appealing is untenable. Sorting out why we watch films and other media forms depicting characters who exhibit callous disregard for others in the form of violence requires analysis of the portrayal, audience, and the context in which the violence is viewed. Research to date does not support the theory that we are processing our underlying anxieties and using violent media images to work out our fears. Rather the evidence suggests that

---

[9] There have been a large number of studies that have produced findings directly counter to the catharsis hypothesis, which has resulted in a "virtual abandonment" (Sparks & Sparks, 2002, p. 278) of catharsis theory by the research community. However, most of these studies have been laboratory studies focusing on aggression in children (as opposed to juvenile or adult criminal behavior) in response to viewing a violent TV or film. Research involving virtual violence and catharsis (in particular with first-person shooter games) is just beginning to be explored. Although the consensus in the media effects literature is that there is little to no support for catharsis theory (Bryant & Zillman, 2002), recent research on video game violence has found that playing violent video games reduces depression and hostile feelings in players through mood management, suggesting that consuming particular forms of violent media may have particular cathartic effects.

we continue to consume violent media even when we are disturbed and disgusted. The following are some of the reasons Goldstein (1998) offers as to why we watch:

- ***Social identity:*** Violent images appeal primarily to males and mostly in groups and serve a social bonding function. The group activity of viewing violence appears to be differentially experienced and dependent on cultural expectation of toughness—individuals watch to show they are tough enough to handle it, and this has a social bonding effect.
- ***Mood management:*** Violent imagery offers an occasion to express emotions in ways generally prohibited. Anxious, more empathic individuals may watch and enjoy violent media and experience identification with the good guy to control anxieties. On the other hand, individuals who enjoy the violence for the sake of itself are likely to be those who have experienced violence in their own lives.
- ***Sensation seeking and excitement:*** Watching violence is a way to fill the void left by the civilizing process in which there is diminished opportunity to experience the real thing.[10] Individuals who experience higher levels of sensation seeking will be more attracted to violent images.
- ***Emotional expression:*** Aggressive games and entertainment offer males or others with social pressures on them not to be intimate or emotional and the opportunity to express emotions in a hypermasculine context. A violent film, like a rock concert, sports, or other social event, provides an opportunity for expression of intense emotion not available in other arenas.
- ***Fantasy:*** Violent entertainment is appealing because it allows the consumer to become totally immersed in the activity in a way that is not possible in real life. Suspension of disbelief and immersion in an imaginary world is a powerful element in consuming media violence and explains the tolerance for, if not the attraction, to it.
- ***Context:*** Whether or not we will enjoy watching depends on the degree to which we feel safe to do so culturally and situationally, and the degree to which violence is validated in our own lives (e.g., personal experience with violence may desensitize prime violence in a way that makes it feel safer and more familiar to watch). People go to the movies to see danger and feel safe. If factors exist to support this, they will watch. If not, they won't.
- ***Justice:*** Violent entertainment offers an opportunity to see justice prevail. People bring a sense of generalized injustice with them to the theater. When

[10] See Elias (1982) and Elias and Dunning (1986). Garland (1990) also offers in-depth discussion of cultural support for the death penalty as a result of these diminished opportunities to see violence in public, including public executions.

good wins over evil, justice is restored. Even just the act of viewing violence and wrongdoing elicits affective response that is mediated by moral judgment. Experiencing feelings of hatred and fear toward a protagonist allows us to enjoy the violence.

- ***Social control:*** Violent images serve a function of creating the "mean world theory."[11] The dangers and evils of the world are displayed on the screen to remind people to watch out and to make clear the boundaries of good and evil, safe and dangerous. People are frightened into obedience, truthfulness, and honesty when they are reminded of the consequences of disregard for the social contract.

Thus the reasons why we watch violent media may depend on a number of individual, social, and cultural factors—different people may watch for different reasons—but on a broad cultural level, we all have the potential to be attracted to violent images to emotionally regulate, socially bond, and to be reminded of the cultural boundaries of human behavior.

Although these theories pertain to violent imagery in general, much the same could be said for media representations of psychopathy. Many depictions of psychopathy are in the form of violent characters. Even psychopathic characters who are not blatantly violent tend to serve the functional storyline of good versus evil. Cultural images of psychopathy reflect a scientifically sterilized and modernized symbol of evil that serves an important function in society. Myth is a cultural expression of mass consciousness that is as close to absolute truth as can be expressed in words, and the more modern and removed we are from ancient mythic participation, the less recognizable are our myths (Hill, 1992). Film (and other forms of popular culture) are modern manifestations of myth that, like ancient myths, reinforce our defenses against what haunts us and, at the same time, make what haunts us more conceivable. Popular culture representations of psychopathy and violence provide a collective opportunity to defend ourselves against what we fear and our desire to confront it to maintain psychic balance (Natoli, 1994).

Conceptualization of the mass media as modern myth offers insight into the cultural fascination with psychopathy and the function of this fascination. In *Without Conscience*, Hare (1993) presents the following theories regarding the function of the psychopathic image in culture:

1. Visual experiencing of the psychopath allows viewers to participate with the psychopath, or as the psychopath, in a manner that is not possible through science.

[11] See Gerbner (1984, 1994a, 1994b).

2. We all identify with and are attracted to psychopaths because we want to understand the internal dynamics we share with them (i.e., we are searching for psychic balance).
3. The psychopathic image reminds psychologically healthy people of the dangers and destructiveness of psychopathy.
4. Psychopaths may recognize themselves through media images and may be compelled to seek help.
5. Media images may serve as role models for individuals with serious psychopathological disturbances.

Black (1991) offers evidence to support several of these theories (specifically 1, 2, and 5) in his book *The Aesthetics of Murder: A Study in Romantic Literature and Contemporary Culture* through analysis of the cases of Mark David Chapman (who was convicted in 1981 of the murder of John Lennon) and John Hinckley (who was acquitted in 1982 under the insanity defense for the attempted assassination of Ronald Reagan). According to Black, the figure of the criminal is "all that remains in the modern age of the sacred and demonic characters of the age of myth" (p. 30). Black argues that the ways in which individuals react to artistic representations of aggression and violence need to be studied and accounted for to learn what specific cultural conditions help to bring about media-related murder. Using Chapman and Hinckley as examples, he contends that the boundaries between the figurative and literal criminal have become blurred in contemporary society:

> Is the individual in these cases really a psycho- or sociopath who mistakes fantasy for reality, fiction for fact, art for action? Or should we regard him rather as an artistic illiterate who is unable to recognize the figural and fictive suspension from the real that art entails? Might such an individual even be a rigorous idealist or supreme literalist who detects a deeper reality hidden beneath the veil of art, and who responds iconoclastically tearing away those media-mediated appearances that bear no relation to the real? In the postindustrial, postmodern society of the late twentieth century, where violence is routinely sublimated into art and where almost every aspect of reality has been thoroughly aestheticized by advertising and the mass media, the criminal sociopath may be the individual who desperately tries to see the worlds as it "really" is, in all its unsublimated, sublime violence. Artistic representations of slayings provide fictional displacements for or simulacra of the act of murder for everyone except the artistically illiterate. Such persons are unable to recognize art as art, not simply because they live in a private world of make-believe fantasy, or because they have not received the proper "aesthetic education," but because they are absolute Realists who find no truth or meaning whatsoever either in

> their own private fantasies (the Imaginary) or in the collective fantasies of art and the media (the Symbolic). (Black, 1991, p. 25)

From this perspective, images of psychopathic characters may have a particular effect on artistically illiterate media junkies who lack an integrated identity serving as role models, but for the rest of us these images offer a kind of vicarious voyeurism that helps us work out our anxieties and make some sense of the world.

In her book *Romantic Outlaws, Beloved Prisons*, Duncan (1996) argues that our relationship to images of crime and outlaws in culture is paradoxical and complex—and deeply psychological with simultaneous feelings of attraction and hatred. Duncan speaks generally about the function of images of criminal justice and criminals, and the psychopathic criminal can be seen as the extreme end of the criminal outlaw continuum. From a psychological standpoint, the law is viewed as the parent and the criminal as child. And the criminal is the "perpetual child" we all, at times, wish to be. "The criminal's allure flows partly from their childlike qualities—their 'charming' unscrupulousness, their refusal to accept responsibility, and their embodiment of freedom" (p. 189). Lesser (1993) similarly argues that there is a tendency toward identification with cultural images of murder. The murder plots in literature and film are those that we are allowed to identify with the murderer, even if sometimes this identification is unconscious and disguised, but that this identification is crucial to the story's plot. She suggests that this identification is clear in viewer responses to the film *The Silence of the Lambs*—"*The Silence of the Lambs* plays on our fears of people like Hannibal Lecter, but it also plays on our even deeper sympathies with them" (p. 51). Lesser suggests that we identify with the murderer because we see him as a victim of the misrepresenting systems of justice and psychiatry:

> [T]he justice system and the psychiatric system have a natural affinity with each other because both prefer diagrammatic, black-and-white, instantly comprehensible renderings of reality to the messy, difficult tangles of truth. I think we identify with the murderer partially because we see him as the victim of both of these misrepresenting systems. The justice system needs to misrepresent, for its own purposes, exactly what he did . . . and the psychiatric system inevitably misrepresents why he did it. The reductive machinery, the inexorable cog in the wheel, makes the accused murderer a figure we can identify with on our own terms; for we too have felt trapped, in one context or another, by the machinery of our social setting. We don't have to imagine ourselves as murderers to identify with him. We need only imagine ourselves as victims. (Lesser, 1993, p. 86)

This paradoxical, love/hate relationship with the cinematic psychopath invites the media consumer to learn about psychopathy that may not be possible through scientific explanations of the condition.

Copycat Psychopaths

There is a growing literature on the phenomenon of copycat crime that examines this blurred boundary between fictional and actual representations of crime, violence, and murder (Coleman, 2004; Helfgott, 2008; Surette, 1990, 2002, 2006, 2013). Copycat crime is crime inspired by another crime that has been publicized in the news media or fictionally or artistically represented whereby the offender incorporates aspects of the original offense into a new crime (Surette, 2002, 2006, in press). A number of offenders who have incorporated copycat aspects in their crimes exhibit characteristics of psychopathy suggesting that psychopathy may be a risk factor for copycat crime (Helfgott, 2008). Historical copycat criminals Mark David Chapman and John Hinckley have been referred to as "artistically illiterate media junkies" who blurred the boundary between fantasy and reality in their quest for identity integration (Black, 1991). Both Chapman and Hinckley exhibited features of psychopathy. Chapman has been called a "sociopath at best, a psychopath at worst" (Duffy, 2010), and evidence presented during the Hinckley trials by the prosecution argued that Hinckley possessed features of psychopathy, including narcissistic and antisocial personality disorders (Low, Jeffries, & Bonnie, 1986).

The relationship between psychopathy and copycat crime has not been empirically explored, but given the theoretical connections in the literature and anecdotal evidence of cases involving psychopaths, this is an intriguing area for future research. Cleckley (1941, 1988) suggests that if in fact a psychopath was able to technically produce art, the rendering of aspects of life would be a "counterfeit." "Whatever he might express would probably be as spurious, as little representative of the authentic human experience, as his convincing but empty promises, his eloquent protestations of love he does not feel" (p. 305). Black's analysis of the Hinckley and Chapman cases suggests that their crimes were the product of an attempt to hijack the identities of their victims in a media-mediated psychological process that involved media immersion, identity disturbance, and a culture characterized by aestheticized hyperreality. According to Black, Hinckley and Chapman were both "frustrated middle-class youth engaged in a desperate quest for social identity and recognition" (p. 144) who operated "under the influence of mass media" (p. 138):

> In the world of the hyperreal, identity is contingent upon image, and individuals exist insofar as they are able to identify themselves with an image generated by the mass media. The individual who lacks a sense of

> identity may seize upon the image of a public figure that can serve him as a model. Such behavior is quite innocuous when the celebrity-model is already dead. . . . The problem arises when an anonymous individual tries to appropriate the image of a living celebrity as his own. The progress from celebrity qua model to celebrity qua double culminates in celebrity qua victim. This is to be expected in an age of mass-(re)production when uniqueness seems impossible to achieve: the anonymous individual tries to appropriate the celebrity's unique aura for himself. It takes a violent act of self-creation to transform the anonymous individual from a Nobody to a Somebody. (Black, 1991, p. 144)

There is a growing body of anecdotal evidence suggesting that copycat crime is a very real phenomenon exacerbated by the central role played by media and popular culture in particular in the lives of youth. The following are some of the most notable copycat cases, all of whom involved offenders who were referred to in trials or news reports as possessing features of psychopathy:

- ***Catcher in the Rye (1951):*** Mark David Chapman believed himself to be Holden Caulfield, the main character in the book. He murdered John Lennon in 1980 after years of fixation on both Lennon and Caulfield. He is believed to have murdered Lennon because he viewed him as a "phony," a term Caulfield used to refer to people.
- ***Clockwork Orange (1971):*** A film associated with the rape of a 17-year-old girl by male youths singing "singing in the rain" and a string of brutal rapes and murders in Britain by men dressed similarly to the characters attributed to either the film or the book. Kubrick pulled the film in Britain in 1972, and it wasn't rereleased there until 2000.
- ***Grand Theft Auto Vice City (2002):*** 18-year-old Devin Moore allegedly played the game for hours before stealing a car and gunning down two police officers and a 911 dispatcher in 2003. When captured he said, "Life is like a video game. Everybody's got to die some time." At trial, it was revealed that he was a compulsive violent video game player who suffered from childhood abuse–related post-traumatic stress disorder. Moore's attorneys argued the "GTA defense"—that he lost touch with reality and was acting out the virtual violence in GTA. Despite his attorney's efforts, the GTA defense was unsuccessful, and Moore was sentenced to death in 2005. ("Can a video game lead to murder?," 2005)
- ***Taxi Driver (1976):*** John Hinckley's 1981 assassination attempt on Ronald Reagan was associated with the film. Hinckley was found not guilty by reason of insanity after his attorneys argued he was fixated on the film, its characters, and actors (Jodi Foster), and that his obsession with the film was evidence that he had lost the distinction between reality and fiction. Hinckley was said to have used *Taxi Driver* as a primary script and John Lennon's

murder by Mark David Chapman as a secondary script in his assassination attempt. The film was played for jurors at his trial.

- ***The Last Seduction (1994):*** Prosecutors in the Mechele Linehan murder trial argued that Linehan, a former Alaskan exotic dancer turned Olympia, Washington, soccer mom, was influenced by the film to conspire with then boyfriend John Carlin to kill her ex-fiancé Kent Leppink in a 1996 murder-for-insurance plot. Prosecutors argued that Linehan committed the crime after viewing the film and used her sexuality to manipulate men, just like the film's main character played by Linda Fiorentino. Linehan, who in the 11 years between the crime and her arrest married a doctor and had a daughter, was convicted of first-degree murder on October 22, 2007. Her conviction was overturned in February 2011, and she was released on bail until her retrial in 2012.
- ***Natural Born Killers (1994):*** Linked to a dozen murders in the United States, Canada, and Europe and to school shooter cases including Columbine. Three copycats involved male/female pairs who went on murder sprees including the 1995 robbery/murder spree of 18-year-old Benjamin Darras and Sarah Edmondson that led to a civil suit against NBK director Oliver Stone that went to the U.S. Supreme Court before it was dismissed in 2001; four murders committed by 19-year-old Florence Rey and her 22-year-old boyfriend Audry Maupin dubbed "France's natural born killers"; and the 1998 case involving Veronique Herbert and Sebastien Paindavoine who murdered a 16-year-old boy in a sex setup right out of the film.
- ***The Matrix (1999, 2003):*** Associated with a half a dozen murders. In several of the offenders' trials (including DC sniper shooter Lee Boyd Malvo), *The Matrix* was woven into the defendant's insanity defense. In at least two cases (Lynne Ansley in Ohio in 2002 and Vadim Mieseges in San Francisco in 2003) the "matrix defense" resulted in a finding of not guilty by reason of insanity.
- ***Dark Night Rises (2012):*** Associated with the mass shooting in the Aurora, Colorado, movie theater where 24-year-old James Holmes threw tear gas canisters into the audience and opened fire, killing 12 and wounding 70 people.
- ***Manchester by the Sea (2016):*** Linked to the 2017 death of a special needs teenager whose parents were indicted for arson and second-degree murder. Prosecutors found evidence that the parents had watched the film just before the crime, which depicts a couple whose children were accidentally killed in a house fire.

These and other documented cases offer anecdotal evidence showing that actual serial murderers and school shooters have mimicked and/or altered their behavior based on media stories of actual or fictional killers.[12]

---

[12] See Helfgott (2008, pp. 379–384) for a more comprehensive list of copycat crime.

Many of these copycat offenders have been referred to as psychopaths and/or exhibit features of psychopathy. For example, in interviews with police two of the most notorious serial killers in history—Gary Ridgway, the Green River Killer, and Dennis Rader, the BTK Killer—made reference to following other serial killers in the media.[13] Similarly, Columbine School shooters Eric Harris and Dylan Klebold boasted on video about inflicting "the most deaths in U.S. history" in an attempt to one-up other school shooters and Timothy McVeigh's actions in the Oklahoma bombing (Cullen, 2004). The 2002 DC sniper shootings by John Muhammad and Lee Malvo inspired a series of sniper attacks around the world, and Lee Malvo himself was said to have watched the film *The Matrix* more than 100 times to prepare himself for the sniper attacks (CNN Transcripts, 2003). And just days before the eighth anniversary of the Columbine murders, Seung-Hui Cho mailed a video of himself to NBC news, ranting about Columbine killers Klebold and Harris before going on to murder 32 students and professors on the Virginia Tech campus later that day (Cullen, 2007), committing the ultimate one-up of his Columbine predecessors.

Elliot Rodger, who committed mass murder on the University of California Santa Barbara campus in 2014, shared videotaped narrations and a 141-page manifesto to publicly communicate his motive, thought processes, and omnipotence. His behavior was media-mediated to an extent rarely seen before in human history. Psychopaths need an audience to threaten, intimidate, and put down in order to build themselves up. Elliot Rodger engaged in a mass media display of mental mechanisms necessary for psychopaths to kill without remorse—a complex process of idealizing and devaluing their victims and making them into monsters they are entitled to control, while seeing themselves as victims and denying the harm they have caused. Rodger likely suffered from mental illness beyond having features of a personality disorder. However, his video rant in his retribution video contained verbalizations that are associated with features of psychopathy similar to the verbalizations that come from the mouths of actual psychopaths. Regardless of what clinical diagnosis Rodger may have had, his thinking process made it possible for him to kill without remorse. He was operating under the influence of mass media, celebrity culture, and the glorification of psychopathic values (Helfgott, 2014, 2015; O'Toole et al., 2014).

Individual, environmental, situational, and media-related factors interact in a unique way to influence whether or not an individual or group of

---

[13] In videotaped interviews with police (*State of Washington v. Ridgway*, 2004), Gary Ridgway mentions having followed other serial killers in the media such as Ted Bundy. Dennis Rader specifically mentions the Green River Killer and Son of Sam in interviews regarding how he embraced the acronym BTK because it was like the "Green River Killer" and "Son of Sam" ("Secret confessions of BTK," 2005, August 12).

individuals will mimic criminal behavior they see in the media and popular culture (see Figure 5.1, Factors That Influence Copycat Crime), and the copycat effect on criminal behavior can be best understood along a continuum of influence (see Figure 5.2, Continuum of Influence of Media and Pop Culture on Criminal Behavior).

On one end of the continuum, media and pop cultural influences may play only a minor role in criminal behavior—for example, an offender who picks up an idea from a movie that makes its way into a component of the modus operandi during the commission of a crime. On the other end of the continuum are individuals who may have a severe psychopathological disturbance and have experienced a loss of boundary between fantasy and reality that becomes a major trigger for criminal behavior. On this extreme end of the continuum are the psychopaths—isolated, personality-disordered media junkies for whom pop cultural imagery plays a critical role in the formation of violent fantasy and resulting criminal behavior. Cases in which an offender seeks to become both celebrated and celebrity are an example of the extreme end of the continuum of media influence in shaping criminal behavior (e.g., John Hinckley and Mark David Chapman).

Another issue to consider in examining the role of psychopathy in copycat crime is celebrity obsession. A number of the notorious copycat cases involved individuals with psychopathic character traits who were obsessed with celebrities. Obsessional following, stalking behavior, and surveillance activities are sanctioned in American popular culture through TV, films, music, comics, jokes, visual art, and advertisements (Marx, 1995).[14] Cultural obsession with celebrity plays a powerful role in the dynamics of copycat crime. Despite known cases of harm and death resulting from obsessed fans and paparazzis, little research attention has been given to the ways in which mass media technology creates new targets for criminal victimization. Media technology creates a false familiarity with strangers. The more visible and accessible a person is, the more likely he or she is to be a target of crime. From a routine activities perspective, "Any activity that separates those who are prone to violence from each other, or from potential victims, is likely to decrease the incidence of violence" (Felson, 1996, p. 116). TV and other forms of media have the potential to reduce crime if potential offenders stay at home watching and away from potential victims, and vice versa. However, media technology brings individuals who we would otherwise not know figuratively into our worlds,

---

[14] Marx (1995) offers examples such as Sting's song "Every Breath You Take" and the Santa Christmas song "He knows when you are sleeping, he knows when you're awake." Meloy (1998) suggests that films such as *Fatal Attraction*, *Play Misty for Me*, the *Charlie Brown* comic where Sally is always following Linus, the perfume Obsession, etc., offer cultural support for stalking as the "dark heart of the romantic pursuit" (p. 6). Other examples of pop cultural images of surveillance and stalking include the films *Sliver*, *Taxi Driver*, and *The Fan*.

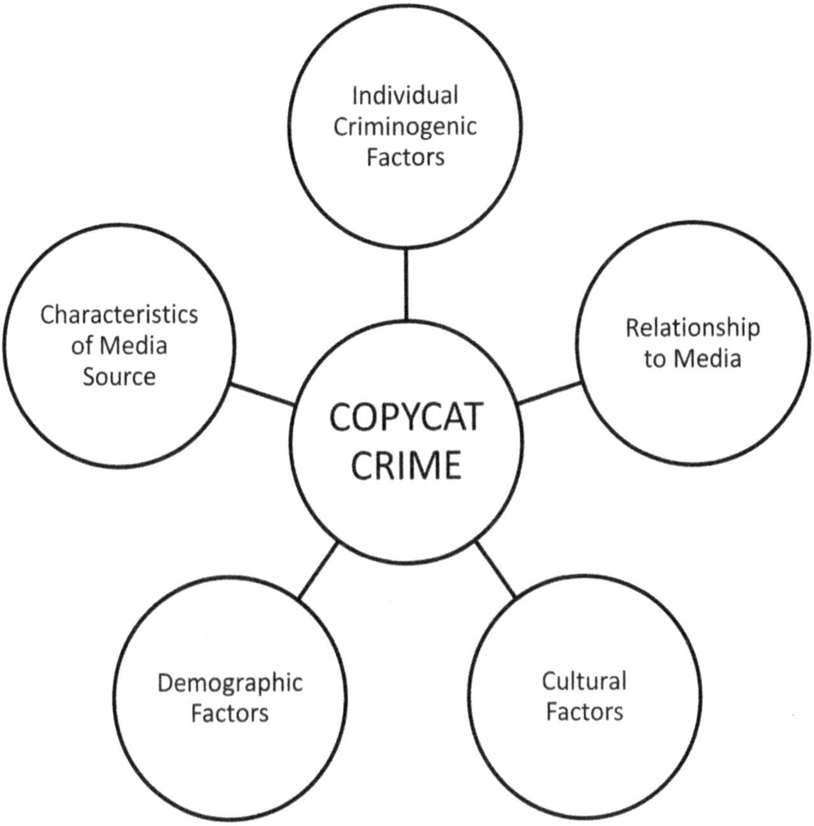

Individual Criminogenic Factors

Characteristics of Media Source

Relationship to Media

COPYCAT CRIME

Demographic Factors

Cultural Factors

Figure 5.1 Factors That Influence Copycat Crime

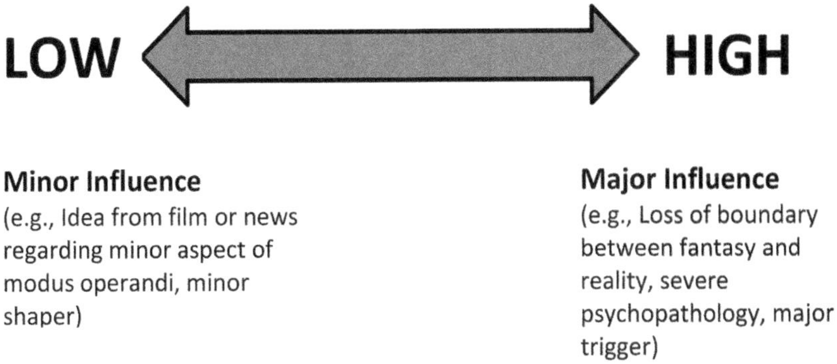

Minor Influence
(e.g., Idea from film or news regarding minor aspect of modus operandi, minor shaper)

Major Influence
(e.g., Loss of boundary between fantasy and reality, severe psychopathology, major trigger)

Figure 5.2 Continuum of Influence of Media and Popular Culture on Criminal Behavior

and this overexposure to media celebrities and the pseudo-familiarity that many people experience with them adds an entirely new dimension to the notion of routine activity. While media technology physically separates people, it also has the potential to reduce virtual distance and increase virtual accessibility, thus creating a new type of victimization target, especially for psychopaths who are media junkies. Most victims are selected because they are familiar and accessible. The pseudo-familiarity with strangers created by celebrity culture creates the potential for an increased number of stranger-victims.

Individuals who are psychopathic who suffer from attachment pathology take the usual familiarity with celebrities many steps further, developing elaborate fantasies about a particular celebrity—a "narcissistic link" between themselves and the object of their admiration that can turn into dangerous or deadly stalking behavior (Meloy, 1992, 1998). There are generally three types of stalking perpetrators: simple obsessionals, love obsessionals, and erotomaniacs. *Simple obsessionals* have some prior (usually intimate) relationship with the victim and are the most common; *love obsessionals* have no existing relationship with the victim and usually target celebrities; *erotomaniacs*, the rarest type, delusionally believe that the victim loves them (Zona Palarea, & Lane, 1998). Stalking perpetrators are likely to have criminal, psychiatric, and drug abuse histories, and show evidence of a range of DSM Axis I and Axis II (primarily Cluster B) disorders, though most are not psychotic at the time of their offense (Meloy, 1998).[15]

There is a long list of celebrity stalking victims, including most notably in recent years:

- Singer Taylor Swift was stalked in 2017 by 29-year-old Mohammed Jaffar who called Swift's management company 60 times before showing up at her home and sent tweets about sweets he planned to give to her and poetry in which he said, "There is nothing I love more than you" (Beaumont-Thomas, 2017).
- Singer Christina Grimmie was shot dead on June 10, 2016, by fan Kevin Loibl who was stalking her online without her knowledge and who showed up at an Orlando, Florida, concert armed with two handguns. Loibl shot Grimmie at close range in the autograph line after the show and then shot himself when her brother Marcus Grimmie went after him just after the shooting (Moriarty, 2017).
- In 2017, singer Selina Gomez was stalked by a superfan who showed up at her home in San Fernando, California, with food, flowers, and gifts, including a penis-shaped flower bouquet (Farley, 2017). Prior to this she had also

[15] Early research assumptions suggested that the majority of stalkers suffered from delusional disorders, in particular the erotomanic subtype. However, recent research indicates that this is an unlikely primary diagnosis among stalkers (Meloy, 1998).

been stalked by a homeless man who jumped her fence at her home and was convicted in 2014 and sentenced to psychological treatment (Associated Press, 2014).

These recent cases show how relentless celebrity stalking is even after years of legal activism to improve stalking laws after highly publicized cases that occurred in the 1980s including:

- Actress Theresa Saldana who was brutally stabbed multiple times by a fan in 1982. Saldana survived the attack and founded the Victims for Victims Organization. Her case led to the California Driver's Policy Protection Act because the perpetrator found her home address through driver's license records.
- Actress Rebecca Schaeffer who starred in the 1980s sitcom *My Sister Sam*, who in 1989 at age 21 was shot dead at her own front door by obsessed fan Robert Bardo. Schaeffer's case indirectly led to stalking laws and specialized stalking units within law enforcement agencies (Harvey, 2002; Orion, 1997).
- Actress Jodie Foster who has long been the subject of John Hinckley's fantasies and whose attention he sought when he attempted to assassinate President Ronald Reagan in 1981. Hinckley sent detailed letters to Foster while she attended Yale and indicated to authorities after the assassination attempt that his primary motivation was to win Foster's affection.
- Musician and former Beatle John Lennon who was murdered at his home in 1980 by Mark David Chapman, an obsessed identity disordered fan who, after reading Salinger's *Catcher in the Rye*, became angry with Lennon for becoming a "phony" (Black, 1990).

Add to this list Madonna, Brad Pitt, Jennifer Aniston, Steven Spielberg, Gianni Versace (Harvey, 2002), Halle Berry, Whitney Houston, Sharon Gless, Janet Jackson, Suzanne Sommers, Paula Abdul, Justine Bateman, Cher, Olivia Newton-John, Vanna White, Kathie Lee Gifford (Orion, 1997), Avril Lavigne (Sullivan, 2004), and Sandra Bullock (Therolf, 2007), all of whom have been the victims of celebrity stalkers or, in some cases, multiple stalkers who formed obsessive media-mediated pseudo-relationships with them. David Letterman was the victim of two serious celebrity-related offenses, one involving a female stalker[16] and the other involving the attempted kidnapping for ransom of his son ("Heartfelt Thanks from Letterman," 2005; Wolf, 2005). Sandra Bullock

[16] Margaret Rey, a.k.a. "The David Letterman Stalker," was mentally ill, served time in a mental institution as a result of convictions for trespassing on Letterman's property, and committed suicide at age 46 in Colorado in 1998 by kneeling in front of a train.

was also the victim of two stalkers, a man from Michigan in 2003, and in 2007, a woman who tried to run her husband Monster Garage producer and motorcycle mogul Jesse James over multiple times with her car in the couple's driveway. The woman was charged with assault with a deadly weapon.

The celebrity obsession phenomenon helps to better understand psychopathic copycat offenders in two ways. First, media plays a central role in crime involving celebrities and copycat crime. Both find inspiration in a media source and are driven by and dependent on the cultural power of fame and notoriety. Second, technology gives potential copycats wide access to information that validates and can be used to mimic the behavior of notorious offenders and well publicized cases, in particular those involving celebrities. For example, there are tribute web pages devoted to celebrity stalkers such as Mark David Chapman and Andrew Cunanan that detail their methods and beliefs available for anyone who may be an aspiring celebrity stalker (Harvey, 2002). Copycats of celebrity stalking incidents are perhaps the crimes that most clearly and blatantly reveal the role of media and quest for notoriety. Harvey (2002) describes the case of Sarah Lockett, a news reporter for Meridian Television in England, who was stalked by Jeremy Dyer, a fan who sent her more than 80 letters from 1998 to 1999 and was sentenced to prison for two years for harassment. The letters included numerous references to the well publicized celebrity murder of BBC news reporter Jill Dando. Dando was shot in the head at close range at her doorstep in 1999 by Barry George, a media-obsessed celebrity stalker who had a history of obsession with a number of celebrities (including Princess Diana and Freddie Mercury, lead singer from the band Queen). The letters by Dyer to Lockett specifically referenced the Dando murder with threatening passages such as:

> You looked a bit miserable on the Monday show. I suppose you would be considering Jill Dando just got her brains blown out by a probable stalker. (Harvey, 2002, p. 149)
>
> If I was stalking Jill Dando I'd have kidnapped her or done something else to her rather than shooting her in the head—unless you hate them of course? It seems a waste of a victim if you ask me. He could have used her before killing her eg, by raping or assaulting her, getting his money's worth as it were. . . . Telling it as I see it. (Harvey, 2002, p. 151)

Dyer used the Dando murder to threaten his victim and to validate and reinforce his own stalking behaviors. Visibility made both Dando and Lockett targets of celebrity stalkers whose fantasies and behaviors were influenced by the cultural emphasis on fame and celebrity voyeurism and facilitated by media technology. The cultural forces that make it appealing to become a notorious celebrity killer are crucial to understanding copycat crime.

The research on copycat crime, celebrity stalking, and the high incidence of Axis II, Cluster B disorders among known copycat offenders suggests that psychopathy and/or characteristics of the disorder may play a central role in media-mediated mimetic crime. Although important work has been done on the role of psychopathy and predatory aggression in stalkers (Meloy, 1998; Meloy, Sheridan, & Hoffman, 2008; O'Toole, Smith, & Hare, 2008), there are no known studies that specifically focus on psychopathy and copycat crime. This is an important and intriguing area for future research.

The Cultural Function of Mythical Monsters and the Psychopathic Imagination

In 1971 Philip Zimbardo conducted the now famous Stanford prison experiment. Also during that time Stanley Milgram (1974) conducted a series of studies on obedience to authority. Both studies showed regular (nonpsychopathic) people engaging in acts of callous cruelty. In 2007 Zimbardo wrote the book *The Lucifer Effect* comparing the heinous acts of cruelty committed against prisoners by U.S. Army military corrections personnel at Abu Ghraib and other acts of extreme cruelty around the world in genocide, war, and everyday life. These and other studies suggest that there is an extraordinary human capacity for one individual to objectify another even in the face of perception of extreme distress in the other person or people. And the ability to create the psychological distance necessary to engage in extreme acts of cruelty toward others is mastered by people who are and are not psychopaths.

Could it be then that images of psychopaths in popular culture provide the rest of us with a scapegoat for our own ability to objectify, cognitively neutralize, and psychologically defend ourselves against our own feelings of aggression toward others? Some writers have suggested that one function of the projection of the psychopathic image in literature, film, TV, and music is that the image of the psychopath symbolizes the human ability to survive at all costs. This function is related to theories that view psychopathy as an adaptive survival strategy (e.g., Glenn, Kurzban, & Raine, 2011; Hall & Benning, 2006; Harrington, 1972; Rieber & Green, 1989; Smith, 1978). Throughout history, biblical and mythical images of characters very similar to the psychopath have "rescued" particular groups from survival-endangering passivity by being willing to engage in acts of violence and callous disregard. For example, the medieval Jewish mythical figure, the golem, is said to have shown the Jewish people the value of aggressive response in times of violent threat. Peretz (1973) tells the tale of the golem:

> When the ghetto of Prague was being attacked, and they were about to rape the women, roast the children, and slaughter the rest; when it seemed that the end had finally come, the great Rabbi Loeb put aside his *Gemarah*, went into the street, stopped before a heap of clay in front of the teacher's house, and molded a clay image. He blew into the nose of the *golem*—and it began to stir; then he whispered the Name into its ear, and our *golem* left

the ghetto. The rabbi returned to the House of Prayer, and the golem fell upon our enemies, threshing them as with flails. Men fell on all sides.

Prague was filled with corpses. It lasted, so they say, through Wednesday and Thursday. Now it is already Friday, the clock strikes twelve, and the Golem is still busy at its work.

"Rabbi," cries the head of the ghetto, "the golem is slaughtering all of Prague! There will not be a gentile left to light the Sabbath fires or take down the Sabbath lamps."

Once again the rabbi left his study. He went to the altar and began singing the psalm "a song of the Sabbath."

The *golem* ceased its slaughter. It returned to the ghetto, entered the House of Prayer, and waited before the rabbi. And again the rabbi whispered into its ear. The eyes of the *golem* closed, the soul that had dwelt in it flew out, and it was once more a *golem* of clay.

To this day the *golem* lies hidden in the attic of the Prague synagogue, covered with cobwebs that extend from wall to wall. No living creature may look at it, particularly women in pregnancy. No one may touch the cobwebs, for whoever touches them dies. Even the oldest people no longer remember the *golem*, though the wise man of Zvi, the grandson of the great Rabbi Loeb, ponders the problem: may such a *golem* be included in the congregation of worshipers or not?

The *golem*, you see, has not been forgotten. It is still here! But the Name by which it could be called to life in a day of need, the Name has disappeared. And the cobwebs grow and grow, and no one may touch them.

What are we to do? (pp. 245–246)

The story of the golem is just one of many tales told across time and culture that reflect the imaginative need for aggressive response as a human survival strategy and the struggle a community must face in the decision to accept or reject, as a member of the community, a character as horrendous as the golem. The golem represents a projection of evil that allowed the Jewish people to reconcile the psychological conflict between the urge to destroy the enemy and the spiritual love of (and attachment to) humanity. If the urge to destroy is projected onto a lump of clay, the guilt associated with the experience of this urge is relieved. The "person who can orchestrate the destruction of another human being and have no remorse, no feeling for his or her victim or external need to defend his or her actions exemplifies the term *golem*" (Hickey, 2002, p. 24).

Mythical characters like the golem from all cultures—the Nordic warrior, the Roman god Saturn, the vampire, the werewolf, and the zombie—represent the callous ability to destroy the innocent without conscience. European Christians in the 13th through 15th centuries projected evil onto the witch. Witches were considered to be empowered by the devil. They were said to kill children, cast spells, and were generally seen as the cause of every private and social malady. Unlike the golem, the witch existed in human form. This presented a problem because the witch could not easily be identified or silenced like the clay golem. One of the functions of early European Catholicism was to identify and destroy witches. In 1486, Pope Innocent VIII commissioned two Dominican monks, Jacob Springer and Heinrich Kramer, to write a handbook on the identification, apprehension, and punishment of witches. The book was called the *Malleus Maleficarum* (Witch's Hammer). Unlike the golem, the witch was associated with the female gender. Faith (1993) cites an excerpt from the *Malleus Maleficarum*:

> [Women] are feebler in mind and body . . . more carnal than a man. When a woman weeps, she labours to deceive. . . . The world now suffers from the malice of women. . . . Woman is beautiful to look upon, contaminating to the touch, and deadly to keep. . . . [Woman is a] liar by nature. . . . They cast wicked spells on men and animals. All witchcraft comes from carnal lust, which is in the woman unsatiable. They consort even with the devils. It is no matter for wonder that there are more women than men found infected with the heresy of witchcraft. (Kramer & Sprenger, 1496/1948, pp. 42–44, in Faith, 1993, p. 18)

An important distinction between the golem and the witch is that the golem was not human and it used its aggressive abilities to destroy the Jews' enemies. The witch was a human being who was supposedly capable of destroying the community of which she was a part. The inability to easily identify the witch created ambiguity and anxiety that were resolved by projecting evil onto an identifiable segment of the population—women.

This projection of evil onto a particular group is a tactic historically used during times of political upheaval and social instability. "From a functionalist point of view, community solidarity is strengthened when authorities (of the state, church, universities, medicine, law) can covertly or overtly identify a single consensual enemy, against which 'the people' can rally" (Faith, 1993, p. 13). Mythical projections of evil like the golem, the vampire, and the werewolf are relatively "safe" in the sense that anxiety about evil (and the guilt over its recognition in ourselves) is alleviated through imagination and art. In our minds, these "others" are containers of evil that provide relief in the safety of a book or a film (Zweig & Abrahms, 1991), or, in the case of the golem, a story. The projection of evil becomes problematic when the object of the projection looks too much like an ordinary human being. As individuals are educated less through religion and myth and more through science and politics, new conceptions of evil develop. Women are evil by nature, Jews wear the tail of the devil, communists are villains, homosexuals are infectious, Blacks are violent criminals, and so on. Without the mythical monster, we must defend ourselves by scientifically or politically identifying an evil "other," or else we will be terrorized or destroyed by the violence, aggression, and chaos within ourselves.

Political and historical consciousness over the past century has left a cultural void. It is no longer socially acceptable to vilify marginalized groups and individuals. However, psychopaths are still fair game. The psychopath is a modern cultural projection of the human urge to destroy, of the dark shadow of the psyche. Sterilized and neutralized through science, the psychopath is an empirically identifiable monster.[17] And in contemporary culture, the psychopath appears live, on the motion picture screen, on the TV set, in interactive computer games, and in real life, in the form of a human being, who appears physically as not only normal, but as charming and attractive, and not necessarily distinguishable by gender, race, ethnicity, or social class. The American media glorification and dramatization of the psychopath differs from the legend of the golem in that the urge to destroy is not "successfully" projected onto a lump of clay. The legend of the golem clearly reminded the Jewish people of the need to detach from other human beings at times when survival is at stake. However, in the story, the Jews recognize the horror of the golem, and its conclusion implies that the golem can never again be brought to life, and that if it is looked upon the looker will die. This suggests a willing and deliberate projection of the evil the golem represents *with the solemn recognition that the golem is intrinsic to human nature.* The 15th-century Witch's Hammer successfully projected evil onto women. A more appropriate term for what has occurred in American culture may be what psychodynamic theorists call *projective identification*—a primitive defense mechanism used by the psychopath (and the psychotic) that differs from *projection* in that the unwanted feeling is not successfully projected onto the object. In other words, as "bad, evil, criminal, aggressive, destructive" drives are *projected* onto the image of psychopath, the image is simultaneously identified with, and the drives are unsuccessfully mediated.

The result of this defensive process is the collective inability to articulate, and to integrate, ego identity. The salience of media violence coupled with the seductive power of fiction appears to have exacerbated individual and cultural displays of the psychopathic dynamic in 20th- and 21st-century America and perhaps all of Western culture. Black (1991) likens the media to the Indian hemp that the original assassins, the Moslem *hashashin*, consumed to prepare for their deeds and provides strong evidence to support his contention that

---

[17] Research indicating that primary psychopaths incapable of experiencing (and of developing) human emotion implies that psychopaths are more like robots than humans. Meloy (1988) has gone so far as to refer to the psychodynamic structure of the psychopath as a "reptilian state" lacking those qualities that distinguish humans and mammals (Meloy, 1988).

"the social norm in postindustrial society and in postmodern culture is no longer the ethical world of the real, but the aesthetic realm of the hyperreal" (pp. 138–139). The 20th- and 21st-century American monster is projected onto the screen; sometimes the boundary between media images and real life is blurred to the point where the projection bounces back and becomes the unsuspecting viewer. The modern projection of evil is a long shot away from the stilled, cobweb-covered clay figure of the medieval Jews that can only be awakened by a rabbi's secret whisper. Psychopathy is a modern cultural projection of evil that is "unsuccessful" relative to the mythical and biblical projections of earlier times. This contemporary blurring of boundaries and unsuccessful projection of evil raises questions about the relationship between the scientific and popular conceptions of psychopathy and the implications of these conceptions for criminal justice policy. When scientific and popular conceptions of psychopathy are intertwined with conceptions of criminality, what role does psychopathy (the construct, the clinical condition, and the personality dynamic) play in the criminal justice process?

The Scientific versus Popular Conception of the Psychopath

The scientific conception of psychopathy has become clear in recent years as researchers have reached consensus regarding the understanding and assessment of the condition, and psychometric tests to measure the condition have been developed, standardized, and validated (Hare, 1991, 2003). There has been an enormous amount of research on aspects of psychopathy from psychometric properties of the PCL-R to brain structure and function and manifestation of the condition across culture (Patrick, 2006) to philosophical perspectives and the moral responsibility of the psychopath (Malatesti & McMillan, 2010). In the last 15 years, there have been more than 500 scientific publications and many books and edited volumes on the subject, and the condition is now considered by many to be the most useful psychological constructs applied in the criminal justice system and the most important forensic concepts in the 21st century (Babiak et al., 2012; Hare & Neumann, 2006, 2010; Hare, Neumann, & Mokros, 2018).

On the other hand, the popular conception of the psychopath is not so clear. Psychopaths depicted in media and popular culture are an interesting mix of cold-blooded, evil, likable, genius, and bizarre. Popular TV shows like *Dexter* show a likable character who carries a baby around to crime scenes who, after putting the little one to bed, sneaks off to bind, torture, and eviscerate deserving victims. *American Psycho*'s Patrick Bateman appears to be increasingly distressed the more people he kills trying to contain his murderous identity. The femme fatale character in the *The Last Seduction* is a glamorous woman who outsmarts and out-seduces every man in her path. The diverse range of psychopathic characters in popular culture are a far cry from the psychopathic icon, *The Silence of the Lambs*' (Bozman et al., 1991) cinematic psychopath posterboy Hannibal Lecter.

Film and other media representations of all psychopathologies are often inaccurate because the media has to conform to the constraints of art, not science (Hesse, 2009; Miller, 1987; Wilson, 1999). For example, Epstein (1995) suggests that serial murderers are presented in film with partial accuracy, but that the film industry has to make decisions about how serial killers are presented based on what the public can handle at the time. In the 1980s and early 1990s serial killers tended to be presented as supernatural for the purpose of leaving out that which people were ready to accept (and to buy a movie ticket to see), female serial murderers were portrayed as avengers whose victims are adult males, and few films portrayed serial murderers or psychopaths as male homosexuals or minorities, while in reality the victims of female murderers are usually children, the sick, or the elderly, and many serial murderers have been male homosexuals and/or minorities.[18] As Epstein (1995) suggests, one hypothesis is that the general public are perceived (by filmmakers) as not ready to handle male homosexuality or images of women (grandmothers, mothers, sisters, and daughters) killing children, the elderly, and the sick. It is safe to view women as a threat to adult men because it is generally believed that a man cannot be easily harmed by women.[19] This may be changing with increasingly widespread media attention to high-profile real-life cases (and the books and movies made about them) that boy or girl next door types of individuals engaged in violent crime such as Kevin Coe, Ted Bundy, Dennis Rader (aka the BTK Killer), Gary Ridgway (aka the Green River Killer), Diane Downs, and Susan Smith.

Fictional psychopaths such as *The Silence of the Lambs*' Hannibal Lecter and *American Psycho*'s Patrick Bateman exhibit characteristics atypical of the average psychopath (Fersch, 2006), which may contribute to a confused understanding of psychopathy among the general public. FBI profilers consulted in the making of the film *The Silence of the Lambs* have said that the character of

---

[18] In the case of race and ethnicity, the increasing concern about presenting information that is politically correct may influence decisions to portray violent criminals as white to avoid exacerbating the problematic stereotype of the black male criminal. According to true crime writer Jack Olsen (Personal communication, 1994, March 15), choosing a case about a psychopath who is black for a true-crime novel is a touchy subject given the political atmosphere of the times. The domination of the mass media by white film and television personalities may also play a role in the lack of minority representation among fictional psychopaths.

[19] Interestingly, many of the main characters of film noir were psychopathic women. However, most of these characters were either killed or defeated in the final scenes. The female psychopath returned with the reemergence of film noir in the 1990s (e.g., *The Last Seduction, Natural Born Killers, Basic Instinct*), and in these films the characters prevail (Helfgott, 1995).

Hannibal is a conglomeration of a range of psychopathic serial killers in the annals of true crime. The character of Bateman in the book (Ellis, 1991) and film *American Psycho* is an even more salient example of a film (and literature) depiction of psychopathy that reflects a disconnect between scientific and popular culture conceptions of the condition. Bateman's character exhibits severe defect in affect in his everyday interactions and his violent behavior; however, in the end of the story he has trouble maintaining what he refers to in the film as his "mask of sanity" and behaves more like he is psychotic than psychopathic. This perplexing depiction has been noted by some authors (Fersch, 2006). Representations of psychopathy that blur the distinction between psychopathy and psychosis perhaps contribute to the discrepancy between popular and scientific conceptions of the condition. In fact, just the title of *American Psycho* and similarity to the original film *Psycho* whose main character Norman Bates was clearly psychotic, not psychopathic, contributes to the blurring of the distinction between psychopathy and psychosis in the public mind.

In addition to discrepant depictions of psychopathy and psychosis in popular culture is the disproportionate number of depictions of psychopaths who are serial killers. Most psychopaths are not in fact serial killers, and many serial killers are not psychopaths (Meloy, 2000). Overrepresentation of psychopathic serial killers contributes to the popular notion that all psychopaths are serial killers or have the potential to be. When thinking about the impact of popular conception of psychopathy on decisions made in the criminal justice system (e.g., jury decision making involving expert testimony on PCL-R scores), this discrepancy between the scientific and popular conceptions of psychopathy can be problematic.

The Popular Conception of the Psychopath

The cultural meaning of the term "psychopath" has received minimal attention in the literature. Helfgott (2013c) conducted a random telephone survey of the general public to answer the question, "What is the popular conception of the psychopath?" Respondents ($n = 353$) were asked questions including, "When you hear the word 'psychopath,' what is the first thing that comes to mind?" and "If I asked you to think of a typical psychopath who would come to mind." Respondents were also asked whether they strongly agree, somewhat agree, somewhat disagree, or strongly disagree with 20 statements about psychopaths. Statements included in this section were designed to solicit information about attitudes and beliefs regarding the etiology, nature, and prevalence of psychopathy (e.g., "Some children are psychopaths," "Psychopaths can't tell the difference between right and wrong," "Psychopaths feel remorse and guilt, they just don't show it," "Female psychopaths are rare,"

"It's hard to tell who is and who is not a psychopath," "Some nonpsychopaths engage in psychopathic acts"). An additional Likert Scale question was asked pertaining to the PCL-R:

> There is a test called the Psychopathy Checklist that social scientists agree can confidently determine whether or not a person is a psychopath. This test is beginning to be used to make various criminal justice decisions. I am going to read you a list of examples of the ways in which this test might be used and I would like you to tell me if you strongly agree, somewhat agree, somewhat disagree, or strongly disagree.

Respondents were asked to rate 17 examples ranging from use of the test in police interrogations to sentencing decisions to correctional classification, to child custody decisions.

This study found that the popular conception of the psychopath is someone who is mentally ill, out of control, out of touch with reality, violent, and dangerous. The majority of the respondents associated psychopathy with mental disorder and serial murder. Most reported that the first thing that came when they heard the word "psychopath" was a real-life serial killer and specifically named Ted Bundy as the most popular real-life psychopath and Hannibal Lecter as the most popular fictional psychopath. The study also found that there were significant differences in beliefs about how the PCL-R and the construct of psychopathy should be used in the criminal justice system between respondents who viewed psychopaths as mentally ill versus those who viewed psychopaths as criminal with the latter more likely to agree with statements regarding punitive sanctions.

If, as Helfgott's (2013c) findings suggest, that the popular conception of the psychopath is mentally ill and out of touch with reality, this conception markedly differs from the scientific conception of the psychopath in that the personality organization of the clinical psychopath is characterized by adequate reality testing (Kernberg, 1967; Meloy, 1988), and psychopaths who meet the criteria for antisocial personality disorder are specifically exempt from the insanity defense in most states (Smith & Meyer, 1987). However, the popular conception is consistent with research findings (e.g., Cleckley, 1941, 1988; Gacono & Meloy, 1994; Gorenstein, 1991; Meloy, 1988; Rieber & Green, 1989; Rieber & Vetter, 1995) that suggest that the classification of psychopaths as "sane" is an oversimplification of the dynamics of the condition.

The study also found a significant difference between respondents who viewed psychopaths as mentally ill versus those who viewed psychopaths as criminal with the latter more likely to agree with statements regarding punitive sanctions suggests that when people view psychopaths as mentally ill they are more inclined to favor more lenient treatment in the criminal justice system. The more people believe that psychopaths are cognitively intact, the more likely they are to agree with statements regarding punitive sanctions such as capital punishment and habitual offender laws. This finding has direct implications for forensic practice given the studies that have found juror inclinations to enter guilty verdicts when psychologist and psychiatrist testimony on psychopathy is presented in court (Edens, 2001; Edens & Cox, 2012; Edens et al., 2005; Edens et al., 2013) and the tendency of courts to use psychopathy as an aggravating rather than mitigating factor (Lyon & Ogloff, 2000; Lyon, Ogloff, & Shepherd, 2016).

The finding that Ted Bundy, Jeffrey Dahmer, and Charles Manson head the pack as examples of the "typical" psychopath in the public mind is not surprising and suggest that the popular news media is a primary influence of the popular conception of the psychopath, and that real-life images of psychopathy and serial murder may have a more powerful impact on people than do their fictional counterparts, which offers some empirical data to the literature media effects and copycat crime (Coleman, 2004; Surette, 1990, 2002, 2006, 2013, 2014) where some have suggested that perhaps fictional representations may be more powerful than real life (Black, 1991; Fister, 2005). Perhaps, fictional representations of serial killers, psychopathic criminals, and other offenders are more influential to a small percentage of individuals who, as some have suggested in the literature, have lack of identity integration and blurred boundaries between reality and fantasy (Black, 1991; Helfgott, 2008).

The study also found that most of the respondents did not associate psychopathy with females and that there were gender differences in attitudes and beliefs about psychopaths. The terms "femme fatale" and "histrionic personality"[20] were the least popular terms used to refer to a psychopath. Men were more likely than women to agree that female psychopaths are more violent than male psychopaths, and to disagree that female psychopaths are rare. Given the discourse in the 1990s that has continued through today on the rise of the violent and "deadlier than the male" female (Kirsta, 1994; Valentis & Devane, 1994) and issues raised in the literature regarding media distortion of motive in male/female copycat offenders with attribution of blame and agency placed on male perpetrators even when factual evidence to the contrary (Boyle, 2001), further examination of the ways in which female psychopaths are portrayed and perceived by the public may offer valuable information that would have particular relevance in real-life cases involving jury trials, parole board decisions, or death penalty cases involving female offenders who are referred to by expert witnesses or others as psychopaths

[20] Histrionic personality disorder has long considered to be a sex-typed manifestation of psychopathy (see Ford & Widiger, 1989; Horowitz, 1977, 1991; Kass, Spitzer, & Williams, 1983; Spalt, 1980; Verona & Vitale, 2006; Warner, 1978).

(e.g., Diane Downs, Susan Smith, Amanda Knox, Casey Anthony, Aileen Wuornos).

Regarding the questions specific to the PCL-R and criminal justice decision making, the majority of respondents agreed with the use of the PCL-R in police investigations, prosecutorial decisions, sentencing, community supervision, and in child custody and civil commitment. The findings suggest that the popular media shapes the public's conception of the psychopath and attitudes and beliefs about psychopaths may influence criminal justice policy and practice.

Results from this study offer a glimpse of how the public viewed psychopaths during a particular time period and in a location of legislative change involving high-risk offenders presented by the media as psychopathic criminals and conducted during a time of rapidly rising research attention to the construct of psychopathy, publication, and widespread use of forensic assessment tools in the criminal justice system (designed to measure psychopathy—e.g., the PCL-R to predict dangerousness, the VRAG, SORAG, RRASOR, LSI-R, Static-99, and others).

Popular versus Scientific Conceptualizations of Psychopathy: Implications for Criminal Justice

In an era of hyperinformation, hyperconnnectivity, and hyperreality, gone are the days where popular culture can be brushed off as mere entertainment. The instant connectivity and widespread availability of information and dissemination of ideas on the Internet, in film, on television, in computer games, in mainstream academic discourse, in the self-publishing industry, music industry, comics, outsider art, and so on call to question the nature of "legitimate" information upon which decisions are made in the social sphere in informal and formal realms. In other words, the circulation of powerful constructs like psychopathy in science, art, and popular makes their way into decisions in everyday life and in the criminal justice system.

The popular conception of the psychopath may influence public support for the use of the concept of psychopathy at virtually every discretion point in the criminal justice system (Bailey & Hale, 1998; Keesler & DeMatteo, 2017; Surette, 2006). A large amount of literature exists reflecting the importance of attending to media presentation of a wide realm of crime- and justice-related issues. Analysis of media impact on public views of law and the legal system suggests that the media presents a distorted view of law, crime, and justice (Hans & Dee, 1991) and that media exposure to psychopathy results in a mixed understanding of psychopathy that has a range of legal, practical, and ethical implications (Keesler & DeMatteo, 2017). These distortions may impact criminal justice policy and practice. Durham, Elrod, and Kinkade (1996) found that true-crime novels present a seriously distorted picture of homicide in the United States and that such depictions significantly impact public perceptions of crime. Media images differ from the reality of crime (Surette, 2014). For example, television crime dramas depict higher clearance rates in solving crimes than is typical in real life (Rhineberger-Dunn, Briggs, & Rader, 2016). News media are strongly oriented toward law enforcement rather than toward the judiciary and corrections. Consumption of television news and crime-based reality programs is associated with increase in support for punishment, deterrence, and incapacitation rather than rehabilitation (Rosenberger & Callahan, 2011). High media consumption is associated with support for capital punishment in particular when nuanced options are not offered (Britto & Noga-Styron, 2014), and research shows that punitiveness is not significantly associated with crime rates, prior victimization, vicarious victimization, or higher perceived risk of victimization. Rather, it is media exposure to crime that makes people more supportive of punitive policies toward individuals who commit crime (Kleck & Jackson, 2017). Heavy exposure to media violence increases viewers' fear of crime (Hollis et al., 2017) and perceptions of crime waves and "epidemics," such as the increase in crack cocaine use and associated violent crime (Belenko, Fagan, & Chin, 1991). Jurors' decisions may be influenced by legally relevant information presented in newspaper reports, radio and TV news, TV crime shows and courtroom scenes, advertising, and movies. For example, a mock juror study conducted during the gag order preceding the Andrea Yates[21] case found that when jurors were given unsympathetic media stories about the case, they were more likely to find her "guilty" (Jacquin & Hodges, 2007).

Depending on how the psychopath is depicted in popular culture, the general public may be willing to support infringement of due process rights, harsher crime control initiatives, and more punitive sanctions for individuals who score high on psychometric assessments of psychopathy. In an era that relies so heavily on forensic assessment and actuarial tools in criminal justice decision making, "the term 'psychopath' is a powerful label that can have a profound impact on how individuals are perceived and treated in the legal system" (Edens & Petrila, 2006, p. 585). Further exploration is needed on the popular conception of the psychopath, the ways in which ideas and beliefs people hold about psychopathy influence their decisions in the voting booth, on juries, in everyday life, and (for those who work in the criminal justice, social service, mental health, or forensic settings) in the workplace, and the reflexive relationship between criminal justice legislation, sanctions, and

---

[21] Andrea Yates was charged with capital murder in 2001 for the deaths of her four children by drowning. She was convicted of the crime in 2002, which was then overturned on appeal, and she was found not guilty by reason of insanity in 2006 (see Denno, 2003; O'Malley, 2004, 2005).

punishment practices and culture (Garland, 1990, Garland, 2002; Ferrell, 1995; Ferrell, Hayward, & Young, 2008, 2015; Ferrell & Sanders, 1995). Additional research is needed on the nature and dynamics of the reciprocity between the concordance of scientific and popular conceptions of psychopathy and the impact of both in criminal justice legislation, policy, and practice.

Furthermore, popular culture depictions of psychopathy may contribute to a more comprehensive understanding of psychopathy than is offered through science. Film presentations of psychopathy have been used by various authors to more vividly illustrate its clinical manifestations. Meloy (1988) acknowledges the absence of the understanding of psychopathic visual predation in the research literature and refers readers to news photographs and film portrayals of the "reptilian stare" to capture the essence of such predation:

> The popular media, both fictional and nonfictional, is quite adept, however, at capturing the reptilian, predatory, and emotionless stare of the psychopath. The reader is encouraged to study newspaper and magazine photographs of such contemporary sexual psychopaths as Charles Manson, Theodore Bundy, and Richard Ramirez. Steve Railsback's portrayal of Manson in the film "Helter Skelter" was an exquisite capturing of the reptilian stare. Other popular film actors such as Clint Eastwood, Charles Bronson . . . , Bruce Dern, Anthony Perkins, and Rutger Hauer . . . have successfully exploited the larger-than-life visual image on the screen to convey the absence of emotion and the presence of more primitive instinct in their eyes. (Meloy, 1988, p. 71)

Miller (1987) has also emphasized the importance of using artistic presentations to understand psychopathology in general, pointing out that clinical disorders can be studied from both scientific and artistic perspectives. Miller (1987, 1989a, 1989b, 1989c) considers film noir[22] to be the motion picture analogue of psychiatry and psychology, and suggests that antisocial personality disorder is the psychopathology most represented in classic and contemporary film noir. College faculty use media presentations of psychopathy to supplement what cannot be conveyed through the research literature. Hare (1993) cites a college course titled "The Psychopath in Fact and Film"[23] that explores film as a form of identification where moviegoers can participate

---

[22] Film noir (dark or black film) refers to group of black-and-white American films with consistent, cohesive themes and a distinctive style expressing a black vision of despair, loneliness, and dread. The film noir period ran from 1940 to 1959.

[23] This course is taught by psychiatrist Joanne Intrator at the Mount Sinai Medical Center in New York.

vicariously in psychopathic arousal, and many courses utilize images of both fictional and real-life psychopaths to convey the subject to students.

These examples of the utilization of art to understand psychopathological phenomena within the scientific community suggest that artistic expression of psychopathology offers researchers a powerful explanatory tool and that art may provide viewers with a more comprehensive and cohesive understanding of psychopathology (Miller, 1987). We love our monster stories, and it is the supernatural, superhuman aspects of Hannibal Lecter and other cinematic psychopaths and their ability to generate civic dissonance and resolution that may be responsible for their appeal (Oleson, 2005, 2006). The boundaries between actual psychopathology and aesthetic psychopathology have become blurred (Black, 1991), and this participatory experience with media violence illustrates the unique contribution of art in the understanding of psychopathy and psychopathic expression. Miller (1987) emphasizes the concept of a "personality science" whereby psychopathology can be studied using methods from a variety of disciplines, including the arts. Scientific psychology can contribute to artistic representations of behavior and personality and vice versa, and this combined approach to understanding psychopathologies may be more reflective of individual aspects of such conditions, including interaction between pathology in society and pathology within the individual (Miller, 1989b). The complementary use of art and science in the understanding of psychopathology and the evidence of the blurred boundaries that may exist between art and reality highlight the need for study of the relationship between artistic and scientific presentations of the psychopath. If students and researchers rely on art to supplement their studies; if individuals identify with and model the behaviors of fictitious and nonfictitious psychopaths in the media; if images of psychopathy in film are helping people to understand their own sicknesses; and if people are using artistic replicas of violence to express their dark sides in relatively safe ways, continued examination of the popular and scientific conceptions of psychopathy and the relationship between them is critical to understanding how the construct of psychopathy is used in everyday life and the criminal justice system.

CHAPTER SIX

Psychopathy and Criminal Justice Practice

There is a "horrible cunning pathological monster" behind these crimes.
—John Walsh, *America's Most Wanted* (Fooksman, 2008)

"He (or she) showed no remorse." These four words reflect the essence of what the public expects from the criminal justice system. Wrongdoing, lawlessness, and social disrespect unaccompanied by expression and display of remorse are an appalling violation of the social contract. In cases of extremely heinous crimes, lack of remorse in the individuals who have committed these crimes is particularly outrageous. Laws are created to protect the law-abiding from those among us who cross and fail to respect social and legal boundaries. Tools, strategies, policies, and legislation are enacted to effectively determine who among us is dangerous, who can be treated and released, and who will benefit from an official "time-out." We do our best to make sure the most dangerous are convicted and imprisoned and never released. Ultimately, we hope that those who harm us have a conscience, emotion, remorse—some feeling deep inside that can be drawn out through treatment, time in prison, or change of heart. Those who don't feel—the remorseless—are human monsters we must protect ourselves against at all cost.

Remorse is so central to the way in which any given criminal event is ultimately experienced and understood that it has the potential to influence the way in which a defendant is perceived throughout the criminal justice process. The importance of remorse in public expectations of the criminal justice system is apparent at any given time in news accounts of cases involving defendants who are referred to in terms of the degree of remorse they display in the aftermath of crime:

- "Two friends of a 19-year-old [Brok Junkermeier] on trial for allegedly killing his friend's grandmother testified Monday that he showed no remorse when he confessed to them shortly afterward." (Ross, 2014)

- "U.S. District Judge Donald Molloy said he saw no remorse from Jordan Graham, 22, in the killing of Cody Johnson, 25." ("Judge: Bride showed no remorse in husband's death," 2014, March 27)
- "[Brynton Warren] grinned through much of his arraignment." "He laughed. He didn't show no remorse, no nothing." "It was a joke." (Feldscher, 2014)
- "There's no remorse from him. . . . He shot my son in the back. I don't get it." (Hayes, 2014)
- "It struck me as if he was giving us a lecture in serial murder 101, because he's not human and has no soul or conscience." "He's up there kind of cavalierly describing how he had his 'hit kit' with him and how his 'projects' were proceeding. . . . There's the lowest form of human filth that ever crawled out of the gene pool masquerading as a human being." (Jeff Davis, son of Delores Davis the last known victim of BTK Killer Dennis Rader) ("Rader details how he killed 10 people," 2005, June 28)

Convicted offenders who have displayed a relentless lack of remorse have gone down in history as human monsters. Few can forget individuals like Richard Allen Davis who when given the death sentence flipped off the cameras and hurled insults to his victim's father or the BTK Killer Dennis Rader whose comments when he was sentenced to life without parole resembled an Academy Awards speech after which the son of his last victim referred to him as a "walking cesspool," "social sewage" ("BTK sentenced to 10 life terms," 2005, August 18).

The primary objective of the criminal justice system is to restore order—to protect public safety through the enforcement of law, the conviction and sanctioning of people who violate the law, and careful decision making regarding when and who to release from the system and how to supervise them. When an individual commits a crime, that person violates the social contract. Some crimes are understandable (e.g., stealing food if one does not have money to feed his or her family). Some crimes are not (e.g., sexual homicide, serial murder). But regardless of the nature of a criminal event, the charge of the criminal justice system to regulate social life and to determine how best to increase public safety by ensuring that the offending individual will either (1) not offend again or (2) be sanctioned in a fair, efficient, and effective manner to ensure that the person's behavior will not result in future harm.

Remorse is one of the most important factors in the regulation of social life, criminal justice decision making, and in informal and formal determinations of who is and who is not dangerous:

> [P]ublic occasions in which there is both communal interest in and communal reaction to a purported wrongdoer's remorse or absence of remorse are significant events in the moral regulation of social life. The public and official focus on the inner life of the transgressor—whether it pertains to

wrongs that have mobilized the outrage of the whole community or less sensational transgressions—informs us not just about the wrong itself but also about how someone who committed the wrong should feel about their own actions. (Weisman, 2009, p. 48)

Of all human psychopathological conditions, psychopathy is the condition most fundamentally characterized by lack of remorse. The defect in affect, absence of conscious, lack of empathy, lack of attachment and affectional bonding, and interpersonal, lifestyle, antisocial, and affective features of psychopathy make psychopathy of critical importance in the criminal justice system. BTK Killer Dennis Rader seen by experts as a classic psychopath (Mann, 2005) was referred to after he was sentenced as the "the lowest form of human filth that ever crawled out of the gene pool masquerading as a human being"—a "classic, textbook sociopath" who had "no conscience, just a black hole inside the shell of a human being" ("BTK victim's son: Rader 'the lowest form of human filth,'" 2005, June 28)

The centrality of psychopathy to criminal justice is evidenced by the attention that has been given to the PCL-R in criminal justice practice on an international level and the explosion of scientific research on psychopathy, violence, and crime in recent years. Psychopathy represents the crux of the intersection of the criminal justice and mental health systems. Psychopathy is one of the most paradoxical conundrums in sorting out the issue of culpability, free will, determinism, and the individual's ability to control behavior in particular with recent research leading to the conclusion that psychopathy has neurobiological origins and psychopaths cannot in fact control their behavior (Kiehl & Buckholtz, 2010).

The Role of Psychopathy in the Criminal Justice System

The advent and standardization of the *Psychopathy Checklist–Revised* (Hare, 1991, 2003) made it possible for research to be conducted utilizing a common definition. The vast and growing body of research linking psychopathy to violent recidivism (Blair, Mitchell, & Blair, 2005; Gacono, 2000; Häkkänen-Nyholm, 2012; Hare, 2007; Patrick, 2006) and recognition that psychopathy research has led to the beginnings of a *mini-theory of crime of human predatory violence* (Report of the Committee on Serious Violence and Sex Offenders, 2000; Steadman et al., 1994) has put the construct of psychopathy at the center of criminal justice decision making. Psychopathy has been referred to as the "single most important clinical construct in the criminal justice system" (Hare, 1996a, 1998, p. 189) and the "Most important forensic concept of the early 21st century" (Monahan, 2006). Scholars are now calling for increased collaboration between researchers and practitioners and communication and training for criminal justice professionals where research on psychopathy meets practice, in particular with respect to recent findings and implications of biosocial research on psychopathy (Glenn & Raine, 2014; Kiehl, 2014). The utilization of the construct of psychopathy in law and all components of the criminal justice system on national and international levels is historically unprecedented.

In July 2012, the *FBI Bulletin* published a report on psychopathy entitled "Psychopathy: An Important Forensic Concept for the 21st Century" by leading psychopathy scholars and law enforcement professionals (Babiak et al., 2012). This report highlighted the relevance of the construct of psychopathy for law enforcement and criminal justice:

> Many psychopaths exhibit a profound lack of remorse for their aggressive actions, both violent and nonviolent, along with a corresponding lack of empathy for their victims. This central psychopathic concept enables them to act in a cold-blooded manner, using those around them as pawns to achieve goals and satisfy needs and desires, whether sexual, financial, physical, or emotional. Most psychopaths are grandiose, selfish sensation seekers who lack a moral compass—a conscience—and go through life taking what they want. They do not accept responsibility for their actions and find a way to shift the blame to someone or something else. . . . The psychopath's egocentricity and need for power and control are the perfect ingredients for a lifetime of antisocial and criminal activity. The ease with which a psychopath can engage in violence holds significance for society and law enforcement. Often, psychopaths are shameless in their actions against others, whether it is murdering someone in a calculated, cold-blooded manner, manipulating law enforcement during an interview, or claiming remorse for actions, but blaming the victim for the crime. (Babiak et al., 2012, para. 5, 8)

This connection between the theory and research on the features of psychopathy and criminal justice implications for law enforcement, civil and criminal court processes, corrections, juvenile justice, and criminal justice policy has been noted over the years by psychopathy scholars (Gacono, 2000; Hare, 1996a, 2016; Herve & Yuille, 2007; Millon et al., 1998; Patrick, 2006; Raine & Sanmartin, 2001) and is more recently beginning to be systematically recognized, documented, and discussed in the academic literature (Häkkänen-Nyholm & Nyholm, 2012). The recognition of the concept of psychopathy as central to law enforcement and criminal justice practice in a publication such as the *FBI Bulletin* and by key psychopathy scholars represents a historical shift in thinking about psychopathy as a critical issue of relevance to criminal justice recognized as such not just within the psychological literature and clinical practice but also within the discipline and practice of criminal justice.

Understanding psychopathy is a key piece in untangling the complexities of offender motivation. If the psychopath's grandiosity, lack of remorse, lack of empathy, egocentricity, and other personality traits and behaviors provide the perfect mix to fuel antisocial and criminal behavior; if psychopathy is empirically linked to general and violent recidivism, does psychopathy hold the key to understanding offender motivation more generally? Can understanding psychopathy also help to understand criminal behavior committed by people who are not psychopaths? Determination of the nature of offender motivation is a key question at every stage of the criminal justice process from police investigations to bail decisions to adjudication to sentencing to release and supervision in the community. The question "What type of offender are we dealing with?" directs criminal justice resources, decision making, and professional practice (Helfgott, 2008). In law enforcement, the concept of psychopathy is used in investigations (Babiak et al., 2012; Hervé et al., 2004; Logan & Hare, 2008) and hostage negotiation training (Greenstone, Kosson, & Gacono, 2000), criminal profiling (Turvey, 2002), and in crime scene (O'Toole, 2007) and offense pattern analysis (Häkkänen, Hurme, & Liukkonen, 2007; Häkkänen et al., 2009). In the courts, expert testimony on whether or not a defendant is a psychopath makes its way into adjudication and sentencing decisions (Edens, 2001; Freedman, 2001), correctional classification, management, treatment, and prediction of dangerousness and release decisions (Wong & Hare, 2005). Waiver decisions in juvenile court consider childhood precursors of psychopathy (Ells, 2005), and knowing the psychopathy level of a perpetrator has implications for victim services (Bowie et al., 1990). All crimes are not committed by psychopaths. However, understanding how psychopathically motivated crime differs from crime motivated by other factors and psychopathological conditions and understanding the connection between the nature of psychopathy and criminal behavior more generally have important implications for criminal justice practice.

There are two ways of looking at the role psychopathy plays in the criminal justice system. First, the condition itself presents special challenges for criminal justice decision makers. Individuals who have been referred to in the academic literature and popular culture as psychopaths such as Ted Bundy, Gary Ridgway, Dennis Rader, Jeffrey Dahmer, Kevin Coe, Susan Smith, and Aileen Wuornos[1] are, for legal purposes, cognitively intact, know the difference

---

[1] These individuals have been referred to as psychopaths in either the academic literature or popular culture. However, given that some may not have been administered a PCL-R (e.g., Bundy was executed in 1989 one year prior to the publication of the PCL-R) and there are not published PCL-R scores for most, reference to these individuals as primary psychopaths is speculative and used here for purpose of example. Of these individuals, a published PCL-R score can be found for Wuornos (Myers, Gooch, & Meloy, 2005), and some scholars have noted that others such as Gary Ridgway may score as a secondary psychopath rather than as a primary (Atherley, 2013).

between right and wrong, and have been found culpable for their criminal behavior, and thus have not been determined not guilty by reason of insanity. On the other hand, it is difficult to make sense of their extreme violent behaviors that appear to be rooted in severe psychopathology. In the correctional system, such individuals can be difficult to manage and present as much of a threat to other prisoners and correctional staff as they did to society at-large prior to incarceration. The complex nature of the condition commands sophisticated decisions about how these individuals should be interrogated by the police, understood by the courts, and managed in correctional settings. Second, conceptions of the psychopath influence decisions at every stage of the criminal justice process and are at the root of laws of insanity (Goldstein, 1967; Low, Jeffries, & Bonnie, 1986) and sexual predator/psychopath statutes (Minnesota Office of the Legislative Auditor, 1994),[2] are used in police profiling (Harcourt, 2007; Holmes & Holmes, 2002; O'Toole, 2007; Turvey, 2011), predictions of dangerousness in release decisions (Harris, Rice, & Cormier, 1991; Quinsey, 1995; Serin & Amos, 1995; Serin, Peters, & Barbaree, 1990), adjudication (Häkkänen-Nyholm & Hare, 2009; Lee, 2007; Lyon & Ogloff, 2000; Vitacco, Lishner, & Neumann, 2012) and capital sentencing decisions (Edens et al., 2005; Ewing, 1983), in correctional classification (Van Voorhis, 1994), treatment (Stevens, 1994), and other legal and forensic contexts (Edens & Petrila, 2006; Lyon & Ogloff, 2000; Malatesti & McMillan, 2010).

In the past two decades there has been widespread application of the construct of psychopathy in the criminal justice system with increased attention to issues associated with expert testimony on the relationship between psychopathy and general and violent recidivism in criminal and civil courts (Häkkänen-Nyholm & Nyholm, 2012; Lyon & Ogloff, 2000; Lyon, Ogloff, & Shepherd, 2016), misuses of the PCL-R in court (Edens, 2001), the use of the label, "psychopath" as a legal synonym of evil (Ruffles, 2004), and the impact of the negative connotation of the term "psychopath" in correctional contexts (Rhodes, 2002, 2004, 2009), the juvenile justice system (Murrie, Cornell, & McCoy, 2005), and on juries and in death penalty decisions (Edens et al., 2005).

However, the extent to which the construct of psychopathy is being used in the criminal justice system and the ways it is being used is unclear. Research suggests that there is a discrepancy between popular and scientific

---

[2] Many states have sexual psychopath statutes whereby sex offenders deemed to be psychopathic or predatory can be sentenced indeterminately. For example, Washington State's Community Protection Act of 1990 states that "sexual predators" can be civilly committed for an indeterminate period of time. Minnesota has a similar law called the "Psychopathic Personality Commitment Law." Both laws have been (and continue to be) challenged in court, and to date, have been upheld.

conceptions of psychopathy (Helfgott, 2013c; Leistedt & Linkowski, 2014) and that even though there is consensus in the scientific literature on psychopathy, this may not be the case in the practitioner realm or in some organizations, institutions, or geographical regions. In Stevens (1994) study on correctional and forensic practitioners' understanding of psychopathy and antisocial personality disorder a psychiatrist said, "If you asked 15,000 psychiatrists for their definitions (of antisocial personality disorder), you would probably get 15,000 definitions" (p. 169). With the explosion of research on psychopathy in the academic domain and the increasingly educated discourse in popular culture, there is clearly greater general understanding of the nature of psychopathy. However, Patrick (2013) has noted that though historical conceptions of psychopathy have evolved considerably, questions regarding the scope and boundaries of the psychopathy construct continue to generate controversy and debate. Controversy and debate continue over issues such as whether there are subtypes of psychopathy (e.g., low/high anxious, primary/secondary), whether aggression and criminal behavior are central features of psychopathy, and if there is such a thing as "adaptive" or "successful" psychopaths.

So why does the historical discourse, controversy, consensus, research, and theory on psychopathy matter for criminal justice? There are three critical reasons: *(1) As theory and research on psychopathy has exploded, it has made its way into criminal justice practice in ways that have not been systematically documented nor clearly understood. (2) There are ethical and legal implications of applying the construct of psychopathy to criminal justice practice that have profound consequences for due process and crime control. (3) As criminological theory has become more integrative and interdisciplinary and as biosocial theories have resurfaced and gained widespread support, there are important criminological gains to be made by integrating theory and research on psychopathy with traditional criminological theory and research that has the potential for direct impact on criminal justice decision making.*

Police

Understanding the role of psychopathy in offense behavior has important implications for police behavior and officer safety, criminal profiling, and interviewing and interrogation. Formal acknowledgment of the importance of psychopathy to law enforcement in the 2012 *FBI Bulletin* on psychopathy (Babiak et al., 2012) highlights the relevance of the construct of psychopathy to law enforcement practice. The predatory nature of the psychopath (McEllistrem, 2004; Meloy, 1988, 2012; Palermo, 2013; Porter & Woodworth, 2006), the threat of the personality type to law enforcement and public safety (Hare, 2012; Logan, 2012; Logan & Hare, 2008), and the importance of a nuanced understanding of the condition for police investigations and security professionals are highlighted in the special bulletin who alert, "The ease with which a psychopath can engage in violence holds significance for society and law enforcement" (Babiak et al., 2012, p. 7). Psychopathic offenders are remorseless and predatory and superoptimistic about their ability to successfully get away with crime, which can pose a great threat to police. Psychopathic offenders have a distinct personality type characterized by aggressive narcissism and antisocial lifestyle that influences the evidence they leave at crime scenes, their behaviors before, during, and after committing a crime, and the ways in which they behave interpersonally. For these reasons understanding the nature of psychopathy (as well as the ways in which the media miscasts offenders as psychopathic) is important in police-citizen interactions and can aid investigation of crimes that potentially involve psychopathic suspects.

Psychopathy, the Individual Monster Model, and Police Behavior

Media depiction of criminals as psychopathic superpredators combined with the potentially dangerous working reality of law enforcement has the potential to influence police behavior. Although most law enforcement officers recognize that the majority of offenders are not dangerous predators, police culture, training, and professional publications that support the "warrior model" of law enforcement (Asken, 2012; Norcross, 2003; Weber, 1999) create a dynamic that has the potential to dichotomize law enforcement and criminals in ways that suggest that police on the street need to be relentlessly on guard against predators who jeopardize public safety.[3] For example, in an *FBI Bulletin* article titled "Offender's Perceptual Shorthand: What Messages Are Law Enforcement Officers Sending to Offenders?," Pinizzotto and Davis (2000) state:

[3] The warrior model of law enforcement does not prescribe a particular view of offenders, citizens, or potential suspects. The model emphasizes a paramilitary/combat mentality that focuses on mental toughness, physical and psychological strength, and confidence. This approach in conjunction with a media-mediated view of offenders as psychopathic has the potential to influence police behavior and interactions with citizens in particular in the face of crisis incidents. Though some research exists showing that officer perceptions of suspect or citizen mental disorder has the potential to influence officer views of the person with mental illness (specifically schizophrenia) as more dangerous but less responsible and more deserving of assistance (Neidhart, 2013), there is a lack of research attention to the effects of officer perception of offenders on police behavior. The connection made here between warrior model, police perceptions of offenders, and police behavior is theoretical. Future research is needed to provide empirical support for the proposed relationship between media-mediated police perceptions of offenders as potentially psychopathic combined with the warrior model of law enforcement and police behavior.

> Much like predators found tracking the untamed jungles for easy victims, human predators stalk human jungles for equally vulnerable targets. Similar to the beasts of the jungle, human predators look into crowds and search, consciously or unconsciously, for some weakness. Unlike the leopard who kills only for physical nourishment, however, human predators pick their prey for a variety of reasons. Law enforcement officers know all too well the unpredictability of the human predator, but do they realize that they, the public's protectors, can become victims through their own actions? (p. 1)

The authors urge law enforcement to:

> protect themselves against such individuals who search for easy prey and strike with little or no warning . . . and must ban together to make officers aware of the importance of understanding how their behaviors and actions impact their survival even when performing the most basic and sometimes mundane official duties. Only then will officers no longer fall victim to predatory offenders using perceptual shorthand to select the most vulnerable targets. (p. 4)

Thus, perception of offenders as psychopathic predators that prey on weakness may contribute to a law enforcement stance that minimizes behavioral nuances that could potentially be perceived as weakness. This concern is magnified by research findings that show that almost half of the perpetrators of line-of-duty officer murders have psychopathic traits (Logan & Hare, 2008; Hare, 1993). Robert Hare warns, "When officers do not know or suspect psychopathy during first contacts with individuals, the results can prove deadly" (Hare, 2012, p. 2). These cautionary findings have implications for law enforcement training and practice around issues of officer safety. On the one hand, empirical support empirically linking psychopathy with assaults against police and line-of-duty deaths (Hare, 2012; Logan, 2012; Logan & Hare, 2008) is of alarming concern. On the other hand, a law enforcement stance that trains officers to be warriors on the lookout for predators who prey on the slightest show of weakness has the potential to impact citizens and nonpsychopathic offenders more broadly.

The popular depiction of crime in the media as violent crime perpetrated by psychopathic superpredators creates an image in the public mind of criminals as dangerous psychopaths. Police officers and criminal justice policy makers are not immune to the effects of media representations (Bailey & Hale, 1998; Ferrell, 1995; Ferrell, Hayward, & Young, 2008; Ferrell & Sanders, 1995). This "individual monster model of crime accepted by a large proportion of the public and criminal justice policy makers leads naturally to the position that the criminal does not deserve the care we accord to full human beings" (Sanders & Lyon, 1995, p. 37). The view of criminals as the dangerous other (as opposed to the view of crime as a normal part of everyday life (Garland, 2002) committed by regular people who are not psychopathology disturbed) has the potential to influence police behavior in ways that can, on one hand lead to more accurate targeting of police resources through risk assessment and scientifically based profiling, but on the other hand has the potential to backfire when stereotypes about offenders are disguised by science-based risk assessment and profiling strategies (Harcourt, 2003, 2007).

On the other hand, consider the potential danger that psychopathic offenders pose for law enforcement. Many of the perpetrators of violence against police and line-of-duty officer murders are individuals known to have features of psychopathy. Individuals such as James Roszko in Alberta, Canada, Johnny Simms in Miami, Florida, Hydra Lacy Jr. in St. Petersburg, Florida, Maurice Clemmons in Lakewood, Washington (Logan, 2012), Christopher Dorner in Los Angeles, California, and Christopher Monfort in Seattle, Washington, are examples of individuals who possess personality disorders with features of psychopathy including early or previous violence, use of weapons in violent acts, and aggression toward authority. Individuals who are bold enough to threaten and murder police and the "revenge-oriented, nothing-more-to-lose psychopath" are the "nemesis for law enforcement" (Logan, 2012, p. 27) and require proactive vigilance to protect street-level officers.

Research in crisis intervention and hostage negotiation suggests that law enforcement officers can benefit from training on mental health, mental disorder, and psychopathology particularly in incidents involving behavioral crisis and hostage negotiation. Training regarding mental health problems, mental disorder, and psychopathology can help law enforcement officers feel informed and confident in their interactions in incidents involving individuals who may have a psychiatric disorder (Silverstone, Krameddine, DeMarco, & Hassel, 2013). Understanding the nature of a subject's mental condition is critical in incidents involving hostage (crisis) negotiation (Eddy & Patrzalek, 2013; Greenstone, Kosson, & Gacono, 2000). Law enforcement officers increasingly have to play the role of street-corner psychiatrists in situations where they have to make quick decisions to assess criminal culpability and to evaluate the individual's mental state or condition to determine the best course of action, and some studies suggest that officer perceptions of a subject's mental illness (specifically schizophrenia) influence officer perceptions of how dangerous a subject is and how culpable and deserving of services the person is (Neidhart, 2013). However, most of the findings on officer perceptions of mental illness and police behavior have focused on mental illness generally with specific attention to disorders such as schizophrenia. There is limited research examining officer perceptions of psychopathy, how these perceptions may be mediated by the media, and the impact of officer perceptions on police discretion, case disposition, and police behavior.[4]

Understanding psychopathy can also have an impact on law enforcement officer and victim advocate responses to victims. Bowie, Silverman, Kalick, and Edbril (1990) found that the psychological impact of rape on the victim differs with respect to type of rape/rapist. Rapists differ with respect to their motivation and modus operandi. Power assertive rapists who have characteristics closely associated with psychopathy (Keppel & Walter, 1999) are more inclined to use what's called a "confidence" approach, while power reassurance rapists may assault the victim using a "blitz" attack. Rape victims attacked by a confidence versus a blitz offender have different needs in the aftermath of the crime. The immediate concerns of blitz rape victims include sense of safety and dealing with fear that the rapist may return, while confidence rape victims tend to feel guilt and self-blame. Blitz rape victims may respond with flashbacks, nightmares, sleep and appetite disturbances, anxiety, heightened startle responses, and depression and usually seek treatment soon after the rape, while confidence rape victims often delay seeking help. Confidence rape victims need to be assured that they deserve help, need clarification of the definition/meaning of rape, and may have doubts about their ability to judge who is and who is not trustworthy. Treatment for blitz rape victims may include psychotherapy, medication, and behavioral desensitization. Similarly, research on domestic violence differentiating types of spouse abusers also has important implications for public safety and victim services. Studies show that batterers who stalk their victims are much more dangerous than batterers who do not stalk. Stalking behavior implies an added level of dangerousness suggesting a different psychopathology. Stalking behavior and predatory fantasy associated with psychopathy (Meloy, Sheridan, & Hoffman, 2008; O'Toole, 2007; Smith, O'Toole, & Hare, 2012) are associated with repetitive and escalating domestic violence and batterers who stalk tend to create increased victim fear (Burgess et al., 2001). Studies of spouse abusers revealing different types of abusers suggest that preventing further victimization depends on best practices that target specific subtypes of spouse abuse offenders (Dixon & Browne, 2003). Understanding the role of psychopathy in offender motivation has important implications for victim services to respond to the special needs of victims.

---

[4] Cooper (2001) suggests that "No term, other, perhaps than 'psychopath' has been more undiscriminatingly used and abused in our times than the word 'terrorist'" (p. 53). His reference to psychopathy in this context, in particular given that terrorist typologies have characterized terrorist subtypes as psychopathic (Eddy & Patrzalek, 2013) or as having personality styles closely associated with psychopathy such as aggressive externalizing (Dingley, 1997) and antisocial or borderline personality (Miller, 2006), further highlights the potential for perceptions to influence police behavior and the need for law enforcement training on mental disorder and psychopathy.

The Use of the Concept of Psychopathy in Investigations, Interrogations, and Criminal Profiling

Criminal investigation and criminal profiling are key areas identified in the 2012 *FBI Law Enforcement Bulletin* report on psychopathy and in other publications in which the construct of psychopathy has been utilized in law enforcement (Babiak et al., 2012; O'Toole, 2007; O'Toole & Häkkänen-Nyholm, 2012). There is a long history, dating back to the early days of the FBI behavioral sciences unit, of the application of the concept of psychopathy in criminal investigation and interrogation (Douglas, Burgess, Burgess, & Ressler, 1997; Douglas, Ressler, Burgess, & Hartman, 2004; Ressler, Burgess, & Douglas, 1992). "Knowing and understanding an offender's personality traits can help officers develop appropriate strategies for complex and unusual investigations" (Babiak et al., 2012, p. 1).

Criminal profiling is the process of inferring offender personality traits from crime scene evidence using theory and research to reach back in time to determine what occurred at the scene and make inferences from crime scene evidence about the characteristics of an unknown offender. Douglas et al. (1992) refer to the profiling process as a "form of retroclassification" whereby, rather than classifying a known entity into a particular category (e.g., DSM diagnosis), inferences are made from crime evidence to infer characteristics that place the unknown offender into a particular category. Profiling is used to supplement other investigative and forensic science techniques based on the idea that a small group of psychopathologically distinct offenders are responsible for a disproportionate amount of social harm. Offenses/offenders considered most suitable for profiling are those in which the offense appears to be motiveless (Douglas, Ressler, Burgess, & Hartman, 2004) and includes serial murderers, rapists, sexual predators, spree killers, mass murderers, family annihilation murderers, bombers, terrorists, stalkers, and arsonists who leave crime scenes that reflect the offender's psychopathology (Holmes & Holmes, 2002). The profiling process fundamentally involves applying criminological theory and criminal typologies to law enforcement investigations. The construct of psychopathy is of particular relevance to key criminological concepts used in the profiling process because the types of crimes for which profiling is most relevant tend to involve distinctions between offender types and the nature of offense motivation and behavior (Helfgott, 2008, 2013b).

There are many different terms used to describe profiling, a range of approaches to profiling, and the general process of profiling has been extensively reviewed (Annon, 1995; Cook & Hinman, 1999; Daéid, 1997; Davis, 1999; Egger, 1999; Godwin, 1998; Homant & Kennedy, 1998; O'Toole, 1999; Pinizzotto & Finkel, 1990; Wilson, Lincoln, & Kocsis, 1997). Terms and variants of profiling include investigative profiling, crime scene assessment, criminal investigative analysis, psychological profiling, criminal personality profiling, sociopsychological profiling, offender profiling, behavioral evidence analysis, investigative process management, crime scene analysis, crime scene profiling, geographical profiling, equivocal death analysis, and applied criminology. There are six general approaches to profiling that have been documented in the literature (Helfgott, 2008; Kocsis, 2013) and are shown in Table 6.1.

All profiling approaches involve the attempt to infer characteristics and patterns from crime scene evidence with focus on offender motivation, signature, and case linkage. Identification of the offender "type," including the nature of the psychopathological disturbance of the offender, in particular level of psychopathy, is critical to profiling, interviewing and 2012; Rossmo, 2000; Smith, O'Toole, & Hare, 2012; Turvey, 2011; Woodworth et al., 2012).

While there are many different approaches to profiling involving different theories, lines of research, and methodology (Kocsis, 2013), there are fundamental concepts of central importance when making inferences about offender characteristics from crime scene evidence that are applicable to all profiling models. All of these concepts require understanding theory and research on psychopathy. For example, one of the most fundamental starting points in profiling violent crime is classification of the crime scene as "organized" or "disorganized" with determination of the degree to which the violence is "predatory" or "affective." In addition, central to profiling process is the identification of modus operandi of the offender and signature elements and classification into typologies. Classification of crime scene evidence with inference regarding what "type" of offender committed the crime is an example of the identification of class characteristics in crime scene evidence, while identifying signature elements are individual characteristics that further individualize the offender for purpose of case linkage and investigative direction (Helfgott, 2008). Table 6.2 lists concepts and typologies central to the profiling process.

Psychopathy is used in profiling concepts and typologies as part of the conceptual language with which to discuss, explain, and classify that provides a foundation upon which inferences can be made upon which a profile can be constructed to aid in investigation, interrogation, risk assessment, and case linkage. Crime scene evidence that reflects modus operandi involving a high level of planning, boldness on the part of the offender, objectification of the victim, and signature elements that show extreme callousness and lack of remorse may provide investigative leads that the perpetrator may have psychopathic characteristics.

Concepts and typologies used in profiling differentiate types based on features of psychopathy in contrast with other psychopathological conditions. For example, the FBI organized/disorganized typology associates "organized" crime scenes with psychopathy and "disorganized" crime scenes with psychosis. More sophisticated typologies such as the compulsive/catathymic

Table 6.1 Profiling Approaches

Concept/ Typology	Description
Personality Profiling/ Diagnostic Evaluations	Personality theory and clinical diagnostic categories used to construct a "personality profile" representing the type of offender most likely to have committed the crime. Generally conducted by psychiatrists, psychologists, and academic criminologists.
Criminal Investigative Analysis	Crime scene patterns, crime scene indicators, victimology, and data collected from interviews with offenders used to determine type (organized/disorganized) of offender who committed the crime. Generally thought of as the method developed by the FBI. Done by law enforcement officers trained in profiling.
Investigative Psychology	Techniques and theories from psychology, psychiatry, and criminology to develop a profile based on statistical probability. Conducted primarily by academic psychologists and criminologists without investigative training who use typologies and empirical studies to construct profiles. Term used primarily in reference to the work of David Canter and the investigative psychology program at the University of Liverpool.
Behavioral Evidence Analysis	Method of criminal profiling involving deductive reasoning and critical thinking with focus on hypothesis testing through analysis of forensic evidence. Approach proposed by Brent Turvey (2011). In contrast with other methods, emphasizes integrating forensic psychology and forensic science in the profiling process.
Geographical Profiling	Geographic profiling aids investigations by predicting a serial offender's probable location. Using information from a series of related crimes, a mathematical model is used to analyze the locations of the crimes and characteristics of local neighborhoods to produce a map showing the areas in which the offender most likely lives, works, entertains, and travels (routes). Developed by Detective Inspector Kim Rossmo, author of *Geographic Profiling.*
Crime Action Profiling	A hybrid model of profiling utilizing concepts from criminal investigative analysis and investigative psychology that focuses on investigator operational goals. This model, developed by Kocsis (2006), is applied specifically to aberrant violent crime and is based on the correlation of specific criminal behavior with offender characteristics that are then used to profile future crimes. CAP models have been developed for sexual murder, serial rape, and serial arson.

Adapted from Kocsis (2013) and Helfgott (2008).

Table 6.2 Profiling Concepts and Typologies

Concept/ Typology	Description
Organized/ Disorganized Typology	Developed by FBI profilers (Douglas, Burgess, Burgess, & Ressler, 1997; Ressler, Burgess, & Douglas, 1988). Whether or not the crime scene is left organized or disorganized is said to provide information about the offender's criminal sophistication and personality. Organized crime scenes are said to reflect an offender who is motivated by a need for power and is associated with psychopathy. Disorganized crime scenes are said to reflect an offender who is motivated by passion, compulsion, frustration, or anxiety and is associated with psychosis. Although Resler, Burgess, and Douglas (1988) acknowledge a "mixed-type" involving both organized and disorganized types, this dichotomizing of crime types and broad oversimplified application of the concepts of psychopathy and psychosis has been criticized (Turvey, 2011) and has not been empirically validated (Canter, Alison, Alison, & Wentink, 2004). However, the organized/disorganized typology is part of the history of criminal profiling and continues to be widely cited, used as an organizing framework for analysis of crime scene evidence, and integrated into more sophisticated typologies (e.g., Meloy, 2000).
Predatory/ Affective Aggression	Aggression is shaped by emotional states—most commonly anger. Aggression can be motivationally categorized into two broad categories: *affective* (also: expressive, defensive) and *predatory* (also: instrumental, appetitive). Predatory aggression is characterized by lack of perceived threat, planned/purposeful violence, goal oriented, lack of conscious experience of emotion, increased self-esteem, and unimpaired reality testing. Affective aggression is characterized by perceived threat with goal of threat reduction, conscious experience of emotion, reactive/ unplanned violence, decreased self-esteem, and possible loss of reality testing (Meloy, 1988).
M.O. and Signature	M.O. is a Latin term meaning *method of operation*. M.O. reflects *how* the offender committed the crime, what he/she had to do to successfully complete it, and tells about the experience/state of the offender and situational/contextual factors involved in the crime. *Signature* is the *psychological calling card* (Keppel & Birnes, 1997) consisting of behavior/expression of violent fantasy the killer *must* leave at the scene to satisfy emotional/psychological needs. Signature goes beyond what's necessary to commit the crime and tells about the offender's emotional/psychological needs and motivation for committing the crime.

(*continued*)

Table 6.2 *(continued)*

Concept/ Typology	Description
Serial Murder and Sexual Homicide Typologies	Frequently cited sexual homicide typologies utilized in the profiling process include the power assertive, power assurance, anger excitation, anger retaliatory typology (Keppel & Walter, 1999); the power/control, visionary, hedonistic, mission typology (Holmes & Holmes, 2002); and Meloy's (2000) compulsive/catathymic typology.

sexual homicide typology offered by Meloy (2000) differentiate sexual homicide types by nature of homicide as organized/disorganized, DSM diagnosis, level of psychopathy, attachment pathology, autonomic nervous system, and early trauma, and characteristics of subtypes of other sexual homicide typologies include features of psychopathy (e.g., power assertive and power/control types).

The core relevance of psychopathy to criminal profiling is the notion that criminal behavior and evidence left at crime scenes by psychopaths are distinct. Crime and violence by psychopaths are "multifaceted and very different from that of other offenders" (Porter & Woodworth, 2006, p. 490) and are reflected in all aspects of a crime from initial motivation and offense planning to M.O. and signature behaviors and interactions with victims and post-offense behavior:

> Violent crime scenes always tell a story—a story written by the offender, the victim, and the unique circumstances of their interaction. That story makes crime scenes dynamic events that will vary in complexity, and, like any narrative, will have a beginning, middle, and end. Of the many possible criminal narratives, those that involve psychopaths have a distinct tone and intent, set apart the way science fiction stands out from other literature. (O'Toole, 2007, p. 302)

The tone and intent in crimes committed by psychopaths are characterized by the distinct interpersonal, affective, lifestyle, and antisocial factors associated with psychopathy that render psychopaths "a breed apart" (O'Toole, 2007, p. 304) from nonpsychopathic offenders with direct implications for criminal investigation. The psychopath's lack of affect, empathy, and remorse, instrumental/predatory nature, selective impulsivity, grandiosity, superficial charm, conning and manipulative nature, penchant for thrill seeking, criminal versatility, and the contemptuous delight they feel in creating shock in others influence their crimes and the crime scenes they leave behind.[5]

Given the long history of utilizing the concept of psychopathy in profiling, researchers have attempted to empirically investigate specific links between psychopathy, criminal behavior, and crime scene evidence. In a study of 125 homicide offenders, Woodworth and Porter (2002) found that psychopaths were "selectively impulsive"—and twice as likely as nonpsychopaths to have engaged in instrumental homicides with 93.3 percent of instrumentally motivated homicides committed by psychopaths compared to 48.4 percent by nonpsychopaths. The authors found that Factor 1 rather than Factor 2 PCL-R was associated with the instrumentality of the homicides and concluded that given the high stakes of perpetrating a homicide, the psychopathic homicide offenders were able to refrain from impulsivity and calculatingly plan their actions.

Häkkänen, Hurme, and Liukkonen (2007) examined distance patterns, disposal sites, and offender characteristics in 50 homicides that took place in rural areas of Finland from 1994 to 2005. The researchers considered various offender characteristics, such as intelligence, gender, relationship to the victim, criminal history, and psychopathy. The findings showed no correlation between the presence of psychopathy and distance patterns and disposal sites in homicides, leading the researchers to suggest that the findings may be due to the traits of impulsivity and egocentricity characteristic of psychopaths, stating that "psychopathic offenders do not want to make an extra effort to conceal their crime, not even in homicide cases" (p. 194). Häkkänen, Hurme, and Liukkonen (2007) also found that offenders who mutilated their victims were no more psychopathic than offenders who did not, noting that a psychopath in their study who had thought about mutilating his victim's body but did not, said when interviewed, "Why would I bother?" (p. 194). In a subsequent study specifically focusing on victim mutilation, they found that while offenders who mutilated their victim's bodies[6] did not significantly

[5] The complex nature of the psychopath's deficient emotional experience is reflected in the unique nature of the psychopath's impulsivity, motivation of power and control, and the commission of crime for shock value. The psychopath's impulsivity has been described as "instrumental impulsivity" (Meloy, 1988) or "selective impulsivity" (Woodworth & Porter, 2002). Perri (2011) notes that one should not extrapolate from what appears to be impulsive behavior committed by a psychopath to mean that psychopathic aggression is random and lacking in reflection. This selective, instrumental, (and emotionless) impulsivity combined with "contemptuous delight" (Meloy, 1988) in harming others (one of the few emotional experiences psychopath's are known to display), entitlement (Yochelson & Samenow, 1976) and omnipotent control (Gacono & Meloy, 1988; Helfgott, 1997, 2003) and dispassionate display of conscienceless behavior to control others (Perri, 2011) are key aspects of the psychopath's emotional void that distinctively manifest in criminal behavior and crime scene evidence.

[6] Only 13 of the 700 homicides in this study involved victim mutilation.

differ on total PCL-R scores, there was a correlation between interpersonal and affective factors and victim mutilation, which the authors attributed to the thrill-seeking nature of psychopathy.

Researchers have also examined the relationship between psychopathy and different types and subtypes of criminal behavior. Goncalves (1999) examined the relationship between psychopathy and offender types (classified as crimes against persons, property, and society) in a Portuguese prisoner sample and found highest levels of psychopathy in offenders who committed theft followed by sex crime and robbery with drug traffickers rated with the lowest mean psychopathy score. Hervé et al. (2004) found that 75 percent of a sample of 66 offenders convicted of unlawful confinement scored above 23 on the PCL-R suggesting that in cases of unlawful confinement that investigators should consider the possibility that the perpetrator is likely to be a psychopath. Spidel et al. (2007) examined the records of 22 offenders who had been charged with pimping and found that 36 percent of the offenders had PCL-R scores greater than 30 and 75 percent had scores over 22.1 with Factor 1/interpersonal and affective items explaining the differences between pimps and general offenders. The researchers concluded that the results offer further evidence to suggest that psychopaths are drawn to crimes that involve manipulation and predatory aggression—"crimes that involve the feeling of being in control of others" (p. 197). Studies have also found that psychopathy is associated with sexual aggression (Seto & Lalumiere, 2000) and rape myths that facilitate sexual assault (Mouilso & Calhoun, 2013), predatory violence (Declercq, Willemsen, Audenaert, & Verhaeghe, 2012; Hodges & Heilbrun, 2009; Meloy, 2012; Porter & Woodworth, 2006), sadistic sexual homicide (Jones, Chan, Meyers, & Heide, 2013), sexual sadism and juvenile sexual homicide (Meyers et al., 2010), violent sex crimes against children (Rosenberg, Abell, & Mackie, 2005), and subtypes of terrorists (Cooper, 2001; Eddy & Patrzalek, 2013), bombers (Meloy & McEllistrem, 1998), hostage takers (Greenstone, Kosson, & Gacono, 2000), white collar (Perri, 2011), fraud offenders (Haapasalo, 1994), and corporate criminals (Pardue, Robinson, & Arrigo, 2013, 2014).

Having knowledge about whether or not a suspect could have a high number of psychopathic character traits or could potentially be a primary psychopath has direct implications for law enforcement investigations, in particular with respect to interviewing and interrogating suspects. Villar, Arciuli, and Paterson (2014) found that the presence and nature of remorseful written statements and utterings are useful in identifying true versus false confessions. Traditional approaches such as the Reid Technique are not appropriate when interviewing suspects who could potentially be psychopathic, and the definition of what constitutes a successful interview (e.g., obtaining a confession) may have to be altered for psychopathic suspects (Perri, 2011). Understanding how psychopathic characteristics manifest themselves in criminal behavior and during investigative interviews is important in informing law enforcement conducting interviews with suspects. Quayle (2008) notes that for suspect interview purposes, the goal is not to clinically assess an individual as a primary psychopath through psychometric assessment on the PCL-R, but rather to consider whether the suspect displays psychopathic traits that will assist the interviewer in determining the appropriate interview strategy to ensure that valuable information can be gleaned from the interview. For example, whereas an emotion-based approach that involves attempts to bond and/or to provoke an emotional response may work when interviewing someone with few psychopathic characteristics, this interview style would not be effective with someone who is a psychopath or who possesses a high number of psychopathic traits. Attempts to encourage a psychopathic suspect to talk, divulge facts, or to confess will likely prove futile. In interviewing a psychopathic suspect, an alternative approach that attempts to elicit inconsistent and implausible information that is contradictory to the facts of the case can yield important information that, coupled with a suspect's display of lack of affect, can provide information to establish deception, lack of credibility that can aid a case (Perri, 2011).

Furthermore, an understanding of psychopathy (and the level of psychopathy of a suspect) has the benefit of informing the interviewer of the appropriate interviewing approach and can assist in avoiding an approach that could backfire if the suspect is a psychopath. For example, Perri (2001) analyzes the interview of Christopher Porco, a 21-year-old who murdered his father and attempted to murder his mother with an ax in Delmar, New York, in 2004. The approach used by the detective in interviewing Porco involved attempted to illicit emotion. The case is illustrative of how not to conduct an interview with an individual who is potentially psychopathic. Perri (2011, p. 48) offers the following excerpt of the Porco interview:

Detective: Listen to me. It's not—it's not—it's a crime of passion, okay? Like an emotional thing. You know, that's what it is.

Porco: That's not the (inaudible one word)—

Detective: An emotional flare up or something, you know, maybe. That's what I'm looking for. Give me something to grasp here. Let me get through the night.

Porco: Nothing happened.

Detective: And you understand what I've been telling you, that this is not a robbery. This is a crime of emotions.

Porco: I know what you are telling me. I—I don't know. I have absolutely no idea.

Detective: I mean, like I told you, in my estimation, that situation, the way I'm seeing it, was something that happened out of a passionate moment.

Porco: You told me they were in bed, so I don't know how passionate that could be, honestly.

Detective: And then afterwards, those emotions subside and the thought is, what's happened? What have I done? What has happened here? What an awful thing.

Porco: I agree it's an awful thing.

Detective: Sometimes your emotions get the best of you, overtake you.

Porco: True.

Detective: Your stomach is going to burn a hole in it. The only way to stop it is to be a man.

Porco: I can't help you.

The Porco interview is an example of how a confrontational, emotion-oriented interview approach can have the effect of shutting down any opportunity for a suspect to reveal investigative information. Attempts to tap into the suspect's emotion or to elicit information about reactive or easily understood motivation are incompatible approaches when interviewing a psychopathic suspect. Table 6.3 lists strategies offered by Perri (2011) to consider when interviewing a psychopathic suspect based on a synthesis of the research on psychopathy and police interrogations.

The construct of psychopathy clearly has direct implications for law enforcement. Knowledge and understanding about psychopathy enhances officer safety and informs interactions with suspects in hostage negotiation situations and aid in investigations, interrogations, and interviewing. Basic law enforcement training and advanced training for specialized units such as crisis intervention, hostage negotiation, and homicide investigation would be strengthened with the addition of a training component on psychopathy.

> [W]ith the proper preparation, knowledge, and understanding of psychopathy, law enforcement investigators can go behind the mask and see the true psychopathic personality beneath. Using dynamic and subtly changing strategies during interviews can create an environment where psychopaths less likely will predict the next steps and more likely will talk about their offenses and criminal superiority. (O'Toole, Logan, & Smith, 2012, p. 19)

It is critical that those in law enforcement understand as much as possible about the nature and manifestations of psychopathy. Knowledge about psychopathy can potentially be a critical element in an investigation, in resolving a crisis or hostage event, or in saving an officer's life (Logan, 2012; Logan & Hare, 2008).

Table 6.3 Strategies for Interviewing Psychopaths

Strategy	Explanation
1. Use a strategy tailored to suspect characteristics.	Interviews with suspects who are potentially psychopathic call for a creative approach tailored to suspect characteristics. Relying on traditional or past strategies (e.g., the Reid Technique) can backfire with a psychopathic suspect.
2. Utilize a nonemotional format.	Psychopaths do not respond to appeals for emotion. Attempts to elicit regret, remorse, social obligation, or sympathy will be a waste of time. Dialogue must center around the facts of the case, specific evidence, and must use a nonemotional format and tone.
3. Avoid projecting emotion.	Psychopaths do not react to emotional or horrific incidents in the same way that nonpsychopaths do. However, as human beings it is difficult to imagine that a person can participate in or witness an emotional incident such as a heinous crime. Interviewers must be conscious of this tendency and avoid projecting their own emotions on the suspect.
4. Do not belittle suspect.	Attempts to belittle a psychopathic suspect will result in the suspect shutting down or becoming superficially angry. Evidence against the suspect should be presented in a straightforward, matter-of-fact, and nonconfrontational manner.
5. Consider incorporating post-offense behavior displayed by the suspect as a possible indicator of psychopathic traits.	Psychopaths will rarely express traumatic reaction to an emotional event. Post-offense behaviors that are indicative of the absence of emption should be considered as indicative of psychopathic traits.
6. Know thyself.	Psychopaths are master manipulators who spend their entire lives learning and perfecting their skills in figuring other people out, learning their weaknesses, and using people's insecurities as a tool to gain control. In order to avoid this trap, the interviewer has to know himself or herself, be aware of his or her own weaknesses, and be prepared to maintain control of the interview even if this means creating the appearance that the suspect is the one in control.

(continued)

Table 6.3 (*continued*)

Strategy	Explanation
7. Avoid overconfidence.	Overconfidence can hinder an investigation. It is important to recognize that detecting deception is extremely difficult, and many studies have shown that criminal justice practitioners are no better at detecting deception than the average person.
8. Present facts of case with the goal of collecting inconsistent and implausible facts from suspect, not a confession.	It is unlikely that a psychopathic suspect will confess. In an interview with a psychopathic suspect the goal of the interview needs to be altered to obtain as much inconsistent and implausible information as possible in response to presenting known facts and details about the case. Psychopaths have no shame. Thus, they may unwittingly offer extraordinarily implausible information when presented with indisputable facts. This information is the most valuable information that can be obtained from a psychopathic suspect.
9. Be aware of the suspect's use of superficial expression of emotion as a form of manipulation.	Psychopaths are masters at mimicry. They know how to display emotion, in some cases more effectively than nonpsychopaths. Beware, in the presence of evidence that the suspect is potentially psychopathic, that expression of emotion is a manipulative tool.
10. Understand the nature of the crime.	Every crime is different in terms of its nature, dynamics, and victimology. The interviewer should have knowledge and understanding of the profile of individuals who commit the specific type of crime in question—characteristics of offenders, M.O., and signature behavior of past offenders, motives, victimology, and crime scene features. Knowing the research of the types of individuals who perpetrate types and subtypes of crime, whether it is a crime that is inclined to be committed by psychopaths, to involve predatory or affective aggression, and so on can provide important information as a framework for individualizing the interview strategy to the individual and the crime.

Adapted from Perri (2011).

Courts

No other area of the criminal justice system is more intertwined with the construct of psychopathy than the courts. The impact of characterization of an offender as remorseful or not to judicial outcomes has been acknowledged within the legal realm and has received empirical support (Weisman, 2008). Expert testimony on psychopathy and forensic use of the PCL-R has been increasing in a range of legal proceedings, including witness credibility, competency to stand trial, guilt determination, habitual offender sentencing, sexually violent predator civil commitment, sentence enhancement and sentence mitigation, capital sentencing, juvenile transfers to adult court, child custody cases, and parole hearings (Lyon & Ogloff, 2000; Walsh & Walsh, 2006). From the earliest cases in the history of modern criminal law to the most notorious cases in history, psychopathy, or, its historical conceptual predecessor, "moral insanity," has played a fundamental role in the origin, development, and boundaries of criminal law and the earliest roots of criminological thought. In fact, "the roots of scientific criminological thought lie in the late 18th- and early 19th-century discourses on the phenomenon of moral insanity, or uncontrollable, remorseless criminal behavior" (Rafter, 2004, p. 979) and texts on moral insanity that focus on the identification of recidivistic and violent crime committed by offenders who appeared incapable of remorse and explained in terms of mental abnormality represent the earliest scientific writings on the causes of crime.[7]

The concept of moral insanity forced psychiatry and the courts to deal with issues of free will and determinism and understanding of the nature of evil in the early formation of criminal law and the law of insanity. Rafter (2004) notes:

> Moral insanity theory emerged in the period between the flowering of 18th-century rationalism and the onset of 19th-century hereditarianism, a time when criminals were assumed to be normal human beings with free will and the capacity for utilitarian cost-benefit analyses. . . . By the 1870s, however, criminals seemed irrational and undeterrable, governed by a malignant heredity over which they had no control. Moral insanity theory, picturing the arch criminal as intellectually sane but morally mad, hovered between these two poles. (Rafter, 2004, pp. 1002–1003)

This exception to criminal rationality was the first step in the conceptualization of the jurisprudence of insanity, and moral insanity became a "key

[7] Moral insanity theory and writings originated in independent writings of physicians Benjamin Rush (United States, 1745–1813) on "moral derangement," Philippe Pinel (France, 1745–1826) on "Mania sans delire," and James Cowles Prichard (England, 1786–1848) on "moral insanity" (Rafter, 2004).

concept in the hereditarian criminologies of the late 19th century . . . the basis for the psychiatric theory of psychopathy. . . . The only criminological concept to have thus survived from the late 18th into the 21st century" (Rafter, 2004, pp. 1002–1003).

Psychopathy, and with it the notion of moral insanity and remorseless criminal behavior, has become a hinge pin in criminal law and the courts. Introduction of psychopathy as assessed through the PCL-R has increased exponentially since the publication of the PCL-R in 1990 (Walsh & Walsh, 2006). The nature of psychopathy—predatory aggression, instrumental behavior, and intact cognition—has been used as a legal basis for exclusion from defense of insanity, introduced in expert testimony in civil and criminal cases, and has been the basis for legal decisions in pretrial detention, adjudication, sentencing, and civil commitment. Psychopathy has been introduced into the courts in cases involving witness credibility, competency to stand trial, habitual offender and sexual predator legislation, juvenile waivers to adult court, child custody, civil commitment, parole hearings, and capital sentencing and has shown to be "a powerfully pejorative diagnostic label that can exert a profound influence over the legal decisions rendered by the courts (Lyon & Ogloff, 2000, p. 139).

There has been increasing attention in recent years to controversy and issues in the utilization of the construct of psychopathy in the courts (Bernat, Helfgott, & Godlove, 2013; DeMatteo & Edens, 2006; Edens, 2001; Edens & Cox, 2012; Edens & Petrila, 2006; Edens et al., 2005; Häkkänen-Nyholm & Hare, 2009; Kiehl & Sinnott-Armstrong, 2013; Lee, 2007; Lloyd, Clark, & Forth, 2010; Lyon & Ogloff, 2000; Malatesti & McMillan, 2010; Sandys, Pruss, & Walsh, 2009; Walsh & Walsh, 2006). The judicial response to psychopathy has historically revolved around two contrasting approaches—the retributive view of psychopathy as a mitigating factor (that psychopaths have a mental disorder that decreases culpability and renders them deserving of mercy and empathy) versus the utilitarian view of psychopathy as an aggravating factor (that psychopaths are a dangerous threat to public safety, are unamenable to treatment, and removing them from the community as long as possible serves the greatest good for the greatest number) (Lee, 2007). However, psychopathy has continued to be predominantly viewed as a condition of "badness" over "madness" and seen in court as an aggravating rather than a mitigating factor to establish criminal intent and premeditation, enhance sentences, and influence determination of dangerousness (Lyon & Ogloff, 2000).

Psychopaths, Psychotics—What's the Difference? Insanity, Legal Competence, and Criminal Responsibility

Psychopathy has had a long history of controversy in medico-legal debates over criminal responsibility and presents important implications for criminology and psychiatry (Vitacco, Lishner, & Neumann, 2012; Ward, 2010). After over 200 years of discourse on the nature of insanity, the existence of the condition of moral insanity, and the distinction between the two, confusion and controversy continue and are reflected in both popular culture and legal discourse. The 1960 movie *Psycho* and 40 years later the 2000 film *American Psycho* further confused the terms "psychopath" and "psychotic" and the fallacious link between mental illness and violence (Kondo, 2008) in the public mind. Film and media depictions of psychotics, psychopaths, pseudopsychopaths (Leistedt & Linkowski, 2014), and strange and unrealistic mixtures of extremes that complicate the relationship between psychopathy and psychosis have done little to clarify the line between psychotics and psychopaths and have direct implications for academic and popular understanding of criminal justice (Helfgott, 2013c).

Although psychological conceptions of mental illness are considered and presented as part of expert testimony in reaching a determination of insanity (e.g., in determining the mental state of a defendant, what type of mental illness the defendant possesses), insanity is a legal standard, not a psychological concept. Like all legal standards, the insanity defense—"not guilty by reason of insanity" (NGBRI)—has changed over time and differs across cultures and jurisdictions. In the United States, there are different versions of insanity defense in the federal and state court systems and in different states. In the 1980s following the trial of John Hinckley, there was widespread reform of the insanity defense in the United States with the majority of the states and the federal system moving to a more restrictive M'Naghten standard. Table 6.4 shows the different versions of the insanity defense that have been used over time and currently in use.

The insanity defense is based on the historical belief that crime can only be committed by rational persons and that those who commit a criminal offense who are not aware of what they are doing do not possess criminal intent and therefore deserve treatment rather than punishment. Tests of insanity have been criticized because they do not recognize that mental processes are interrelated and interdependent (Goldstein, 1967), and there is a long discourse on problematic aspects of excluding certain types of mental conditions like psychopathy and other personality disorders, suggesting insanity tests "unscientifically abstract out of the mental make-up but one phase or element of mental life, the cognitive, which, in this era of dynamic psychology, is beginning to be regarded as not the most important factor in conduct and its disorders" (McCord & McCord, 1964, p. 178). Former Supreme Court justice Benjamin Cordozo said long ago that "Everyone recognizes that the present [legal] definition of insanity has little relation to the truths of mental life" (Cordozo, 1930). However, it has been, and remains, extremely difficult to resolve the opposing objectives of the criminal justice system's demand for responsibility in the law and the mental health system's desire to treat mental illnesses that manifest in criminal behavior.

The understanding of psychopathy as a condition of "moral insanity" that renders those so afflicted cognitively able to determine the difference between

Table 6.4 Legal Tests for Insanity

The M'Naghten Rule	The historic origin of the insanity defense is the 1843 case of Daniel M'Naghten. Daniel M'Naghten shot and killed British prime minister Sir Robert Peel's secretary Edward Drummond. The jury in the case acquitted M'Naghten with a finding "not guilty by reason of insanity." The ruling was controversial at the time and resulted in the establishment of an official process by which insanity was to be determined. This process, developed by the English common law judges came to be known as the M'Naghten rule. The M'Naghten rule required evidence that at the time of the offense, the defendant's actions were committed under a defect of reason, a disease of the mind, resulting in the defendant's *inability to know what he or she was doing and/or that what he or she was doing was wrong*. The M'Naghten rule, sometimes called the "right/wrong" test, is the historical foundation of the insanity defense in Britain and the United States.
The Durham Rule	The M'Naghten rule was criticized because it did not take into account individuals who knew the difference between right and wrong when committing an act, but who could not control their behavior and stop themselves from committing the act. As a result of this dissatisfaction with the M'Naghten rule, the District of Columbia Federal Court of Appeals formulated a new rule called the Durham rule in 1954 in the case *Durham v. United States*. The Durham rule, also known as the "irresistable impulse test," required that to be determined "not guilty by reason of insanity" the defendant's act must be the *product of a mental disease or defect that rendered the accused incapable of controlling his or her behavior*. The Durham rule was criticized because of concerns over the interpretation of "mental disease or defect." Critics argued that the Durham rule left open the possibility of a broad range of minor mental disorders in the *Diagnostic and Statistical Manual of Mental Disorders* to be considered under the rule and gave psychologists and psychiatrists too much power in the courtroom. The Durham rule was abandoned by the DC Federal Court of Appeals in the 1972 case *United States v. Brawner*.

(continued)

Table 6.4 (*continued*)

The American Law Institute Model Penal Code and Brawner Rule	The M'Naghten rule was replaced in most jurisdictions in the 1960s with the adoption of the American Law Institute (ALI) standards, which were included in the 1962 Model Penal Code. The Model Penal Code *combined the principles of the M'Naghten and Durham rules with specification of the type of mental disease or defect that could be considered to establish insanity.* After the 1972 case *United States v. Brawner* that dealt with the murder trial of Archie Brawner, the Model Penal Code excluded a specific type of mental disease or defect—antisocial personality disorder or any abnormality manifested only by repeated criminal and/or antisocial conduct. Under the Model Penal Code, a defendant could be considered not guilty by reason of insanity if at the time of the conduct, as a result of mental disease or defect, the defendant lacked the substantial capacity to appreciate the wrongfulness of the conduct or conform to the requirements of the law. The Model Penal Code included a major caveat—that the mental disease or defect could not be solely manifested by antisocial or repeated criminal conduct. The Model Penal Code can be seen as an attempt to exclude antisocial personality disorder and/or psychopaths from the insanity defense. However, because the law requires that the mental disease or defect be manifested *only* by antisocial or criminal behavior and most psychopaths and antisocial personality disordered individuals behaviorally manifest their personality disorder in other types of conduct, some question whether or not this caveat can technically ever apply to anyone.
The Insanity Reform Act of 1984	Public outrage over the 1982 acquittal of John Hinckley prompted a barrage of legislation at the federal level and throughout the country intended to abolish or severely restrict the use of the insanity defense. John Hinckley was tried in federal court in the District of Columbia, which at the time used the Model Penal Code as the test of insanity. Critics of the Model Penal Code and Hinckley acquittal argued that Hinckley clearly knew what he was doing when he plotted to assassinate then president Ronald Reagan and that the current formation of the insanity defense allowed offenders to get away with murder.

(*continued*)

Table 6.4 *(continued)*

The Insanity Reform Act of 1984 (*continued*)	The Insanity Reform Act of 1984 was a compromise between insanity defense abolitionists and legal and psychiatric professionals who argued for modification rather than abolition. The Insanity Reform Act of 1984 removed the volitional prong of the ALI test that excused a defendant who could not control his or her behavior and narrowed the definition of mental disease or defect to include only severe mental disease or defect. In addition, the Insanity Reform Act shifted the burden of proof to the defendant, limited the scope of expert psychiatric testimony, and established procedures for the hospitalization and release of acquittees. The Insanity Reform Act of 1984 was essentially a return to a test more closely resembling the original M'Naghten rule.
Guilty but Mentally Ill	As a result of public reaction to the acquittal of John Hinckley in 1982, a number of states developed an alternative to the determination of "not guilty by reason of insanity." The "guilty but mentally ill" (GBMI) alternative was developed requiring that *defendants deemed mentally ill at the time of their offense would be treated in a psychiatric facility until they are determined to be no longer mentally ill and then would be transferred to a correctional facility to serve the remainder of their sentence.* The states that allow for the GBMI verdict provide GBMI as an alternative to NGRI whereby the jury is given four verdict options: guilty, not guilty, guilty but mentally ill, and not guilty by reason of insanity. Thus the defendant is given a criminal sentence, but mental health and correctional professionals determine if treatment is needed and where the offender will reside during the course of his or her sentence.

right and wrong, yet unable or unwilling to engage in behavior directed by moral or social concern, led to the exclusion of psychopathy from the defense of insanity. After years of discourse on the notion of moral insanity, the exclusion of mental conditions that produce repeated antisocial and criminal conduct were officially excluded from the insanity defenses. The American Law Institute's (ALI) 1962 Model Penal Code and subsequent 1972 Brawner rule specifically and purposefully excludes any mental disease or defect manifested by repeated criminal or antisocial conduct from the defense. These legal definitions of insanity have historically resulted in the courts' exclusion of psychopathy from the insanity defense either explicitly by statute or by judicial interpretation (Goldstein, 1967; Morse, 2010), although some courts have continued to struggle with the problematic attempt to make legal determinations involving psychological conditions (Smith & Meyer, 1987; Slate, Buffington-Vollum, & Johnson, 2013), and there has been a recent resurgence in discourse supporting the inclusion of psychopathy in the insanity defense (Morse, 2010; Ward, 2010).

The crux of the issue lies in the fact that the insanity defense is based on the notion that individuals who do not understand the difference between right and wrong and do not appreciate the wrongfulness of their acts should not be held responsible and should be treated and released when restored to healthy functioning. The problem with psychopaths is that they appreciate the wrongfulness of their acts, the very evidence of their psychological condition is evidenced by their criminal acts, and they are known to be very difficult if not impossible to treat. This creates a fundamental conundrum for including them in the insanity defense. If psychopaths are included in the insanity defense when they know what they are doing, they don't care, and the evidence of their disorder is their criminal act, then it would follow that anyone who intentionally commits a remorseless unexplainable crime could use the defense of insanity.

The historical case of Henriette Cornier in Paris in 1926 was told and retold in England and the United States amid the discourse on moral insanity and represented a turning point in the relationship between law and psychiatry regarding the demarcation of criminal responsibility and insanity. Henriette Cornier was a 27-year-old servant in Paris who in 1826 went to a neighborhood shop to buy some cheese for the family she worked for. When she arrived at the cheese shop, she asked the shopkeeper if she could take her infant daughter (who she was known to be fond of) for a walk. However, instead of taking the child for a walk, she took her to her mistress's house, laid the child across her own bed, and severed the girl's head off with a kitchen knife. After the act she was reported to show no emotion. When the mother came for her child two hours later, Cornier was said to have told her coldly, "Your child is dead." When the mother who did not believe her went looking for the child and found her mutilated body, Cornier picked up the child's head and threw it into the street from the open window. When Cornier was asked why she did it, she said it was to attract public attention so that people might come to her room and see that she alone was responsible for the murder. This was the first time in Europe or North America that a new category for insanity in which the act itself was used as a defense against criminal culpability was used. However, because no motive could be ascertained, her violent act could not be situated within the conventional parameters of criminal misconduct and criminal law. Cornier knew what she did was wrong but offered no motive as to why she did it. The only evidence of her insanity was what she had done (Weisman, 2008).

The Cornier case represented a critical demarcation in the history of criminal law with long-term implications for how the condition of psychopathy came to be seen by the courts in particular with respect to the law of insanity. If Cornier's heinous act was to be used as evidence of insanity even though she knew the wrongfulness of her act, how could the courts ever distinguish a cognitively unimpaired murderer whose actions were willful and deliberate from the cognitively unimpaired insane offender whose wrongdoings were caused by a mental affliction? Although there was discourse, discussion, and understanding of the distinct form of moral insanity represented by Cornier and others like her throughout 19th-century discourse, by the early-20th-century publication of Krafft-Ebing's (1906) *Text-Book of Insanity,* the view of moral insanity came closer to the view of psychopathy today—with the behavior of the offender an expression of the essence of personality pathology with lack of remorse at its core that is hereditary, untreatable, and a relentless danger to others (Weisman, 2008).

Expert testimony on psychopathy has historically been used to exclude a defendant from the insanity defense. Notorious court cases throughout history have involved battles between prosecution and defense teams that use experts on the side of the prosecution who paint a picture of the defendant as a remorseless predatory psychopath, while the experts for the defense describe the defendant as a psychotic who is out of touch with reality and incapable of appreciating the wrongfulness of the criminal act. The insanity trial of John Hinckley in 1981, which led to widespread changes in how the insanity defense is applied in the United States, illustrates the classic dynamic in the war of the experts when the topic of psychopathy is introduced. In the Hinckley case, the defense psychiatrists testified that Hinckley was psychotic, while the prosecution experts disagreed, testifying that he suffered from various personality disorders (Low, Jeffries, & Bonnie, 1986).

Psychopathy is the perfect prosecutorial weapon. Psychopathy has been historically represented as the antithesis of insanity and barred from the insanity defense because the condition does not entail cognitive defect that would render an individual with the disorder incapable of understanding right from wrong. Because of the way in which criminal law is applied through the fundamental concept of "mens rea" (evil mind) and "actus reus" (the actual, voluntary performance of a criminal act), individuals (e.g., psychopaths) who do not exhibit lack of cognitive defect must be held responsible for their acts. Furthermore, the notion of the "successful" or "adaptive" psychopath and view of psychopathy as an adaptation rather than a clinical disorder (e.g., Hall &

Benning, 2006; Babiak & Hare, 2006) negate the application of the insanity defense for psychopaths (Lee, 2007). Long before the advent of the PCL-R, evidence regarding whether or not a defendant is psychopathic has been used by prosecutors to rebut evidence of mental illness, and evidence on psychopathy continues to be used in NGRI cases (Rendell et al., 2010).

DeMatteo and Edens's (2006) survey of the use of psychopathy in court found that testimony that a defendant is a psychopath has been offered in court as explanation for a defendant's violent criminal conduct and invoked to support the conclusion that the defendant was not mentally disordered at the time of the offense but rather were malingering symptoms of serious mental illness. Other insanity defense trials throughout history (such as Andrea Yates, Mark David Chapman, Jeffrey Dahmer) have involved a similar battle of experts who present evidence of the planned, predatory nature of the defendant from the prosecution side versus the unplanned, reactive, affective, and psychotic nature on the defense side.[8] Rendell et al. (2010) examined whether or not juror attitudes toward the insanity defense are influenced by the term "psychopath" in comparison with information regarding the trait it represents and have found that mock jurors were more likely to find the defendant NGRI when the prosecution testimony labeled the defendant a psychopath than when the prosecution described the defendant as not mentally ill. The study also found that that mock jurors were more likely to find the defendant NGRI if the defense expert testimony was based on biological rather than psychological evidence.

However, there have been questions and controversy regarding the nature of the psychopath's impairment in moral responsibility and ability to control or make decisions to control morally irresponsible and antisocial behavior (Duff, 2010).

Ward (2010) asks:

> Suppose that psychopaths as described by Cleckley, "subtly constructed reflex machine[s]" that lack some essential element of fully human personality, really exist. How is a court to know that any particular defendant is such a specimen? The fact that someone attains a certain score on a checklist of the observable symptoms of psychopathy does not of itself afford any deep insight into his moral experience or lack of it. Even if personality, rather than the outward behavior that makes up what the law

[8] Some of these cases did not involve expert testimony specifically on psychopathy or PCL-R scores because either they occurred before the PCL-R was published and widely used in forensic assessment and/or before there was widespread consensus on the definition and research on psychopathy. However, testimony on predatory nature versus psychosis illustrates the relevance of expert testimony on psychopathy in insanity defense cases.

> defines as "character," is a proper subject of psychiatric study and treatment, is it something that courts are equipped to investigate? If psychiatrists claim to be so equipped, are courts justified in accepting their claims? "We are," Cleckley concluded, "not competent to serve in such a role nor are we responsible" for determining such momentous legal issues. (Ward, 2010, p. 20)

Recent research suggests that the value of testimony on psychopathy at insanity trials is weak and that there are issues with the view that the presence of psychopathy rules out the possibility that a defendant suffers from a major mental disorder such as psychosis. DeMatteo and Edens (2006) argue that psychopathy and psychosis are not mutually exclusive, nor is a high PCL-R score an acceptable standard for assessment of malingering. The authors pose what is essentially the central question in making sense of the value of expert testimony on psychopathy in insanity trials: "[C]an a high score on the PCL-R aid in determining that a defendant does or does not meet the cognitive prong of M'Naughten or American Law Institute criteria?" The authors respond:

> [T]here is nothing about psychopathy per se that rules out the presence of psychosis or other factors that may strongly impact whether a defendant understands the wrongfulness of his or her actions at the time of the offense. Moreover, the examiner's attempt to explain the defendant's criminal conduct by invoking the psychopath label arguably goes well beyond the purpose of a sanity evaluation, in which the role of the examiner is to attempt to inform the court about the defendant's mental state at the time of the offense. (DeMatteo & Edens, 2006, p. 230)

With the proliferation of biological and neuropsychological research on psychopathy that present issues regarding the ability of psychopathic defendants to control their inclinations and behavior, controversy and discourse on the use of psychopathy as a prosecutorial rebuttal against the insanity defense will likely continue for some time to come.

Adjudication and Legal Decision Making: Expert Testimony, Competency Determinations, Criminal Trial, and Jury Decision Making

The notion that psychopathy and psychosis are distinct and that psychopaths do not suffer from cognitive impairment that disrupts their ability to understand the nature and consequences of their criminal acts also has implications in the courts beyond the rare cases that involve the insanity defense. The courts are increasingly admitting evidence on the PCL-R to address issues at the pretrial, trial, and dispositional stages in the criminal and civil courts (DeMatteo & Edens, 2006). Pretrial competency determinations, adjudication, jury decision making, sexually violent predator determinations, and expert testimony of all components of the court process are impacted by the inclusion of research and theory on psychopathy.

Courts employ one of two standards for admitting scientific evidence: the Frye standard and the Daubert standard. The Frye standard, established in *Frye v. United States* (1923), requires that scientific evidence has gained general acceptance in the scientific community. The Frye standard is used in over half of the state courts. In *Daubert v. Merrill Dow Pharmaceuticals* (1993), the U.S. Supreme Court set forth a new standard, further articulated in *Kumho Tire Ltd v. Carmichael* (1999). The Daubert standard outlined four factors that needed to be considered in admitting expert testimony: (1) whether the theory/technique could be/has been subject to testing, (2) whether error rates are known, (3) whether the issues have been subjected to peer review and publication, and (4) general acceptance in the relevant scientific community. The federal system and approximately half the states use the Daubert standard (Calhoun, 2008; Keierleber & Bohan, 2005).

In *Barefoot v. Estelle* (1983), a capital case involving Thomas Barefoot convicted of the murder of a police officer in Bell County, Texas, the U.S. Supreme Court ruled that clinical opinions given by psychiatrists could be introduced in court, arguing that mental health experts had not been proved to be less reliable than other experts in predicting dangerousness. This opened the door to what has been referred to as the "age of the mental health expert" (Smith, 1989), with increasing reliance on expert testimony involving forensic assessment of offender risk. The empirical evidence linking the PCL-R to violent recidivism has exponentially increased the degree to which the concept of psychopathy is introduced in court decisions and has made the PCL-R one of the most prominent forensic assessment instruments noted by expert witnesses in a range of situations in criminal and civil courts in particular in cases involving the prediction of dangerousness.

The courts have generally spoken in favor of admitting PCL-R evidence under both Daubert and Frye admissibility standards, and in many cases where PCL-R testimony is offered, the PCL-R is the only forensic assessment measure introduced (Walsh & Walsh, 2006). At the pretrial stage, forensic evaluation results are sometimes introduced as evidence of a defendant's competency to stand trial and for purposes of pretrial detention (Lyon & Ogloff, 2000; Rendell et al., 2010; Walsh & Walsh, 2006). For example, Walsh and Walsh (2006) found a California state court case in which a defendant was evaluated as competent to stand trial after twice being found incompetent based on testimony that the defendant demonstrated behaviors associated with psychopathy. At the trial stage, expert testimony on psychopathy has been introduced to discredit witnesses, for case linkage and understanding offender motivation (Häkkänen-Nyholm & Hare, 2009), and assessment of dangerousness (Lee, 2007).

In recent years a number of studies have been conducted to examine the nature of expert testimony on psychopathy in court proceedings. Lloyd, Clark, and Forth (2010) suggest that PCL-R scores, particularly within the context of testimony related to treatment amenability, are moderately related to trial outcome. Walsh and Walsh (2006) identified four cases from 1991 to 2004 in which PCL-R testimony was presented to comment on the issue of guilt based on the notion that the PCL-R indicated a tendency toward violence. PCL-R testimony has also been used to argue that a defendant was unlikely to have committed a sexual assault based on testimony that he was a nonpsychopath. Häkkänen-Nyholm and Hare (2009) found that psychopathic offenders are prone to certain post-offense behaviors such as leaving the scene of the crime, denying responsibility, denying charges, shifting blame to external forces, and making good impressions and successfully manipulating the courts, which lead to reduction of charges and/or a more lenient sentence. In general, these post-offense behaviors reflect "strategic self-presentation to prevent others (e.g., police officers) from considering them as suspects, to mitigate the seriousness of the crime, or to influence court proceedings" (p. 773). Although some studies indicate that expert agreement in adversarial court process is low and consistently biased toward partisan allegiance (Murrie et al., 2007), others suggest that expert testimony on psychopathy accurately reflects what is currently known in the research literature.

However, misuses of the psychopathy construct in court have been identified and have raised a number of questions about ethical issues associated with expert testimony on psychopathy. For example, Edens (2001) provides case study examples to illustrate how the presence and absence of psychopathy have been misused in court—a capital case in which a defendant's PCL-R score was presented as evidence of psychopathy by a prosecution expert and used as an aggravating factor and a case where a defendant's absence of psychopathy was presented by a defense expert in a highly unusual manner through reference to specific items on the PCL-R and used as evidence of the absence of psychopathy as a mitigating factor in a sexual violence case to suggest that the defendant was not capable of sexual violence. In both of these cases conclusions were made that were not supported by the existing literature, and in the sexual violence case there were numerous issues with the expert's testimony, including lack of adequate information to administer and score the PCL-R and presentation of the results in a nonstandardized and unusual manner.[9]

---

[9] The outcomes in both of these cases illustrate the issues with expert testimony on the PCL-R. In the first case, the prosecution withdrew the examiner's report after the defense submitted a

Sentencing and Civil Commitment: Dangerous Offenders, Sexual Psychopaths/ Sexually Violent Predators, Three-Strikes Legislation, and the Death Penalty

At the sentencing and civil commitment stage of the criminal justice process, theory and research on psychopathy have been incorporated at the front and back ends of the sentencing process—incorporated into risk assessment instruments in sentencing schemes, in the sentencing phase in death penalty cases, and civil commitment (Luna, 2013). Although theoretical and philosophical arguments have been raised to support consideration of psychopathy as both an aggravating and mitigating factor, psychopathy has primarily been used to establish a case that a defendant is dangerous, unamenable to treatment, and therefore in need of long-term indefinite incarceration or death to protect public safety (Luna, 2013; Lyon & Ogloff, 2000; Lyon, Ogloff, & Shepherd, 2016). The strong empirical link between psychopathy and violent recidivism and research suggesting that psychopaths cannot be successfully treated has provided information to the courts as an aggravating factor at sentencing and to support preventative detention, civil commitment, and indefinite confinement of offenders legally designated as dangerous and/or sexually violent predators. In capital sentencing, expert testimony on the link between psychopathy and institutional misconduct has been used to support the death sentence as opposed to life without possibility of parole (LWOP) on the grounds that a defendant's psychopathy presents a dangerous threat to the safety of the prison population and staff.

One of the most prominent areas in which psychopathy has made its way into the courts is to support indeterminate sentences and civil detention for dangerous offenders and sexually violent predators. There is a long history dating to before the turn of the 20th century linking psychopathy to habitual offender legislation with the notion that psychopaths are among the group of persistent chronic offenders that represent a small percentage of offenders but are responsible for large percentage of crime. The idea was revived in the 1970s in sociological terms as the "6 percent solution" based on the Wolfgang study *Delinquency in a Birth Cohort* (Wolfgang, Figlio, & Sellin, 1972) that found that 6 percent of a cohort of 10,000 young men in Philadelphia born in 1945 were responsible for more than 50 percent of total crime. More recently psychopathy has been integrated into interdisciplinary models and empirical research examining and explaining serious offender trajectories (Moffit, 1993) and the

---

motion *in limine* to exclude the PCL-R results and all references to psychopathy including affidavits from researchers on the lack of clear association between psychopathy and institutional violence. In the second case, rebuttal testimony was offered that presented the irrelevance of the testimony to the case, and the defendant was found not guilty after several hours of deliberation (Edens, 2001).

role of psychopathy in explaining persistent offending patterns and pathways (e.g., Shaw & Porter, 2012; Vincent et al., 2003).

There has also been a historical intertwining of psychopathy and sexual psychopathy and sexually violent predator (SVP) legislation (Janus & Prentky, 2008; Sutherland, 1950). Current SVP laws are a revival of the old "sexual psychopathy" laws of the early 1900s.[10] Jenkins (1998) notes that the term "predator" originated in popular writings of Jack Olsen and Andrew Vachss and made its way from popular culture into the habitual offender and civil commitment laws with the help of highly publicized and heinous crimes and criminals that were used to launch legislative changes.[11] This transfer of the use of the term "predator" from pop culture to law coincided with the exponential accumulation of research in the area of psychopathy, sexual deviancy, and violent crime (Helfgott, 2008).

Like the habitual offender laws, the purpose of sexual predator laws is to protect the public by identifying the subtype of offenders deemed most dangerous. Sexually violent predator laws requiring civil commitment of sexually violent offenders after serving their sentence were deemed constitutional in *Kansas v. Hendricks* (1997). Washington State was the first state to revive the old sexual psychopath laws. The current Washington law, enacted as part of the Community Protection Act of 1990, is called the sexually violent predator (SVP) statute (RCW 71.09.020). The way the law works is that the prosecuting attorney or attorney general will petition the court for an end-of-sentence review of an offender and probable cause hearing to determine whether or not he or she[12] meets the legal definition of "sexually violent predator." The legal

---

[10] "Sexual psychopath" is (like "sexually violent predator") a legal term used to impose civil commitment. The definition and adoption of the laws between 1937 and 1957 reflect the historical conceptual connection between psychopathy and sexual deviancy. Some states (e.g., Minnesota) still refer to "sexual psychopathic personalities" and "sexually dangerous persons" in the modernized version of the older sexual psychopath laws. However, "sexual psychopathy" and "sexually violent predator" as used in civil commitment statutes are legal, not psychological terms. The terminology and definitions used in civil commitment legislation in different states may not correspond to the scientific conceptualization of psychopathy, antisocial personality, pedophilia, and other disorders. In fact, the U.S. Supreme Court noted (in *Kansas v. Hendricks*, 1997) the distinction between law and science stating that the two need not always agree: "States have, over the years, developed numerous specialized terms to define mental health concepts. Often, those definitions do not fit precisely with the definitions employed by the medical community. The legal definitions of 'insanity' and 'competency,' for example, vary substantially from their psychiatric counterparts. . . . Legal definitions . . . need not mirror those advanced by the medical profession" (*Kansas v. Hendricks*, 1997).

[11] For example, posterboy superpredators were used in Washington State (e.g., Earl Shriner, Westley Dodd, and Charles Campbell) and California (e.g., Richard Allen Davis in California) to launch three-strikes legislation (see Helfgott, 2008, pp. 203–205, for a history of sexual predators in Washington State whose cases informed Washington State three-strikes legislation).

[12] Although most offenders civilly committed under this law are male, some female offenders have been deemed sexual predators and have been civilly committed. At the time of this writing,

definition of sexually violent predator in Washington State is "any person who has been convicted of or charged with a crime of sexual violence and who suffers from a mental abnormality or personality disorder which makes the person likely to engage in predatory acts of sexual violence if not confined in a secure facility" (RCW 71.09.020). If there is probable cause that the offender meets the legal definition, the offender is civilly committed for an indefinite length of time. An offender may be released from confinement to the community to less restrictive community custody after participating in treatment and when mental health staff determine the offender has made treatment gains that reduce the likelihood of reoffense and risk to public safety. Approximately 16 other states have similar civil commitment laws for sexual predators.

In 1994 the state of Kansas enacted the sexual predator law that was patterned after the Washington State law. Prior to this the state had a civil commitment law pertaining to the mentally ill. Like the Washington SVP law, the Kansas sexual predator law defines sexual predators as "any person who has been convicted or charged with a sexually violent offense and who suffers from a mental abnormality or personality disorder which makes the person likely to engage in the predatory acts of sexual violence" (Kan. Stat. Ann. §59-29a01, 1994, cited in *Kansas v. Hendricks*, 1997). Both the Washington and Kansas laws draw on theory and research regarding the nature of sexual violence and treatment amenability for predatory offenders. According to the Kansas state legislator:

> [A] small but extremely dangerous group of sexually violent predators exist who do not have a mental disease or defect that renders them appropriate for involuntary treatment pursuant to the [general involuntary civil commitment statute]. . . . In contrast to persons appropriate for civil commitment under the [general involuntary civil commitment statute], sexually violent predators generally have antisocial personality features which are unamenable to existing mental illness treatment modalities and those features render them likely to engage in sexually violent behavior. The legislature further finds that sexually violent predators' likelihood of engaging in repeat acts of predatory sexual violence is high. The existing involuntary commitment procedure . . . is inadequate to address the risk these sexually violent predators pose to society. The legislature further finds that the prognosis for rehabilitating sexually violent predators in a prison setting is poor, the treatment needs of this population are very long term and the treatment modalities for this population are very different than the traditional treatment modalities for people appropriate for

---

there is one female offender who has been civilly committed currently serving time at the Washington State Special Commitment Center.

commitment under the [general involuntary civil commitment statute]. (Kan. Stat. Ann. §59-29a01, 1994, cited in *Kansas v. Hendricks*, 1997)

PCL-R assessments of psychopathy are more frequently used in U.S. courts in sexual predator hearings than in any other area of the courts. As a group SVPs display higher levels of psychopathy than offenders generally as measured through the PCL-R, with rapists having significantly higher psychopathy scores than other offender categories (e.g., child molesters) (Vess, Murphey, & Arkowitz, 2004). Jackson and Richards (2007) found that the PCL-R scores in a sample of Washington State SVPs were higher than published norms for male offenders with a mean PCL-R score of 24.12 with a range of 9 to 39 with 27.5 percent exceeding the cutoff for primary psychopathy of ≥ 30 (36 of the 131 for which PCL-R scores were available). The study also found that PCL-R scores were higher for mixed offenders than for child molesters, but there was no difference between mixed offenders and rapists.

The PCL-R is a standard part of the forensic assessment process included among risk assessment tools and has been used in SVP determinations used with increasing frequency (Bernat, Helfgott, & Godlove, 2013; DeMatteo & Edens, 2006; DeMatteo et al., 2014). Walsh and Walsh's (2006) review of U.S. court cases from 1991 to 2004 involving testimony on the PCL-R found that 75 percent of cases involving PCL-R assessments were sexual predator determinations, and in most of these cases (heard in state courts of New Jersey, Illinois, Wisconsin, Florida, California, Minnesota, Ohio, Texas, North Dakota, Washington, the U.S. District Court for the Western District of Wisconsin) PCL-R evidence was used to argue that a defendant posed a high risk of sex offense recidivism. In only 6 percent of cases was evidence presented by the defense that a defendant was a nonpsychopath to argue that a defendant was not likely to reoffend.

Psychopathy and expression of remorse can potentially impact on sentence length. Research on the influence of remorse on sentencing and parole recommendations for sexual assault cases has found that jurors give longer sentences to defendants who do not show remorse (McKelvie, 2013). Testimony on psychopathy has been used as an aggravating factor to support indeterminate sentences in Canada (Lloyd, Clark, & Forth, 2010), in the United Kingdom to civilly detain dangerous offenders, and in the United States to civilly commit sexually violent predators. In the United Kingdom between 1991 and 2003 legislation was enacted to make it easier to preventatively detain dangerous offenders indefinitely. In 2001 the dangerous offenders with severe personality disorders (DSPD) program was launched, inspired by a similar system in the Netherlands rooted in the "Psychopath Act" that was introduced in 1928. The DSPD program and the Dutch program upon which it is based makes it possible to civilly detain offenders beyond their prison sentence if they have a mental disorder that is linked to their offense and are determined to be a high risk of reoffending (de Boer, Whyte, & Maden, 2008).

However, recent research has questioned the role and reliability of expert testimony on the PCL-R and other actuarial tools in civil commitment SVP evaluations. Issues have been raised regarding the use of testimony on high PCL-R scores as a blanket red flag indicative of dangerousness, low reliability across experts, and discordance between the conceptual and theoretical knowledge about the instrumental nature of psychopathy and the ways in which it is used in the courts to prove lack of volitional control to justify civil commitment. Bernat, Helfgott, and Godlove (2013) found that expert testimony on actuarial instruments to predict dangerousness including the PCL-R have been used in the appellate courts to uphold decisions in the name of public safety even in cases where clinical judgment concludes low risk. DeMatteo et al. (2014) examined 214 SVP civil commitment trial cases and found low reliability of scores across cases and significant differences in the scores reported by prosecution and defense witnesses. The study found that the average PCL-R score reported by prosecution experts was significantly higher than the average PCL-R score reported by defense experts with more than 50 percent of cases scoring above 30 reported by prosecution experts, while defense experts reported only 10 percent scoring above 30. The authors conclude that the use of the PCL-R in SVP cases as an indicator of impaired volitional control is "ironic, if not downright contradictory" and "raises concerns about the ability of mental health professionals to differentiate between impaired volition and poor decisions" (DeMatteo et al., 2014, p. 253).

In the landmark case *Furman v. Georgia* (1972) the U.S. Supreme Court ordered a moratorium on capital punishment in America, ruling that, as applied, the practice violated the Eighth Amendment protection against cruel and unusual punishment and the equal protection clause of the Fourteenth Amendment. In the subsequent case *Gregg v. Georgia* (1976), the Supreme Court ruled that guided discretion schemes that weighed mitigating and aggravating factors in arguments regarding whether or not the death penalty should be imposed sufficiently minimized the arbitrary sentencing practices identified in *Furman*. The federal system and most state statutes have multiple mitigating and aggravating factors that can be considered such as a defendant's impaired ability to conform to the requirements of the law (mitigating) or substantial threat of future dangerousness (aggravating). Nearly all states and the federal system include future dangerousness as an aggravating factor, and it has played a substantial role in post-Furman executions (Cunningham, Reidy, & Sorensen, 2008; Luna, 2013).

The nature of psychopathy lends itself to prosecutorial arguments for the sentence of death. In particular, "the attribute of remorse plays a pivotal role in portraying the offender as deserving of death or worthy of life" (Weisman, 2008, p. 189). Given the extreme nature of death penalty cases and the crimes they involve, there is a long history of capital cases that have involved testimony on psychopathy and antisocial personality disorder since the door to future dangerousness testimony was opened in *Barefoot v. Estelle* (1983), which itself involved psychiatric testimony that Thomas Barefoot was a severe and dangerous "criminal sociopath." Theoretically, as is the case in other areas of sentencing,

> psychopathy could serve as mitigation at sentencing based on an offender's diminished capacity for rational decision-making. But the disorder might also offer good reason to increase punishment, given the high rate of recidivism among psychopaths and lack of effective treatment. Psychopathy thus provides a near perfect example of the perpetual conflict between consequentialist and nonconsequentialist theories of punishment. The precise attributes that a retributist might point to as a justification for a reduced sentence—the long-term cognitive and affective deficits of the psychopath—may offer the utilitarian a good reason for enhanced punishment. The issue epitomizes the more general clash among punishment rationales, the disagreement among scholars, and the theoretical uncertainty in sentencing schemes across the nation. (Luna, 2013, p. 376)

However, as was the case in *Barefoot* where testimony on the defendant led to a one-hour deliberation that resulted in a sentence of death for Thomas Barefoot, psychopathy has primarily been introduced as an aggravating factor in capital sentencing cases.

The extent to which expert testimony on psychopathy has been introduced in capital sentencing has spurred considerable research attention in recent years. Edens and Cox (2012, p. 247) found that in virtually every capital case where any mental health evidence was presented in a study surveying 41 practitioners attending a legal seminar, evidence pertaining to APD and psychopathy was presented and was described as having a "considerable" or "extensive" (p. 247) impact on the outcome of cases by the majority of respondents. Edens, Guy, and Fernandez (2003) found that psychopathy testimony appears to cause jurors to disregard important mitigating factors in mock death penalty cases. Jurors are most persuaded for death by evidence of future dangerousness when that evidence is couched in terms of psychopathy, while defendants who are perceived as suffering and/or experiencing traumatic life events that are out of their control are more likely to receive a life sentence and perceptions of future dangerousness and are also closely associated with perceptions of remorse (Sandys, Pruss, & Walsh, 2009).

Research findings on studies of mock jurors have raised questions regarding the implications of PCL-R testimony in death penalty cases. From 1991 to 2004 PCL-R testimony was introduced in four death penalty sentencing cases in federal courts to argue that the defendant was likely to commit future violence in prison and thus should receive the death penalty. In one of these cases (U.S. District Court for the Northern District of Indiana) the court held that the admission of the defendant's PCL-R score was improper based on research that was critical of its use to predict dangerousness in capital sentencing proceedings (Walsh & Walsh, 2006). Furthermore, Edens et al. (2005) found that only 5 percent of capital defendants predicted by experts to constitute a threat to society committed subsequent acts of violence and argued that prosecution experts in capital cases draw conclusions that go beyond what is empirically defensible. Specifically, prediction measures cannot predict with accuracy post-conviction prison misconduct that would warrant a death sentence rather the LWOP. Critics continue to take issue with the accuracy of the PCL-R and the weight the courts have given to expert testimony on psychopathy in capital cases, in particular with respect to the ability of the PCL-R to predict institutional violence (Lee, 2007) and predictive accuracy in general assertions of future dangerousness (Cunningham, Reidy, & Sorensen, 2008), which is what is generally at issue when making the determination between LWOP and the death sentence.

The controversy over the use of psychopathy in the courts is ongoing. The derogatory nature of the psychopathic label and the associated stigma and extreme implications of the diagnosis raise numerous ethical and philosophical issues. Questions remain regarding the relevance of the construct to particular judicial questions. The research that has uncovered the potential for the psychopathic label to increase dangerousness ratings and the identification of serious misuses in court (DeMatteo & Edens, 2006; Edens, 2001; Lloyd, Clark, & Forth, 2010; Walsh & Walsh, 2006) raise serious due process issues that are only beginning to be examined. Furthermore, recent biological research on psychopathy (e.g., Glenn & Raine, 2014; Kiehl, 2014) is increasing the divide regarding its use as an aggravating or mitigating factor in court decision making (Cunningham, Reidy, & Sorensen, 2008; Lee, 2007; Luna, 2013) further highlighting the need for more empirical research and discourse on the implications of testimony on psychopathy in the courts in particular in capital sentencing where the potential for misuse of future dangerousness testimony has irreparable consequences.

Corrections

Psychopathy is of particular relevance in correctional management, treatment, and release decisions because of the link between psychopathy and predatory aggression and violence, the dangers that psychopaths present to staff and other inmates, and the widespread belief that psychopaths are difficult if not impossible to treat. Psychopathy is associated with violent disciplinary infractions and institutional violence (Edens, Poythress, Lilienfeld, & Patrick, 2008; Forth, Hart, & Hare, 1990; Guy, Edens, Anthony, &

Douglas, 2005). Psychopaths are "responsible for crime far out of proportion to their numbers" and represent approximately 20 percent of prison populations (Hare, 1993, p. 87). Psychopaths are able to present themselves in a highly positive light, which makes it difficult for correctional authorities to identify psychopathic offenders who are a potential threat to institutional safety and security. Psychopaths are more likely to escape from prison, have a higher number of institutional infractions, and have unique treatment needs and low treatment, all of which have implications for correctional decision making.

Correctional Classification, Institutional Management, and Treatment

Before publication and widespread acceptance of the PCL-R, lack of consensus in terminology and overlapping constructs of sociopathy, antisocial personality disorder, and psychopathy resulted in one-size-fits-all approaches in offender classification, treatment, and management in correctional contexts, making it difficult to evaluate the effectiveness of therapeutic approaches in prison treatment. Martinson's (1974) article "What Works? Questions and Answers about Prison Reform," well known in the criminal justice field as "The Martinson Report" and the single publication most associated with the demise of correctional rehabilitation era,[13] found that correctional treatment was generally ineffective. In the years since its publication, a large body of research has accumulated replacing "nothing works" with an "evidence-based corrections" paradigm emphasizing empirically correctional initiatives firmly grounded in science, methodological rigor, and specific attention to what works and what doesn't (Cullen & Gendreau, 2001; Farrington, Petrosino, & Welsh, 2001; Gendreau, 1996; Sherman et al., 1997).

Sophisticated meta-analyses now show that when highly structured cognitive-behavioral correctional interventions target criminogenic needs and offender risk, and are delivered with attention to the relationship between staff and offenders and individual offender differences, treatment is effective with many offenders in a range of contexts (Andrews & Bonta, 2006; Andrews & Dowden, 2006; Cullen & Gendreau, 2001; Dowden & Andrews, 2004; Dowden, Antonowicz, & Andrews, 2003; Gendreau, Cullen, & Bonta, 1994;

---

[13] Martinson was a coinvestigator on a study that reviewed findings of 230 correctional treatment studies (Lipton, Martinson, & Wilks, 1975). The Lipton et al. study actually revealed that correctional treatment does work for some offenders under some conditions; however, liberal and conservative politicians took hold of the findings to argue against rehabilitation (Andrews & Bonta, 2003) with liberals contending that treatment was infringing on the rights of offenders and conservatives arguing that rehabilitation was a waste of resources and too soft on crime. In 1979, a year before Martinson died, he recanted the "nothing works" conclusion, restating the findings stating that some treatment programs do show an effect on recidivism (Martinson, 1979).

Gendreau, Little, & Goggin, 1996; Gendreau & Ross, 1987; Phipps, Korinek, Aos, & Lieb, 1999; Serin & Kennedy, 1997) and that identification of risk factors can operate as a correctional classification, programming, and management tool reducing the risk for and incidence of institutional violence (Belfrage, Fransson, & Strand, 2004; Clements, 1996). Gains in what is known about treatment effectiveness have been largely the result of understanding that all offenders are not alike (including greater awareness of the distinctions between psychopathic and nonpsychopathic offenders) and that treatment interventions have to target offender risk, need, and responsivity (Andrews & Bonta, 2006). Understanding the unique characteristics of offender types has important implications for correctional supervision and treatment. For example, spouse abusers include heterogeneous subtypes whose risk characteristics need to be differentially targeted in treatment (Burgess et al., 2001; Dixon & Browne, 2003), and child molesters have different treatment needs than sadistic rapists (Prentky, 2003; Prentky, Janus, & Seto, 2003).

The empirical link between psychopathy and institutional misconduct, lack of amenability in treatment, and general and violent recidivism has implications for distinguishing psychopathic offenders within correctional populations. Treatment strategies that seek to develop empathy in offenders are not likely to be effective with offenders who score high on measures of psychopathic traits (Thornton & Blud, 2007), and the lack of remorse of the psychopath presents significant countertransference issues in treatment (Huffman, 2013a, 2013b). Furthermore, research suggests that effective interventions for different types of offenders who have psychopathic traits differ in terms of treatment efficacy. Psychopathic offenders present unique correctional management concerns. For example, treatment approaches for narcissistic stalkers differ from those that would be effective with stalkers with delusional disorders (Kamphuis & Emmelkamp, 2005). Mentally ill, psychopathic, and sadistic sex offenders are not deterred by increased surveillance and monitoring; however, with specialized supervision programs they are better able to be managed in correctional contexts to detect new sex offenses when they occur to identify which offenders may be best placed in custodial settings (Stalans, 2004).

In 2005 Wong and Hare published *Guidelines for a Psychopathy Treatment Program* offering guidelines for a treatment delivery model for psychopaths. The publication synthesizes the important work done over the past three decades on "what works" in correctional rehabilitation and accumulated research on the assessment, treatment, and management of psychopaths. The recommendations for a psychopathy treatment are to utilize the risk-need-responsivity model as the foundation for a treatment program while taking into account the unique cognitive and personality characteristics of psychopaths as responsivity factors that must be addressed through program delivery, the risk for violence that must be addressed through management that preserves program integrity, and identification of criminogenic factors unique to psychopathy as treatment targets. According to the authors:

> The clinical lore that treatment of psychopaths is doomed to fail or that treatment can make psychopaths worse is based on traditional treatment programs that are not suitable for these individuals. An appropriately designed and implemented treatment program for institutionalized psychopaths has yet to be implemented. Violence and antisocial behaviors are the primary reasons for incarcerating or legally detaining psychopaths. The focus of their treatment should be to reduce the risk of violent and antisocial behaviors rather than to modify their core personality features. Treatment of psychopaths can be considered a special case of general correctional treatment. (Wong & Hare, 2005, p. 55)

The authors recommend the transtheoretical model for change to conceptualize and measure treatment readiness through a three-phase treatment delivery model: (1) looking in the mirror, (2) breaking the cycle, and (3) preventing relapse. This model informs staff about what needs to be done at points throughout the treatment delivery process using practices that have been implemented and tested in offender treatment programs with high-risk, high-need offender groups. While the authors acknowledge that there is currently no known successful treatment for psychopaths, this model is "a small step in the right direction, but there is still a long way to go in the development and evaluation of effective programs for the treatment of psychopaths" (Wong & Hare, 2005, p. 55).

One of the most important areas of theory and research on criminal behavior with implications for treatment has been the bimodal classification of aggression into predatory and affective categories. Many researchers and theorists have noted the importance of distinguishing between predatory and affective motivations for criminal behavior with important implications for treatment (Geen & Donnerstein, 1998; McEllistrem, 2004; Meloy, 1988). Raine et al.'s (1998) findings that affective murderers lack prefrontal control over emotion regulation and aggressive impulses while predatory murderers have good prefrontal functioning and Woodworth and Porter's (2002) research linking psychopathy and predatory aggression are examples of research highlighting the need for different treatment strategies for predatory versus affectively motivated offenders. A common application of the bimodal classification of aggression to treatment are anger management programs that target offenders who have high anger and low self-control and that targeting anger reduces recidivism in impulsively aggressive offenders (Wang & Diamond, 1999). Offenders who are instrumental, predatory, and/or psychopathic show diminished success after receiving anger management treatment because violent behavior committed by these offenders is generally not emotionally reactive. On the other hand, violent offenders who are low in anger control and high in anger show the greatest gains from anger management programs (Howells et al., 2002). Thus research aggression and the emotional experience of psychopaths (e.g., Porter & Woodworth, 2006; Steuerwald & Kosson, 2000) are a critical piece in determining appropriate treatment interventions.

Offenders who are more psychopathic are less amenable to treatment and present special challenges in interpersonal interactions with correctional staff charged with treatment and management. Meloy (1988) suggests that there needs to be clear role clarification with a distinction between clinical evaluation and treatment, that for treatment purposes psychopathy should be a conceptualized process along a hypothetical continuum and that it is important to acknowledge severity of the disturbance with potential implications for a decision not to treat. Lloyd, Clark, and Forth (2010, p. 334) suggest that experts may implicitly use psychopathy ratings as a measure of treatment amenability and may influence treatment outcomes by suggesting a clear relation between psychopathy and untreatability that may trigger a more intense supervision approach and less inclination to treat even in situations where there may be some benefit (e.g., in the case of younger offenders) (Vidal & Skeem, 2007). Research on the interpersonal markers of high-level and potentially dangerous psychopaths can be used to aid decisions about treatment amenability and risk to correctional staff in the treatment and management of psychopaths (Helfgott, 2004; Kosson, Gacono, & Bodholdt, 2000). Given the level of severity of personality disorder in offenders who score high on measures of psychopathy, there is potential for these individuals to be screened out of treatment programs as a result of low treatment amenability, limited resources for treatment in most correctional settings, and dangers and difficulties presented for correctional staff and other offenders in treatment program delivery. However, advances in knowledge and research on psychopaths coupled with the accumulated knowledge on what works in correctional treatment offer potential for programs that specifically target the risk-need-responsivity features that are unique to psychopathic offenders.

Psychopathy as a Predictor of Violent Recidivism and Dangerousness in Parole and Release Decisions and in Community Supervision of Offenders

Forensic risk assessment tools have been increasingly used to predict dangerousness at all stages of the criminal justice process (Scott & Resnick, 2006). Nowhere is forensic assessment of risk more pronounced than in parole and release decisions. The strong empirical relationship between psychopathy and general and violent recidivism has had broad implications for the use of the construct of psychopathy in parole and release decisions:

> Most of the specialized risk instruments do what they were designed to do, which is to assess risk for recidivism. Evidence for their validity is derived almost exclusively from recidivism research. The PCL-R, on the other hand, measures a construct with important and far-reaching theoretical and practical implications for the criminal justice system; its utility and explanatory power extend well beyond the assessment of risk. (Hemphill & Hare, 2004, p. 206)

The PCL-R was not developed as a risk assessment tool. However, it has come to be known as one of the single best predictors of general and violent recidivism and as a result has been used in conjunction with risk assessment tools and forensic evaluations to predict dangerousness and risk in the parole and release process (Guy, Packer, Kusaj, & Douglas, 2015). The PCL-R assesses the clinical construct of psychopathy, while risk assessment instruments include a range of risk factors (often both static and dynamic) that provide a comprehensive offender risk/needs assessment. The construct of psychopathy has been determined to be important as the single disorder most predictive of recidivism, and the PCL-R is included in risk assessment instruments including the Historical, Clinical, Risk-20 (HCR-20), Level of Service Inventory–Revised (LSI-R), and subsequent Level of Service/Case Management Inventory (LC/CMI), the Violence Risk Appraisal Guide (VRAG), and in forensic evaluations of risk.

Research is just beginning to examine the extent to which psychopathy and the PCL-R are being used in parole and release decisions. Walsh and Walsh (2006) identified five parole determination cases in the United States where PCL-R evidence was used in the U.S. District Court for the District of Oregon and one in New Jersey state court from 1991 to 2004. All five of these cases used PCL-R testimony to argue that the parolee was likely to reoffend as a result of assessed psychopathy level. In a study of parole suitability decisions in California for a sample of 5,187 offenders indeterminately sentenced to life, Guy, Packer, Kusaj, and Douglas (2015) found that when the PCL-R is used in conjunction with the HCR-20 and LC/CMI PCL-R, scores had little influence on parole suitability decisions beyond the HCR-20 and LS/CMI. The authors, however, note the content overlap between the HCR-20 and the LS/CMI:

> [I]nterpreting the contribution of the PCL-R to parole board decisions is confounded by the fact that analyses of the HCR-20 Historical scale included item H7 (Psychopathy), our results suggest that the PCL-R had a

> negligible impact on BPH decisions compared with other risk indices. There is substantial overlap between constructs represented on the PCL-R and HCR-20 (and to a lesser extent, the LS/CMI) such as impulsivity, instability, hostility, substance use problems, and so forth. Therefore, we interpret our findings regarding the apparent smaller contribution of the PCL-R to parole suitability decisions to be reflective of the fact that important constructs tapped by the PCL-R likely would have been considered via assessment using the HCR-20.

These findings suggest that further research is needed to determine the ways in which the PCL-R is being used in parole and release decisions, to further investigate the content overlap between forensic tools to predict dangerousness, and to identify the role and utility of psychopathy in relation to other risk factors predictive of future violence.

Researchers are just beginning to unravel the potential role of psychopathy used in conjunction with risk/needs assessment tools to provide information regarding risk among specific offender types and subtypes. The interaction between psychopathy and other risk factors such as sexual deviance is a robust predictor of great significance (Hemphill & Hare, 2004). For example, psychopathic child molesters who have a specified target type may be at a particularly high risk for reoffense given the combination of their callous nature, vulnerable target type, and lengthy offense history (Porter, Brinke, & Wilson, 2009). Research examining the role of psychopathy in conjunction with risk assessment instruments has particular implications for utilizing the psychopathy construct in assessing risk for specific criminal types and subtypes.

Research on psychopathy also has important implications for training parole board members and correctional professionals charged with release decisions. Häkkänen-Nyholm and Hare (2009) found that psychopathic offenders engage in impression management. Psychopaths have the ability to make a good impression to parole boards, and parole board members need to be alert to the superficial presentation that often can lead to a decision to release that could potentially result in a false negative decision error (e.g., predicting an offender will not reoffend who ends up reoffending). In a study of male Canadian federal offenders, Porter, Brinke, and Wilson (2009) found that offenders with high levels of psychopathy were 2.5 times more likely to be granted conditional release than nonpsychopathic offenders. The authors concluded that offenders with high levels of psychopathy are more proficient at persuading parole boards to release them and recommend specialized training for correctional professionals in dealing with psychopathic offenders.

Knowledge about psychopathy also has important implications for community supervision of offenders. In one of the first studies of its kind, Blumenthal, Craissati, and Minchin (2009) examined high-risk personality-disordered offenders in a community supervision context in a hostel in England and Wales. The PCL-R was completed for 76 men in the study, with 17 scoring below 12, 40 between 12 and 24, and 19 scoring 25 or higher. PCL-R scores were the most useful tool in predicting overall failure with only one-third of the psychopathic group succeeding with increased failure among those with sexual and violent convictions. In addition to the high recidivism of psychopathic offenders on community supervision, the authors found that staff members were more likely to make negative comments in psychopathic residents' files. Thus, in addition to psychopathy increasing offender risk, staff countertransference responses to psychopathic residents appeared to have a negative effect in terms of the way in which staff viewed residents. This suggests that psychopathy may play a role in responsivity in addition to risk and that staff training in recognizing and managing countertransference responses to negative affect is critical in working with psychopaths in community corrections contexts (Blumenthal, Craissati, & Minchin, 2009).

Tools exist to assist correctional staff who work with psychopathic offenders. For example, in addition to assessment of offenders using the PCL-R, researchers have suggested that additional tools may be helpful to determine the level of danger present in interactions with offenders through interpersonal cues and language used by offenders. For example, Kosson, Gacono, and Bodholdt (2000) offer the Interpersonal Measure of Psychopathy (IM-P) as a tool that can be used to supplement the PCL-R to evaluate potential dangerous interpersonal situations that may potentially confront staff when they are working with psychopathic offenders. Furthermore, Helfgott (2004) suggests that verbalizations and written narratives of psychopathic offenders and identification of primitive defenses in the language used by offenders can be used as concrete information to score the IM-P items and can be considered red flags for staff who must make on-the-spot judgments about personal safety when working with dangerous offenders. These tools offer qualitative information to supplement actuarial predictors of dangerousness that may be an aid to correctional staff in having to make decisions about who among the offenders they are working with may require additional precautions and specialized management and treatment tactics and interactions.

The implications of psychopathy for corrections, release decisions, and community supervision of offenders are profound given the association between high levels of psychopathy and institutional conduct and general and violent recidivism. Understanding the level of psychopathy in conjunction with offender risk, need, and responsivity offers correctional professionals greater knowledge of who they are dealing with for correctional management, treatment decisions with direct implication for security and custody decisions, specialized treatment and staff training, and release decisions and community supervision plans.

Juvenile Justice

The notion of the psychopathic child has long been recognized in media and popular culture. In 1956 the film *The Bad Seed* (LeRoy, 1956)[14] featured pigtailed eight-year-old Rhoda Penmark who murdered her schoolmate Claude Daigle for the penmanship medal she believed she deserved. Little Rhoda Penmark could put Hannibal Lecter to shame for her ability to charm and manipulate and murder without remorse. Almost 40 years later in the 1993 film *The Good Son*, Page and Ruben (Producers) and Ruben (Director) (1993), Macaulay Culkin played Henry Evans, a young boy who dropped "Mr. Highway" manikin onto freeway traffic as a fun gag, causing a multiple car traffic accident while his cousin watched in horror. And in 2011, the film *We Need to Talk about Kevin*—Fox, Roeg, and Solerno (Producers) and Ramsey (Director) (2011)—depicted "Kevin," a little boy who delighted in engaging in callous and remorseless acts toward his mother that ultimately culminated in a gruesome bow and arrow mass murder of his father and sister followed by a mass murder at his high school.

Beyond these fictional pop cultural depictions of psychopathic children, it wasn't until the mid-1990s that researchers began to direct attention to psychopathy in youth. This lack of attention to psychopathy in childhood is surprising given findings on the biological roots of psychopathy (Blair, Mitchell, & Blair, 2005; Blair, 2013; Glenn & Raine, 2014; Raine, 2013), its developmental origins (Meloy, 1998), and the historical depictions of the psychopathic child in film and popular culture. The notion of the child psychopath has long been acknowledged in discussions of the early childhood origins of the condition; however, few scholars have focused on the child psychopath to venture into empirical examination of the subject.

In 1996 Donald Lynam coined the term "fledgling psychopath" in his landmark article "Early Identification of Chronic Offenders: Who Is the Fledgling Psychopath?" Lynam identified a subpopulation of children with symptoms of hyperactivity, impulsivity, and attention problems with concurrent conduct problems that closely resemble psychopathic adults (Lynam, 1996, 1998). Lynam's work questioned the early stability of psychopathy, suggesting that the stability of the disorder in adulthood is the result of inadequate early identification and intervention.

Childhood disorders with features associated with the construct of psychopathy such as lack of attachment, affect, remorse, callous-unemotional

---

[14] A remake of this film premiered on September 9, 2018 on the Lifetime Channel (Greene, J., Kahn, H. [Producers] & Lowe, R. [Director] [2018]. *The Bad Seed* [Motion Picture]. USA: Front Street Pictures). The remake of the Bad Seed features Patty McCormack, the actress who was nominated for an Oscar for playing Rhoda Penmark in the original 1956 film. In the remake, McCormack plays a psychiatrist who treats the young girl (named Emma in the remake).

traits, and early behavioral problems have been examined to inform early identification of psychopathy and potential interventions to alter its developmental pathway. Researchers have examined the relationship between childhood disorders such as attention-deficit/hyperactivity disorder, conduct disorder, oppositional defiant disorder, autism, and alexithymia, and other disorders with attention to comorbidity, features that involve impaired empathy, and homogeneous features that distinguish a subset of children who may be at risk for adult psychopathy. Literature on the childhood predictors, risk factors, and antecedents of psychopathy continues to build (Fontaine et al., 2011; Hughes, Gacono, Tansy, & Shaffer, 2013; Ullrich & Marneros, 2007).

Childhood Antecedents to Psychopathy

Researchers, clinicians, and criminal justice practitioners have been hesitant to apply the term "psychopath" to children and youth. However, research conducted over the past 20 years provides answers regarding the early childhood precursors, diagnoses, and developmental pathway of psychopathy. Knowledge of the early childhood precursors, the diagnostic differentiation between children who are identified as having these precursors and children who do not, and the developmental pathway to psychopathy offers information with which to potentially alter the development of psychopathy in adulthood.

Childhood diagnostic categories in the DSM that have historically been associated with psychopathy in adulthood include DSM disruptive disorders—conduct disorder (CD) and oppositional defiant disorder (ODD) and attentional disorders—attention-deficit/hyperactivity disorder (ADHD). Conduct disorder in particular has been most commonly considered the early childhood precursor to antisocial personality disorder (APD) and psychopathy. However, like APD, the diagnostic classification category of conduct disorder is heterogeneous with respect to the developmental pathway to psychopathy. Researchers have examined features of conduct-disordered children with attention to age of onset (childhood v. adolescence, socialization (socialized or not), aggression (low/high levels of aggression), social behavior (solitary or group), and comorbidities (CD + ADHD). Increasingly, researchers have focused on a severe subgroup within these diagnoses called the "psychopathic conduct cluster" of severely conduct-disordered children who display callous and unemotional traits (CUs). These early onset, undersocialized, aggressive, solitary, CD + ADHD children with CU traits represent a homogeneous subgroup of children more prone to develop adult psychopathy (Frick, Barry, & Bodin, 2000; Salekin, 2006).

Fledgling psychopaths are typically diagnosed with conduct disorder, oppositional defiant disorder, and attention-deficit/hyperactivity disorder, or some combination of these three DSM diagnoses, and the diagnosis of these three co-occurring disorders is considered to carry a more severe risk profile for antisociality and dangerousness (DeLisi et al., 2013). Although features such as callousness, lack of remorse, and unemotionality have been theorized to characterize the fledgling psychopath, recent research has found that impulsivity and thrill seeking are the strongest variables in differentiating delinquency and violent delinquency. The features that distinguish the fledgling psychopath suggest that there may be differential manifestation of psychopathy related to particular characteristics.

Assessment of Psychopathy in Youth

In 1997 Lynam developed the Childhood Psychopathy Scale (Lynam, 1997), and other instruments followed including the Antisocial Process Screening Device (Frick & Hare, 2002) and the *Psychopathy Checklist: Youth Version* (PCL:YV) (Forth, Kosson, & Hare, 2003) providing a means of assessing psychopathy in youth ages 12–18. However, recent research has questioned the stability of psychopathy scores in adolescents versus adults given the changes in personality and identity formation in adolescence (Cauffman, Skeem, Dmitrieva, & Cavanaugh, 2016).

Implications for Juvenile Justice

Walsh and Walsh (2006) identified one case from 1991 to 2004 (U.S. District Court for the Southern District of New York) where a juvenile was transferred to adult court based on expert testimony on his PCL-R score and inferred dangerousness. Boccaccini, Murrie, Clark, and Cornell (2008) found that juvenile probation officers have decision-making and supervision approaches that are affected by a youth's psychopathic traits (Vidal & Skeem, 2007). In a study of judicial perceptions and recommendations in response to a hypothetical case, Jones and Cauffman (2008) found that when judges were presented with cases in which juveniles were labeled as psychopaths or ascribed psychopathic traits, they were more likely to perceive the juveniles as dangerous, not amenable to treatment, and recommend more restrictive placement.

Based on these and other findings, it is clear that labeling a child a psychopath has significant and potentially severe implications (Flexon, 2018). In a special issue on juvenile psychopathy, Petrila and Skeem (2003) caution:

> Application of the label "psychopath" to youth could do significant harm, particularly given that many of the adolescents to whom the label might be applied are already involved in juvenile proceedings. The label may drive decision making in the legal setting in a punitive direction. Moreover, its presence in legal and medical records that will follow the adolescent may have collateral impact throughout his or her life. (p. 691)

On the other hand, while research still has a long way to go toward identifying a coherent syndrome analogous to psychopathy in adults in children (Johnstone & Cooke, 2004; Petrila & Skeem, 2003), the growing body of research that has identified the psychopathic conduct cluster, callous and unemotional traits, and co-occurring disorders that make up the severe risk profile found in fledgling psychopaths suggest that identification of these features is important to identify and treat children on the pathway to adult psychopathy with hope that this pathway can be altered.

Victimology, Victim's Rights, and Restorative Justice

Very little has been written on the implications of understanding psychopathy for victims and victims services. What has been written has been for the general mass market audience by people who have suffered at the hands of people in their lives they believe are psychopaths (e.g., Brown, 2009; MacKenzie, 2015; Rule, 2013) and self-help books by psychologists to help people who have found themselves in relationships with psychopaths (e.g., Simon, 2010; Simon, 2011). The nature of psychopathy as a condition that enables people to harm others with no remorse has particular implications for victims. Victims who are harmed by psychopaths may have a need for distinct types of services and support as a result of the nature of their victimization. The evidence of lack of amenability to treatment in individuals who are assessed as psychopaths has implications for the use of victim-centered approaches that have been used in many areas in the criminal justice system. Legislation and policy that has been enacted with focus on victim's rights and public safety has passed historically under the guise of protecting individuals from cold-blooded remorseless psychopaths when in practice the legislation disproportionally affects disadvantaged groups and individuals most of whom are not psychopaths. The ways the construct of psychopathy impacts criminal justice and community response to victims is an important and understudied area that needs attention.

Organizations such as *Aftermath: Surviving Psychopathy Foundation, Psychopath Free*, and *Psychopath Victims* have been launched to assist victims of psychopaths.[15] Aftermath was founded by David Kosson and other psychopathy experts including Robert Hare and Paul Babiak to provide a resource and referral service to individuals who are survivors of psychopathy. Aftermath offers referrals, workshops, and support for victims of psychopaths and is the only organization of its kind founded and directed by leading psychopathy experts. Additional support available to victims of psychopaths has been offered by authors who

---

[15] See Aftermath: Surviving Psychopathy: http://aftermath-surviving-psychopathy.org, Psychopath Free: https://www.psychopathfree.com, and Psychopath Victims: http://psychopathvictims.com.

have written on the subject such as the website Psychopath Free, which offers a discussion forum for subscribers, and other sites produced by victims of psychopaths such as Psychopath Victims offer help to those affected by psychopathy.

There are two features of psychopathy that have particular implications for victims—the psychopath's ability to pick up on the vulnerabilities of potential victims and the absence of emotional responsivity psychopaths have in response to expressions of victim pain and suffering. Research has shown that the ability to identify vulnerabilities in potential victims is associated with psychopathy levels. For example, Wheeler, Book, and Costello (2009) found that individuals with psychopathic traits were better able to identify victim vulnerability after viewing short clips of people walking. Young et al. (2012) found that psychopaths are more likely than nonpsychopaths to judge accidents where one person harmed another unintentionally to be morally permissible suggesting failure to appreciate the emotional aspect of harm to victims. Furthermore, the deficits that psychopaths have been found to have in the violence inhibition mechanism (VIM) is particularly important in understanding the nature of the psychopath's victimization (Blair, Mitchell, & Blair, 2005). Individuals with high psychopathic traits have reduced responsiveness to expressions of sadness and fear in others, are not inhibited by expressions of victim pain and suffering, and are particularly impaired when it comes to victim fearful vocal affect (Blair, 2007b; Blair et al., 2002; Blair, Mitchell, & Blair, 2005).

To be victimized by a psychopath can mean being subjected to harm that is remorseless and cruel, and in the case of nonviolent harms, can involve psychological and emotional abuse that can span years or decades. Psychopaths are also more likely to harm others using conning and manipulation, which can have potential impact on victims in terms of self-blaming. For example, power assertive rapists (who are more likely to be psychopaths) are more inclined to attack their victims using a "confidence" ruse, while power reassurance rapists are more likely to use a "blitz" type of attack, and this has implications for victims. The immediate concern of blitz attack victims is generally about feeling safe and dealing with the fear that the rapist may return, whereas confidence rape victims tend to feel guilt and self-blame. Blitz rape victims often have flashbacks, nightmares, sleep disturbance, startle responses, and depression and tend to seek help soon after the attack, while victims of confidence attacks are more likely to delay seeking help (Bowie, Silverman, Kalick, & Edbril, 1990). Understanding offense dynamics and offender type is important in delivering services to victims (Helfgott, 2008). Victims who are harmed by psychopaths, whether it be a crime of rape or other violent crime, or a nonviolent crime or other form of harm, will have particular needs in the aftermath of the harm if the person who victimized them was a psychopath. More research is needed to better understand how best to help victims of psychopaths deal with the distinct forms of harm they experience at the hands of individuals who have high levels of psychopathic traits.

Do Psychopaths Give All Offenders a Bad Rap? Remorse, Accountability, and the Role of Psychopathy in the Victim's Rights Movement

Victims of psychopaths are more likely to be strangers (Williamson, Hare, & Wong, 1987) and to have a victim who is male and not a family member or intimate acquaintance (Häkkänen-Nyholm & Hare, 2009). Their crimes are more likely to be predatory and instrumental (Woodworth & Porter, 2002), their motivations more likely to be power-control rather than anger, and their modus operandi more con rather than blitz form of attack (Bowie, Silverman, Kalick, & Edbril, 1990; Silverman et al., 1988), and individuals who score higher on measures of psychopathy have been found to be more accurate at perceiving victim vulnerability (Wheeler et al., 2009). Psychopaths are less amenable to treatment (Harris & Rice, 2006; Wong & Hare, 2005) and are more at risk for institutional misconduct in correctional facilities (Edens & Campbell, 2007). There is a long history of loose application of the term "psychopath" to offenders in general, and for these reasons, it is important to think about the impact that the notion of psychopathy has on victims, victim services, and legislation and criminal justice policy and practice enacted to protect public safety.

Historical criminal justice legislative activity in the United States such as the discourse around the enactment of three-strikes legislation, civil commitment of sexually violent predators, sex offender registration, and efforts to abolish capital punishment have centered around superpredators, most of whom would score high on measures of psychopathy. For example, the movements to enact three-strikes legislation in Washington, California, the federal system, and around the country featured atrocity tales involving high-profile predatory offenders such as Richard Allen Davis in California and Westley Allan Dodd in Washington State. These sorts of dramatic changes in criminal justice policy, practice, and law can be heavily influenced by the popular view of psychopathy, confusion in the general public about offenders in general and the belief that many or most are psychopaths (Helfgott, 2013c), and can result in draconian laws being passed that ultimately have questionable impact on public safety and result in sentencing disparity and injustice (Moore, 1999).

Retributive versus Restorative Justice for Psychopaths: Would You Want a Psychopath in a Sentencing Circle?

Criminal justice policies and practices that are more restorative rather than retributive in nature have taken hold in many components of the criminal justice system (Braithwaite, 1989, 2002; Daly, 2016; Zehr, 2005, 2015).

Victim-offender mediation (Dhama, 2016; Umbreit, Coats, & Vos, 2004), prison encounter programs that involve victims, citizens, and offenders (Helfgott, Lovell, Lawrence, & Parsonage, 1999; Helfgott, Lovell, & Lawrence, 2000), and sentencing circles (Bazemore & Griffiths, 1997) have become an increasing part of the criminal justice landscape rising in popularity with the rise in the victim's rights movement and community justice alternatives to traditional adversarial approaches to crime and justice (Clear, Hamilton, & Cadora, 2011; Garland, 2002). Beyond traditional restorative justice initiatives, treatment programs are increasingly utilizing empathy-building techniques that sometimes involve role playing and/or the use of victim-impact panels.

Given the nature of psychopathy—the lack of empathy and ability to understand and respond to the experience of victims—restorative justice-oriented initiatives and treatment programs that involve victim-offender encounters and center around developing empathy in the offender and reparation of harm through expression of remorse and accountability may not be appropriate for individuals who possess high levels of psychopathic traits. Research has shown that individuals with levels of psychopathy do not exhibit increased victim empathy the longer they are in treatment. In fact, a study by Roche et al. (2011) that examined psychopathy as a moderating effect in sex offender treatment found that the higher levels of psychopathic personality traits resulted in lower empathy scores the longer they were in treatment. Researchers have cautioned the use of restorative justice-oriented treatment with offenders who have proclivity to engage in manipulation because restorative justice programs center on the needs and interests of victims and reparation of harm. Programs such as mediation, prison encounter programs, and sentencing circles that focus on the goal of healing, reparation, and empathy building have the potential to create new harms for victims if offenders in these programs do not have the capacity for empathy. Belknap and McDonald (2010) caution the use of sentencing circles in intimate partner abuse cases in part because of the opportunity for manipulation and abuse of the community and victims. Other researchers have similarly noted the importance of screening out offenders who are not willing to take responsibility for their crimes and those who have been involved in crimes that involve interpersonal manipulation and boundary crossing such as sex offenses and domestic violence (Helfgott, Lovell, & Lawrence, 2000).

As discussed throughout this chapter, psychopathy has enormous implications for all components of the criminal justice system—policing, the courts, corrections, reentry, and victim services. Remorse is a concept that is central to the administration of justice. Crimes that involve an absence of remorse are particularly brutal, lack of remorse alters modus operandi and signature behaviors, and impacts amenability to treatment. Victims and community members have indicated that expression of remorse by an offender is one of the single most important factors in healing in the aftermath of crime. The psychopath's absence of remorse and the constellation of interpersonal, affective, antisocial, and lifestyle features of psychopathy present unique challenges throughout the criminal justice process with implications for criminal justice practice.

CHAPTER SEVEN

New Research and Emerging Issues

I've done terrible things, that's for sure. And I am a woman and it's very rare for a woman to do the kinds of things I have done.

—Karla Homolka (Transcript of Homolka interview with Radio-Canada reporter Joyce Napier, 2005)

My orchestration of the Day of Retribution is my attempt to do everything, in my power, to destroy everything I cannot have. All of those beautiful girls I've desired so much in my life, but can never have because they despise and loathe me, I will destroy. All of those popular people who live hedonistic lives of pleasure, I will destroy, because they never accepted me as one of them. I will kill them all and make them suffer, just as they have made me suffer. It is only fair.

—Elliot Rodger (*My Twisted World*, p. 137)

[S]ociety's willingness to firmly grasp the neoethical nettles that entangle neurocriminology, and to sensibly and cautiously integrate innovative clinical neuroscience findings with public policy, will be a critical ingredient for our future success in violence prevention.

—Adrian Raine (2013, p. 371)

No remorse. This fundamental feature of psychopathy has enormous implications for theory and research and criminal justice practice. The notion that psychopaths are a remorseless variant of humanity has made its way into the collective psyche—in media and popular culture, in scientific literature, and in criminal justice policy and practice. The scientific understanding of psychopathy has come far. However, complex historical-theoretical issues remain that are necessary to examine and unpack to move forward in ways that advance scientific advances and build on the more nuanced understanding of psychopathy we have today after more than 200 years of scholarly and popular discourse on the subject. Key aspects of our understanding of psychopathy are still left unresolved—psychopathy and gender; issues of criminal responsibility raised by new research findings on biology, neuroanatomy, and psychopathy; and ethical implications of the use of the term "psychopath" in criminal justice policy and practice.

Since 1801 when Pinel first raised the notion of psychopathy with the term "manie sans délire," there has been extraordinary scholarly advancement in the study of psychopathy. From the 1800s discourse around psychopathy and criminal responsibility, to early 1900s discussion of psychodynamic origins in the development of psychopathy, to the late 1900s consensus on the definition and the development of the PCL-R, to the recent increased attention in the 21st century to biological and neuropsychological underpinnings of psychopathy, the use of the psychopathy to predict dangerousness, and understanding of the criminal justice implications of the diagnosis of psychopathy, we have come a long way toward understanding the nature and dynamics of this human condition that has long been a focus of popular intrigue and a conundrum for scholars and practitioners in mental health and criminal justice.

Psychopathy and Gender

It is long and well established in the criminological literature that criminal behavior is more prevalent in males than females. Gender is the strongest predictor of criminality. Being born male is considered among the top five risk factors for committing a serious criminal offense (Office of the Surgeon General, 2001), and across all time periods and cultures, the vast majority of crime is committed by men (Messerschmidt, 1993). Hypermasculinity and hostile masculinity have been associated with violent and sex crime (Abbey et al., 2011; Katz, 2006; Reidy, Shirk, Sloan, & Zeichner, 2009). Psychopathy is a key moderating factor that contributes to sexual aggression given the strong empirical link established between psychopathy, crime, violence, and sexual aggression (Knight & Guay, 2006; Knight & Sims-Knight, 2003) and because psychopathy-related personality traits encourage hostile masculinity.[1]

This gender gap in criminal behavior and the complex interplay of traits and characteristics associated with masculinity, psychopathy, crime, and violence are an ongoing focus of research. What is important moving forward, and noted by a number of authors (e.g., Abbey et al., 2011; Helfgott, 2008; Lobo de la Tierra, 2016; McFarlane, 2013; Naffine, 1997; Ogilvie, 1996), is to deconstruct cultural stereotypes that have made their way into the gendered nature

[1] This research investigates the confluence model that integrates risk factors for sexual aggression and violence into two construct constellations—hostile masculinity and impersonal sexual orientation found to be empirically associated with sexual aggression and violence (Abbey et al., 2011). It has been suggested that psychopathy is an important addition to the confluence model because of the strong empirical relationship between psychopathy and sexual aggression.

of crime and to untangle the roles played by personality factors, gender socialization, and biological sex differences. There is no question that crime and victimization are gendered. Crime and victimization are socioculturally constructed with the view of masculinity as antisocial and threatening (McFarlane, 2013) and femininity as prosocial and helpless (Dirks, Heldman, & Zack, 2015). Gender is a risk factor for criminal behavior and for the social construction of crime and victimization that has direct implications for understanding the role of psychopathy in criminal behavior.

Recent research has examined the complex interaction between biological, social, and cultural variables that may be at play. Violence is one of the central forms of expression traditionally associated with masculinity, while vulnerability is central to notions of femininity (Heber, 2017). This "predator-prey" dichotomy—the notion that males are criminal-predators and females are victim-prey—is central to patriarchal societies and intimately embedded in the interaction between biology and environment in the development of antisocial and criminal behavior (Helfgott, 2008). With this long-standing notion of the male as criminal and female as victim, it is difficult to disentangle stereotyped sociocultural projections, gender socialization, and biological sex differences in understanding the role of gender in criminal behavior.[2]

Psychopathy, Crime, and Masculinity

Psychopathy, like crime, also has long been associated with masculinity. Features of psychopathy such as glibness/superficial charm, grandiosity, need for stimulation, lack of remorse or guilt, stimulation seeking, and shallow affect are aligned with masculine values that promote getting ahead at all costs in contrast with feminine values that have been historically and culturally values that promote the nurturance of social relationships and caretaking of others. Constructions of masculinity and crime in many respects map directly to features of psychopathy. For example, Lobo de la Tierra (2016) examines features of "perilous masculinity"—"the constitution of manhood via avenues full of ominous risk" (p. 379) evident in popular criminological ethnographies.[3] Features of perilous masculinity—constant

[2] This predator-prey dichotomy manifests in strange ways in cultural discourse. For example, Dirks, Heldman, and Zack (2015) discuss a "Mug Shot of the Day" contest in which the mug shots of white female offenders received the most votes and discusses the perception of these women as victims of circumstance rather than criminals who deserve empathy and opportunity for redemption.

[3] Lobo de la Tierra (2016) examines three popular ethnographies—Randol Contrera's *The Stickup Kids*, Alice Goffman's *On the Run*, and Victor Rios's *Punished*. These ethnographies focus on a range of issues in the lives of youth engaged in violent crime including social class, racial/ethnic oppression, marginalization, drugs, and law enforcement and are not stories of individuals who would

scheming, male chauvinism, and savage violence—are closely aligned with features of psychopathy and specific PCL-R items: need for stimulation/proneness to boredom, pathological lying, grandiosity, poor behavioral controls, juvenile delinquency, lack of remorse or guilt, and lack of empathy.

It is difficult to unravel the complex interaction between biological sex differences, gender socialization, psychopathology and personality traits, and antisocial and criminal behavior. For example, Choy et al. (2017) found that the lower heart rate in males is partially responsible for higher rates of crime with the total effect of gender on crime mediated by resting heart rate ranging from 5.4 to 17.1 percent. This antisocial behavior–heart rate is widely viewed as a risk factor for antisocial behavior, reactive and proactive aggression, child psychopathy, and as a biological factor that interacts with social adversity (Raine et al., 2014). So which is the primary risk factor for antisocial and criminal behavior—low resting heart rate attributed to biological sex difference, personality traits (aka psychopathy), or other masculine character traits that are the product of gender role socialization? How are biological sex differences intertwined with developmental pathways to psychopathy and crime?

Researchers have attempted to better understand the confluence of masculinity, hypermasculinity, and hostile masculinity with mental health pathology, psychopathic traits, negative character traits, and criminal behavior. For example, Brown (2016) raises the issue of rapidly changing gender norms and the disorienting (and potentially harmful) conflation of masculine identity and antisocial traits for empathetic, nonviolent boys and men, and asks, "what is excessively masculine about the perceived threat to control, respect, and power?," and how did masculinity come to serve as a proxy for characteristics such as hatred toward women, control, domination, and cruelty when there are gender-neutral constructs such as misogyny and sadism that embody these characteristics? (p. 122). These questions are of central importance in sorting out the relationship between gender, psychopathy, and crime.

There is an extensive discourse on the sex-typed pathways of psychopathy (Ford & Widiger, 1989; Horowitz, 1977; Jackson & Richards, 2007; Lilienfeld et al., 1986; Spalt, 1980; Warner, 1978; Verona & Vitale, 2006). Psychopathy has been associated with hostile masculinity, negative attitudes toward women, impersonal sex, and sexual dominance. Specific psychopathic personality traits are predictive of hostile masculinity with anger predictive of hostility toward women, erratic lifestyle predictive of interpersonal sexual

---

necessarily be forensically assessed as primary psychopaths (given the contexts of their lives, it is more likely they would score as secondary psychopaths on the PCL-R). However, conceptually, the features that characterize perilous masculinity noted in these ethnographies conceptually overlap with features of psychopathy and specific PCL-R items.

behavior and attitudes, and entitlement predictive of sexual dominance and negative attitudes toward women (LeBreton, Baysinger, Abbey, & Jacques-Tiura, 2013).

Theory development and additional research are needed to untangle the relationship between biology and socialization in the gendered development and manifestation of psychopathy. Given the research on the links between masculinity, crime, and psychopathy and the limited research on the ways in which psychopathy develops in girls and women, this area of research is of great importance in the advancement of research on psychopathy and crime. There is a growing body of research suggesting that there are biological differences in the male and female brain (Baron-Cohen, 2003). Women empathize more and men systemize more (Baron-Cohen, 2003; Svedholm-Hakkinen, Ojala, & Lindemann, 2018). With empathy and the absence of remorse the essential feature of psychopathy and the centrality of the construct of psychopathy to crime and criminal justice, the psychopathy-masculinity-crime nexus is a critical area of importance for future research. Questions such as: *How does biological sex influence the development and manifestation of psychopathy? How do sociobiological processes differ across sex and gender to influence the development and manifestation of psychopathy? How is childhood abuse and trauma differentially experienced across gender, and how does this gendered experience influence the development and manifestation of psychopathy? What is the relationship between psychopathy and gender identity and gender expression? Does sexual orientation influence the manifestation of psychopathy?*

The stark omission of research on girls and women in criminology, even more so in the research on female psychopaths, has left substantial gaps in the literature. Psychopathy is now recognized as more prevalent in females than originally thought, and there has been a growing number of studies on the predictive utility of psychopathy as a risk factor for crime and violence; however, theory development and ongoing research are needed. Although it is still believed that the base rate of psychopathy in incarcerated women is less than that of men, with mean PCL-R scores lower for incarcerated women (Beryl, Chou, & Vollm, 2014; Logan & Weizmann-Henelius, 2012), in recent years there has been an increasing number of studies using female samples conducted around the world in an attempt to investigate lines of research that have historically focused solely on male samples. Research on female psychopathy has examined prevalence rates of female psychopaths, gender differences in externalizing traits and the manifestation of psychopathy, the validity and measurement of female psychopathy, and gender differences in the development of psychopathy, and what is needed now are "uniquely female theories of psychopathic and antisocial behavior" (Verona & Vitale, 2006, p. 431).

Researchers from around the world have utilized female samples examining well-established areas of research that have largely focused on men. Some of this research has found that females are similar to males with respect to aspects of psychopathy. For example, abnormalities in emotional processing associated with psychopathy have been found to be the same in both men and women (Sutton, Vitale, & Newman, 2002). For women, like men, the cognitive processes of psychopathy versus antisocial personality disorder are different with psychopaths characterized by low anxiety and callous-emotional traits and antisocial personality disorder characterized by higher rates of anxiety and substance abuse (Anton et al., 2012). Eisenbarth et al. (2012) examined brain activity in response to emotional facial expressions in 28 women in Italy and found evidence of significant cortical reduction activity while processing emotional faces similar to what has been found in male samples. In a study of adolescent girls in Portuguese detention facilities and schools, Pechorro et al. (2014) found that psychopathic trait scores are associated with early onset crime in adolescent girls just as they are in boys.

On the other hand, there have also been findings showing significant differences between males and females with high psychopathic traits. Verona, Bresin, and Patrick (2013) found that female inmates who score high on the PCL-R have diminished startle response in response to victim pictures though adequate response to threatening images suggesting that the deficit for women who possess psychopathic traits may be more in empathy rather than fear. An interesting study by Vitale and Newman (2001) compared findings between male and female psychopaths on response perseveration and found that when female psychopaths are presented with a gambling card game where the odds of winning decrease with every round, male psychopaths persevere (play more rounds and win less money) than nonpsychopaths, but that female psychopaths do not play more cards and lose more money than nonpsychopaths and play fewer cards than male psychopaths. This suggests that response perseveration may not be a core feature of psychopathy in female psychopaths and that tasks such as gambling that have historically been used in studies involving male samples may not be sufficient to elicit psychopathic traits in women and that psychopathic traits may manifest differently in women such as decreased sensation seeking and disinhibition.

A number of authors have suggested special consideration in administering forensic assessment instruments with female populations (Cunliffe, Gacono, Meloy, & Taylor, 2013; Falkenbach, 2008; Verona & Vitale, 2006). The predictive power of the PCL-R is weaker for women (Eisenbarth et al., 2012). Women tend to score lower on the PCL-R than men in self-report and interview-based assessments, in particular on Factor 2 items, and scores are not associated with conduct problems in childhood and aggression in women (Verona & Vitale, 2006, 2018). Differences in assessment scores for women may be the product of differential gender manifestation and gender bias in diagnosis (Falkenbach, 2008; Ford & Widiger, 1989; Forouzan & Cooke, 2005). Gender differences in the manifestation of psychopathy may actually be the result of improper scoring of females and the result of instruments that were originally developed on male samples reflecting antisocial behaviors traditionally seen in males and not females (Strand & Belfrage, 2005). Based on the differential gender manifestation of psychopathy and potential gender bias in diagnosis, researchers have urged extreme caution in evaluating psychopathic traits and in using the PCL-R to predict violence in women and reevaluation of PCL-R items to better reflect female manifestations of these traits (Falkenbach, 2008). Cunliffe, Gacono, Meloy, and Taylor (2013) identified nine PCL-R items that require special consideration in scoring women—glibness/superficial charm, grandiose sense of self-worth, conning/manipulative, callous/lack of empathy, parasitic lifestyle, sexual promiscuity, early behavioral problems, juvenile delinquency, revocation of conditional release, and criminal versatility. Verona and Vitale (2006, 2018) raise similar concerns suggesting that though the PCL-R shows adequate reliability and validity with female populations but that with the skepticism that exists regarding whether or not the PCL-R adequately taps the characteristics that discriminate psychopathic from nonpsychopathic women, that other indicators may be needed that identify uniquely female expressions of antisocial-externalizing tendencies measured through Factor 2 items on the PCL-R—for example, prostitution, intimate partner violence, child abuse and maltreatment, forms of relational aggression, and comorbid psychopathology (e.g., histrionic personality disorder and somatization).

Crime, Aggression, and Sex-Typed Pathways and Diagnoses of Psychopathy

The suggestion that women may score lower on the PCL-R overall, in particular on Factor 2 behavioral items, raises questions regarding the sex-typed behavioral pathway of psychopathy as well as gender bias in clinical assessment and diagnoses. The sex-typed pathway and differential manifestation of psychopathy across gender has been discussed by multiple authors (Anton et al., 2012; Cale & Lilienfeld, 2002; Cunliffe, Gacono, Meloy, & Taylor, 2013; Cunliffe et al., 2016; Flanagan & Blashfield, 2005; Forouzan & Cooke, 2005; Forouzan & Nicholls, 2015; Kreis & Cooke, 2011; Miller, Watts, & Jones, 2011; Rogers, Jordan, & Harrison, 2007; Sevecke, Lehmkuhl, & Krischer, 2009; Strand & Belfrage, 2005; Sutton, Vitale, & Newman, 2002; Verona & Vitale, 2006, 2018; Visser, Pozzebon, Bogaert, & Ashton, 2010; Weizmann-Henelius et al., 2010). Research suggests that male psychopaths engage in more externalizing behaviors, while female psychopaths engage in more internalizing behaviors. Female psychopathy may best resemble secondary psychopathy, while male traits are more associated with primary psychopathy (Sevecke, Lehmkuhl, & Krischer, 2009).

Studies examining the developmental pathway to psychopathy have found differences across gender with respect to the links between psychopathy and childhood trauma and abuse. Women who score high on psychopathic traits are more likely to have been exposed to diverse forms of victimization, including paternal parental abuse and to manifest psychological, cognitive, and behavioral dysfunction in early childhood (Forouzan & Nicholls, 2015). A study conducted in Finland by Weizmann-Henelius et al. (2010) found that in a sample of 102 female and 457 male homicide offenders, childhood victimization increased the risk of psychopathy in both males and females; however, there was a significant relationship between physical abuse and psychopathy in males (but not females) and between sexual abuse and psychopathy in females (but not males) and that the impact of abuse on psychopathy was significantly greater for females in particular with respect to affective and lifestyle traits, suggesting that sexual abuse impacts the ability to experience emotions such as empathy and guilt as well as lifestyle traits such as impulsivity.

Other studies have focused on gender differences in the manifestation of psychopathy and measurement of psychopathic traits through items on the PCL-R (Beryl, Chou, & Vollm, 2014; Chouinard, 2009; Cunliffe, Gacono, Meloy, & Taylor, 2013; Cunliffe et al., 2016; Holm, 2004; Logan, 2011; Miller, Watts, & Jones, 2011; Setoodeh, 2011; Strand & Belfrage, 2005; Verona & Vitale, 2006, 2018; Wahid et al., 2016). Males manifest higher mean levels of psychopathy with certain types of behaviors more associated with high-scoring males versus females. For example, child abuse is more strongly linked to criminality in females, and Factor 2 psychopathy scores are more strongly related to gambling for men, while Factor 2 scores in women are more strongly associated with difficulty in resisting urges (Miller, Watts, & Jones, 2011). Gender differences have also been noted in media depictions of psychopaths with female psychopaths portrayed as lacking empathy in their interpersonal relationships, displaying cruelty and manipulation and relational aggression through intimate relationships with partners, children, family, and friends, while male psychopaths are portrayed as engaging in physical aggression and violence (Chouinard, 2009; Holm, 2004; Logan, 2011; Setoodeh, 2011; Wahid et al., 2016). In a study conducted in Sweden, Strand and Belfrage (2005) found that among those found to be psychopaths using the PCL:SV, women scored higher on measures of deceitfulness and poor behavioral controls, while men scored higher on adolescent and adult antisocial behavior. Specifically, men scored higher on both personality and behavioral measures of psychopathy on superficiality, grandiosity, lack of remorse, lack of empathy, lack of goals, adolescent antisocial behavior, and adult antisocial behavior, while women scored higher in terms of impulsivity and poor behavioral controls. Beryl, Chou, and Vollm (2014) found that women scored lower than men on glibness/superficial charm, grandiose sense of self-worth, and pathological lying, and higher on sexual promiscuity, many short-term martial relationships, and criminal versatility and suggest that women manifest manipulative behavior in the form of flirtation and sexual promiscuity rather than through overt behavioral expressions of aggression such as criminal and antisocial behavior. In a study examining psychopathy in male and female college students, Poy et al. (2013) found that men scored higher on boldness, meanness, and disinhibition, while women scored higher on neuroticism, agreeableness, and conscientiousness. An interesting study conducted by Visser, Pozzebon, Bogaert, and Ashton (2010) found that increased levels of psychopathy are significantly associated with increased sexual partners and having an affair for both men and women, but for men, psychopathy level was associated with high self-rated and peer-rated attractiveness, decreased body shame, and appearance-related anxiety, while for women, psychopathy level was associated with lower self-esteem and increased body shame and was unrelated to self and peer ratings of attractiveness. This research suggests that psychopathy has been an evolutionarily effective mating strategy for men but not for women.

Implications of Gender-Based Models of Aggression and Crime

There are a number of important considerations in making sense of the relationship between gender, psychopathy, and crime. Gender differences in the development, manifestation, and assessment of psychopathy are influenced by a complex interplay of biological sex differences, sex-role socialization, and gender-related bias. There is much research still to be done to explain the gendered nature of psychopathy and crime. First, the traits associated with masculinity, psychopathy, crime, and violence need to be further examined to determine whether or not stereotypes have influenced the confluence of the masculinity-psychopathy-crime construct. Second, the ways in which the manifestation of psychopathy have been influenced by sex-role socialization need further examination. Finally, changing conceptions of gender and sexual identity and cultural gender stereotypes may influence the development, manifestation, and assessment of psychopathy over time. Could it be that with changing conceptions of gender, there will be a narrowing of the gender gap in the manifestation of psychopathy? Should age and culture be taken into consideration when understanding the ways in which the pathway to psychopathy is shaped across gender? How have cultural gender stereotypes made their way into risk assessment instruments and forensic assessment tools such as the PCL-R and clinical evaluation? These and other questions need to be explored in future research to better understand the relationship between gender, psychopathy, crime, and violence.

There are a number of cases that illustrate gender differences in psychopathy in women. Cases such as Diane Downs who shot her three children in 1983, Susan Smith who drowned her two children in 1995, Andrea Yates who drowned her five children in 2001, and other "killer moms"

(Sokmensuer, 2017), Jodi Arias who murdered her husband in 2008, and Karla Homolka who with her husband Paul Bernardo raped, tortured, and murdered three teenage girls in the early 1990s including Homolka's sister have all been depicted as having psychopathic character traits in the popular media. These women exemplify the ways in which psychopathy may manifest in women in terms of aggression and violence directed toward children and family members. Their crimes are examples of extreme forms of relational aggression that need to be examined closely to better understand the ways in which psychopathy develops and manifests in women as well as the ways in which psychopathy and psychopathic traits interact with co-occurring disorders such as borderline personality disorder, postpartum depression, and bipolar disorder to produce criminal behavior. Specific crime categories that are particularly cruel and brutal committed solely by women such as fetal abduction/cesarean kidnapping (Arquette, 2012; Burgess, Baker, & Rabun, 2002; Helfgott, 2008; Porter, 2015; Walters, 2015) also need to be explored to better understand the unique ways in which psychopathy may manifest in females. Cesarean kidnapping case histories show evidence that the individuals who commit these crimes have largely been found to have primitive rather than psychotic personality organization and Cluster B personality disorders whose M.O. involves conning, deception, and elaborate preplanning with the dual motive of bolstering a relationship with a partner and fulfilling a childbearing and delivery fantasy and mothering identity (Burgess, Baker, & Rabun, 2002). The abductors in all 21 cases reported worldwide since 1987 have been women (Porter, 2015). Although the findings on this crime given it is such a low-base-rate criminal behavior have been case study histories, the findings suggesting the personality organization, method, and motive in these cases demonstrate that this crime in particular has something to offer in the way of understanding extreme female manifestation of psychopathy. For individuals who suffer from severe psychopathology with psychopathic traits, sex-role socialization that teaches girls and women that female success involves relationships and motherhood can result in uniquely female fantasy development that results in exclusively female crime that has much to offer in terms of comparison with uniquely male fantasy development and crime (e.g., mass shooting and sexual homicide) and the role psychopathy plays in these traditionally male crimes.

Future research is also needed on women who commit crimes that are traditionally associated with males and masculinity to better understand the role psychopathy plays in these crimes and the ways in which gender stereotypes may influence the discourse around women who commit these crimes and the forensic assessment of psychopathy given the issues scholars have raised regarding changes necessary to the PCL-R and other assessment tools when assessing women. For example, female serial killer Aileen Wuornos engaged in a traditionally male crime (serial murder/sexual homicide[4]) using traditionally male methods (murder by firearm) and has been described as borderline and antisocial personality disordered and psychopathic (Arrigo & Griffin, 2004; Myers, Gooch, & Meloy, 2005; Shipley & Arrigo, 2004). Wuornos was arrested in 1991 for the murders of seven men who solicited prostitution from her during a one-year period when she was 34 years old in 1989–1990. She was sentenced to death and executed in 2002 amid unprecedented media attention before, during, and after her trial, conviction, sentencing, and execution.[5] Myers, Gooch, and Meloy (2005) describe a PCL-R assessment for Wuornos with a score of 32. A score of 30 and above is indicative of primary psychopathy. Wuornos's case presents a notable example of the interaction between biological predisposition, early childhood trauma, environmental conditions and risk factors for criminal behavior, and how the manifestation of psychopathy and its assessment are potentially shaped by gender stereotypes. Myers, Gooch, and Meloy (2005) give Wuornos a score of 32 with high ratings of 1 and 2 on both Factor 1 and Factor 2 items (see Table 7.1).

Although women generally tend to score lower on the PCL-R in particular on Factor 2, Wuornos's rating of 32 is high, placing her in the range of 30 or above, indicative of primary psychopathy. Given Wuornos's history of poverty, early childhood trauma, abuse, and victimization, her case and PCL-R ratings offer opportunity to examine potential gender stereotypes that may influence PCL-R assessment. Wuornos's case was extraordinary in terms of the media attention she received and the ways in which she was viewed in popular culture—by forensic and criminal justice professionals and throughout the criminal justice process. Wuornos's PCL-R rating is consistent with these findings that show that women tend to score higher on promiscuity, criminal versatility, impulsivity, and poor behavioral controls, and lower on glibness/superficial charm and grandiose sense of self-worth.

It is important to think through the ways in which gender stereotypes have potentially made their way into the PCL-R itself and into the case file history of Wuornos, the interviewer subjective perception of her, and ultimately her

[4] The degree to which Aileen Wuornos can be considered a sexual homicide offender is discussed by Myers, Gooch, and Meloy (2005), who note the ambiguity of the evidence and multiple competing hypotheses about the motivation for her crimes. The authors suggest that there is insufficient evidence to label Wuornos a sexual predator or sexual sadist; however, her crimes fit the definition of sexual homicide found in the forensic science literature because they involved intentional killing during which there was sexual activity by the perpetrator.

[5] See *Overkill: The Aileen Wuornos Story*, a made-for-TV movie featuring Jean Smart (Beaudine & Levin, 1992), two documentaries by Nick Broomfield—*Aileen Wuornos: The Selling of a Serial Killer* (Broomfield & Oord, 1992) and *Aileen: Life and Death of a Serial Killer* (Human, Broomfield, & Churchill, 2003), and the Hollywood film *Monster* (Damon et al., 2003) for which Charlize Theron won an Academy Award for Best Actress for playing Wuornos.

Table 7.1 Aileen Wuornos PCL-R Ratings

PCL-R Item	Rating	Factor 1	Factor 2	Interpersonal	Affective	Lifestyle	Antisocial
1. Glibness/superficial charm	1	1		1			
2. Grandiose sense of self-worth	1	1		1			
3. Need for stimulation	2		2			2	
4. Pathological lying	2	2		2			
5. Conning/manipulative	2	2		2			
6. Lack of remorse or guilt	2	2			2		
7. Shallow affect	2	2			2		
8. Callous/lack of empathy	2	2			2		
9. Parasitic lifestyle	2		2			2	
10. Poor behavioral controls	2		2				2
11. Promiscuous sexual behavior	2						

12. Early behavioral problems	1		1				1
13. Lack of realistic, long-term goals	2					2	
14. Impulsivity	2		2			2	
15. Irresponsibility	2		2			2	
16. Failure to accept responsibility	1	1			1		
17. Many short-term marital relationships	1						
18. Juvenile delinquency	1		1				1
19. Revocation of conditional release	0		0				0
20. Criminal versatility	2						2
TOTAL	**32**	**13**	**12**	**6**	**7**	**10**	**6**

Adapted from Myers, Gooch, and Meloy, 2005.

assessment. Myers, Gooch, and Meloy (2005, p. 4) report that Wuornos rated a 2 on the PCL-R Item 9, parasitic lifestyle, because "She worked as a prostitute as needed, spending much of her money on alcohol while her girlfriend worked a regular job to help support them. Although able-bodied, she consistently avoided steady, gainful employment, PCL-R Item 11. Promiscuous sexual behavior because "she had innumerable casual sexual encounters for many years as a prostitute," and PCL-R Item 20, criminal versatility, "based on the broad range of legal charges (≥ 6) she accrued during her life." On PCL-R Item 10, poor behavioral controls, she was rated a 2 because she "had a bad temper as a child, was rebellious as a teenager (e.g., she attacked a friend with a shish-ka-bob after a trivial disagreement), and had multiple adult charges consistent with poor self-control," and PCL-R Item 14, impulsivity, "Based on multiple examples of poor impulse control throughout her life."

Research by feminist criminologists has called attention to the ways in which violence is seen as the polar opposite of femininity and behavior by women that falls outside of traditional gender norm of the feminine good girl is more likely to be sanctioned and come to the attention of law enforcement and has raised questions about the patriarchal lens and laws through which women's bodies and behaviors are controlled (Campbell, 1993; Chesney-Lind, & Jones, 2010; Naffine, 1997; Robinson & Ryder, 2013). Girls growing up in distressed environments and communities reject and resist the dominant gender discourse that dictate that girls are good, peaceful, and nonviolent and are punished harshly for their gender norm violations (Irwin & Adler, 2012). Furthermore, research and discourse on prostitution offer an alternative lens through which to reexamine the assessment of promiscuity on the PCL-R. One view of prostitution contends that prostitution is a form of sexual liberation, expression, and women's agency (Delacoste & Alexander, 1988; Swanson, 2016) and a means to alleviate poverty whereby women use prostitution to escape poverty while simultaneously being dependent on men for social and material survival (Phoenix, 2004). If prostitution is seen as an occupational opportunity for women in disadvantaged financial circumstances in a culture that rewards and values women for their sexuality rather than their accomplishments, is it reasonable to score Wuornos a 2 on PCL-R Item 11, promiscuous sexual behavior, based on her work as a prostitute? If prostitution can be seen as an occupation, is Wuornos's work as a prostitute meaningful basis to score the PCL-R Item 9, parasitic lifestyle?

These and other questions are important to explore to sort out the complex relationship between psychopathy, gender, and crime and the ways in which biological sex differences, sex-role socialization, and gender stereotypes influence the development, manifestation, and assessment of psychopathy. Continued research is critical to better understand Aileen Wuornos (her developmental history, how she was culturally perceived, her forensic assessment, and how all of this ultimately played into her disposition in the criminal justice system) and other female offenders. Future research is needed to sort through the ways in which male-focused criminological theory and assessment of psychopathy and criminogenic risk through instruments that were originally constructed and normed on male criminal populations have impacted the ways in which we understand the relationship between sex, gender, crime, violence, and female psychopathy.

The Biology and Neuroanatomy of Psychopathy: New Research Findings and Implications for the Way We Think about Psychopathy and Criminal Responsibility

The long-held view of the psychopath as a cognitively intact dangerous and aggressive variant of antisocial personality disorder not amenable to treatment and the empirical link between psychopathy and general and violent recidivism has resulted in the use of psychopathy as an aggravating factor in criminal justice decision making. Much of this view is associated with an understanding of psychopathy as a condition that does not render an individual with a high level of psychopathic traits behaviorally helpless and rejection of the positivist view that criminal behavior is determined by biology or personality. In other words, psychopaths, because they are cognitively intact, can make premeditated decisions about when to commit and when not to commit an antisocial or criminal act, understand the difference between right and wrong, and thus should be held accountable for the crimes they commit.

In 1941 Cleckley wrote in *The Mask of Sanity* that the psychopath is "incompetent but not insane" (p. 98)—"socially incompetent in the sense that he cannot carry out a sane plan of life or avoid repeated antisocial acts and other acts seriously damaging to himself" (p. 429). This view of the psychopath as incompetent in terms of not being able to control behavior has historically not taken hold in the criminal justice system where expert testimony on psychopathy has been consistently used as evidence to show premeditation, capacity for reality testing, and is considered an aggravating rather than mitigating factor in sentencing decisions (Edens, 2001; Edens & Cox, 2012; Edens, Petrila, & Kelley, 2018; Lee, 2007; Ling & Raine, 2018; Mowle, Edens, Clark, & Sörman, 2016; Sandys, Pruss, & Walsh, 2009; Verdun-Jones & Butler, 2013). However, the growing biosocial research on psychopathy raises questions as to whether the psychopath's volitional control is in fact a scientific truth and whether neurological evidence will impact juror decision making to view psychopathy as cause for mitigation (Phillips, 2013; Umbach, Berryessa, & Raine, 2015).

After a 70-year ban of biological explanations of crime in many of the social sciences, biosocial criminology is now seen by many leading scholars as the dominant paradigm of the 21st century (Walsh & Wright, 2015a). Although biosocial criminology is still seen by many as a serious threat to the social constructionist and critical criminology paradigm, there has been a resurgence of attention to biological roots and neurobiological factors associated with psychopathy. Much of this work specific to psychopathy has come from the psychological literature (e.g., Blair, Mitchell, & Blair, 2005; Glenn & Raine, 2014; Kiehl, 2014; Raine, 2013); however, there has been increasing attention to biosocial perspectives in the criminological literature as well (Beaver, 2008, 2015; DeLisi, 2015; Rocque, Welsh, & Raine, 2012; Walsh & Beaver, 2009; Walsh & Vaske, 2011). This research represents a significant paradigm shift that raises questions about the legal competence and criminal responsibility of psychopaths.

Almost 50 years ago Hare's (1970) *Psychopathy: Theory and Research* presented empirical findings from experimental psychology on psychopathy, autonomic reactivity, and executive function. Twenty-five years ago, Raine (1993) suggested in *The Psychopathology of Crime* that evidence of the biological, genetic, neurochemical, and psychophysiological roots of criminal behavior offer support to consider crime a clinical disorder. In the years since publication of these seminal works there has been exponential growth in theory and research on the biology of crime and psychopathy, producing findings in areas including genetics, hormones, psychophysiology, and neuropsychology. Although there has historically been much more acceptance of biological theories of crime and psychopathy in the discipline of psychology, which has supported scientific advancement in physiological psychology and neuroscience, criminology/criminal justice is an interdisciplinary discipline that examines crime and its response from sociological, psychological, cultural, and legal perspectives. The interdisciplinary nature of criminology/criminal justice has until relatively recently stalled scientific advancement in biosocial criminology within the discipline. However, in recent years, a large body of research has accumulated showing that assumptions that criminal behavior is devoid of biological influences are demonstrably wrong, that biosocial criminology adds to the field, and that the historical skepticism of biosocial research is the result of a clash between theoretical paradigms with the biosocial theory and research rooted in positivism, empiricism, and reductionism pit against the social constructionist, radical, postmodernist scholarship. Advances in criminology/criminal justice now give way to a disciplinary understanding that biology is intricately intertwined with human agency and human behavior (Walsh & Wright, 2015a, p. 136).

This paradigm shift in criminology/criminal justice coupled with the exponential growth in theory and research in physiological psychology and neuroscience has led to a more sophisticated understanding of the complex interplay between biological mechanisms and environmental influences that shape the development and manifestation of psychopathy and its role in criminal behavior. Research now suggests that approximately half of the variation in psychopathic traits is genetic and half is environmental (Glenn & Raine, 2015). A biosocial model of criminal behavior and violence, which posits that "biological is not the equivalent of innate" (Glenn & Raine, 2015, p. 196), reveals the reflexive relationship between genes and environment, biological and social, that influence cognition, emotion, and executive function to produce mental health issues and psychological disorders and their behavioral manifestations, including antisocial and criminal behavior (Raine, 2013). This integrated, interdisciplinary, dynamic model that recognizes the relationship between hormonal and motivational imbalance (low sensitivity to punishment/high sensitivity reward) and its effect on neuroanatomical structure and function (van Honk & Shutter, 2006) offers support for a compatibilist perspective (Blair, 2007a; Cuypers, 2013; Smilansky, 2007). This perspective offers an alternative to the strict biological determinism that has historically been incompatible with free will models of criminal responsibility and has resulted in exclusion of antisocial personality disorder and psychopathy from defenses that involve diminished capacity and insanity and have in fact viewed psychopathy as an aggravating factor in criminal justice decision making.

Psychopathy, Legal Competence, and Criminal Responsibility

If psychopathy is the outcome of biological predisposition, shaped by environmental forces, and empirical evidence shows that the brains of psychopaths are distinct from the brains of nonpsychopaths rendering afflicted individuals remorseless, without conscience, and unamenable to change, then is it just to consider psychopaths competent and criminally responsible for their criminal antisocial acts?

Theory and research have led to the conclusion that brain deficits in the frontal cortex in the orbitofrontal and ventromedial regions of the frontal lobe, and the temporal cortex, amygdala and hippocampus, corpus callosum, and the striatum are associated with psychopathy (Glenn & Raine, 2014; Kiehl, 2014; Lushing, Gaudet, & Kiehl, 2016; Raine, 2013; Yang & Raine, 2018) and behaviors associated with psychopathy such as response perseveration (Hiatt & Newman, 2006; Newman, Schmitt, & Voss, 1997; Vitale & Newman, 2001; Vitale et al., 2016), deficits in empathy related to externalizing behavior and the violence inhibition mechanism (Blair, 2007b; Blair et al., 1997; Blair et al., 2002; Blair, Mitchell, & Blair, 2005; Blair, Meffert, Hwang, & White, 2018), genetic influences (Waldman, Rhee, LoParo, & Park, 2018), and physiological responses to emotional stimuli (Hare, 1966a, 1968a, 1970, 1982; Wang et al., 2012). This research evidence from experimental psychology and neuroscience has persuaded many legal experts and philosophers to revisit the long-held legal conceptualization of psychopathy as a condition that does not remove criminal responsibility (Godman & Jefferson, 2017).

Although the science on the etiology, development, manifestation, and assessment of psychopathy has advanced considerably and the accumulation of knowledge about the condition is vast and has achieved consensus, decisions about how to legally treat psychopaths and the degree to which they are held criminally responsible are social decisions based on the social will, not science (Ortega-Escobar, Alcázar-Córcoles, Puente-Rodríguez, & Peñaranda-Ramos, 2017). In other words, whether we want to view psychopaths as responsible for their behavior does not depend solely on whether science determines psychopathy to be the product of sociobiological forces beyond the individual's control. Ultimately, the decision regarding whether or not to hold psychopaths criminal responsible is beyond a scientific or legal decision—it is an ethical one (Duff, 2010).

Although psychopaths know the difference between right and wrong and their aggression is predominantly instrumental, mounting neuroscientific evidence suggests that psychopathy is the product of biological and environmental forces and that the psychopath's defect is so deeply ingrained that afflicted individuals do not possess awareness or the ability to control their behavioral impulses—"The thinking of psychopaths is frequently irrational at a deeper level, so much so that their cognitive capacity is often impaired" (Palermo, 2013, p. 173). Yet, psychopaths continue to be held responsible for their criminal behaviors (Godman & Jefferson, 2017), and a diagnosis of psychopathy is generally considered as an aggravating factor that results in increased probability of a guilty verdict, enhanced sentence length, exclusion from treatment, and increased security and custody levels in confinement and supervision. Taking this further, Duff (2010) suggests that psychopathy can be understood as a "radical deficiency in rational capacities" (p. 209) whereby the psychopath has some, but not all, reasoning abilities such as the cognitive capacity for decision making that involves non-normative beliefs and reasoning. However, when it comes to matters of value that involve normative judgment of worth and emotions that normative judgment informs, the entire dimension of practical rationality is absent for the psychopathy:

> He can see how others have strong feelings about various matters, including about his conduct towards them; he can see that they recognize, discuss, appeal to, and are motivated by reasons that he does not share: but he has no grasp of those kinds of reason or those kinds of concern. He cannot understand how the interests or the suffering of others could have a claim on him, a claim that might outweigh his own inclination; or how honesty could matter in any terms other than those of immediate self-interest. He cannot understand what it is to love someone, or to be angered by injustice, or to be moved by compassion; he cannot grasp the kinds of reason that ground or are grounded by such emotions as these. (Duff, 2010, p. 209)

Thus, the psychopath's absence of emotion severely limits range of rationality and reason to decision making that involves actions that self-satisfy or that rely on imitation of others; however, the psychopath is an outsider to any reasoning and decision making informed by emotion and values.

Reconceptualizing Free Will and Determinism with Psychopathy in Mind

Given this understanding of the psychopath's partial cognitive capacity, a number of authors suggest that the recent findings in neuroscience call for a rethinking of the lines of criminal responsibility when it comes to psychopaths (Godman & Jefferson, 2017; Malatesti & McMillan, 2010; Ortega-Escobar, Alcázar-Córcoles, Puente-Rodríguez, & Peñaranda-Ramos, 2017; Palermo, 2013). For example, prominent forensic psychiatrist, criminologist, and scholar George Palermo who served as a state expert in the Jeffrey Dahmer case, testifying that Dahmer suffered from personality disorders so severe that "he could not have used sheer willpower to stop himself from killing" (Washington Post, 1992), argues that punishment should be proportionate to the crime and the purpose of punishment to reflect on past misdeeds and make sure the behavior is not repeated in the future (Palermo, 2013). However, psychopaths are impaired when it comes to learning from punishment, do not benefit from it, and need an alternative criminal justice response, perhaps more lenient punishment that does not treat the psychopath as sane, but rather addresses the unique factors that contributed to their criminal misconduct. Palermo concludes:

> [P]sychopathic criminal behavior is due not only to a personal decision to act (or a decision not to act), but also to predisposing factors—biological, genetic, and environmental. Therefore their aggressive behavior should be viewed within a compatibilistic theoretical approach (the coexistence of free will and determinism) and, if found guilty, the question of diminished responsibility should be considered before deciding their punishment. (Palermo, 2013, p. 355)

Similarly, Duff (2010) refers to psychopathy as a "responsibility-negating disorder" (Duff, 2010, p. 210) because of the psychopath's incapacity to understand the moral practices, is not guided by moral reasons, and cannot explain his antisocial actions. Other authors (Fox, Kvaran, & Fontaine, 2013; Levy, 2014; Nelkin, 2015) suggest that blameworthiness comes down to moral awareness and because psychopaths are not morally aware, they should not be held responsible.

Alternatively, other authors contend that there are important reasons to hold psychopaths accountable including the instrumental premeditated nature of their acts and the harm and dangers they pose to public safety (Erickson & Vitacco, 2012). Blair (2007a) asks, "Does the antisocial behavior of individuals with psychopathy reflect free will?" (p. 327), suggesting that, from a compatibilist perspective, both reactive and instrumental aggression involve some element of choice, but episodes of reactive aggression can occur in the absence of free will, while instrumental aggression must involve free will. However, from a hard determinist perspective, prior experience absolves free will and "the details of this debate remain currently philosophical and empirically impervious" (p. 328). Godman and Jefferson (2017) note that there is evidence to suggest that at least some psychopaths do not satisfy "desert-based" arguments because they "are insensitive to moral considerations which would typically move normal individuals" (p. 133). However, the authors suggest that there are compelling reasons to hold psychopaths criminally responsible, including public trust and the legitimacy of the judicial system (if the worst of the worst aren't punished then who should be?), prevention of future harm to society, and concerns about harm to patients in forensic settings if psychopaths met the requirements for the insanity defense and were housed in forensic populations (Godman & Jefferson 2017). Morse (2010) suggests that psychopaths be held under "involuntary quasi-criminal commitment" whereby their personality disorder and risk for future dangerousness would be used as rationale for civil commitment—thus, despite the deterministic forces that potentially impair the free will of psychopaths. If research findings that support biological determinism and the psychopath's inability to understand the moral meaning of antisocial conduct mitigate responsibility of psychopaths for the harm they cause, this potentially carries enormous consequences for the foundations of criminal law. All human behavior is the product of deterministic forces. If psychopaths are not considered to be responsible for their actions, then who among us could be held responsible? In addition, there are grave public safety implications if dangerous psychopaths are not kept from harming future victims and the only way to ensure public safety may be to hold them accountable and incapacitate them.

Whether the call for psychopaths to be deemed incompetent and responsible (as Cleckley and others have proposed), or at minimum, for psychopathy to be considered seen as a mitigating versus aggravating condition in the courts, remains to be seen. Studies conducted to date suggest that it is not likely that the common view of psychopathy as an aggravating factor will change any time soon. Mowle, Edens, Clark, and Sörman (2016) found that testimony on neuroscience evidence did not significantly influence juror perceptions of psychopathy and their tendency to view the defendant negatively resulting in determination of guilt determination and longer sentences. On the other hand, Marshall, Lilienfeld, Mayberg, and Clark (2017) found that when mock jurors are presented with neurological or psychological research with neuroscientific explanations, that jurors did not alter their sentencing judgment; however, they did consider the defendant more treatable and less dangerous and recommended less severe punishment.

CHAPTER EIGHT

Future Implications of the Psychopathy Construct for Criminology and Criminal Justice Policy and Practice

I would like to make it crystal clear I do not regret what I did. I am not sorry. I have not shed a tear for the innocent people I killed.
—Dylann Roof, convicted and sentenced to death for the mass murder of nine people in 2015 at the Emanuel African Methodist Episcopal Church in Charleston, South Carolina

For that lack of remorse. . . . Roof deserves the death penalty.
—Nathan Williams, assistant U.S. attorney, prosecutor, in the federal capital trial of Dylann Roof

[N]o normal person is so unevolved and no ordinary criminal so generally unresponsive and distorted, that he does not seem to experience satisfaction, love, hate, grief, and a general participation in life at human personality levels much more intense and more substantial than the affective reactions of the psychopath.
—Hervey Cleckley (1941, p. 374)

Beyond the issue of how psychopathy should be seen in the courts as a result of the research evidence that shows that the impairment the psychopath experiences may be beyond the control of the individual who is so afflicted are other issues to consider. The label "psychopath," while clinically defined as a personality disorder made up of a constellation of traits and behaviors, has a cultural meaning that goes far beyond the clinical diagnosis and is by no means a neutral diagnosis. The term "psychopath" has had a negative meaning throughout history, and the ethical implications of the use of the term as a diagnostic label used in the criminal justice system are extraordinary in terms of the potential for deprivation of liberty of individuals so labeled. Issues that are of particular importance to consider include the use of the term "psychopath" with children and adolescents, whether or not legal consent should be required before people are administered instruments such as the PCL-R, expert testimony on psychopathy in the courts, and the use of psychopathy to predict dangerousness in pretrial, sentencing, and release decisions.

Ethical and Legal Issues

There are a number of salient legal and ethical issues that deserve attention in future research. Although the construct of psychopathy has ethical-legal implications across the criminal justice process from law enforcement to the courts to corrections to reentry, there are particular issues that have risen to the level of critical importance in terms of examining who is impacted, how, and to what extent. Very limited research has been conducted to date examining how people have been harmed by the psychopathy construct and label in comparison with how many people have been protected given the strength of the link between psychopathy and general and violent recidivism and predatory aggression. What is ultimately needed is a cost-benefit analysis of the degree to which knowledge, theory, research, and assessment of psychopathy benefits society in comparison with any potential harm caused.

One of the most concerning applications of the construct of psychopathy in criminal justice decision making is labeling children as psychopaths. Although most psychopathy scholars who study psychopathy in childhood and adolescence caution the use of the label "psychopath" applied to children, the existence of instruments available to assess psychopathy in children and youth and the knowledge accumulation on the "psychopathic conduct cluster" in conduct-disordered children (Frick, Barry, & Bodin, 2000) create potential for misuse. Future research examining the extent to which instruments such as the *Psychopathy Checklist: Youth Version* (Forth, Kosson, & Hare, 2003), the Childhood Psychopathy Scale (Lynam, 1997), and the Antisocial Process Screening Device (Frick & Hare, 2002) are used in practice and their impact is needed.

Another important area for future research is the issue of legal consent to be administered the PCL-R and other instruments that measure psychopathy. When offenders in criminal justice contexts are assessed using the PCL-R and other forensic instruments, more often than not, the individuals who are being assessed do not know they are being assessed. This is also an issue for youth who are assessed even in cases where parents may be informed by clinicians about the instruments psychologists and psychiatrists are using in assessments where parents may not have enough knowledge or even time to process what it actually means for their child to be assessed for psychopathy. Books published such as Ronson's (2011) *The Psychopath Test* and Gentry's (2011) *Pass the PCL-R* reflect growing concerns around the potential harms that can come from a psychopathy assessment. Although the issue of informed consent is an ethical one and psychologists and psychiatrists should never conduct an assessment without first obtaining informed consent (Lyon, Ogloff, & Shepherd, 2016), in the criminal justice context where assessments are mandated, there are situations in which individuals who are being assessed may not fully understand the instruments they are consenting to and in some situations may not give informed consent at all or may do so in the context of consenting to a battery of instruments that they know little about. There is also the issue of whether or not individuals in a correctional context can give informed consent in the first place given that they are under control of the criminal justice system and are not truly free to make decisions that will not in some way have implications for their liberty.

Psychopathy has potentially become a scientifically supported legal synonym for evil when experts testify on the condition in the courts (Ruffles, 2004). The large body of research that indicates that psychopathy is used in the courts as an aggravating factor to predict dangerousness (e.g., DeMatteo & Edens, 2006; Edens, 2001; Edens & Cox, 2012; Edens, Guy, & Fernandez, 2003; Lloyd, Clark, & Forth, 2010; Lyon & Ogloff, 2000; Lyon, Ogloff, & Shepherd, 2016; Sandys, Pruss, & Walsh, 2009; Walsh & Walsh, 2006) highlights a range of issues that deserve further examination when the PCL-R and other forensic instruments that assess psychopathy are used to predict dangerousness. Issues such as training (Campbell, 2006), familiarity with the research literature (Lyon & Ogloff, 2000; Lyon, Ogloff, & Shepherd, 2016) and scoring, interpretation, and reporting practices (Boccaccini, Chevalier, Murrie, & Varela, 2017) present significant potential ethical concerns when forensic assessment of psychopathy is used in criminal justice decision making. For example, in a comprehensive study of the use of the PCL-R in sexually violent predator (SVP) determinations, Boccaccini, Chevalier, Murrie, and Varela (2017) found that the PCL-R is second only to the Static-99 in sex offender risk assessment and evidence of "adversarial allegiance" and "bias blind spot" in PCL-R and other risk assessment scoring and significant gaps between research and routine practice and caution evaluators to be cognizant of the ways in which the adversarial context may influence and bias their assessments and interpretation of scores. The widespread use of expert testimony on psychopathy in criminal justice contexts is only beginning to be explored. Given the implications of testimony on psychopathy in the criminal justice contexts, future research is needed to continue to examine the ways in which psychopathy is used as an aggravating factor in criminal justice decisions and the prediction of dangerousness.

Categorical versus Dimensional Models of Psychopathy

The notion of the categorically distinct primary psychopath who is qualitatively different from nonpsychopaths draws a line between individuals who are and are not psychopaths. This distinction is of great importance in the criminal justice system where definitive lines are needed for the purpose of legal decisions to protect public safety. This distinction is apparent in the history of the evolution of the construct of psychopathy where the disentangling of primary psychopathy from antisocial personality disorder and secondary psychopathy has long been discussed with accumulated support and consensus with recognition that the harm that can come to an individual who has been labeled "psychopath" is considerable and has particularly dire consequences in the criminal justice system.

When the first edition of the PCL-R was published in 1991, the manual recommended that a cutoff score of 30 be used to classify individuals as psychopaths (Hare, 1991). Subsequently, researchers used this cutoff score that was conceptually constructive to make sure studies were on the same page in terms of differentiating psychopaths from nonpsychopathic antisocial personality disordered individuals or "secondary psychopaths" who scored 20–29 on the PCL-R. With the large amount of research using the 30 cutoff score, consensus appeared to be moving toward the notion that only "primary" or "true" psychopaths who scored above 30 on the PCL-R should be considered psychopaths, and individuals who scored 20–29 should be considered "secondary psychopaths" who were essentially antisocial personality disordered individuals and not psychopaths.

However, in the second edition of the PCL-R, Hare (2003) indicates that "The PCL-R provides a dimensional score that represents the extent to which a given individual is judged to match the 'prototypical psychopath'" (p. 30) and notes that there is no completely satisfactory solution to the problem of cutoff scores. Hare offers a descriptive scheme for those who wish to avoid diagnostic labels or categories converting PCL-R scores to *T*-scores describing a range of severity from very low (0–8), low (9–16), and moderate (17–24) to high (25–32), and very high (33–40) levels of psychopathy. Hare also notes the practical implications of cutoff scores, the importance of taking gender, culture, and context into consideration, and cautions that the meaning of the cutoff scores is different in different settings and cultures and implications need to be considered. For example, a conservative higher cutoff score of 33 or 34[1] makes sense if the concern is about the effects of a false positive (incorrectly predicting that someone will reoffend when he or she does not reoffend)

[1] This takes into consideration the standard error of measurement for PCL-R ratings—3.0 in the second edition of the PCL-R and 3.25 in the first edition of the PCL-R.

rather than a false negative (incorrectly predicting that someone will not reoffend when he or she does reoffend).

The trend toward the dimensional model of psychopathy is the result of a number of factors. First, while categorical cutoffs are made in psychological assessments all the time (e.g., DSM-5 classifications require evidence of a specific number of criteria to diagnostically classify), there is no sharp dividing line between a PCL-R score of 30 and a score of 29 that definitively indicates that that person is a "psychopath." There are errors in measurement across raters and ratings and differences in assessments across gender, culture, and context that have the potential to affect scores. Second, there has been an increasing amount of research examining psychopathy outside of criminal justice contexts such as in the workplace (e.g., Babiak & Hare, 2006) and in community samples (e.g., Uzieblo, Verschuere, Van den Bussche, & Crombez, 2010) using the PCL-R and other instruments such as the B-Scan and the Psychopathic Personality Inventory–Revised (PPI-R) where the dimensional model makes more sense because there would be expected to be fewer individuals who would be considered primary psychopaths in these contexts. Third, primary psychopathy is a low-base-rate condition that is difficult to study even in large offender samples where a sample of 100 would likely only yield 15–20 primary psychopaths who score above 30 on the PCL-R, making the accumulation of research that differentiates primary psychopathy from secondary and nonpsychopathy difficult and slow. Finally, and most importantly for the use of the construct of psychopathy in criminal justice contexts, is that there are serious implications of the label "psychopath" in criminal justice contexts that may result in extended deprivation of liberty, exclusion from treatment, or even a death sentence.

Although there is ample evidence to support that primary psychopathy is a distinct construct and research should continue to further examine and better understand the demarcation between primary psychopathy and nonpsychopathy (and there is good reason to argue abandoning the term "secondary psychopathy" altogether[2]), psychopathy may be best viewed along a continuum. Meloy (1988) suggests that psychopathy be viewed along a "hypothetical continuum" for the purpose of treatment because given the research on the lack of treatment amenability for primary psychopaths, if psychopathy is viewed categorically there would be no point in attempting to treat. This hypothetical continuum also makes sense to make room for the possibility of assessment error and to be cognizant of the civil liberty implications of the

[2] The term "secondary psychopath" refers to individuals who would score 20–29 on the PCL-R. Since most antisocial personality disordered individuals would likely score in this range, and there has long been consensus that antisocial personality disorder is not the same clinical entity as psychopathy, the term "secondary psychopath" has a pejorative connotation and should be abandoned.

label "psychopath" when it is used in criminal justice and forensic contexts. For example, clinicians who offer expert testimony in criminal justice contexts tend to communicate risk assessment results in categorical terms, and there is discrepancy in terms of the score cutoffs used by prosecutors who tend to use a lower cutoff score than defense attorneys (Boccaccini, Chevalier, Murrie, & Varela, 2017). It also makes a difference in terms of a more negative impression on jurors if experts refer to a defendant as a psychopath as opposed to describing offenders as having a high level of psychopathic traits (Guy & Edens, 2003, 2006). In other words, even though research suggests that primary psychopathy does in fact exist and is associated with lack of remorse, predatory aggression, and a particular constellation of traits, the conservative approach from a due process perspective would be to view psychopathy along a hypothetical continuum while recognizing that a very high PCL-R score of 33 and above (using the conservative cutoff score taking into account standard error) is likely indicative of a categorically distinct clinical condition associated with lack of remorse, predatory aggression, lack of amenability to treatment, and future dangerousness.

Pemment (2013) suggests that neurological failures in the empathy circuit of the brain distinguish psychopathy from sociopathy and that given the implications of both conditions in the criminal justice system, sociopathy needs its own neurological correlate. From this perspective, sociopathy is analogous to secondary psychopathy and antisocial personality disorder. Unlike primary psychopaths, sociopaths engage in antisocial behavior but have a conscience and experience empathy and remorse. Their antisocial behavior and sociopathy, rather than the product of biological predisposition and lack of attachment in infancy, is acquired through some sort of trauma, dementia, or brain injury (similar to the case of the 19th-century railway worker Phineas Gage who became violent after a metal spike impaled his frontal lobe). This distinction between primary psychopathy and antisocial personality disorder or sociopathy is an important one. Research is needed to further examine the ways in which primary psychopathy is distinct with recognition that the majority of individuals in criminal justice contexts are not primary psychopaths who do not have the capacity to experience empathy and remorse.

The discussion over whether psychopathy is dimensional or categorical will no doubt continue. However, research has led most scholars to the view that both models have something to offer in understanding the role psychopathy plays in criminal behavior. The construct of psychopathy accommodates both dimensional and categorical approaches to studying antisocial behavior (DeLisi, 2009). The dimensional model is important in understanding how psychopathy level is associated with increased risk for criminal behavior, and the categorical model is important in moving forward to examine how primary psychopathy is conceptually and practically distinct in better understanding the role psychopathy plays in predatory aggression, future dangerousness, and treatment amenability.

What to Do with the Worst of the Worst? Ethics and Public Safety: Balancing the Limits of Psychological Predictors and Humane Treatment with the License to Protect Society

Is the psychopath still, as Cleckley (1941, p. 16) claimed, the "forgotten man" of penology and psychiatry?" Is there a place in the mental health or criminal justice system to house, manage, and treat the psychopath? Historically, given the association between psychopathy and general and violent recidivism and dangerousness as well as lack of amenability to treatment, the options for managing and treating individuals with high levels of psychopathic traits or those officially or unofficially labeled as "psychopaths" in criminal justice and forensic settings[3] include housing in general forensic or correctional populations, confinement in segregation units or "supermax" facilities, therapeutic treatment programs, specialized treatment in correctional or forensic settings, or, as the research showing the juror inclination to sentence psychopaths to death, execution. Issues faced in determining what to do with psychopaths who tend to be considered the worst of the worst in criminal justice and mental health systems ultimately deal with balancing the need for safety with humane and appropriate treatment.

Currently, there are few places in the criminal justice or mental health systems that specifically focus on the treatment and management needs of psychopaths, and those treatment programs that do exist show minimal to no success (Edens & Petrila, 2006; Thornton & Blud, 2007; Young, Justice, Gacono, & Kivisto, 2016). In addition, despite promising approaches put forth more than 50 years ago (e.g., Cleckley, 1941; Yochelson & Samenow, 1976), few treatment programs are specifically dedicated to the treatment of primary psychopaths who score above 30 on the PCL-R so research on treatment amenability for this group consistent with the risk-need-responsivity model (Andrews & Bonta, 1994, 2003, 2006; Andrews & Dowden, 2006; Dowden & Andres, 2004; Serin & Kennedy, 1997; Wong & Hare, 2004) for correctional

[3] Beyond an official score on the PCL-R or other forensic assessment instruments, offenders in correctional contexts are sometimes referred to in their institutional files by clinicians and/or correctional counselors as "cold-blooded," "predatory," as possessing "psychopathic traits," or even referred to as "psychopaths" without an accompanying forensic assessment. These references can carry through a person's institutional sentence with each subsequent evaluation referring to prior references. This can have the effect of a long-standing "unofficial" reference to an individual as psychopathic that persists over time that can potentially be based on a reference made even before there were validated and standardized assessment instruments to measure psychopathy such as the PCL-R.

treatment is sorely lacking. Much of the reason as to why some of the early treatment programs such as Yochelson and Samenow's (1976) "criminal personality" program implemented at Saint Elisabeth's Hospital in the 1970s (Samenow, 1984, 2013) has not taken hold[4] is likely the significant cost of these sorts of programs when economic decisions made in correctional contexts must necessarily meet the needs of the majority of offenders rather than targeting the small number with such severe psychopathological disturbance that they show limited to no hope for treatment and rehabilitation.

Although findings to date offer a relatively pessimistic view of treatment for psychopaths (Harris & Rice, 2006; Young, Justice, Gacono, & Kivisto, 2016) with a great deal of therapeutic nihilism in particular with respect to individuals with PCL-R scores in the very high range (Wong et al., 2012) and some view psychopathy as an incurable disorder (Meloy & Gacono, 2000), there is some hope for continued exploration of possibilities for treating individuals with high levels of psychopathic traits. For example, de Ruiter, Chakhssi, and Bernstein (2016) describe treatment efforts in the Netherlands using schema therapy (ST) and betrayal trauma theory (BTT),[5] a departure from other cognitive-behavioral treatments of psychopathy that assume it is impossible to change psychopathic personality. According to ST, patients with psychopathy use maladaptive coping styles that involve attempts to con and manipulate, self-aggrandizement and devaluation of others, and attempts to bully and intimidate, focusing of attention to detect a hidden threat, and cold-calculating aggression aimed at eliminating the threat. This maladaptive coping schematic mode is hypothesized to originate in adverse early childhood experiences and temperament whereby an individual who suffers maltreatment in childhood makes sense of the world through the lens of abuse, neglect, abandonment, and rejection, and then later in adulthood, early maladaptive schemas are triggered by life events that are unconsciously experienced as similar to the early childhood experience which then effect emotional processing, the interpretation of social cues, and behavior. Betrayal trauma theory (BTT), heavily influenced by attachment theory, builds on ST to explain the unique hypothetical reaction in

---

[4] While the study of the Yochelson and Samenow treatment program has been heavily criticized, the "criminal personality" treatment approach has evolved into one of the most publicized cognitive-behavioral therapy for antisocial personality disordered offenders (Reid, 1998).

[5] Laws and practices in the Netherlands make for a particularly rich opportunity to examine treatment of psychopaths in forensic hospitals. In the Netherlands, two-thirds of patients in forensic hospitals have a personality disorder without a concomitant clinical mental disorder. Under Dutch criminal law, offenders who have mental disorders including personality disorders can be civilly involuntarily committed to forensic hospitals and remain indefinitely with two-year review as long as the offender is deemed a danger to society. It is estimated that up to 35 percent of these civilly committed offenders in the Netherlands have been diagnosed as psychopaths using the European cutoff score of 26 and 21 percent using the North American cutoff score of 30 (de Ruiter, Chakhssi, & Bernstein, 2016).

individuals with high levels of psychopathic traits suggesting that the degree to which early childhood abuse represents a betrayal by a trusted and needed attachment mediates the way in which abuse-related information is remembered and processed. Used together, ST and BTT offer a promising approach to treating individuals with psychopathic traits. Although the authors note that to date there have been no randomized controlled trials of treatments for psychopaths published in the literature, they note that there is also no good evidence that individuals with high psychopathic traits cannot be treated effectively. The authors provide a case example of an individual named "Andy" whose PCL-R score, after a four-year treatment program and three-year follow-up using ST and BTT, dropped from 27 to 14. The authors suggest that what appears to be lack of remorse, emotional callousness, and hypoarousal and indifference to harm may be a biologically based unconscious defensive reaction to complex trauma such that "posttraumatic amnesia, emotional numbing, and identification with the aggressor could be seen as mechanisms of coping with complex/betrayal trauma" (p. 396).

Although these and other findings are certainly promising, it should be noted that de Ruiter, Chakhssi, and Bernstein's (2016) "Andy" received a pretreatment PCL-R score of 27 which, while indicative of primary psychopathy in European samples, is still below the 30 cutoff in North American samples and with the standard error, Andy may not be categorically a primary psychopath, which could potentially explain his amenability to treatment. Betrayal trauma may be applicable to individuals who are antisocial personality disordered secondary psychopaths and may be less applicable to primary psychopaths who score in the very high PCL-R range of 33–40. Future research is needed to examine the use of this and other promising treatment programs in terms of whether or not treatment effects differ by psychopathy level and the effect in particular with individuals who score in the very high range and who are considered to be primary psychopaths.

But what then can be done with individuals who score in the very high range who are primary psychopaths whose lack of remorse is rooted in neurobiological etiology and whose developmental process has left them with a complete incapacity for remorse and empathy? Are there individuals for whom the disorder is so extreme that there is no hope for treatment? Is the behavior of these individuals so dangerous and their sentences so severe that there is no reason to even discuss or consider the possibility of treatment and rehabilitation? Are these individuals rightly sentenced to death given the severity of their crimes and danger to society? For those who are not sentenced to death, is incapacitation in intensive management, supermax facilities, and/or civil commitment the only answer to how we should deal with these individuals in the criminal justice and mental health systems?

What we do with psychopaths in any given society or culture is ultimately not a psychological question. Rather, how we deal with psychopaths in society is a legal-ethical-philosophical choice that can only be determined through discourse and decision making that weighs the cost and benefits of crime control (punishment and incapacitation) and due process (protection of individual liberty and humane treatment). Ultimately, the question is not—Can psychopaths be treated? Rather it is—Do we choose to view psychopaths as people or monsters? Rhodes (2002) discusses how the category of psychopathy is used, through the merging of clinical and moral discourses, to designate prisoners as dangerous and confine them to supermax facilities in many cases using material from their institutional files, which is regurgitated and repurposed over time by multiple criminal justice and clinical actors.[6] She notes that:

> For correctional staff . . . the main issue in all this is the boundary these distinctions establish between treatable conditions and untreatable traits. This boundary helps them reserve their time and resources for the overwhelming numbers of mentally ill people in prison . . . The rehabilitation and naturalization of psychopathy also allows differentiation, not only between the mentally ill and the personality disordered, but also between run-of-the-mill and exceptional criminals. The diagnosis gains respectability from its association with criminal profiling and marks an arena of particular expertise for forensic psychologists specializing in corrections and policing. (Rhodes, 2002, pp. 447–448)

Thus the term "psychopath" is a critical marker in the criminal justice system in the critical decision-making processes that guide public safety and release decisions as well as safety and security, custody and management, and resource allocation decisions within correctional facilities.

The question of what to do with psychopaths is society in general and how to treat individuals with high levels of psychopathic traits in the criminal justice system in particular is an extremely difficult question to answer. For the public, the words "He/she showed no remorse" as the individual is led in handcuffs off to prison marks the "end" of the problem. However, this is not the end. Psychopathic individuals who are sentenced to custody in jails, prisons, and even death row or supermax facilities, continue to present custody and management dilemmas, threats to the safety of other inmates and correctional and mental health staff, can harm potential victims from prison, and can eventually be released on parole, appeal, or changes in law. For example, Dennis Rader, otherwise known as the BTK Killer (for "Bind, Torture,

---

[6] For example, Rhodes (2002) provides participation observation data showing that prison officials charged with writing reports on inmates use and reuse information in institutional files labeling offenders as psychopaths. She describes this as the "looping effect" whereby influence flowing back and forth between a diagnostic category and the people who are described by it is mutually reinforcing (Rhodes, 2002, p. 448).

and Kill"), was sentenced in 2005 to 10 consecutive life sentences for the murder of 10 people who he predatorily stalked, tortured, and killed in Kansas between 1974 and 1991. Rader is well known for his grandiosity (when asked if he had something to say at his sentencing, launched into an academy award–like speech), for his ability to allude law enforcement for 30 years while living life as a devoted father and churchgoer, who had a degree in administration of justice, and worked as a security and animal control officer. In the 1970s, Rader wrote a letter to the news media, which was eventually published in the *Wichita Sun* newspaper:

> When this monster enter my brain, I will never know. But, it here to stay. . . . Society can be thankfull [*sic*] that there are ways for people like me to relieve myself at time by day dreams of some victim being torture and being mine. It a big compicated [*sic*] game my friend of the monster play putting victims number down, follow them, checking up on them waiting in the dark, waiting, waiting. . . . Maybe you can stop him. I can't. He has aready [*sic*] chosen his next victim—BTK. (Henkel, 2005)

If Rader is correct, that he could not stop himself, maybe it is time we listen, and do what is needed to stop him, or to continue to advance scientific knowledge with increasingly sophisticated understanding of the origins, development, and manifestation of psychopathy with attention and awareness to the ways in which our popular conceptions of psychopathy—both popular and scientific, inform and guide criminal justice decisions at every stage of the criminal justice process. There is much at stake. If the criminological life course of one individual with high levels of psychopathic traits like Rader is derailed or shortened, even by a day, month, or year, that developmental halt will protect the "next victim" and will potentially save someone's life, whether that next victim is in the community, a fellow prisoner, or correctional staff member in a prison or mental health facility.

This book opened with the example of Richard Allen Davis, a repeat offender who in 1993 broke into a house during a slumber party, abducted 12-year-old Polly Klaas at knifepoint during her slumber party with her mother sleeping and younger sister asleep down the hall and her friends watching, took her to a remote location, raped and murdered her and dumped her body at the edge of a highway miles away, and then at his sentencing hearing caused a dramatic courtroom scene when he accused Polly Klaas's dad Marc Klaas of molesting Polly. Davis, who flipped off the media cameras as he left the courtroom after his conviction, has been diagnosed with antisocial personality disorder, is widely considered a psychopath and was the media superpredator largely responsible for the passing of three-strikes legislation in California, was sentenced to death in 1996, and he remains on death row in San Quentin today more than 20 years later with no execution date in sight (Moya, 2015). Davis continues to appeal his sentence, has a website hosted by the Canadian

Coalition against the Death Penalty through which he seeks a female pen pal, and was resuscitated in 2006 after an opiate overdose in his prison cell (Romney, 2006). Similarly, Kevin Coe, aka the "South Hill Rapist," served a 25-year sentence after his arrest and conviction for three rapes in Spokane, Washington, was the subject of Jack Olsen's book *Son: A Psychopath and His Victims* and a made-for-TV movie *Sins of the Mother* (Patterson & Siegel, 1991), and, along with a number of other notorious predators influenced the enactment of three-strikes legislation in Washington State (Helfgott, 2008), and then in 2008 sentenced to civil commitment as a sexually violent predator in Washington State has refused treatment and continues to challenge his civil commitment (Pulkkinen, 2013) only to be denied (Mischke, 2014). Other known psychopaths such as Diane Downs who shot her three children, killing one of them in 1983, and was sentenced to life plus 50 years was most recently denied parole in 2010 and will not get another chance until 2020 (Terry, 2010); and Susan Smith, who killed her two sons in 1994 and will be up for parole after 30 years in 2024, has committed multiple infractions while in prison including infractions for having sex four times with a 50-year-old corrections officer and has been repeatedly placed in protective custody (Field, 2017). Davis, Coe, Downs, and Smith are examples of the many individuals with high levels of psychopathic traits who, though they have been removed from the public sphere, continue to be housed in correctional and civil commitment contexts for decades.

Some of these severely psychopathic individuals will never be released from prison; however, some will, and these cases raise the question of what to do with individuals in society who represent the worst of the worst. Karla Homolka, for example, was released from prison in 2005 after serving a 12-year sentence in Canada for the 1992 sexual homicide–torture of two teenage girls and her sister she committed with her ex-husband Paul Bernardo (who is currently in prison and up for parole in 2018) (Basa, 2018). For every notorious psychopath, there are hundreds of thousands sitting in jails and prisons and in civic commitment facilities, and many would argue in boardrooms and White Houses (Dutton, 2012, 2016; Lilienfeld et al., 2012; Wallis, 2016) that beg the question of how to view and what to do in response to these individuals in society.

In thinking about what to do with the worst of the worst in the criminal justice system, an answer may be found in future technological advances. Research in artificial intelligence and affective computing (Schwark, 2015; Terkle, 2008, 2011) may offer answers that have not been possible until now. Thinking about the applications of artificial intelligence research to psychopathy, it is difficult to forget Cleckley's description of the psychopath as a "machine" when he said, "we are dealing here not with a complete man at all but with something that suggests a subtly constructed reflex machine which can mimic the human personality perfectly" (p. 369). If psychopaths are more like machines than humans, and computers can be made to feel and to be sensitive to other people's feelings, then why can't that same technology be used to enable psychopaths to feel?

Although the primary objective of affective computing research has been to give future robots socioemotional skills, affective computing research has potential implications for the assessment and treatment of psychopathy and other conditions such as autism and alexithymia associated with the absence or deficits in emotional processing (Baron-Cohen, 2011; Bird, 2014). For example, researchers are beginning to examine how affective computing and autism research can be merged. Since the late 1990s, affective computing researchers have been working on the development of technologies that have advanced understanding of and approach to affective neuroscience and autism. New techniques have been created that have the potential to infer affective or cognitive states. Sensors and machine learning algorithms have been designed that can measure affective information through gestures, gaze, facial expressions, tone of voice, physiology. Machines have been developed that respond adaptively and affectively to a person's state, and personal technologies have been created that improve awareness of affective states and its selective communication to others (El Kaliouby, Picard, & Baron-Cohen, 2006). The affective computing research has particular promise in terms of helping people with autism, and autism research can help technologists in their efforts to design smart machines that can aid individuals who have difficulties in empathizing and recognizing social cues and nuances of social interactions with socioemotional interactions.

Future research is needed to examine how affective computing and psychopathy research can be merged to explore the ways in which forensic assessment of psychopathy can be improved with the use of sensors that more accurately measure empathy than can existing forensic assessment instruments. In addition, artificial intelligence advances that can make robots "feel" so to speak, have particular implications for treatment of psychopathy, in particular for individuals who score in the very high PCL-R range who are primary psychopaths who are not amenable to traditional treatment approaches. In other words, if robots can be made to feel and to respond to people's feelings, then why can't this same technology be used to treat psychopaths to "teach" them how to feel and engage in appropriate interactions that will reduce the harm that comes from their antisocial interactions? Of course, there are a range of ethical issues to consider in moving in this direction with respect to using affective computing research for good rather than bad (Beavers & Slattery, 2017),[7] but if the choice or inclination societally is to treat psychopaths as humans rather than monsters and to work toward

[7] For example, psychopaths already do well in tapping into other people's emotions. If affective computing technology is able to assist psychopaths in gauging other people's feelings and only simulating, but not truly feeling their own emotions, then would this technology potentially create more opportunities for psychopaths to harm others rather than assisting them with socioemotional interactions that will reduce antisocial behavior?

developing ways to enable individuals who do not experience empathy or show remorse to get along in society through socioemotional interactions, then this is a promising direction to consider.

Conclusion: Remorse Revisited

The term "psychopath" continues to be associated with an individual who "shows no remorse." In science, popular culture, and in the minds of laypeople, psychopathy is a condition that represents the extreme absence of emotion and an inability to take responsibility. Remorse is what the public wants from offenders in the aftermath of crime, and psychopathy reflects the incapacity to experience and express this key element of criminal redemption. Jury panel members view the prototypical psychopath as responsible for their own actions, capable of determining right from wrong, as not "insane" and as highly dominant, self-focused, and lacking in empathy and remorse (Smith et al., 2014), and offenders have concerns that their expression of remorse is scrutinized and used as a key piece in parole and release decisions and public perceptions of them (Helfgott & Strah, 2013; Helfgott, Lovell, & Lawrence, 2000, 2002; Helfgott, Lovell, Lawrence, & Parsonage, 1999).

Remorse has been defined as an "unpleasant affective event after a transgression" though it is unclear from research and case law as to the specific emotions and cognitions that characterize remorse and the focus of the emotions and cognitions, and questions have been raised regarding whether remorse can be seen as equivalent to constructs of emotions similar to remorse such as conscience and empathy (Spice, Viljoen, Douglas, & Hart, 2015). Brooks and Reddon (2003) pose the question, "What is remorse?" and examine people's opinions about the nature of remorse in a sample of probation officers in which the Remorse Construct Rating Form (RCRF) and Jackson Personality Inventory–Revised (JPI-R) were administered. Results show that probation officers identified 668 items linked to remorse. The authors conclude that the single item that measures remorse on the PCL-R—Item 6, lack of remorse or guilt—oversimplifies the concept of remorse and creates opportunities for errors that result in concluding that remorse is lacking when it is present and concluding that remorse is present when it is feigned or absent. The authors call for a comprehensive assessment to measure remorse that takes into account two independent dimensions of remorse identified in the research findings—internal remorse related to morality and ethical behavior and external remorse related to fear of authority and shame.

Remorse is integral to justice, has been throughout history in humans and primates, and restorative justice approaches that hinge on reconciliation, empathy, and reciprocal altruism are evolutionarily favorable. Empathy can partially be explained by mirror neurons that enable the ability to interpret the actions of others in conjunction with reflection enabled by the prefrontal cortex (DeLisi & Vaughn, 2015). Psychopathy is characterized by lack of remorse (Spice, Viljoen, Douglas, & Hart, 2015), and psychopaths experience cognitive empathy which gives them the ability to understand others' intentions and to take advantage of others but do not experience affective empathy, which allows them to feel no remorse (Dutton, 2012).

Criminologists have raised the importance of future research on empathy and crime (Jolliffe & Murray, 2012). Although some have questioned whether psychopathy can be considered a general theory of crime while noting the value of the construct in generally advancing criminological theory (e.g., Walters, 2004), psychopathy has increasingly been incorporated into criminological theory by criminologists who have integrated the theory and research on psychopathy into life course criminology (Fox, Jennings, & Farrington, 2015; Lynam, Charnigo, Moffitt, & Raine, 2009), self-control theories (DeLisi et al., 2018), biosocial criminology (DeLisi, Umphress, & Vaughn, 2009; Weibe, 2012), and career criminality (McCuish, Corrado, Hart, & DeLisi, 2015; Vaughn & DeLisi, 2008). According to DeLisi (2009), whose work has been particularly impactful in the integration of psychopathy into mainstream criminological theory:

> In addition to its theoretical and empirical significance, psychopathy is also critically important in practice and should be included in every handbook of every practitioner position in the juvenile and criminal justice systems. . . . For virtually any research question centering on antisocial behavior, psychopathy is relevant. And it should, for it is the unified theory of crime. (pp. 267–268)

DeLisi (2009, p. 256) contends that, "Of all the theories emanating from the social, behavioral, and criminological sciences, psychopathy is superior to its competitors," that psychopathy is the "purest and explanation of antisocial behavior" and the "unified theory of delinquency and crime." Similarly, Fox, Jennings, and Farrington (2015) suggest that "criminology as a discipline needs to broaden its view of criminological theorizing to be more open to theoretical integration in general and theoretical integration with focus on psychopathy specifically" (p. 285).

Some very recent work in criminology has begun to examine the role of regret in crime desistance (Warr, 2016).[8] This work further marks the closing

[8] Interestingly, Warr (2016) uses Camus's Mersault in *The Stranger* in his concluding comments about the importance of regret in crime desistance, noting that Mersault indicated that he has never been able to regret anything in his life. This harks back to almost 40 years ago when Duff (1977) argued that Mersault's lack of remorse and regret were indicative of psychopathy. However, as discussed in Chapter 4, this is an oversimplified reading of *The Stranger* and Mersault's character. As Smith (1978) suggested, Mersault's inability to understand others also rendered him unable to

of disciplinary gaps that have existed for years where psychologists have long studied the role of emotion, attachment, aggression, and antisocial behavior, while criminology has largely omitted this work in theoretical and empirical study of crime. In a publication of findings from a study of remorse in serious adolescent offenders in *Justice Quarterly*, the journal of the *Academy of Criminal Justice Sciences*, Piquero (2017) notes that while the role of emotions has long been studied in the social sciences, emotions have not received empirical attention in criminology and criminal justice, and "empirical research in criminology focusing on regret/remorse has been virtually absent" (p. 354). While this study did not employ the PCL-R so there is no way of knowing the level of psychopathy of participants in terms of PCL-R scores and cutoffs—the study utilized the Youth Psychopathic Traits Inventory (YPI)—the results from a sample of 1,354 adolescents found guilty of a serious offense show that that lack of remorse was associated with a higher frequency of rearrest at the end of the seven-year study, with the conclusion that "remorse resistance" is related to more offending, while "remorse-proneness" is related to less offending. This is one of the first empirical studies in mainstream criminological and criminal justice theory to fully integrate psychopathy research with focus on the role of remorse in criminal behavior, and a sign that the time has officially come for the construct of psychopathy to be a central focus in criminology and criminal justice.

Twenty years ago, Hare (1998) suggested that psychopathy is such a robust and important risk factor for violence that failure to consider it may constitute professional negligence. It is a promising development in the social sciences that in the early part of the 21st century after hundreds of years of discourse, theory development, and research on the subject of psychopathy and the many points of historical and theoretical intersection in the disciplines of psychology, criminology/criminal justice and in crime, criminal law, and criminal justice, that scholars in criminology, criminal justice, psychology, sociology, and other behavioral sciences and cultural studies disciplines are now integrating theory and research that will advance knowledge to an entirely new level. The construct of psychopathy should hold a central place in criminological theory, integrated and situated within interdisciplinary criminology, and recognized as a construct with significant implications for criminal justice practice. The empirical association with general and violent

---

exploit others, which distinguishes Mersault from individuals with high levels of psychopathy who are natural manipulators. Mersault was not a psychopath; he was an existentialist with intense personal awareness who took full responsibility for his actions and for who he was. This ongoing discussion and debate of Mersault in the literature on psychopathy and now in criminology in reference to regret and crime desistance suggests that there is still far to go to examine the role of emotion in crime, which types of emotions play a role in crime desistance, and how the disciplinary links and gaps between emotion-crime and the psychopathy-crime empirical associations.

recidivism, and implications of psychopathy for law enforcement, the courts, corrections, juvenile justice, and victim services, examination of psychopathy as central to criminology and criminal justice is important moving forward to better understand and respond to this condition that has so many implications for public safety, criminal justice decision making, law, and due process.

A final point. It is only fitting to end this book with a final quote from Hervey Cleckley. In his concluding comments in *The Mask of Sanity,* Cleckley said, "If we consider . . . the vast number of similar people in every community who show the same behavior pattern in milder form but who are sufficiently protected and supported by relatives to remain at large, the prevalence of this disorder is seen to be appalling" (p. 452). This is an important thought to keep in mind when thinking about the ways in which psychopathy has made its way into the criminal justice system, which has been historically fraught with issues impacting the selective enforcement of law that result in disparity and discrimination rooted in socioeconomic status, race/ethnicity, and gender at every stage of the criminal justice process.

Another important final thought, while the PCL-R, IM-P, risk assessment tools, clinical assessment, and other tools available in the criminal justice and mental health systems have become increasingly sophisticated in terms of their ability to empirically predict dangerousness, these tools only offer insight regarding the probability of future dangerousness, not the 100 percent accurate prediction of who will and who will not engage in antisocial and criminal acts. Remorse is an emotion that sits beneath the surface of overt behavior and conscious cognition. Remorse is almost impossible to definitely measure and identify, and its behavioral expression is highly dependent on a range of factors including gender, race, socioeconomic status, culture, subculture, temperament, situation, context, individual-environmental interactions, and other unknown factors. Many individuals who enter and make their way through the criminal justice process are told by their attorneys to refrain from making public statements in court. Boys and men are socialized to keep their feelings to themselves. Women with psychopathic traits who lack remorse often present as overly emotional. Some cultures reinforce more emotional displays of interpersonal interactions, and some subcultures help to reinforce the suppression of remorse in otherwise empathy-oriented people. Research that shows that the presence of remorseful utterances and written statements are indicative of true confessions, while the lack of remorse is associated with false confessions (Villar, Arciuli, & Paterson, 2014) and that jurors are more likely to give longer sentences to defendants who show remorse (McKelvie, 2013) should make us all very concerned about how or whether we have the capacity to show remorse if we are ever arrested for a crime or find ourselves convicted of one. How can we be sure that the police who are doing the arresting are capable of evaluating suspect displays of remorse? What about jurors, attorneys, judges, clinicians, forensic evaluators, correctional staff, and other justice professionals at every stage of the criminal justice process? Jon Ronson (2011) cautions in his book *The Psychopath Test*, that instruments like the PCL-R have the potential to make us all into "psychopath spotters." On the other hand, the PCL-R has been instrumental in advancing scientific research to better understand the condition and to get us to a place far from the confusion over the condition that existed even just a generation ago. *Is there a way we can make use of the vast amount of theory and research on psychopathy to reduce crime and violence and protect potential victims from future harm, while recognizing our limitations and the inherent opportunities for injustice in criminal justice decision making when searching for signs of remorse in individuals processed through the criminal justice system? Can remorse be measured? What factors influence the expression of remorse? And how important is remorse in criminal behavior and its response?* These and other questions deserve continued discussion, exploration, and empirical examination.

Science has come an incredibly long way to help us understand the role psychopathy plays in crime, violence, and antisocial behavior, how to forensically assess the condition, and its developmental pathways and manifestations. We are beginning to see promising work that offers hope for treatment possibilities and for a more nuanced and sophisticated understanding of the disorder that may help merge psychological realities with the needs of public safety—to arrive at definitive determinations of guilt, innocence, and sentence length in ways that are ethically just, legally sound, and informed by science. However, all individuals with psychopathic traits will not be treated alike. Some will never be identified, and some who find themselves in the criminal justice system may be treated more harshly than they otherwise would as a result of the identification of psychopathic traits, in particular the absence of remorse, which is ultimately very difficult if not impossible to definitely identify and measure. Ideally, theory and research and knowledge on psychopathy will help to correctly identify psychopathologically disturbed remorseless individuals among us to protect public safety and to minimize the harm caused by this devastating condition. However, it is critical that the use of the psychopathy construct for the purpose of enhancing public safety be balanced with an equal push to find ways to help those afflicted with a predisposition for psychopathy to alter its developmental pathway with the recognition that while individuals with high levels of psychopathic traits may commit monstrous acts that afflict harm on individuals and society, the people who commit these acts are ultimately human. Psychopathy is a human condition. Finding ways to better understand psychopathy—its origins, mechanisms, manifestations, pathways, and amenability for treatment—and how the psychopathy construct can be used to help and not to harm, should be the driving force for future research, policy, and practice.

References

Abbey, A., Jacques-Tiura, A. J., & LeBreton, J. M. (2011). Risk factors for sexual aggression in young men: An expansion of the confluence model. *Aggressive Behavior, 37*(5), 450–464.

Abrahams, J., & Zweig, C. (Eds.). (1991) *Meeting the shadow: The hidden power of the dark side of human nature.* New York: G. P. Putnam's Sons.

Adler, F., Mueller, G. O. W., & Laufer, W. S. (1994). *Criminal justice.* New York: McGraw-Hill.

Agnew, R. (1994). The techniques of neutralization and violence. *Criminology, 32*(4), 555–580.

Ainsworth, M. D. S. (1989). Attachments beyond infancy. *American Psychologist, 44*, 709–716.

Alexander, F., & Staub, H. (1931, 1956). *The criminal, the judge, and the public: A psychological analysis.* Glencoe, IL: Free Press.

Allen, H. (1987). *Justice unbalanced.* Milton Keynes, UK: Open University Press.

American Psychiatric Association. (1952). *Diagnostic and statistical manual of mental disorders* (DSM). Washington, DC: American Psychiatric Association.

American Psychiatric Association. (1968). *Diagnostic and statistical manual of mental disorders* (2nd ed.) (DSM-II). Washington, DC: American Psychiatric Association.

American Psychiatric Association. (1980). *Diagnostic and statistical manual of mental disorders* (3rd ed.) (DSM-III). Washington, DC: American Psychiatric Association.

American Psychiatric Association. (1987). *Diagnostic and statistical manual of mental disorders* (Rev. 3rd ed.) (DSM-III-R). Washington, DC: American Psychiatric Association.

American Psychiatric Association. (1994). *Diagnostic and statistical manual of mental disorders* (4th ed.) (DSM-IV). Washington, DC: American Psychiatric Association.

American Psychiatric Association. (2000). *Diagnostic and statistical manual of mental disorders* (4th ed., text rev.) (DSM-IV-TR). Washington, DC: American Psychiatric Association.

American Psychiatric Association. (2013). *Diagnostic and statistical manual of mental disorders* (5th ed.) (DSM-5). Washington, DC: American Psychiatric Association.

Anderson, C. A., Berkowitz, L., Donnerstein, E., Huesmann, L. R., Johnson, J. D., Linz, D., Malamuth, N. M., & Wartella, E. (2003). The influence of media violence on youth. *Psychological Science in the Public Interest, 4*(3), 81–110.

Andrews, D. A., & Bonta, J. (1994, 2003, 2006, 2010). *The psychology of criminal conduct.* Cincinnati: Anderson.

Andrews, D. A., & Dowden, C. (2006). Risk principle of case classification in correctional treatment: A meta-analytic investigation. *International Journal of Offender Therapy and Comparative Criminology, 50*(1), 88–100.

Annon, J. S. (1995). Investigative profiling: A behavioral analysis of the crime scene. *American Journal of Forensic Psychology, 13*(4), 67–75.

Anton, M., Baskin-Sommers, A., Vitale, J., Curtin, J., & Newman, J. (2012). Differential effect of psychopathy and antisocial personality disorder symptoms on cognitive and fear processing in female offender. *Cognitive Affect Behavioral Neuroscience, 12,* 761–776.

Arquette, K. E. (2012). *Fetal attraction: A descriptive study of patterns in fetal abductions* (Unpublished master's thesis). Retrieved from Regis University ePublications, https://epublications.regis.edu/cgi/viewcontent.cgi?referer=https://www.google.com/&httpsredir=1&article=1245&context=theses

Arrigo, B. A. (2000). *Introduction to forensic psychology: Issues and controversies in crime and justice.* San Diego: Academic Press.

Arrigo, B. A., & Griffin, A. (2004). Serial murder and the case of Aileen Wuornos: Attachment theory, psychopathy, and predatory aggression. *Behavioral Sciences and the Law, 22,* 375–393.

Arrigo, B. A., & Shipley, S. (2001a). The confusion over psychopathy (I): Historical considerations. *International Journal of Offender Therapy and Comparative Criminology, 45*(3), 325–344.

Arrigo, B. A., & Shipley, S. (2001b). The confusion over psychopathy (II): Implications for forensic (correctional) practice. *International Journal of Offender Therapy and Comparative Criminology, 45*(4), 407–420.

Asken, M. J. (2012). *Warrior mindset: Mental toughness skills for a nation's peacekeepers.* Millstadt, IL: Human Factor Research Group.

Associated Press. (2014, March 26). Judge: Bride showed no remorse in husband's death. *San Diego Union-Tribune.* Retrieved from http://www.sandiegounion tribune.com/sdut-bride-faces-sentencing-for-glacier-park-killing -2014mar26-story.html

Associated Press. (2014, June 21). Selena Gomez stalker sentenced to treatment. *Billboard.* Retrieved from https://www.billboard.com/articles/columns/pop -shop/6128691/selena-gomez-stalker-sentenced-to-treatment

Astor, M. (1963). *The incredible Charlie Carewe.* New York: Dell.

Atherley, L. (2013). Profiling psychopathic traits in serial sexual homicide: A case study of the personality and personal history of the Green River killer Gary

Leon Ridgway. In J. B. Helfgott (Ed.), *Criminal psychology* (Vol. 3, pp. 229–252). Santa Barbara, CA: Praeger.

Babiak, P., Folino, J., Hancock, J., Hare, R. D., Logan, M., Leon Mayer, E., Meloy, J. R., Häkkänen-Nyholm, H., O'Toole, M. E., Pinizzotto, A., Porter, S., Smith, S., & Woodworth, M. (2012, July). Psychopathy: An important concept for the 21st century. *FBI Law Enforcement Bulletin, 81*(7). Retrieved from http://www.fbi.gov/stats-services/publications/law-enforcement-bulletin/july-2012/July-2012

Babiak, P., & Hare, R. D. (2006). *Snakes in suits: When psychopaths go to work.* New York: HarperCollins.

Bailey, F. Y., & Hale, D. C. (1998). *Popular culture, crime, and justice.* Belmont, CA: Wadsworth.

Bakan, D. (1989). Power, method, and ethics: A reflection on Bateson's view of moral and national character. In R. W. Rieber (Ed.), *The individual, communication, and society* (pp. 31–47). Cambridge: Cambridge University Press.

Barak, G. (1998). *Integrating criminologies.* Needham Heights, MA: Allyn & Bacon.

Barbour-McMullen, J., Coid, J., & Howard, R. (1988). The psychometric identification of psychopathy in mentally abnormal offenders. *Personality and Individual Differences, 9,* 817–823.

Barefoot v. Estelle (1983), 463 U.S. 880.

Barnes, H. E. (1972). *The story of punishment.* Montclair, NJ: Patterson Smith.

Baron-Cohen, S. (2003). *The essential difference: Male and female brains and the truth about autism.* New York: Basic Books.

Baron-Cohen, S. (2011). *The science of evil: On empathy and the origins of cruelty.* New York: Basic Books.

Bartol, C. R. (1995). *Criminal behavior: A psychosocial approach.* Englewood Cliffs, NJ: Prentice Hall.

Basa, E. (2018). Infamous serial killer Karla Homolka is roaming free in Canada and people are furious. *Narcity.* Retrieved from https://www.narcity.com/news/disgraced-serial-killer-karla-homolka-is-roaming-free-in-canada-and-people-are-furious

Bazemore, G., & Griffiths, C. T. (1997). Conferences, circles, boards, and mediations: The "new wave" of community justice decisionmaking. *Federal Probation, 61*(2), 25–37.

Beaudine, W., Jr. (Producer), & Levin, P. (Director). (1992). *Overkill: The Aileen Wuornos story* [TV movie]. USA: CBS.

Beaumont-Thomas, B. (2017, September 26). Taylor Swift's alleged stalker deemed psychologically unfit to stand trial. *Guardian.* Retrieved from https://www.theguardian.com/music/2017/sep/26/taylor-swift-alleged-stalker-deemed-psychologically-unfit-to-stand-trial

Beaver, K. M. (2008). *The nature and nurture of antisocial outcomes.* El Paso, TX: LFB Scholarly.

Beaver, K. M. (2015). *The nurture versus biosocial debate in criminology: On the origins of criminal behavior and criminality.* Thousand Oaks, CA: Sage.

Beavers, A. F., & Slattery, J. P. (2017). On the moral implications and restrictions surrounding affective computing. In J. Myounghoon (Ed.), *Emotions and affect in human factors and human-computer interaction* (pp. 143–161). San Diego: Elsevier Academic Press.

Becker, E. (1991). The basic dynamic of human evil. In J. Abrahams & C. Zweig (Eds.). *Meeting the shadow: The hidden power of the dark side of human nature* (pp. 186–189). New York: G. P. Putnam's Sons.

Becker, H., Mulvehill, C., Pfeffer, R. (Producers), & Becker, H. (Director). (1993). *Malice* [Motion picture]. USA: Columbia Pictures.

Belenko, S., Fagan, J., & Chin, K. (1991). Criminal justice responses to crack. *Journal of Research in Crime and Delinquency, 28*(1), 55–75.

Belfrage, H., Fransson, G., & Strand, S. (2004). Management of violent behaviors in the correctional system using qualified risk assessments. *Legal and Criminological Psychology, 9,* 11–22.

Belnap, J., & McDonald, C. (2010). Judges' attitudes about and experiences with sentencing circles in intimate-partner abuse cases. *Canadian Journal of Criminology and Criminal Justice, 52*(4), 369–395.

Benning, S. D., Venables, N. C., & Hall, J. R. (2018). Successful psychopathy. In C. J. Patrick (Ed.), *Handbook of psychopathy* (2nd ed., pp. 585–610). New York: Routledge.

Berman, J. J. (Ed.). (1989). *Cross-cultural perspectives.* Lincoln/London: University of Nebraska Press.

Bernat, F. R., Helfgott, J. B., & Godlove, N. (2013). Sexually violent predators and state appellate courts' use of actuarial tests in civil commitments. In J. B. Helfgott (Ed.), *Criminal Psychology* (Vol. 3, pp. 87–112). Santa Barbara, CA: Praeger.

Bernstein, A. J. (2002, 2014). *Emotional vampires: Dealing with people who drain you dry.* New York: McGraw-Hill.

Beryl, R., Chou, S., & Vollm, B. (2014). A systematic review of psychopathy in women within secure settings. *Personality and Individual Differences, 71,* 185–195.

Best, J. (1994). Rhetoric in claims-making: Constructing the missing children problem. In P. A. Adler & P. Adler (Eds.), *Constructions of deviance: Social power, context, and interaction* (pp. 105–121). Belmont, CA: Wadsworth.

Bird, G. (2014). The self to other model of empathy: Providing a new framework for understanding empathy impairments in psychopathy, autism, and alexithymia. *Neuroscience and Biobehavioral Reviews, 47,* 520–532.

Bjorkqvist, K., & Niemela, P. (Eds.). (1992). *Of mice and women: Aspects of female aggression.* New York: Academic Press.

Black, D. W. (1999). *Bad boys, bad men: Confronting antisocial personality disorder.* New York: Oxford University Press.

Black, J. (1991). *The aesthetics of murder: A study in romantic literature and contemporary culture.* Baltimore: Johns Hopkins University Press.

Blackburn, R. (1988). On moral judgements and personality disorders. *British Journal of Psychiatry, 153,* 503–512.

Blackburn, R. (1993). *The psychology of criminal conduct.* New York: Wiley.

Blackburn R. (1998). Psychopathy and personality disorder: Implications of interpersonal theory. In J. Cooke et al. (Eds.), *Psychopathy: Theory, research, and implications for society* (pp. 269–301). Netherlands: Kluwer.

Blackburn, R. (2007). Personality disorder and psychopathy: Conceptual and empirical integration. *Psychology, Crime, & Law, 13*(1), 7–18.

Blair, J., Mitchell, D., & Blair, K. (2005). *The psychopathy: Emotion and the brain.* Malden, MA: Blackwell.

Blair, R. J. R. (2007a). Aggression, psychopathy and free will from a cognitive neuroscience perspective. *Behavioral Sciences and the Law, 25*, 321–331.

Blair, R. (2007b). Empathic dysfunction in psychopathic individuals. In T. Farrow & P. Woodruff (Eds.), *Empathy in mental illness* (pp. 3–16). Cambridge: Cambridge University Press. doi:10.1017/CBO9780511543753.002

Blair, R. J. R. (2013). Psychopathy: Cognitive and neural dysfunction. *Dialogues in Clinical Neuroscience, 15*(2), 181–190.

Blair, R. J. R., Jones, L., Clark, F., & Smith, M. (1997). The psychopathic individual: A lack of responsiveness to distress cues? *Psychophysiology, 34*, 192–198.

Blair, R. J. R., Meffert, H., Hwang, S., & White, S. F. (2018). Psychopathy and brain function insights from neuroimaging findings. In C. J. Patrick (Ed.), *Handbook of psychopathy* (2nd ed., pp. 401–421, 682–709). New York: Guilford Press.

Blair, R. J. R., Mitchell, D. G. V., Kelly, S., Richell, R. A., Leonard, L., Newman, C., & Scott, S. K. (2002). Turning a deaf ear to fear: Impaired recognition of vocal affect in psychopathic individuals. *Journal of Abnormal Psychology, 111*(4), 682–686.

Blumenthal, S., Craissati, J., & Minchin, L. (2009). The development of a specialist hostel for the community management of personality disordered offenders. *Criminal Behavior and Mental Health, 19*, 43–53.

Boccaccini, M. T., Chevalier, C. S., Murrie, D. C., & Varela, J. G. (2017). Psychopathy Checklist–Revised use and reporting practices in sexually violent predator evaluations. *Sexual Abuse, 29*(6), 592–614.

Boccaccini, M. T., Murrie, D. C., Clark, J. W., & Cornell, D. G. (2008). Describing, diagnosing, and naming psychopathy: How do youth psychopathy labels influence jurors? *Behavioral Sciences and the Law, 26*(4), 487–510.

Bok, S. (1998). *Mayhem: Violence as public entertainment.* New York: Basic Books.

Bolt, D. M., Hare, R. D., & Neumann, C. S. (2007). Score metric equivalence of the Psychopathy Checklist–Revised (PCL-R) across criminal offenders in North America and the United Kingdom: A critique of Cooke, Michie, Hart, and Clark (2005) and new analyses. *Assessment, 14*(1), 44–56.

Bolt, D. M., Hare, R. D., Vitale, J. E., & Newman, J. P. (2004). A multigroup item response theory analysis of the Psychopathy Checklist–Revised. *Psychological Assessment, 16*, 155–168.

Boppre, B., & Salisbury, E. (2016). The women's risk needs assessment: Putting gender at the forefront of actuarial risk assessment. *Penal Reform International*. Retrieved from https://www.penalreform.org/blog/womens-risk-needs-assessment-putting-gender-forefront-actuarial

Bowie, S. I., Silverman, D. C., Kalick, S. M., & Edbril, S.D. (1990). Blitz rape and confidence rape: Implications for clinical intervention. *American Journal of Psychotherapy, 44* (2), 180–188.

Boyle, K. (2001). What's natural about killing? Gender, copycat violence and Natural Born Killers. *Journal of Gender Studies, 10*(3), 311–321.

Bozman, R. M., Saxon, E., Utt, K. (Producers), Blake, G., Goetzman, G. (Associate Producers), & Demme, J. (Director). (1991). *Silence of the lambs* [Motion picture]. USA.: Orion Pictures.

Braithwaite, J. (1989). *Crime, shame, and reintegration*. New York: Cambridge University Press.

Braithwaite, J. (2002). *Restorative justice and responsive regulation*. Oxford: Oxford University Press.

Bresin, K., Boyd, R. L., Ode, S., & Robinson, M. D. (2013). Egocentric perceptions of the environment in primary, but not secondary, psychopathy. *Cognitive Therapy and Research, 37*(2), 412–418.

Brinkley, C. A., Bernstein, A., & Newman, J. P. (1999). Coherence in the narratives of psychopathic and nonpsychopathic criminal offenders. *Personality and Individual Differences, 27*, 519–530.

Brinkley, C. A., Newman J. P., Harpur T. J., & Johnson M. M. (1999). Cohesion in texts produced by psychopathic and nonpsychopathic criminal inmates. *Personality and Individual Differences, 26*, 873–885.

Brinkley, C. A., Newman, J. P., & Widiger, T. A. (2004). Two approaches to parsing the heterogeneity of psychopathy. *Clinical Psychology: Science and Practice, 11*(1), 69–94.

Brites, J. A. (2016). The language of psychopaths: A systematic review. *Aggression and Violent Behavior, 27*, 50–54.

Britto, S., & Noga-Styron, K. E. (2014). Media consumption and support for capital punishment. *Criminal Justice Review, 39*(1), 81–100.

Broadbent, G., Czernin, P., McDonagh, M. (Producers), & McDonagh, M. (Director). (2012). *Seven psychopaths* [Motion picture]. USA: CBS Films.

Brooks, J. H., & Reddon, J. R. (2003). The two dimensional nature of remorse: An empirical inquiry into internal and external aspects. *Journal of Offender Rehabilitation, 38*(2), 1–15.

Broomfield, N., Oord, R. (Producers), & Broomfield, N. (Director). (1992). *Aileen Wuornos: The selling of a serial killer.* USA: Lafayette Films.

Brown, A. (2016). Masculinity is not pathology: An exploration of masculinity among juvenile sexual abusers and general delinquents. *Journal of Juvenile Justice, 5*(2), 121–133.

Brown, L. S., & Ballou, M. (1992). *Personality and psychopathology: Feminist reappraisals*. New York: Guilford Press.

Brown, S. L. (2009). *Women who love psychopaths*. Penrose, NC: Mask.

Bryant, J., & Zillman, D. (Eds.). (2002). *Media effects: Advances in theory and research.* Mahwah, NJ: Erlbaum.

BTK sentenced to 10 life terms. (2005, August 18). *CNN.com.* Retrieved from http://www.cnn.com/2005/LAW/08/18/btk.killings

BTK victim's son: Rader "the lowest form of human filth." (2005, June 28). *CNN .com.* Retrieved from http://www.cnn.com/2005/LAW/06/28/victims.son /index.html?eref=sitesearch

Burgess, A. W., Baker, T., & Rabun, J. B., Jr. (2002). Newborn kidnapping by cesarean section. *Journal of Forensic Sciences, 47*(4), 827–830.

Burgess, A. W., Harner, H., Baker, T., Hartman, C., & Lole, C. (2001). Batterers stalking patterns. *Journal of Family Violence, 16*(3), 309–321.

Cale, E. M., & Lilienfeld, S. O. (2002). Sex differences in psychopathy and antisocial personality disorder: A review and integration. *Clinical psychology review, 22*(8), 1179–1207.

Calhoun, M. C. (2008). Scientific evidence in court: Daubert or Frye, 15 years later. *Washington Legal Foundation, 23*(37). Retrieved from http://www.wlf .org/upload/08-22-08calhoun.pdf

Campbell, A. (1993). *Men, women, & aggression.* New York: Basic Books/Harper Collins.

Campbell, K. (2002, October 10). As sniper hunt grows role of media blurs. *Christian Science Monitor.* Retrieved November 4, 2005, from http://www.csmonitor .com/2002/1010/p01s03-usju.htm

Campbell, T. W. (2006). The validity of the Psychopathy Checklist–Revised in adversarial proceedings. *Journal of Forensic Psychology Practice, 64*(4), 43–53.

Camus, A. (1942). *The Stranger.* New York: Vintage Books.

Camus, A. (1955). *The myth of sisyphus.* New York: Vintage Books.

Canter, D., Alison, L. J., Alison, E., & Wentink, N. (2004). The organized/disorganized typology of serial murder: Myth or model? *Psychology, Public Policy, and Law, 10*(3), 293–320.

Caplan, P. J. (1995). *They say you're crazy: How the world's most powerful psychiatrists decide who's normal.* Reading, MA: Addison-Wesley.

Capote, T. (1965). *In Cold Blood.* New York: Random House.

Cauffman, E., Skeem, J., Dmitrieva, J., & Cavanaugh, C. (2016). Comparing the stability of psychopathy scores in adolescents versus adults: How often is "fledgling psychopathy" misdiagnosed? *Psychology, Public Policy, and Law, 22*(1), 77–91.

Cavadino, M. (1998). Death to the psychopath. *Journal of Forensic Psychiatry, 9*(1), 5–8.

CBS/Associated Press. (2009). D.C. sniper John Allen Muhammad executed. Retrieved from https://www.cbsnews.com/news/dc-sniper-john-allen -muhammad-executed

Centifanti, L. C. Muñoz, Kimonis, E. R., Frick, P. J., & Aucoin, K.J. (2013). Emotional reactivity and the association between psychopathy-linked narcissism and aggression in detained adolescent boys. *Development and Psychopathology, 25*(2), 473–485.

Centifanti, L. C. Muñoz, Thomson, N. D., & Kwok, A. H. (2016). Identifying the manipulative mating methods associated with psychopathic traits and BPD features. *Journal of Personality Disorders, 30*(6), 721–741.

Chaplin, J. P. (1975). *Dictionary of psychology.* New York: Dell.

Chesler, P. (1971). *Women and madness.* New York: Avon.

Chesney-Lind, M., & Jones, N. (Eds.). (2010). *Fighting for girls: Critical perspectives on gender and violence.* Albany, NY: SUNY Press.

Chouinard, V. (2009). Placing the "mad woman": Troubling cultural representations of being a woman with mental illness in Girl Interrupted. *Social & Cultural Geography, 10*(7), 791–804.

Choy, O., Raine, A., Venables, P. H., & Farrington, D. P. (2017). Explaining the gender gap in crime: The role of heart rate. *Criminology, 55*(2), 465–487.

Clear, T. R., Hamilton, J. R., & Cadora, E. (2011) *Community justice.* New York: Routledge.

Cleckley, H. (1941, 1976, 1982, 1988). *The mask of sanity.* Augusta, GA: Emily S. Cleckley.

Cleckley, H. (1946). The psychopath viewed practically. In R. V. Seliger, L. L. B. Lukas, & R. M. Lindner (Eds.), *Contemporary criminal hygiene* (pp. 194–217). Baltimore: Oakridge Press.

Clements, C. B. (1996). Offender classification: Two decades of progress. *Criminal Justice and Behavior, 23*(1), 121–143.

CNN Transcripts. (2003, December 9). *Malvo trial.* Retrieved November 4, 2005, from http://transcripts.cnn.com/TRANSCRIPTS/0312/09/ltm.06.html

Cohen, S. (1985). *Visions of social control: Crime, punishment, and classification.* Cambridge: Polity Press.

Coid, J. (1993). Current concepts and classifications of psychopathic disorder. In P. Tyrer & G. Stein (Eds.), *Personality disorder reviewed* (pp. 113–164). London: Gaskell/Royal College of Psychiatrists.

Coleman, L. (2004). *The copycat effect: How the media and popular culture trigger mayhem in tomorrow's headlines.* New York: Paraview Pocket Books.

Conrad, J. (1907, 1953). *The secret agent.* Garden City, NY: Anchor Books.

Contreras-Rodríguez, O., Pujol, J., Batalla, I., Harrison, B. J., Bosque, J., Ibern-Regàs, I., & Pifarré, J. (2014). Disrupted neural processing of emotional faces in psychopathy. *Social cognitive and affective neuroscience, 9*(4), 505–512.

Cook, P. E., & Hinman, D. L. (1999). Criminal profiling: Science and art. *Journal of Contemporary Criminal Justice, 15*(3), 230–241.

Cooke, D. J., & Michie, C. (1999). Psychopathy across cultures: North America and Scotland compared. *Journal of Abnormal Psychology, 108*(1), 58–68.

Cooke, D. J., & Michie, C. (2001). Refining the construct of psychopathy: Towards a hierarchical model. *Psychological Assessment, 13*(2), 171–188.

Cooke, D. J., Michie, C., Hart, S. D., & Clark, D. (2005). Assessing psychopathy in the UK: Concerns about cross-cultural generalizability. *The British Journal of Psychiatry, 186*(4), 335–341.

Coolidge, F. L., Marle, P. D., Van Horn, S. A., & Segal, D. L. (2011). Clinical syndromes, personality disorders, and neurocognitive differences in male and female inmates. *Behavioral Sciences and the Law, 29*(5), 741–751.

Cooper, H. H. A. (2001). Negotiating with terrorists. *Journal of Police Crisis Negotiations, 1*(2), 53–67.

Cooper, S., & Arnow, A. (1988). *The Rorschach defense scales*. National Institute of Mental Health Grant R01 MH34123.

Copes, H. (2003). Societal attachments, offending frequency, and techniques of neutralization. *Deviant Behavior: An Interdisciplinary Journal, 24*, 101–127.

Copjec, J. (1993). *Shades of noir*. London/New York: Verso.

Cordozo, B. (1930). *What medicine can do for the law*. New York: Harpur.

Corrado, R., DeLisi, M., Hart, S. D., & McCuish, E. C. (2015). Can the causal mechanisms underlying chronic, serious, and violent offending trajectories be elucidated using the psychopathy construct? *Journal of Criminal Justice, 43*(4), 251–261.

Cox, J., Edens, J. F., Rulseh, A., & Clark, J. W. (2016). Juror perceptions of the interpersonal-affective traits of psychopathy predict sentence severity in a white-collar criminal case. *Psychology, Crime & Law, 22*(2), 721–740.

Crego, C., & Widiger, T. A. (2016). Cleckley's psychopaths: Revisited. *Journal of Abnormal Psychology, 125*(1), 75–87.

Cullen, D. (2004, April 20). The depressive and the psychopath: At last we know why the Columbine killers did it. *Slate*. Retrieved October 19, 2005, from http://slate.msn.com/id/2099203

Cullen, D. (2007, April 20). Psychopath? Depressive? Schizophrenic? Was Cho Seung-Hui really like the Columbine killers? *Slate*. Retrieved August 17, 2007, from http://www.slate.com/id/2164757

Cullen, F. T., & Gendreau, P. (2001). From nothing works to what works: Changing professional ideology in the 21st century. *The Prison Journal, 81*, 313–338.

Cunliffe, T., Gacono, C. B., Meloy, J. R., & Taylor, E. (2013). Are male and female psychopaths equivalent? A Rorschach study. In J. B. Helfgott (Ed.), *Criminal psychology* (Vol. 2, pp. 423–459). Santa Barbara, CA: Praeger/ABC-CLIO.

Cunliffe, T., Gacono. C. B., Smith, J. M., Kivisto, A. J., Meloy, J. R., & Taylor, E. (2016). Assessing psychopathy in women. In C. B. Gacono (Ed.), *The clinical and forensic assessment of psychopathy: A practitioner's guide* (2nd ed., pp. 167–190). New York: Routledge.

Cunliffe, T., Johnson, E. A., & Weiss, D. E. (2013). Psychopathy, borderline personality disorder, and domestic violence: An empirical review. In J. B. Helfgott (Ed.), *Criminal psychology* (Vol. 2, pp. 461–485). Santa Barbara, CA: Praeger/ABC-CLIO.

Cunningham, M. D., Reidy, T. J., & Sorensen, J. R. (2008). Assertions of "future dangerousness" at federal capital sentencing: Rates and correlates of subsequent prison misconduct and violence. *Law and Human Behavior, 32*, 46–63.

Cuypers, S. E. (2013). Moral shallowness, metaphysical megalomania, and compatibilist-fatalism. *Ethical Theory and Moral Practice, 16*(1), 173–188.

Daéid, N. N. (1997). Differences in offender profiling in the United States of America and the United Kingdom. *Forensic Science International, 90*, 25–31.

Daly, K. (1994). *Gender, crime, and punishment*. New Haven/London: Yale University Press.

Daly, K. (2016). What is restorative justice? Fresh answers to a vexed question. *Victims and Offenders*, 11(1), 9–29.

Damon, M., Kushner, D., Peterson, C., Theron, C., Wyman, B., Silver, N. (Producers), & Jenkins, P. (2003). *Monster* [Motion picture]. USA: Denver & Delilah Films.

Darwin, C. (1859, 1999). *The origin of species*. New York: Bantam Dell.

Daubert v. Merrell Dow Pharmaceuticals, Inc., 509 U.S. 579 (1993).

Davis, J. A. (1999). Criminal personality profiling and crime scene assessment: A contemporary investigative tool to assist law enforcement public safety. *Journal of Contemporary Criminal Justice, 15*(3), 291–301.

De Boer, J., Whyte, S., & Maden, T. (2008). Compulsory treatment of dangerous offenders with severe personality disorders: A comparison of the English DSPD and Dutch TBS systems. *The Journal of Forensic Psychiatry & Psychology, 19*(2), 148–163.

Declercq, F., Willemsen, J., Audenaert, K., & Verhaeghe, P. (2012). Psychopathy and predatory violence in homicide, violent, and sexual offenses: Factor and facet relations. *Legal and Criminological Psychology, 17*, 59–74.

De Fina, B. (Producer), & Scorsese, M. (Director). (1991). *Cape fear* [Motion picture]. USA: Amblin Entertainment.

Delacoste, E., & Alexander, P. (Eds.). (1988). *Sex work: Writings by women in the sex industry*. London: Virago Press.

DeLisi, M. (2009). Psychopathy is the unified theory of crime. *Youth Violence and Juvenile Justice, 7*(3), 53–76.

DeLisi, M., Dansby, T., Peters, D. J., Vaughn, M. G., Shook, J. J., & Hochstetler, A. (2013). Fledgling psychopathic features and pathological delinquency: New evidence. *American Journal of Criminal Justice, 39*, 411–424.

DeLisi, M., Tostlebe, J., Burgason, K., Heirigs, M., & Vaughn, M. (2018). Self control versus psychopathy: A head-to-head test of general theories of antisociality. *Youth Violence and Juvenile Justice, 16*(1), 53–76.

DeLisi, M., Umphress, Z. R., & Vaughn, M. G. (2009). The criminology of the amygdala. *Criminal Justice and Behavior, 36*(11), 1241–1252.

DeLisi, M., & Vaughn, M. G. (2015). Ingredients for criminality require genes, temperament, and psychopathic personality. *Journal of Criminal Justice, 43*(4), 290–294.

DeMatteo, D., & Edens, J. F. (2006). The role and relevance of the Psychopathy Checklist–Revised in court: A case law survey of US courts (1991–2004). *Psychology, Public Policy, and Law, 12*, 214–419.

DeMatteo, D., Edens, J. F., Galloway, M., Cox, J., & Smith, S. T. (2014). The role and reliability of the Psychopathy Checklist–Revised in U.S. sexually violent predator evaluations: A case law survey. *Law and Human Behavior, 38*(3), 248–255.

Demetrioff, S., Porter, S., & Baker, A. (2017). I know how you feel: The influence of psychopathic traits on the ability to identify micro-expressions. *Psychology, Crime, & Law, 23*(3), 274–290.

Denno, D. W. (2003). Who is Andrea Yates? A short story about insanity. *Duke Journal of Gender, Law, & Policy, 10*(1), 1–58.

De Ruiter, C., Chakhssi, F., & Bernstein, D. (2016). Treating the untreatable psychopath. In C. B. Gacono (Ed.), *The clinical and forensic assessment of psychopathy: A practitioner's guide* (2nd ed., pp. 388–402). New York: Routledge.

DeShong, H. L., Helle, A. C., & Mullins-Sweatt, S. N. (2016). Unmasking Cleckley's psychopath: Assessing historical case studies. *Personality and Mental Health, 10*(2), 142–151.

Desola, R. (1982). *Crime dictionary.* New York: Facts on File.

Dexter renewed for 7th and 8th season. (2011, November 18). *Voice of TV.* Retrieved May 23, 2012, from http://thevoiceoftv.com/news-and-gossip/dexter-renewed-for-7th-and-8th-season

Dhami, M. K. (2016). Apology in victim-offender mediation. *Contemporary Justice Review, 19*(1), 31–42.

Dillon, N. (2012, January 29). Halle Berry stalker, Richard Franco, sentenced to 386 days in jail and five years probation. *Daily News.* Retrieved from http://www.nydailynews.com/entertainment/gossip/halle-berry-stalker-richard-franco-sentenced-386-days-jail-years-probation-article-1.1008885

Dingley, J. C. (1997). The terrorist—Developing a profile. *International Journal of Risk, Security, and Crime Prevention, 2*(1), 25–37.

Dinwiddie, S. H. (2015). Psychopathy and sociopathy: The history of a concept. *Psychiatric Annals, 45*(4), 169–174.

Dirks, D., Heldman, C., & Zack, E. (2015). "She's white and she's hot, so she can't be guilty": Female criminality, penal spectatorship, and white protectionism. *Contemporary Justice Review, 18*(2), 160–177.

Dixon, C., & Twomey, J. (2011, March 25). Yard sorry over the Night Stalker's 1000 victims. *Express.co.uk.* Retrieved April 1, 2011, from http://www.express.co.uk/posts/view/236607/Yard-sorry-over-the-Night-Stalker-s-1-000-victims

Dixon, L., & Browne, K. (2003). The heterogeneity of spouse abuse: A review. *Aggression and Violent Behavior, 8*, 107–130.

Doren, D. M. (1987). *Understanding and treating the psychopath.* New York: Wiley.

Dostoevsky, F. (1869, 2003). *The idiot.* New York: Vintage.

Dostoyevsky, F. (1880, 1982). *The brothers Karamazov.* New York: Penguin.

Dostoyevsky, F. (1951). *Crime and punishment.* London: Penguin Books.

Douglas, J. E., Burgess, A. W., Burgess, A. G., & Ressler, R. K. (1992, 1997). *Crime classification manual.* San Francisco: Josey-Bass.

Douglas, J. E., & Olshaker, M. (1999). *The anatomy of motive.* New York: Pocket Books.

Douglas, J. E., Ressler, R. K., Burgess, A. W., & Hartman, C. R. (2004). Criminal profiling from crime scene analysis. In R. Keppel (Ed.), *Offender profiling* (pp. 23–34). Belmont, CA: Wadsworth.

Douglas, K.S., Vincent, G. M., & Edens, J. F. (2006). In C. J. Patrick (Ed.), *Handbook of psychopathy* (pp. 533–554). New York: Guilford Press.

Douglas, K. S., Vincent, G. M., & Edens, J. F. (2018). Risk for criminal recidivism: The role of psychopathy. In C. J. Patrick (Ed.), *Handbook of psychopathy* (2nd ed., pp. 682–709). New York: Guilford Press.

Dowden, C., & Andrews, D. A. (2004). The importance of staff practice in delivering effective correctional treatment: A meta-analytic review of core correctional practice. *International Journal of Offender Therapy and Comparative Criminology, 48,* 203–214.

Dowden, C., Antonowicz, D., & Andrews, D. A. (2003). The effectiveness of relapse prevention with offenders: A meta-analysis. *International Journal of Offender Therapy and Comparative Criminology, 47,* 516–528.

Draguns, J. G. (1980). Psychological disorders of clinical severity. In H. C. Triandis & J. G. Draguns (Eds.), *Handbook of cross-cultural psychology: Vol. 6. Psychopathology* (pp. 99–179). Boston: Allyn & Bacon.

Draguns, J. G. (1989). Normal and abnormal behavior in cross-cultural perspective: Specifying the nature of their relationship. In J. J. Berman (Ed.), *Cross-cultural perspectives* (pp. 235–277). Lincoln/London: University of Nebraska Press.

Drake, J. (Producer), & Harron, M. (Director). (2000). *American psycho* [Motion picture]. USA: Lions Gate Films.

Duff, A. (1977). Psychopathy and moral understanding. *American Philosophical Quarterly, 177,* 189–200.

Duff, A. (2010). Psychopathy and answerability. In L. Malatesti & J. McMillan (Eds.), *Responsibility and psychopathy: Interfacing law, psychiatry and philosophy* (pp. 199–212). Oxford, UK: Oxford University Press.

Duffy, P. (2010, September 16). Mark David Chapman is now 55 years old and has been in prison for almost 30 years. *Huliq.com.* Retrieved May 27, 2012, from http://www.huliq.com/10061/john-lennon-was-easy-target-his-killer-tells-parole-board

Duncan, M. G. (1996). *Romantic outlaws, beloved prisons.* New York: New York University Press.

Durand, G., Plata, E. M., & Arbone, I. (2017). Negative attitudes towards psychopaths: The role of one's own psychopathic traits. *Personality and Individual Differences, 109*(1), 72–76.

Durham, A. M., Elrod, H. P., & Kinkade, P. T. (1996). Public support for the death penalty: Beyond Gallup. *Justice Quarterly, 13*(4), 705–736.

Dutton, K. (2012). *The wisdom of psychopaths: What saints, spies, and serial killers can teach us about success.* New York: Scientific American/Farrar, Straus and Giroux.

Dutton, K. (2016). Would you vote for a psychopath? *Scientific American, 27*(5), 50–55.

Eddy, L., & Patrzalek, S. W. (2013). The elements of hostage (crisis) negotiation. In J. B. Helfgott (Ed.), *Criminal psychology* (Vol. 3, pp. 169–193). Santa Barbara, CA: Praeger.

Edens, J. F. (2001). Misuses of the Hare Psychopathy Checklist–Revised in court. *Journal of Interpersonal Violence, 16*(10), 1082–1093.

Edens, J. F., Buffington-Vollum, J. K., Keilen, A., Roskamp, P., & Anthony, C. (2005). Predictions of future dangerousness in capital murder trials. *Law and Human Behavior, 29*(1), 55–86.

Edens, J. F., & Campbell, J. S. (2007). Identifying youths at risk for institutional misconduct: A meta-analytic investigation of the psychopathy checklist measures. *Psychological Services, 4*(1), 13–27.

Edens, J. F., Clark, J., Smith, S. T., Cox, J., & Kelley, S. E. (2013). Bold, smart, dangerous and evil: Perceived correlates of core psychopathic traits among jury panel members. *Personality and Mental Health, 7*(1), 143–153.

Edens, J. F., & Cox, J. (2012). Examining the prevalence, role and impact of evidence regarding antisocial personality, sociopathy and psychopathy in capital cases: A survey of defense team members. *Behavioral Sciences and the Law, 30*(3), 239–255.

Edens, J. F., Guy, L. S., & Fernandez, K. (2003). Psychopathic traits predict attitudes toward a juvenile capital murderer. *Behavioral Sciences and the Law, 21*(6), 807–828.

Edens, J. F., Lilienfeld, S. O., Marcus, D. K., & Polythress, N. G. (2006). Psychopathic, not psychopath: Taxometric evidence for the dimensional structure of psychopathy. *Journal of Abnormal Psychology, 115*(1), 131–144.

Edens, J. F., Marcus, D. K., & Vaughn, M. G. (2011). Exploring the taxometric status of psychopathy among youthful offenders: Is there a juvenile psychopath taxon? *Law and Human Behavior, 35*(1), 13–24

Edens, J. F., & Petrila, J. (2006). Legal and ethical issues in the assessment and treatment of psychopathy. In C. J. Patrick (Ed.), *Handbook of psychopathy* (pp. 573–588). New York: Guilford Press.

Edens, J. F., Petrila, J., & Kelley, S. E. (2018). Legal and ethical issues in the assessment and treatment of psychopathy. In C. J. Patrick (Ed.), *Handbook of psychopathy* (2nd ed., pp. 732–754). New York: Guilford Press.

Edens, J. F., Poythress, N. G., Lilienfeld, S. O., & Patrick, C. J. (2008). A prospective comparison of two measures of psychopathy in the prediction of institutional misconduct. *Behavioral Sciences and the Law, 26*(5), 529–541.

Egger, S. A. (1999). Psychological profiling: Past, present, and future. *Journal of Contemporary Criminal Justice, 15*(3), 242–261.

Egner, J. (2012, January 5). Defined by a smile and a drawl. *New York Times.* Retrieved from http://www.nytimes.com/2012/01/08/arts/television/timothy-olyphant-in-elmore-leonards-justified-on-fx.html?pagewanted=all

Eichler, M. (1966). The application of verbal behavior analysis to the study of psychological defense mechanisms: Speech patterns associated with sociopathic behavior. *Journal of Nervous and Mental Disease, 141*(2), 658–663.

Eisenbarth, H., Angrilli, A., Calogero, A., Harper, J., Olson, L., & Bernat, E. (2012). Reduced negative affect response in female psychopaths. *Biological Psychology, 94,* 310–318.

Eisenbarth, H., Osterheider, M., Nedopil, N., & Stadtland, C. (2012). Recidivism in female offenders: PCL-R lifestyle factor and VRAG show predictive validity in a German sample. *Behavioral Sciences and the Law, 30,* 575–584.

Elias, N. (1982). *The civilizing process.* New York: Pantheon.

Elias, N., & Dunning, E. (1986). *The quest for excitement.* Oxford: Blackwell.

El Kaliouby, R., Picard, R., & Baron-Cohen, S. (2006). Affective computing and autism. *Annals of New York Academy of Sciences, 1093,* 228–248.

Ellis, B. E. (1991). *American psycho.* New York: Vintage.

Ells, L. (2005). Juvenile psychopathy: The hollow promise of prediction. *Columbia Law Review, 105*(1),158–208.

Emily, J. (2011, April 1). Jurors give father life for abuse that left child blind, deaf, paralyzed. *Dallas News.com.* Retrieved April 1, 2011, from http://www.dallasnews.com/news/crime/headlines/20110401-jurors-give-father-life-for-abuse-that-left-child-blind-deaf-paralyzed.ece

Epstein, S. C. (1995). The new mythic monster. In J. Ferrell & C. R. Sanders (Eds.), *Cultural criminology* (pp. 66–79). Boston: Northeastern University Press.

Erickson, S. K., & Vitacco, M. J. (2012). Predators and punishment. *Psychology, Public Policy, and Law, 18*(1), 1.

Ewing, C. P. (1983). "Dr. Death" and the case for an ethical ban on psychiatric and psychological predictions of dangerousness in capital sentencing proceedings. *American Journal of Law & Medicine, 8*, 407–428.

Faigman, D. L. (1999). *Legal alchemy: The use and misuse of science and law.* New York: W. H. Freeman.

Faith, K. (1993). *Unruly women: The politics of resistance and confinement.* Vancouver, BC: Press Gang.

Falkenbach, D. M. (2008). Psychopathy and the assessment of violence in women. *Journal of Forensic Psychology Practice, 8*(2), 212–224.

Falkenbach, D. M., Mckinley, S. J., & Larson, F. R. R. (2017). Two sides of the same coin: Psychopathy case studies from an urban police department. *Journal of Forensic Psychology Research and Practice, 17*(5), 338–356.

Fanti, K. A., Lordos, A., Sullivan, E. A., & Kosson, D. S. (2018). Cultural and ethnic variations in psychopathy. In C. J. Patrick (Ed.), *Handbook of psychopathy* (2nd ed., pp. 529–569). New York: Guilford Press.

Farley, R. (2017, September 6). A fan tried to send Selena Gomez the most disturbing gift. *Refinery 29.* Retrieved from https://www.refinery29.com/2017/09/171133/selena-gomez-bouquet-fan-gift?bucketed=true

Farrington, D. P. (2006). Family background and psychopathy. In C. J. Patrick (Ed.), *Handbook of psychopathy* (pp. 229–250). New York: Guilford Press.

Farrington, D. P., & Bergstrom, H. (2018). Family background and psychopathy. In C. J. Patrick (Ed.), *Handbook of psychopathy* (2nd ed., pp. 354–379). New York: Guilford Press.

Farrington, D. P., Petrosino, A., & Welsh, B. C. (2001). Systematic reviews and cost-benefit analyses of correctional interventions. *The Prison Journal, 81*, 339–359.

Feihauer, J., Cima, M., Korebrits, A., & Kunert, H. (2012). Differential associations between psychopathy dimensions, types of aggression, and response inhibition. *Aggressive Behavior, 38*(1), 77–88.

Feldscher, K. (2014, April 1). Relative incensed as murder suspect grins during arraignment for fatal stabbing. *MLive*. Retrieved from http://www.mlive.com/news/ann-arbor/index.ssf/2014/04/relative_incensed_as_murder_su.html

Felson, R. B. (1996). Mass media effects on violent behavior. *Annual Review of Sociology, 22*, 103–128.

Ferguson, C. J., & Rueda, S. M. (2010). The hitman study: Violent video game exposure effects on aggressive behavior, hostile feelings, and depression. *European Psychologist, 15*(2), 99–108.

Fernbach, B., Winstead, B., & Derlega, V. (1989). Sex differences in diagnosis and treatment recommendations for antisocial personality and somatization disorders. *Journal of Social and Clinical Psychology, 8*, 238–255.

Ferrell, J. (1995). Culture, crime, and cultural criminology. *Journal of Criminal Justice and Popular Culture, 3*(2), 25–42.

Ferrell, J., & Hamm, M. S. (1998). *Ethnography at the edge: Crime, deviance, and field research.* Belmont, CA: Wadsworth.

Ferrell, J., Hayward, K., & Young, J. (2008). *Cultural criminology: An Invitation.* Thousand Oaks, CA: Sage.

Ferrell, J., Hayward, K., & Young, J. (2015). *Cultural criminology: An Invitation* (2nd ed.). Thousand Oaks, CA: Sage.

Ferrell, J., & Sanders, C. R. (1995). *Cultural criminology.* Boston: Northeastern University Press.

Fersch, E. L. (Ed.). (2006). *Thinking about psychopaths and psychopathy: Answers to frequently asked questions with case examples.* New York: iUniverse.

Fido, D., Santo, M. G. E., Bloxsom, C. A. J., Gregson, M., & Sumich, A. L. (2017). Electrophysiological study of the violence inhibition mechanism in relation to callous-unemotional and aggressive traits. *Personality and Individual Differences, 118*(1), 44–49.

Field, C. (2017, September 28). What's Susan Smith done since she killed her sons: What does she look like now? *WYFF News*. Retrieved from http://www.wyff4.com/article/whats-susan-smith-done-since-she-killed-her-sons-what-does-she-look-like-now/12501584

Fishbein, D. (2001). *Biobehavioral perspectives in criminology.* Belmont, CA: Wadsworth.

Fister, B. (2005). Copycat crimes: Crime fiction and the marketplace of anxieties. *Clues, 23*(3), 43–56.

Flanagan, E. H., & Blashfield, R. K. (2005). Gender acts as a context for interpreting diagnostic criteria. *Journal of Clinical Psychology, 61*(12), 1485–1498.

Fleming, V. (Director), & Selznick, D. O. (Producer). (1939). *Gone with the wind* [Motion picture]. USA: MGM.

Flexon, J. L. (2018). *Juvenile psychopathy: A primer.* Weston, WV: Weston.

Flexon, J. L., & Meldrum, R. C. (2013). Adolescent psychopathic traits and violent delinquency: Additive and nonadditive effects with key criminological variables. *Youth Violence & Juvenile Justice, 11*(4), 349–369.

Fontaine, N. M. G., McCrory, E. J. P., Boivin, M., Moffit, T. E., & Viding, E. (2011). Predictors and outcomes of joint trajectories of callous-unemotional traits and conduct problems in childhood. *Journal of Abnormal Psychology, 120*(3), 730–742.

Fooksman, L. (2008, February 7). Town center murders work of serial killer? *Sun-Sentinel.com.* Retrieved from http://articles.sun-sentinel.com/2008-02-07/news/0802070459_1_serial-killer-nancy-bochicchio-cell-phone

Ford, M., & Widiger, T. (1989). Sex bias in the diagnosis of histrionic and antisocial personality disorders. *Journal of Consulting and Clinical Psychology, 57*, 301–305.

Forouzan, E., & Cooke, D. J. (2005). Figuring out la femme fatale: Conceptual and assessment issues concerning psychopathy in females. *Behavioral Sciences & the Law, 23*(6), 765–778.

Forouzan, E., & Nicholls, T. (2015). Childhood and adolescent characteristics of women with high versus low psychopathy scores: Examining developmental precursors to the malignant personality disorder. *Journal of Criminal Justice, 43*, 307–320.

Forth, A. E., Brown, S. L., Hart, S. D., & Hare, R. D. (1996). The assessment of psychopathy in male and female noncriminals: Reliability and validity. *Personality and Individual Differences, 20*, 531–543.

Forth, A. E., Hart, S. D., & Hare, R. D. (1990). Assessment of psychopathy in male young offenders. *Psychological Assessment, 2*, 342–344.

Forth, A. E., Kosson, D., & Hare, R. D. (2003). *The Hare Psychopathy Checklist: Youth Version (PCL:YV).* Toronto, Ontario, Canada: Multi-Health Systems.

Foucault, M. (1977, 1995). *Discipline and punish: The birth of the prison.* New York: Vintage.

Foulds, G. A. (1965). *Personality and personal illness.* London: Tavistock.

Fowles, D. C. (2018). Temperament risk factors for psychopathy. In C. J. Patrick (Ed.), *Handbook of psychopathy* (2nd ed., pp. 94–123). New York: Guilford Press.

Fowles, D. C., & Dindo, L. (2006). A dual-deficit model of psychopathy. In C. J. Patrick (Ed.), *Handbook of psychopathy* (pp. 14–34). New York: Guilford Press.

Fowles, J. (1999). *The case for television violence.* Thousand Oaks, CA: Sage.

Fox, A. R., Kvaran, T. H., & Fontaine, R. G. (2013). Psychopathy and culpability: How responsible is the psychopath for criminal wrongdoing? *Law & Social Inquiry, 38*(1), 1–26.

Fox, B. H., Jennings, W. G., & Farrington, D. P. (2015). Bringing psychopathy into developmental and life-course criminology theories and research. *Journal of Criminal Justice, 43*(4), 274–289.

Fox, J., Roeg, L., Solerno, R. (Producers), & Ramsey, L. (Director). (2011). *We need to talk about Kevin* [Motion picture]. USA: Oscilloscope Laboratories.

Frankenstein, C. (1959). *Psychopathy.* New York/London: Grune & Stratton.

Franz, M. (1974, 1995). *Shadow and evil in fairy tales.* Boston: Shambhala.

Freedman, D. (2001). False prediction of future dangerousness: Error rates and the Psychopathy Checklist–Revised. *Journal of the American Academy of Psychiatry and Law, 29*, 89–95.

Frick, P. J., Barry, C. T., & Bodin, D. (2000). Applying the concept of psychopathy to children: Implications for the assessment of antisocial children. In C. B. Gacono (Ed.), *The clinical and forensic assessment of psychopathy: A practitioner's guide* (pp. 3–24). Mahwah, NJ: Erlbaum.

Frick, P. J., & Hare, R. D. (2002). *Antisocial process screening device.* Toronto: Multi-Health Systems.

Frye v. United States, 293 F. 1013 (D.C. Cir. 1923).

Furman v. Georgia, 408 U.S., 238 (1972).

Gabor, T. (1994). *Everybody does it! Crime by the public.* Toronto: University of Toronto Press.

Gacono, C. B. (1990). An empirical study of object relations and defensive operations in antisocial personality disorder. *Journal of Personality Assessment, 54*, 589–600.

Gacono, C.B. (Ed.). (2000). *The clinical and forensic assessment of psychopathy.* Mahwah, NJ: Erlbaum.

Gacono, C. B. (2013). Guidelines for the evaluation and interpretation of psychopathy research findings. In J. B. Helfgott (Ed.), *Criminal psychology* (Vol. 2, pp. 341–354). Santa Barbara, CA: Praeger.

Gacono, C. B. (Ed.). (2016). *The clinical and forensic assessment of psychopathy: A practitioner's guide.* New York: Routledge.

Gacono, C. B., Loving, J. L., Evans, F. B., Jumes, M. T. (2002). The Psychopathy Checklist–Revised: PCL-R testimony & forensic practice. *Journal of Forensic Psychology Practice, 2*(3), 33–53.

Gacono, C. B., & Meloy, J. R. (1988). The relationship between conscious cognitive style and unconscious defensive process in the psychopath. *Criminal Justice and Behavior, 15*, 472–483.

Gacono, C. B., & Meloy, J. R. (1994). *The Rorschach assessment of aggressive and psychopathic personalities.* Hillsdale, NJ: Erlbaum.

Gacono, C. B., & Meloy, J. R. (2002). Assessing psychopathic personalities. In J. N. Butcher (Ed.), *Clinical personality assessment: Practical approaches* (pp. 361–375). New York: Oxford University Press.

Gacono, C. B., Meloy, J. R., & Berg, J. L. (1992). Object relations, defensive operations, and affective states in narcissistic, borderline, and antisocial personality disorder. *Journal of Personality Assessment, 59*(1), 32–49.

Gacono, C. B., Meloy, J. R., & Heaven, T. R. (1990). A Rorschach investigation of narcissism and hysteria in antisocial personality. *Journal of Personality Assessment, 55*(1&2), 270–279.

Galang, A. J. R., Castelo, V. L. C., Santos, L. C., Perlas, C. M. C., & Angeles, M. A. B. (2016). Investigating the prosocial psychopath model of the creative personality: Evidence from traits and psychophysiology. *Personality and Individual Differences, 100*, 28–36.

Garland, D. (1990). *Punishment and modern society: A study in social theory.* Chicago: University of Chicago Press.

Garland, D. (2002). *The culture of control: Crime and social order in contemporary society.* Chicago: University of Chicago Press.

Geen, R. G., & Donnerstein, E. (Eds.). (1998). *Human aggression: Theories, research, and implications for social policy.* San Diego: Academic Press.

Gendreau, P. (1996). Offender rehabilitation: What we know and what needs to be done. *Criminal Justice and Behavior, 23*(1), 144–161.

Gendreau, P., Cullen, F. T., & Bonta, J. (1994). Intensive rehabilitation supervision: The next generation in community corrections? *Federal Probation, 58*, 72–78.

Gendreau, P. Goggin, C. & Smith, P. (2002). Is the PCL-R really the "unparalleled" measure of offender risk? A lesson in knowledge cumulation. *Criminal Justice and Behavior, 29*(4), 397–426.

Gendreau, P., Little, T., & Goggin, C. (1996). A meta-analysis of the predictors of adult offender recidivism. What works? *Criminology, 34*, 575–607.

Gendreau, P., & Ross, R. R. (1987). Revivification of rehabilitation: Evidence from the 1980s. *Justice Quarterly, 4*(3), 349–407.

Gendreau, P., & Ross, R. (1987). Revivification and rehabilitation: Evidence from the 1980's. *Justice Quarterly, 4*, 349–407.

Gentry, A. (2011). *Pass the PCL-R: Your guide to passing the Hare Psychopathy Checklist–Revised AKA the psychopath test.* Charleston, SC: CreateSpace.

Gerbner, G. (1984). Science or ritual dance? A revisionist view of television violence effects research. *Studies on Sexual Violence, 34*(3), 164–173.

Gerbner, G. (1994a). Reclaiming our cultural mythology: Television's global marketing strategy creates a damaging and alienated window on the world. *The Ecology of Justice, 38*. Retrieved February 28, 2004, from http://www.context.org/ICLIB/IC38/Gerbner.htm

Gerbner, G. (1994b). Growing up with television: The cultivation perspective. In J. Bryant & D. Zillman (Eds.), *Media effects: Advances in theory and research.* Hillsdale, NJ: Erlbaum.

Gilbert, P. R. (2002). Discourses of female violence and societal gender stereotypes. *Violence against Women, 8*(11), 1271–1300.

Glenn, A. L., Kurzban, R., & Raine, A. (2011). Evolutionary theory and psychopathy. *Aggression and Violent Behavior, 16*, 371–380.

Glenn, A. L., & Raine, A. (2014). *Psychopathy: An introduction to biological findings and their implications.* New York: New York University Press.

Glimcher, A., Perry, S., Rich, L. (Producers), & Glimcher, A. (Director). (1995). *Just cause* [Motion picture]. USA: Warner Brothers Pictures.

Glueck, S. (1927). *Mental disorder and the criminal law.* Boston: Little, Brown.

Glueck, S., & Glueck, E. T. (1950). *Unraveling juvenile delinquency.* Cambridge, MA: Harvard University Press.

Godman, M., & Jefferson, A. (2017). On blaming and punishing psychopaths. *Criminal Law and Philosophy, 11*, 127–142.

Godwin, M. (1998). Reliability, validity, and utility of extant serial murder classifications. *The Criminologist*, 22(4), 195–210.

Goffman, I. (1963). *Stigma: Notes on the management of a spoiled identity.* Englewood Cliffs, NJ: Prentice Hall.

Golden, T. (1996, August 6). Jury recommends death for killer of Polly Klaas. *New York Times.*

Goldstein, A. S. (1967). *The insanity defense.* New Haven/London: Yale University Press.

Goldstein, J. H. (Ed.). (1998). *Why we watch: The attractions of violent entertainment.* New York: Oxford University Press.

Gonçalves, R. A. (1999). Psychopathy and offender types: Results from a Portuguese prison sample. *International Journal of Law and Psychiatry, 22*(3–4), 337–346.

Gorenstein, E. E. (1991). A cognitive perspective on antisocial personality. In P. A. Magaro (Ed.), *Cognitive bases of mental disorders: Annual review of psychopathology* (Vol. 1, pp. 100–133). Newbury, CA: Sage.

Gottfredson, M. R., & Hirschi, T. (Eds.) (1987). *Positive criminology.* Beverly Hills/London: Sage.

Gottfredson, M. R., & Hirschi, T. (1990). *A general theory of crime.* Palo Alto, CA: Stanford University Press.

Grady, M. D., & Shields, J. J. (2018). The relationship between attachment dimensions and emotion regulation in individuals who have committed sexual crimes. *Journal of Sexual Aggression, 24*(1), 51–65.

Greene, J., Kahn, H. (Producers) & Lowe, R. (Director) (2018). *The Bad Seed* [Motion Picture]. USA: Front Street Pictures.

Greenstone, J. L., Kosson, D. S., & Gacono, C. B. (2000). Psychopathy and hostage negotiations: Some preliminary findings. In C. B. Gacono (Ed.), *The clinical and forensic assessment of psychopathy* (pp. 385–403). Mahwah, NJ: Erlbaum.

Gregg v. Georgia (1976), 48 U.S. 153 (1976).

Gregory, B. (2002). Hannibal Lecter: The honey in the lion's mouth. *American Journal of Psychotherapy, 56*(1), 100–114.

Gretton, H. M., Hare, R. D., & Catchpole, R. E. (2004). Psychopathy and offending from adolescence to adulthood: A 10-year follow-up. *Journal of Consulting and Clinical Psychology, 72*(4), 636.

Grossberg, L., Nelson, C., & Treichler, P. A. (Eds.). (1992). *Cultural studies.* New York/London: Routledge, Chapman, & Hall.

Guggenbuhl-Craig, A. (1980). *Eros on crutches: On the nature of the psychopath*. Dallas: Spring.

Guggenbuhl-Craig, A. (1991). Why psychopaths do not rule the world. In J. Abrahms & C. Zweig (Eds.), *Meeting the shadow: The hidden power of the dark side of human nature* (pp. 223–226). Los Angeles: Jeremy P. Tarcher.

Guns N' Roses. (1987). Sweet child o' mine. On *Appetite for destruction*. Santa Monica, CA: Geffen Records.

Guy, L. S., & Edens, J. F. (2003). Juror decision-making in a mock sexually violent predator trial: Gender differences in the impact of divergent types of expert testimony. *Behavioral Sciences and the Law, 21*, 215–237.

Guy, L. S., & Edens, J. F. (2006). Gender differences in attitudes toward psychopathic sexual offenders. *Behavioral Sciences and the Law, 24*, 65–85.

Guy, L. S., Edens, J. F., Anthony, C., & Douglas, K. S. (2005). Does psychopathy predict institutional misconduct among adults? A meta-analytic investigation. *Journal of Consulting and Clinical Psychology*, *73*(6), 1056.

Guy, L. S., Packer, I. K., Kusaj, C., & Douglas, K. S. (2015). Influence of the HCR-20, and PCL-R on decisions about parole suitability among lifers. *Law and Human Behavior*, *39*(3), 232–243.

Haapasalo, J. (1994). Types of offense among the Cleckley psychopaths. *Journal of Offender Therapy and Comparative Criminology*, *38*(1), 59–67.

Habel, U., Kuhn, E., Salloum, J. B., Devos, H., & Schneider, F. (2002). Emotional processing in psychopathic personality. *Aggressive Behavior, 28*, 394–400.

Häkkänen, H., Hurme, K., & Liukkonen, M. (2007). Distance patterns and disposal sites in rural area homicides committed in Finland. *Journal of Investigative Psychology and Offender Profiling*, *4*(3), 181–197.

Häkkänen-Nyholm, H., & Hare, R. D. (2009). Psychopathy, homicide, and the courts working the system. *Criminal Justice and Behavior*, *36*(8), 761–777.

Häkkänen-Nyholm, H., & Nyholm, J. (Eds.). (2012). *Psychopathy and the law*. Malden, MA: Wiley-Blackwell.

Häkkänen-Nyholm, H., Weizmann-Henelius, G., Salenius, S., Lindberg, N., & Repo-Tiihonen, E. (2009). Homicides with mutilation of the victim's body. *Journal of Forensic Sciences*, *54*(4), 933–937.

Hall, J. R., & Benning, S. D. (2006). The "successful" psychopath: Adaptive and subclinical manifestations of psychopathy in the general population. In C. J. Patrick (Ed.), *Handbook of psychopathy* (pp. 459–478). New York: Guilford Press.

Hamilton, R. B., & Newman, J. P. (2018). The response modulation hypothesis: Formulation, development, and implications for psychopathy. In C. J. Patrick (Ed.), *Handbook of psychopathy* (2nd ed., pp. 80–93). New York: Guilford Press.

Hamilton, S., Rothbart, M., & Dawes, R. M. (1986). Sex bias, diagnosis, and DSM-III. *Sex Roles, 5*, 269–274.

Hammer, R. (1990). The biblical perception of the origin of evil. *Judiasm, 39*(3), 318–325.
Hamsher, J., Murphey, D., Townsend, C. (Producers), & Stone, O. (Director). (1994). *Natural born killers* [Motion picture]. USA: Warner Brothers.
Hancock, J. T., Woodworth, M. T., & Porter, S. (2013). Hungry like the wolf: A word-pattern analysis of the language of psychopaths. *Legal and Criminological Psychology, 18*(1), 102–114.
Hans, V. P., & Dee, J. (1991). Media coverage of law: Its impact on juries and the public. *American Behavioral Scientist, 35*(2), 136–149.
Harcourt, B. E. (2003). The shaping of chance: Actual models and criminal profiling at the turn of the twenty-first century. *University of Chicago Law Review, 70*(1), 105–128.
Harcourt, B. E. (2007). *Against prediction: Profiling, policing, and punishing in an actuarial age.* Chicago: Chicago University Press.
Hare, R. D. (1965a). A conflict and learning theory analysis of psychopathic behavior. *Journal of Research in Crime and Delinquency, 2*, 12–19.
Hare, R. D. (1965b). Acquisition and generalization of a conditioned-fear response in psychopathic and non-psychopathic criminals. *Journal of Psychology, 59*, 367–370.
Hare, R. D. (1965c). Temporal gradient of fear arousal in psychopaths. *Journal of Abnormal Psychology, 70*, 442–445.
Hare, R. D. (1966a). Psychopathy, fear arousal, and anticipated pain. *Psychological Reports, 16*, 499–502.
Hare, R. D. (1966b). Psychopathy and choice of immediate versus delayed punishment. *Journal of Abnormal Psychology, 71*, 25–29.
Hare, R. D. (1966c). Preference for delay of shock as a function of its intensity and probability. *Psychonomic Science, 5*, 393–394.
Hare, R. D. (1968a). Psychopathy, autonomic functioning, and the orienting response. *Journal of Abnormal Psychology Monograph Supplement, 73* (Part 2), 1–24.
Hare, R. D. (1968b). Detection threshold for electric shock in psychopaths. *Journal of Abnormal Psychology, 73*, 268–272.
Hare, R. D. (1969). An MMPI comparison of psychopathic and nonpsychopathic criminals. *Journal of Abnormal Psychology, 73*, 268–272.
Hare, R. D. (1970). *Psychopathy: Theory and research.* New York/London: Wiley.
Hare, R. D. (1980). A research scale for the assessment of psychopathy in criminal populations. *Personality and Individual Differences, 1*, 111–119.
Hare, R. D. (1982). Psychopathy and physiological activity during anticipation of an aversive stimulus in a distraction paradigm. *Psychophysiology, 19*(3), 266–271.
Hare, R. D. (1985a). Comparison of procedures for the assessment of psychopathy. *Journal of Consulting and Clinical Psychology, 53*, 7–16.
Hare, R. D. (1985b). *The psychopathy checklist.* Unpublished manuscript. Vancouver, Canada: University of British Columbia.
Hare, R. D. (1991, 2003). *Manual for the Psychopathy Checklist–Revised.* Toronto, Ontario: Multi-Health Systems.

Hare, R. D. (1993). *Without conscience: The disturbing world of psychopaths among us*. New York: Pocket Books.

Hare, R. D. (1996a). Psychopathy: A clinical construct whose time has come. *Criminal Justice and Behavior, 23* (1), 25–54.

Hare, R. D. (1996b). Psychopathy and antisocial personality disorder: A case of diagnostic confusion. *Psychiatric Times, 13,* 39–40.

Hare, R. D. (1996c). *The psychopathic mind* [Videorecording]. Canadian Broadcasting Corporation. Princeton, NJ: Films for the Humanities & Sciences.

Hare, R. D. (1998). Psychopaths and their nature: Implications for the mental health and criminal justice systems. In T. Millon, E. Simonsen, E. Birket-Smith, & R. D. Davis (Eds.), *Psychopathy: Antisocial, criminal, and violent behavior* (pp. 188–212). New York: Guilford.

Hare, R. D. (2001). Psychopaths and their nature: Some implications for understanding human predatory violence. In A. Raine & J. Sanmartin (Eds.), *Violence & psychopathy* (pp. 5–34). New York: Kluwer/Plenum.

Hare, R. D. (2007). Forty years aren't enough: Recollections, prognostications, and random musings. In H. Herve & J. Yuille (Eds.), *The Psychopath: Theory, research, and practice* (pp. 3–28). Mahwah, NJ: Erlbaum.

Hare, R. D. (2012). Focus on psychopathy. *FBI Law Enforcement Bulletin, 81*(7), 2.

Hare, R. D. (2016). Psychopathy, the PCL-R, and criminal justice: Some new findings and current issues. *Canadian Psychology/Psychologie canadienne, 57*(1), 21.

Hare, R. D., & Babiak, P. (2006). *Snakes in suits: When psychopaths go to work.* New York: Ragen Books.

Hare, R. D., Clark, D., Grann, M., & Thorton, D. (2000). Psychopathy and the predictive validity of the PCL-R: An international perspective. *Behavioral Sciences and the Law, 18*, 623–645.

Hare, R. D., Hart, S. D., & Harpur, T. (1991). Psychopathy and the DSM-IV criteria for antisocial personality disorder. *Journal of Abnormal Psychology, 100*, 391–398.

Hare, R. D., and Hervé, H. F. (1999, 2001). *Hare P-Scan Research Version.* North Tonawanda, NY: Multi-Health Systems.

Hare, R. D., McPherson, L. M., & Forth, A. E. (1988). Male psychopaths and their criminal careers. *Journal of Consulting and Clinical Psychology, 56*(5), 710–714.

Hare, R. D., & Neumann, C. S. (2006). The PCL-R assessment of psychopathy: Development, structural properties, and new directions. In C. J. Patrick (Ed.), *Handbook of psychopathy* (pp. 58–88). New York: Guilford Press.

Hare, R. D., & Neumann, C. S. (2010). The role of antisociality in the psychopathy construct: Comment on Skeem and Cooke (2010). *Psychological Assessment, 22*(2), 446–454.

Hare, R. D., Neumann, C. S., & Mokros, A. (2018). The PCL-R assessment of psychopathy: Development, properties, debate, and new directions. In C. J.

Patrick (Ed.), *Handbook of psychopathy* (2nd ed., pp. 39–79). New York: Guilford Press.

Hare, R. D., & O'Toole, M. E. (2006, February 20–24). *Psychopathy and its application to understanding violent criminals and their behavior.* Workshop presentation at the American Academy of Forensic Sciences, Seattle.

Hare, R. D., & Schalling, D. (1978). *Psychopathic behaviour: Approaches to research.* New York: Wiley.

Harlow, H. F. (1961). The development of affectional patterns in infant monkeys. In B. M. Foss (Ed.), *Determinants of infant behaviour* (pp. 75–97). London: Methuen.

Harpur, T. J., Hakstian, R. A., & Hare, R. D. (1988). Factor structure of the psychopathy checklist. *Journal of Counseling and Clinical Psychology, 56,* 741–747.

Harpur, T. J., Hare, R. D., & Hakstian, R. (1989). Two-factor conceptualization of psychopathy: Construct validity and assessment implications. *Psychological Assessment: A Journal of Consulting and Clinical Psychology, 1*(1), 6–17.

Harrington, A. (1972). *Psychopaths.* New York: Simon & Schuster.

Harris, G. T., & Rice, M. E. (2006). Treatment of psychopathy: A review of empirical findings. In C. J. Patrick (Ed.), *Handbook of psychopathy* (pp. 555–572). New York: Guilford Press.

Harris, G. T., Rice, M. E., & Cormier, C. A. (1991). Psychopathy and violent recidivism. *Law and Human Behavior, 15,* 625–637.

Harris, G. T., Rice, M. E., & Quinsey, V. L. (1994). Psychopathy as a taxon: Evidence that psychopaths are a discrete class. *Journal of Consulting and Clinical Psychology, 62*(2), 387–397.

Hart, S., & Hare, R. D. (1989). Discriminant validity of the psychopathy checklist in a forensic population. *Psychological Assessment, 1,* 211–218.

Hart, S. D. (1998). The role of psychopathy in assessing risk for violence: Conceptual and methodological issues. *Legal and Criminal Psychology, 3,* 121–137.

Hart, S. D., Cox, D. N., & Hare, R. D. (1995). *The Hare Psychopathy Checklist: Screening Version (PCL:SV).* Toronto, Ontario, Canada: Multi-Health Systems.

Harte, J. M. (2015). Preventing crime in cooperation with the mental health care profession. *Crime, Law, and Social Change, 64*(4/5), 263–275.

Harvey, D. (2002). *Obsession: Celebrities and their stalkers.* Dublin, Ireland: Merlin.

Hayes, H. (2014, April 7). Isaiah Smith found guilty of voluntary manslaughter. *CBS Pittsburgh.* Retrieved from http://pittsburgh.cbslocal.com/2014/04/07/isiah-smith-found-guilty-of-voluntary-manslaughter

Heber, A. (2017). "You thought you were superman": Violence, victimization and masculinities. *British Journal of Criminology, 57,* 61–68.

Helfgott, J., Lovell, M., & Lawrence, C. (2000). Results from the pilot study of the Citizens, Victims, and Offenders Restoring Justice Program at the

Washington State Reformatory. *Journal of Contemporary Criminal Justice, 16*, 5–31.

Helfgott, J., Lovell, M., Lawrence, C., & Parsonage, W. (1999). Development of the Citizens, Victims and Offenders Restoring Justice Program at the Washington State Reformatory. *Criminal Justice Policy Review, 10*(3), 363–399.

Helfgott, J. B. (1991). *A comparison of cognitive, behavioral, and psychodynamic assessments of psychopathy: Integrative measures of understanding the psychopathic personality in criminal and noncriminal populations* (Unpublished master's thesis). Pennsylvania State University, University Park.

Helfgott, J. B. (1992). *The relationship between unconscious defensive process and conscious cognitive style in psychopaths* (Doctoral dissertation). Penn State University. Dissertation Abstracts International, 54-03A, 1102–1374.

Helfgott, J. B. (1994, March). *Psychopathy in art and science: Is Hollywood moving faster than academe?* Paper presented at the Academy of Criminal Justice Sciences, Chicago.

Helfgott, J. B. (1995, March). *The female psychopath in art versus science: Analysis of film portrayals of the femme fatale.* Paper presented at the Academy of Criminal Justice Sciences, Boston.

Helfgott, J. B. (1997). The relationship between unconscious defensive process and conscious cognitive style in psychopaths. *Criminal Justice & Behavior, 24*, 278–293.

Helfgott, J. B. (2004). Primitive defenses in the language of the psychopath: Considerations for forensic practice. *Journal of Forensic Psychology Practice, 4*(3), 1–29.

Helfgott, J. B. (2008). *Criminal behavior: Theories, typologies, and criminal justice.* Thousand Oaks, CA: Sage.

Helfgott, J. B. (Ed). (2013a). *Criminal psychology* (Vols. 1–4). Santa Barbara, CA: Praeger.

Helfgott, J. B. (2013b). Criminal typologies. In J. B. Helfgott (Ed.), *Criminal psychology* (Vol. 2, pp. 3–42). Santa Barbara, CA: Praeger.

Helfgott, J. B. (2013c). The popular conception of the psychopath: Implications for criminal justice practice. In J. B. Helfgott (Ed.), *Criminal psychology* (Vol. 2, pp. 515–546). Santa Barbara, CA: Praeger.

Helfgott, J. B. (2014). Fame, media, and mass shootings: Culture plays a role in creating these tragedies. *Crosscut.* Retrieved from http://crosscut.com/2014/06/08/crime-safety/120459/fame-media-and-mass-shootings-culture-playing-role/?page=2

Helfgott, J. B. (2015). Criminal behavior and the copycat effect: Review of the literature and theoretical framework for empirical investigation. *Aggression and Violent Behavior, 22*, 46–64.

Helfgott, J. B., Lovell, M. L., & Lawrence, C. F. (2002). Citizens, victims, and offenders restoring justice: Accountability, healing, and hope through storytelling and dialogue. *Crime Victims Report, 6*, 3–4, 11.

Helfgott, J. B., & Strah, B. M. (2013). Actuarial prediction in determinate-plus sex offender release decisions. In J. B. Helfgott (Ed.), *Criminal personality* (Vol. 3, pp. 113–135). Santa Barbara, CA: Praeger/ABC-CLIO.

Hemphill, J. S., & Hare, R. D. (2004). Some misconceptions about the Hare PCL-R and risk assessment: A reply to Gendreau, Goggin, and Smith. *Criminal Justice and Behavior, 31*(2), 203–243.

Hemphill, J. S., Hare, R. D., & Wong, S. (1998). Psychopathy and recidivism: A review. *Legal and Criminological Psychology, 3,* 139–170.

Henderson, D. K. (1947). *Psychopathic states.* New York: Norton.

Henkel, C. (2005, February 27). Killer's letter still haunting 30 years later. *Seattle Times.* Retrieved from https://www.seattletimes.com/nation-world/killers-letter-still-haunting-30-years-later

Herson, M., & Turner, S. M. (Eds.). (1991). *Adult psychopathology and diagnosis.* New York: Wiley.

Hervé, H. F., Mitchell, D., Cooper, B. S., Spidel, A., & Hare, R. D. (2004). Psychopathy and unlawful confinement: An examination of perpetrator and event characteristics. *Canadian Journal of Behavioural Science, 36*(2), 137–145.

Hervé, H. F., & Yuille, J. C. (Eds.). (2007). *The psychopath: Theory, research, and practice.* Mahwah, NJ: Erlbaum.

Hesse, M. (2009). Portrayal of psychopathy in the movies. *International Review of Psychiatry, 21*(3), 207–212.

Hiatt, K. D., & Newman, J. P. (2006). Understanding psychopathy: The cognitive side. In C. J. Patrick (Ed.), *Handbook of psychopathy* (pp. 334–352). New York: Guilford Press.

Hickey, E. W. (1991, 1997, 2002, 2006, 2009, 2015). *Serial murderers and their victims.* Belmont, CA: Wadsworth.

Hickey, E. W., Walters, B. K., Drislane, L. E., Palumbo, I. M., & Patrick, C. J. (2018). Deviance at its darkest: Serial murder and psychopathy. In C. J. Patrick (Ed.), *Handbook of psychopathy* (2nd ed., pp. 570–584). New York: Guilford Press.

Hicks, B. M., & Drislane, L. E. (2018). Variants ("subtypes") of psychopathy. In C. J. Patrick (Ed.), *Handbook of psychopathy* (2nd ed., pp. 297–332). New York: Guilford Press.

Hill, G. (1992). *Illuminating shadows: The mythic power of film.* Boston: Shambhala.

Hirschi, T. (1969). *Causes of delinquency.* Berkeley: University of California Press.

Hodges, H., & Heilbrun, K. (2009). Psychopathy as a predictor of instrumental violence among civil psychiatric patients. *International Journal of Forensic Mental Health, 8,* 131–141.

Hofstede, G. (1980). *Culture's consequences: International differences in work-related values.* Beverley Hills/London: Sage.

Hofstede, G. (1988). *Masculinity and femininity: The taboo dimension of national cultures.* Thousand Oaks, CA: Sage.

Hollis, M. E., Downey, S., del Carmen, A., & Dobbs, R. R. (2017). The relationship between media portrayals and crime: Perceptions of fear of crime among citizens. *Crime Prevention and Community Safety, 19*(1), 46–60.

Holm, K. (2004). The making of a monster. *Journal of Feminist Family Therapy, 16*(1), 83–85.

Holmes, R. M. (1989, 1995). *Profiling violent crimes: An investigative tool.* Newbury Park, CA: Sage.

Holmes, R. M., & Holmes, S. T. (2002). *Profiling violent crimes: An investigative tool.* Thousand Oaks, CA: Sage.

Homant, R. J., & Kennedy, D. B. (1998). Psychological aspects of crime scene profiling: Validity research. *Criminal Justice and Behavior, 25*(3), 319–343.

Hoppenbrouwers, S. S., Neumann, C. S., & Lewis, J. (2015). A latent variable analysis of the Psychopathy Checklist–Revised and behavioral inhibition system/behavioral activation system factors in North American and Swedish offenders. *Personality Disorders: Theory, Research, and Treatment, 6*(3), 251–260.

Horberg, W., Sternberg, T. (Producers), & Minghella, A. (Director). (1999). *The talented Mr. Ripley* [Motion picture]. USA: Paramount Pictures, Miramax Films.

Horowitz, M. J. (1977, 1991). *Hysterical personality style and the histrionic personality disorder.* Northvale, NY: Jason Aronson.

Hort, B. E. (1996). *Unholy hungers: Encountering the psychic vampire in ourselves and others.* Boston: Shambhala.

Hosen, A. (2015, October 16). He showed no remorse. *Daily Star.* Retrieved from https://www.thedailystar.net/frontpage/he-showed-no-remorse-157792

Howard, R. C., Khalifa, N., & Duggan, C. (2014). Antisocial personality disorder comorbid with borderline pathology and psychopathy is associated with severe violence in a forensic sample. *The Journal of Forensic Psychiatry & Psychology, 25*(6), 658–672.

Howells, K., Day, A., Bubner, S., Jauncey, S., Williamson, P., Parker, A., & Heseltine, K. (2002, June). Anger management and violence prevention: Improving effectiveness. *Trends and Issues in Crime and Justice.* Canberra, Australia: Australian Institute of Criminology.

Huffman, E. G. (2013a). The therapeutic relationship, prison, and responsivity. In J. B. Helfgott (Ed.), *Criminal psychology* (Vol. 4, pp. 175–208). Santa Barbara, CA: Praeger.

Huffman, E. G. (2013b). Inside the imprisoned therapeutic relationship. In J. B. Helfgott (Ed.), *Criminal psychology* (Vol. 4, pp. 209–232). Santa Barbara, CA: Praeger.

Hughes, T. L., Gacono, C. B., Tansy, M., & Shaffer, K. (2013). Psychopathy in youth: Treatment of youth in schools. In J. B. Helfgott (Ed.), *Criminal psychology* (Vol. 4). Santa Barbara: Praeger.

Hui, H. C., & Triandis, H. C. (1986). Individualism-collectivism: A study of cross-cultural researchers. *Journal of Cross-Cultural Psychology, 17*(2), 786–792.

Human, J. (Producer), Broomfield, N., & Churchill, J. (2003). *Aileen: Life and death of a serial killer.* USA: Lafayette Films.

Hyatt, C. S., & Willis, J. (2010). *The psychopath's bible.* Reno, NV: New Falcon.

Igoumenou, A., Yang, M., Harmer, C. J., Coid, J. W., & Rogers, R. D. (2017). Faces and facets: The variability of emotion recognition in psychopathy reflects its affective and antisocial features. *Journal of Abnormal Psychology, 126*(8), 1066–1076.

Institute for Bioenergetic Analysis. (1975). *Psychopathic behavior and the psychopathic personality.* Expanded version of a lecture given at the Community Church, New York.

Irwin, K., & Adler, C. (2012). Fighting for her honor: Girl's violence in distressed communities. *Feminist Criminology, 7*(4), 350–380.

Issa, M., Falkenbach, D. M., Trupp, G. F., Campregher, J. G., & Lap, J. (2017). Psychopathy in Lebanese college students: The PPI-R considered in the context of borderline features and aggressive attitudes across sex and culture. *Personality and Individual Differences, 105*(15), 64–69.

Jackson, R. L., & Richards, H. J. (2007). Diagnostic and risk profiles among civilly committed sex offenders in Washington State. *International Journal of Offender Therapy and Comparative Criminology, 51*(3), 313–323.

Jackson, R. L., Rogers, R., Neumann, C. S., & Lambert, P. L. (2002). Psychopathy in female offenders: An investigation of its underlying dimensions. *Criminal Justice and Behavior, 29*(6), 692–704.

Jacquin, K. M., & Hodges, E. P. (2007). The influence of media messages on mock juror decisions in the Andrea Yates trial. *American Journal of Forensic Psychology, 25*(4), 21–40.

Janus, E. S., & Prentky, R. A. (2008). Sexual predator laws: A two-decade retrospective. *Federal Sentencing Reporter, 21*(2), 90–97.

Jenkins, P. (1994). *Using murder: The social construction of serial homicide.* New York: Aldine de Gruyter.

Jenkins, P. (1998). *Moral Panic: Changing concepts of the child molester in modern America.* New Haven, CT: Yale University Press.

Jermyn, D. (1996). Rereading the bitches from hell: A feminist appropriation of the female psychopath. *Screen, 37*(3), 251–267.

Johannessen, C. (Producer). (2006–2013). *Dexter* [Television series]. New York: Showtime.

Johnson, A. E. (1923). The constitutional psychopathic inferiors: A problem in diagnosis. *American Journal of Psychiatry, 21*(1), 467–473.

Johnson, J. (2011, April 1). Koran-burning pastor calls Afghan killings "tragic." *Newser.* Retrieved April 1, 2011, from http://www.newser.com/story/115462/koran-burning-protester-terry-jones-calls-killing-of-un-workers-tragic-but-isnt-sorry-he-burned.html

Johnson, R. (1991). *Owning your own shadow: Understanding the dark side of the psyche.* New York: HarperCollins.

Johnstone, L., & Cooke, D. J. (2004). Psychopathic-like traits in childhood: Conceptual and measurement concerns. *Behavioral Sciences and the Law, 22,* 103–125.

Jolliffe, D., & Murray, J. (2012). Lack of empathy and offending: Implications for tomorrow's research and practice. In R. Loeber & B. C. Welsh (Eds.), *The future of criminology* (pp. 62–69). New York: Oxford University Press.
Jonason, P. K., Foster, J. D., Egorova, M. S., Parshikova, O., Csathó, Á, Oshio, A., & Gouveia, V. V. (2017). The dark triad traits from a life history perspective in six countries. *Frontiers in Psychology, 8*(1), 1–6.
Jones, D. A. (1986). *History of criminology.* New York/London: Greenwood Press.
Jones, D. W. (2017). Moral insanity and psychological disorder: The hybrid roots of psychiatry. *History of Psychiatry, 28*(3), 263–279.
Jones, S., & Cauffman, E. (2008). Juvenile psychopathy and judicial decision making: An empirical analysis of an ethical dilemma. *Behavioral Sciences and the Law, 26*, 151–165.
Jones, S., Chan, H. C., Meyers, W. C., & Heide, K. M. (2013). Proposed sexual homicide category: The psychopathic-sexually sadistic offender. In J. B. Helfgott (Ed.), *Criminal psychology* (Vol. 2, pp. 403–422). Santa Barbara, CA: Praeger.
Jordan, K., Swartz, M. S., George, L., Woodbury, M. A., & Blazer, D. G. (1989). Antisocial and related disorders in a southern community: An application of grade membership analysis. *The Journal of Nervous and Mental Disease, 177*(9), 529–541.
Judge: Bride showed no remorse in husband's death. (2014, March 27). *Associated Press.* Retrieved from no-remorse-husbands-death-000539588 .html
Kafka, F. (1925). *The trial.* New York: Schocken Books.
Kagitcibasi, C. (1989). Family and socialization in cross-cultural perspective: A model for change. In J. J. Berman (Ed.), *Cross-cultural perspectives* (pp. 135–200). Lincoln/London: University of Nebraska Press.
Kamphuis, J. H., & Emmelkamp, P. M. (2005). Twenty years of research into violence and trauma. *Journal of Interpersonal Violence, 20*(2), 167–174.
Kansas v. Hendricks (1997), 521 U.S. 346.
Kaplan, J. (Director), Jaffe, S. R., & Lansing, S. (Producers). (1988). *The accused* [Film]. Hollywood, CA: Paramount Pictures.
Kaplan, M. (1983). A woman's view of DSM-III. *American Psychologist, 38*, 225–248.
Karpman, B. (1941). On the need of separating psychopathy into two distinct clinical types: The symptomatic and the ideopathic. *Journal of Criminal Psychopathology, 3*, 112–137.
Karpman, B. (1946). Psychopathy in the scheme of human typology. *Journal of Nervous and Mental Disease, 103*, 276–288.
Karpman, B. (1948). The myth of the psychopathic personality. *American Journal of Psychiatry, 104*, 523–534.
Kass, F., Spitzer, R., & Williams, J. (1983). An empirical study of the issue of sex bias in the diagnostic criteria of DSMIII Axis II personality disorders. *American Psychologist, 38*, 799–801.

Katz, J. (2006). *The macho paradox: Why some men hurt women and how all men can help.* Naperville, IL: Sourcebooks.
Keesler, M. E., & DeMatteo, D. (2017). How media exposure relates to laypersons' understanding of psychopathy. *Journal of Forensic Sciences, 62*(6), 1522–1533.
Keierleber, J. A., & Bohan, T. L. (2005). Ten years after Daubert: The status of the states. *Journal of Forensic Sciences, 50*(5), 1154–1163.
Keppel, R. D., & Birnes, W. (1997). *Signature killers.* New York: Pocket Books.
Keppel, R. D., & Walter, R. (1999). Profiling killers: A revised classification model for understanding sexual murder. *International Journal of Offender Therapy and Comparative Criminology, 43*(4), 417–437.
Kernberg, O. F. (1966). Structural derivatives of object relationships. *International Journal of Psychoanalysis, 47,* 236–253.
Kernberg, O. F. (1967). Borderline personality organization. *Journal of the American Psychoanalytic Association, 15,* 641–685.
Kernberg, O. F. (1975). *Borderline conditions and pathological narcissism.* New York: Jason Aronson.
Kernberg, O. F. (1976). *Object relations theory and clinical psychoanalysis.* New York: Jason Aronson.
Kernberg, O. F. (1984). *Severe personality disorders: Psychotherapeutic strategies.* New Haven, CT: Yale University Press.
Kernberg, O. F. (1985a). *Borderline conditions and pathological narcissism.* New York: Jason Aronson.
Kernberg, O. F. (1985b). *Internal world and external reality.* New York: Jason Aronson.
Kernberg, O. F. (1987). A psychodynamic approach. *Journal of Personality Disorders, 1*(4), 344–346.
Kernberg, O. F. (1989). The narcissistic personality disorder and the differential diagnosis of antisocial behavior. *Psychiatric Clinics of North America, 12,* 553–557.
Kernberg, O. F. (1992). *Aggression in personality disorders and perversions.* New Haven, CT: Yale University Press.
Kernberg, O., Selzer, M., Koenigsberg, C. A., Carr, A. C., & Appelbaum, A. (1989). *Psychodynamic psychotherapy of borderline patients.* New York: Basic Books.
Kiehl, K., & Sinnott-Armstrong, W. P. (Eds.). (2013). *Handbook of psychopathy and law.* Oxford: Oxford University Press.
Kiehl, K. A. (2014). *The psychopath whisperer: The science of those without a conscience.* New York: Crown.
Kiehl, K. A., & Buckholtz, J. W. (2010, September/October). Inside the mind of a psychopath. *Scientific American Mind,* 22–63.
Kimonis, E. R., Fanti, K. A., Goulter, N., & Hall, J. (2017). Affective startle potentiation differentiates primary and secondary variants of juvenile psychopathy. *Development and Psychopathology, 29*(4), 1149–1160.

King 5 News. (1996, August 5). Interview with Mark Klaas regarding Richard Allen Davis sentencing.

Kirsta, A. (1994). *Deadlier than the male: Violence and aggression in women.* London: HarperCollins.

Kiselyak, C. (Producer, Director). (1996). *Natural Born Killers: Director's cut* [Film]. Available from Pioneer Entertainment.

Kleck, G., & Jackson, D. B. (2017). Does crime cause punitiveness? *Crime & Delinquency, 63*(12), 1572–1599.

Knight, M. L. (2013). Learned monsters: Psychopathic masculinities in contemporary German film and fiction. *In Colloquia Germanica, 46*(1), 4–20.

Knight, R. A., & Guay J. P. (2006). The role of psychopathy in sexual coercion against women. In C. J. Patrick (Ed.), *Handbook of psychopathy* (pp. 512–532). New York: Guilford Press.

Knight, R. A., & Guay, J. P. (2018). The role of psychopathy in sexual coercion against women: An update and expansion. In C. J. Patrick (Ed.), *Handbook of psychopathy* (2nd ed., pp. 662–681). New York: Guilford Press.

Knight, R. A., & Sims-Knight, J. E. (2003). The developmental antecedents of sexual coercion against women: Testing alternative hypotheses with structural equation modeling. *Annals of New York Academy of Sciences, 989*, 72–85.

Kocsis, R. N. (2006). *Criminal profiling: Principles and practice.* New York: Humana Press.

Kocsis, R. N. (2013). An introduction to criminal profiling. In J. B. Helfgott (Ed.), *Criminal psychology* (Vol. 2, pp. 43–62). Santa Barbara, CA: Praeger.

Kohut, H. (1971). *Analysis of the self.* New York: International Universities Press.

Kondo, N. (2008). Mental illness in film. *Psychiatric Rehabilitation Journal, 31*(3), 250–252.

Kopelson, A., Carlyle, P. (Producers), & Fincher, D. (Director). (1995). *Se7en* [Motion picture]. USA: New Line Cinema.

Kosson, D. S., Gacono, C. B., & Bodholdt, R. H. (2000). Assessing psychopathy: Interpersonal aspects and clinical interviewing. In C. B. Gacono (Ed.), *The clinical and forensic assessment of psychopathy* (pp. 203–229). Mahwah, NJ: Erlbaum.

Kosson, D. S., Gacono, C. B., Klipfel, K. M., & Bodholdt, R. (2016). Understanding and assessing psychopathy: Interpersonal aspects and clinical interviewing. In C. B. Gacono (Ed.), *The clinical and forensic assessment of psychopathy* (2nd ed., pp. 252–275). New York: Routledge.

Kosson, D. S., Smith, S. S., & Newman, J. P. (1990). Evaluation the construct validity of psychopathy in black and white male inmates: Three preliminary studies. *Journal of Abnormal Psychology, 99*, 250–259.

Kosson, D. S., Vitacco, M. J., Swagger, M. T., & Steuerwald, B. L. (2016). Emotional experiences of the psychopath. In C. B. Gacono (Ed.), *The clinical and forensic assessment of psychopathy* (2nd ed., pp. 73–96). New York: Routledge.

Krafft-Ebing, R. V. (1906). *Psychopathia sexualis.* Chicago: Login Brothers.

Krafft-Ebing, R. V. (1965). *Psychopathia sexualis.* New York: Stein & Day.

Kreis, M. K., & Cooke, D. J. (2011). Capturing the psychopathic female: A prototypicality analysis of the Comprehensive Assessment of Psychopathic Personality (CAPP) across gender. *Behavioral Sciences and the Law, 29*(5), 634–648.

Kumho Tire Company, Ltd v. Carmichael, 526 U.S. 137 (1999).

Lafarge, L. (1989). Emptiness as defense in severe regressive states. *Journal of the American Psychoanalytic Association, 37,* 965–995.

Leader, C. (2009). The Odyssey—a Jungian perspective: Individuation and meeting with the archetypes of the collective unconscious. *British Journal of Psychotherapy, 25*(4), 506–519.

Leask, A. (2018, May 10). "Sinister, abhorrent, gross" child sex offender jailed. *Newstalk ZB.* Retrieved from http://www.newstalkzb.co.nz/on-air/larry-williams-drive/audio/sinister-abhorrent-gross-child-sex-offender-jailed

LeBreton, J. M., Baysinger, M. A., Abbey, A., & Jacques-Tiura, A. J. (2013). The relative importance of psychopathy-related traits predicting impersonal sex and hostile masculinity. *Personality and Individual Differences, 55,* 817–822.

Lee, C. (2007). The judicial response to psychopathic criminals: Utilitarianism over retribution. *Law & Psychology Review, 31,* 125–136.

Leistedt, S. J., & Linkowski, P. (2014). Psychopathy and the cinema: Fact or fiction? *Journal of Forensic Sciences, 59*(1), 167–174.

Leroy, M. (Producer/Director). (1956). *The bad seed.* [Motion picture]. USA: Warner Brothers.

Lesser, W. (1993). *Pictures at an execution: An inquiry into the subject of murder.* Cambridge: Harvard University Press.

Letendre, J. (2007). "Sugar and spice but not always nice": Gender socialization and its impact on development and maintenance of aggression in adolescent girls. *Child and Adolescent Social Work Journal, 24*(4), 353–368.

Levy, N. (2014). Psychopaths and blame: The argument from content. *Philosophical Psychology, 27*(3), 351–367.

Lilienfeld, S., VanValkenburg, C., Larntz, K., & Akiskal, H. (1986). The relationship of histrionic personality disorder to antisocial personality disorder and somatization disorders. *American Journal of Psychiatry, 143*(6), 718–722.

Lilienfeld, S. O., & Andrews, B. P. (1996). Development and preliminary validation of a self report measure of psychopathic personality traits in noncriminal populations. *Journal of Personality Assessment, 66,* 488–524.

Lilienfeld, S. O., Waldman, I. D., Landfield, K., Watts, A. L., Rubenzer, S., & Faschingbauer, T. R. (2012). Fearless dominance and the U.S. presidency: Implications of psychopathic personality traits for successful and unsuccessful political leadership. *Journal of Personality and Social Psychology, 103*(3), 489–505.

Lindberg, M. A., Fugett, A., & Adkins, A. (2015). Tests of theories of crime in female prisoners: Social bond and control, risk taking, and dynamic systems theories. *International Journal of Offender Therapy and Comparative Criminology, 61*(3), 282–309.

Lindner, R. M. (1945). *Rebel without a cause.* London: Research Books.

Lindner, R. M. (1946). *Stone walls and men.* New York: Odyssey Press.

Lindsay Lohan shows no remorse with tight court outfit. (2011, March 11). *Ace Showbiz.* Retrieved April 1, 2011, from http://www.aceshowbiz.com/news/view/00038968.html

Ling, S., & Raine, A. (2018). The neuroscience of psychopathy and forensic implications. *Psychology, Crime, & Law, 24*(3), 296–312.

Lipton, D., Martinson, R., & Wilks, D. (1975). *The effectiveness of correctional treatment: A survey of treatment evaluation studies.* New York: Praeger.

Lishner, D. A., Hong, P. Y., Jiang, L., Vitacco, M. J., & Neumann, C. S. (2015). Psychopathy, narcissism, and borderline personality: A critical test of the affective empathy-impairment hypothesis. *Personality and Individual Differences, 86*(1), 257–265.

Litwack, T. R., & Schlesinger L. B. (1998). Dangerous risk assessments: Research, legal, and clinical considerations. In A. K. Hess & I. B. Weiner (Eds.), *Handbook of forensic psychology* (pp. 171–217). New York: Wiley.

Lloyd, B. T. (2002). A conceptual framework for examining adolescent identity, media influence, and social development. *Review of General Psychology, 6*(1), 73–91.

Lloyd, C. D., Clark, H. J., & Forth, A. E. (2010). Psychopathy, expert testimony, and indeterminate sentences: Exploring the relationship between Psychopathy Checklist–Revised testimony and trial outcome in Canada. *Legal and Criminological Psychology, 15,* 323–339.

Lobo de la Tierra, A. (2016). Essentializing manhood in the "street": Perilous masculinity and popular criminological ethnographies. *Feminist Criminology, 11*(4), 375–397.

Logan, C. (2011). La femme fatale: The female psychopath in fiction and clinical practice. *Mental Health Review Journal, 16*(3), 118–127.

Logan, C., & Weizmann-Henelius, G. (2012). Psychopathy in women: Presentation, assessment, and management. In H. Häkkänen-Nyholm & J. Nyholm (Eds.), *Psychopathy and the law* (pp. 99–125). West Sussex, UK: Wiley-Blackwell.

Logan, M. (2013). No more bagpipes: The threat of the psychopath. *FBI Law Enforcement Bulletin, 81*(7), 22–29.

Logan, M., & Hare, R. D. (2008). Criminal psychopathy: An introduction for police. In M. St.-Yves & M. Tanguay (Eds.), *Psychology of criminal investigation* (pp. 393–442). Cowansville, QC: Éditions Yvon Blais.

Loomans, M. M., Joke, H. M. T., & van Marle, H. J. C. (2013). The psychophysiology and neuroanatomy of antisocial behavior. In J. B. Helfgott (Ed.), *Criminal psychology* (Vol. 1, pp. 89–115). Santa Barbara, CA: Praeger/ABC/CLIO.

Lovell, M., Helfgott, J., & Lawrence, C. (2002a). Narratives from Citizens, Victims, and Offenders Restoring Justice. *Contemporary Justice Review, 5*(3), 261–272.

Lovell, M., Helfgott, J., & Lawrence, C. (2002b). Citizens, Victims, and Offenders Restoring Justice: Social group work bridging the divide. In S. Henry et al., *Social work with groups: Mining the gold*. New York: Haworth.

Low, P. W., Jeffries, J. C., & Bonnie, R. J. (1986). *The trial of John W. Hinckley, Jr.: A case study in the insanity defense*. New York: Foundation Press.

Lowenstein, J., Purvis, C., & Rose, K. (2016). A systematic review on the relationship between antisocial, borderline and narcissistic personality disorder diagnostic traits and risk of violence to others in a clinical and forensic sample. *Borderline Personality Disorder and Emotional Dysregulation, 3*(1), 14.

Lucchesi, G., Koch, H. W., Jr. (Producers), & Holbit, G. (Director). (1996). *Primal fear* [Motion picture]. USA: Paramount Pictures.

Luna, E. (2013). Psychopathy and sentencing. In K. Kiehl & W. P. Sinnott-Armstrong (Eds.), *Handbook of psychopathy and law* (pp. 358–388). Oxford: Oxford University Press.

Lushing, J. R., Gaudet, L. M., & Kiehl, K. A. (2016). Brain imaging in psychopathy. In C. B. Gacono (Ed.), *The clinical and forensic assessment of psychopathy* (2nd ed., pp. 32–53). New York: Routledge, 32–53.

Lykken, D. T. (1957). A study of anxiety in the sociopathic personality. *Journal of Abnormal and Social Psychology, 55*, 6–10.

Lykken, D. T. (2018). Psychopathy, sociopathy, and antisocial personality disorder. In C. J. Patrick (Ed.), *Handbook of psychopathy* (2nd ed., pp. 22–38). New York: Guilford Press.

Lynam, D. R. (1996). Early identification of chronic offenders: Who is the fledgling psychopath? *Psychological Bulletin, 120*(2), 209–234.

Lynam, D. R. (1997). Pursuing the psychopath: Capturing the fledgling psychopath in a nomological net. *Journal of Abnormal Psychology, 106*(3), 425–438.

Lynam, D. R. (1998). Early identification of the fledgling psychopath: Locating the psychopathic child in the current nomenclature. *Journal of Abnormal Psychology, 107*, 566–575.

Lynam, D. R., Charnigo, R., Moffitt, T. E., & Raine, A. (2009). The stability of psychopathy across adolescence. *Development and Psychopathology, 21*(4), 1133–1153.

Lynam, D. R., & Derefinko, K. J. (2006). Psychopathy and personality. In C. J. Patrick (Ed.), *Handbook of psychopathy* (pp. 133–155). New York: Guilford Press.

Lynam, D. R., Miller, J. D., & Derefinko, K. J. (2018). Psychopathy and personality: An articulation of the benefits of a trait-based approach. In C. J. Patrick (Ed.), *Handbook of psychopathy* (2nd ed., pp. 259–280). New York: Guilford Press.

Lyon, D. R., & Ogloff, J. R. P. (2000). Legal and ethical issues in psychopathy assessment. In C. B. Gacono (Ed.), *The clinical and forensic assessment of psychopathy: A practitioner's guide* (pp. 139–173). Mahwah, NJ: Erlbaum.

Lyon, D. R., Ogloff, J. R. P., & Shepherd, S. M. (2016). Legal and ethical issues in psychopathy assessment. In C. B. Gacono (Ed.), *The clinical and forensic assessment of psychopathy: A practitioner's guide* (2nd ed., pp. 193–216). Mahwah, NJ: Erlbaum.

Macaulay, S. (1987). Images of law in everyday life: The lessons of school, entertainment, and spectator sports. *Law & Society Review, 21*, 185–218.

Maccoby, E. E., & Jacklin, C. N. (1974). *The psychology of sex differences*. Stanford, CA: Stanford University Press.

MacKenzie, J. (2015). *Psychopath Free: Recovering from emotionally abusive relationships with narcissists, sociopaths, and other toxic people*. New York: Berkley.

Maiese, M. (2014). Moral cognition, affect, and psychopathy. *Philosophical Psychology, 27*(6), 807–828.

Mailer, N. (1958). *The white negro: Voices of dissent*. New York: Grove Press.

Mailer, N. (1959). *Advertisements for myself*. New York: G. P. Putnam's Sons.

Malatesti, L., & McMillan, J. (2010). *Responsibility and psychopathy: Interfacing law, psychiatry and philosophy*. Oxford, UK: Oxford University Press.

Mann, D. (2005, July 1). The BTK Killer: Portrait of a psychopath. *FoxNews.Com*. Retrieved from http://www.foxnews.com/story/2005/07/01/btk-killer-portrait-psychopath

Manti, E., Scholte, E. M., Van Berckelaer-Onnes, I. A., & Van Der Ploeg, J. D. (2009). Social and emotional detachment: A cross-cultural comparison of the non-disruptive behavioural psychopathic traits in children. *Criminal Behaviour and Mental Health, 19*(3), 178–192.

Marshall, A., Kassar, M. (Producers), & Verhoeven, P. (Director). (1992). *Basic instinct* [Motion picture]. USA: TriStar Pictures.

Marshall, J., Lilienfeld, S. O., Mayberg, H., & Clark, S. E. (2017). The role of neurological and psychological explanations in legal judgments of psychopathic wrongdoers. *The Journal of Forensic Psychiatry & Psychology, 28*(3), 412–436.

Martin, A. I. (2011). *Laughter effects: Humor and inspiration for victims of sociopaths*. North Charleston, SC: Create Space.

Martin, R., Mutchnick, R. J., & Austin, W. T. (1990). *Criminological thought: Pioneers past and present*. New York: Macmillan.

Martinson, R. (1974). What works? Questions and answers about prison reform. *The Public Interest, 35*, 22–54.

Martinson, R. (1979). New findings, new views: A note of caution regarding sentencing reform. *Hofstra Law Review, 7*, 243–258.

Marx, G. T. (1995). Electric eye in the sky: Some reflections on the new surveillance and popular culture. In J. Ferrell & C. R. Sanders (Eds.), *Cultural criminology* (pp. 106–141). Boston: Northeastern University Press.

Matusiewicz, A. K., McCarthy, J. M., McCauley, K. L., & Bounoua, N. (2018). Current directions in laboratory studies of personality pathology: Examples from borderline personality disorder, psychopathy, and schizotypy. *Personality Disorders: Theory, Research, and Treatment, 9*(1), 2–11

Maugham, W. S. (1915, 1968). *Of Human Bondage*. New York: Penguin.

Maughs, W. S. (1941). A concept of psychopathy and psychopathic personality: Its evolution and historical development. *Journal of Criminal Psychopathology, 2*, 329–356.

Maxwell, T. (2017, January 4). Church shooter Dylann Roof showed no remorse in writings while in jail. *USA Today*. Retrieved from https://www.usatoday.com/story/news/nation-now/2017/01/04/church-shooter-dylann-roof-showed-no-remorse-writings-while-jail/96172486

McCabe, D. L. (1992). The influence of situational ethics on cheating among college students. *Sociological Inquiry, 62*, 365–374.

McCord, W., & McCord, J. (1959). *Origins of crime: A new evaluation of the Cambridge-Somerville Study*. New York: Columbia University Press.

McCord, W., & McCord, J. (1964). *The psychopath: An essay on the criminal mind*. New York: Van Nostrand Reinhold.

McCuish, E. C., Corrado, R. R., Hart, S. D., & DeLisi, M. (2015). The role of symptoms of psychopathy in persistent violence over the criminal career into full adulthood. *Journal of Criminal Justice, 43*(4), 345–356.

McCuish, E. C. & Lussier, P. (2018). A developmental perspective on the stability and change of psychopathic personality traits across the adolescence–adulthood transition. *Criminal Justice and Behavior, 45*(5), 666–691.

McCuish, E. C., Mathesius, J. R., Lussier, P., & Corrado, R. R. (2018). The cross-cultural generalizability of the psychopathy checklist: Youth version for adjudicated indigenous youth. *Psychological Assessment, 30*(2), 192–203.

McDonagh, M. (Writer/Director). (2012). *Seven psychopaths* [Motion picture]. USA: Blueprint Pictures.

McEllistrem, J. E. (2004). Affective and predatory violence: A bimodal classification of human aggression and violence. *Aggression and Violent Behavior, 10*, 1–30.

McFarlane, H. (2013). Masculinity and criminology: The social construction of the criminal man. *The Howard Journal, 52*(3), 321–335.

McGlashan, T., & Heinssen, R. (1989). Narcissistic, antisocial, and noncomorbid subgroups of borderline disorder: Are they distinct entities by long term clinical profile? *Psychiatric Clinics of North America, 12*(3), 653–670.

McKelvie, S. J. (2013). Effects of offender remorse on sentencing and parole recommendations for sexual assault in a mock crime scenario. *Psychology Journal, 10*(1), 2–22.

Meloy, J. R. (1988). *The psychopathic mind: Origins, dynamics, and treatment*. New Jersey/London: Jason Aronson.

Meloy, J. R. (1992). *Violent attachments*. Northvale, NJ: Jason Aronson.

Meloy, J. R. (Ed.). (1998). *The psychology of stalking: Clinical and forensic perspectives*. San Diego: Academic Press.

Meloy, J. R. (2000). The nature and dynamics of sexual homicide: An integrative review. *Aggression and Violent Behavior, 5*, 1–22.

Meloy, J. R. (Ed.). (2001). *The mark of Cain: Psychoanalytic insight and the psychopath*. Hillsdale, NJ: Psychoanalytic Press.

Meloy, J. R. (2012). Predatory violence and psychopathy. In H. Häkkänen-Nyholm & J. Nyholm (Eds.), *Psychopathy and the law* (pp. 159–175). Chichester, West Sussex, UK: Wiley-Blackwell.

Meloy, J. R., & Gacono, C. B. (2000). Psychopathy assessment and report writing. In C. B. Gacono (Ed.), *The clinical and forensic assessment of psychopathy* (pp. 231–250). Mahwah, NJ: Erlbaum.

Meloy, J. R., & Gacono, C. B. (2016). Assessing psychopathy: Psychological testing and report writing. In C. B. Gacono (Ed.), *The clinical and forensic assessment of psychopathy* (2nd ed., pp. 276–292). New York: Routledge.

Meloy, J. R., & McEllistrem, J. E. (1998). Bombing and psychopathy: An integrative review. *Journal of Forensic Sciences, 43*(3), 556–562.

Meloy, J. R., Sheridan, L., & Hoffman, J. (Eds.). (2008). *Stalking, threatening, and attacking public figures: A psychological and behavioral analysis.* New York: Oxford University Press.

Menninger, K. (1968). *The crime of punishment.* New York: Viking Press.

Messerschmidt, J. W. (1993). *Masculinities and crime: Critique and reconceptualization of theory.* Lanham, MD: Rowman & Littlefield.

Meyers, W. C., Chan, H. C., Vo, E. J., & Lazarou, E. (2010). Sexual sadism, psychopathy, and recidivism in juvenile sexual murderers. *Journal of Investigative Psychology & Offender Profiling, 7,* 49–58.

Meyers, W. C., Gooch, E., & Meloy, J.R. (2005). The role of psychopathy and sexuality in a female serial killer. *Journal of Forensic Science, 50*(3), 1–6.

Milgram, S. (1974). *Obedience to authority: An experimental view.* New York: HarperCollins.

Mill, J. S. (1929). *On liberty.* London: C. A. Watts.

Miller, J., Watts, A., & Jones, S. E. (2011). Does psychopathy manifest divergent relations with components of its nomological network depending on gender? *Personality and Individual Differences, 50,* 564–569.

Miller, J. D., Dir, A., Gentile, B., Wilson, L., Pryor, L. R., & Campbell, W. K. (2010). Searching for a vulnerable dark triad: Comparing Factor 2 psychopathy, vulnerable narcissism, and borderline personality disorder. *Journal of Personality, 78*(5), 1529–1564.

Miller, L. (1987). Classification of psychopathology according to a scientific (psychology and psychiatry) and an artistic (film noir) perspective. *Psychological Reports, 61,* 287–299.

Miller, L. (1989a). Laurence Miller on Robert Lang's interpretation of Kiss Me Deadly. *Cinema Journal, 28,* 69–71.

Miller, L. (1989b). The contribution of scientific psychology to artistic representations (film noir) of behavior and personality. *Journal of Social Behavior and Personality, 4,* 17–33.

Miller, L. (1989c). How many film noirs are there? How statistics can help answer this question. *Empirical Studies of the Arts, 7,* 51–55.

Miller, L. (1992). Evidence for a British film noir cycle. *Film Criticism,* 42–51.

Miller, L. (2006). The terrorist mind: II. Typologies, psychopathologies, and practical guidelines for investigation. *International Journal of Offender Therapy and Comparative Criminology, 50*(3), 255–268.

Millon, T. (1980). *Disorders of personality.* DSMIII Axis II. New York: Wiley.

Millon, T., Simonsen, E., Birket-Smith, E., & Davis, R. D. (Eds.). (1998). *Psychopathy: Antisocial, criminal, and violent behavior.* New York: Guilford Press.

Minnesota Office of the Legislative Auditor (1994, February 25). *Psychopathic Personality Commitment Law: Executive summary* [Online]. Retrieved from http://www.auditor.leg.state.mn.us/PSYCHO.htm

Minzenberg, M. J., & Siever, L. J. (2006). Neurochemistry and pharmacology of psychopathy and related disorders. In C. J. Patrick (Ed.), *Handbook of psychopathy* (pp. 251–277). New York: Guilford Press.

Mischke, N. (2014, September 18). Convicted rapist Kevin Coe to remain at McNeil Island. *KHQ Q6.* Retrieved from http://www.khq.com/story/26566153/convicted-rapist-kevin-coe-to-remain-at-mcneil-island

M'Naghten's Case (1843). 10 Cl & F, 200.

Modlin, H. C. (1983). The antisocial personality. *Bulletin of the Menninger Clinic, 47,* 129–144.

Moffit, T. E. (1993). Adolescent-limited and life-course-persistent antisocial behavior: A developmental taxonomy. *Psychological Review, 100*(4), 674–701.

Mokros, A., Neumann, C. S., Stadtland, C., Osterheider, M., Nedopil, N., & Hare, R. D. (2011). Assessing measurement invariance of PCL-R assessments from file reviews of North American and German offenders. *International Journal of Law and Psychiatry, 34*(1), 56–63.

Molinuevo, B., Pardo, Y., González, L., & Torrubia, R. (2014). Memories of parenting practices are associated with psychopathy in juvenile male offenders. *The Journal of Forensic Psychiatry & Psychology, 25*(4), 495–500.

Monahan, J. (2006). Comments on cover jacket. C. J. Patrick (Ed.), *Handbook of psychopathy.* New York: Guilford Press.

Moore, M. J. (Director). (1999). *Legacy: Murder and media, politics and prison* [Video recording]. Princeton, NJ: Films for the Humanities.

Moore, T. (1990). *Dark eros: The imagination of sadism.* Woodstock, CT: Spring.

Moreira, D., Almeida, F., Pinto, M., & Fávero, M. (2014). Psychopathy: A comprehensive review of its assessment and intervention. *Aggression and Violent Behavior, 19*(3), 191–195.

Moriarty, E. (2017, September 2). Stalked. *48 Hours/CBS News.* Retrieved from https://www.cbsnews.com/news/stalked-48-hours-investigates-pauley-perrette-fights-to-change-stalking-laws

Morrison, J. (1989). Histrionic personality disorder in women with somatization disorder. *Psychometrics, 30,* 433–437.

Morse, S. J. (2010). Psychopathy and the law: The United States experience. In L. Malatesti & J. McMillan, *Responsibility and psychopathy: Interfacing law, psychiatry and philosophy* (pp. 41–61). Oxford, UK: Oxford University Press.

Mouilso, E. R., & Calhoun, K. S. (2012). Narcissism, psychopathy and five-factor model in sexual assault perpetration. *Personality and Mental Health, 6*(3), 228–241

Mouilso, E. R., & Calhoun, K. S. (2013). The role of rape myth acceptance and psychopathy in sexual assault, *22*(2), 158–174.

Mowle, E. N., Edens, J. F., Clark, J. W., & Sörman, K. (2016). Effects of mental health and neuroscience evidence on juror perceptions of a criminal defendant: The moderating role of political orientation. *Behavioral Sciences and the Law, 34*, 726–741.

Moya, A. (2015, July 26). In California, a death sentence with no date in sight. *CNN*. Retrieved from https://www.cnn.com/2015/07/26/us/death-row-stories-california-death-penalty/index.html

Muñoz Centifanti, L. C., Thomson, N. D., & Kwok, A. H. (2016). Identifying the manipulative mating methods associated with psychopathic traits and BPD features. *Journal of Personality Disorders, 30*(6), 721–741.

Murphy, J. G. (1972). Moral death: A Kantian essay on psychopathy. *Ethics, 82*(4), 284–298.

Murphy, N. A. (1947). *The story of Mrs. Murphy*. New York: E. P. Dutton & Company.

Murrie, D. C., Boccaccini, T., & McCoy, W. (2007). Diagnostic labeling in juvenile court: How do descriptions of psychopathy and conduct disorder influence judges? *Journal of Clinical Child and Adolescent Psychology, 36*(2), 228–241.

Murrie, D. C., Cornell, D. G., & McCoy, W. K. (2005). Psychopathy, conduct disorder, and stigma: Does diagnostic labeling influence juvenile probation officer recommendations? *Law and Human Behavior, 29*(3), 323–342.

Myers, W. C., Chan, H. C. O., Vo, E. J., & Lazarou, E. (2010). Sexual sadism, psychopathy, and recidivism in juvenile sexual murderers. *Journal of Investigative Psychology and Offender Profiling, 7*(1), 49–58.

Myers, W. C., Gooch, E., & Meloy, J. R. (2005). The role of psychopathy and sexuality in a female serial killer. *Journal of Forensic Science, 50*(3), 1–6.

Naffine, N. (1997). *Feminism and criminology*. Cambridge: Polity Press.

Natoli, J. (1994). *Hauntings: Popular film and American culture, 1990–1992*. New York: State University of New York Press.

Neidhart, E. (2013). Crisis intervention and police interactions with individuals with mental illness. In J. B. Helfgott (Ed.), *Criminal psychology* (Vol. 3, pp. 140–167). Santa Barbara, CA: Praeger.

Nelkin, D. K. (2015). Psychopaths, incorrigible racists, and the faces of responsibility. *Ethics, 125*(2), 357–390.

Neroni, H. (2005). *The violent woman: Femininity, narrative, and violence in contemporary American cinema*. Albany, NY: State University of New York Press.

Neumann, C. S., Kosson, D. S., & Salekin, R. T. (2007). Exploratory and confirmatory factor analysis of the psychopathy construct: Methodological and conceptual issues. In H. Hervé & J. C. Yuille (Eds.), *The psychopath: Theory, research, and practice* (pp. 79–104). Mahwah, NJ: Erlbaum.

Neumann, C. S., Schmitt, D. S., Carter, R., Embley, I., & Hare, R. D. (2012). Psychopathic traits in females and males across the globe. *Behavioral Sciences and the Law, 30*, 557–574.

Neumann, C. S., Vitacco, M. J., & Mokros, V. (2016). Using both variable-centered and person-centered approaches to understanding psychopathic personality. In C. B. Gacono (Ed.), *The clinical and forensic assessment of psychopathy* (2nd ed., pp. 14–31). New York: Routledge.

Newman, J. P., Schmitt, W. A., & Voss, W. D. (1997). The impact of motivationally neutral cues on psychopathic individuals: Assessing the generality of the response modulation hypothesis. *Journal of Abnormal Psychology, 106*(4), 563–575.

Nietzsche, F. (1966, 1973). *Beyond good and evil.* New York: Penguin Books.

Norcross, R. H. (2003). The "modern warrior": A study in survival. *FBI Law Enforcement Bulletin, 72*(10), 20–26.

Nuckolls, C. W. (1992). Toward a cultural history of personality disorders. *Social Science Medicine, 35*, 37–47.

Office of the Surgeon General; National Center for Injury Prevention and Control; National Institute of Mental Health; Center for Mental Health Services. (2001). *Youth violence: A report of the surgeon general.* Rockville, MD: Office of the Surgeon General. Retrieved from https://www.ncbi.nlm.nih.gov/books/NBK44293

Ogilvie, E. (1996). Masculine obsessions: An examination of criminology, criminality, and gender. *Australian & New Zealand Journal of Criminology, 29*(3), 205–226.

Ogloff, J. R. P., Campbell, R. E., & Shepherd, S. M. (2016). Disentangling psychopathy from antisocial personality disorder: An Australian analysis. *Journal of Forensic Psychology Practice, 16*(3), 198–215.

Ogloff, J. R. P., Wong, S., & Greenwood, A. (1990). Treating criminal psychopaths in a therapeutic community program. *Behavioral Sciences and the Law, 8*(2), 181–190.

Oleson, J. C. (2005). King of killers: The criminological theories of Hannibal Lecter, part two. *Journal of Criminal Justice and Popular Culture, 12*(3), 187–210.

Oleson, J. C. (2006). Contemporary demonology: The criminological theories of Hannibal Lecter, part two. *Journal of Criminal Justice and Popular Culture, 13*(1), 29–49.

Olsen, J. (1983). *Son: A psychopath and his victims.* New York: Atheneum.

O'Malley, S. (2004, 2005). *The unspeakable crime of Andrea Yates. "Are you there alone?"* New York: Pocket Books.

Orion, D. (1997). *I know you really love me: A psychiatrist's journal of erotomania, stalking, and obsessional love.* New York: Macmillan.

Ortega-Escobar, J., Alcázar-Córcoles, M. A., Puente-Rodríguez, L., & Peñaranda-Ramos, E. (2017). Psychopathy: Legal and neuroscientific aspects. *Anuario de Psicologia Juridica, 27*, 57–66.

O'Toole, M. E. (1999). Criminal profiling: The FBI uses criminal investigative analysis to solve crimes. *Corrections Today, 61*, 44–46.

O'Toole, M. E. (2007). Psychopathy as a behavior classification system for violent and serial crime scenes. In H. Herve & J. Yuille (Eds.), *The psychopath: Theory, research, and practice* (pp. 301–325). Mahwah, NJ: Erlbaum.

O'Toole, M. E. (Moderator), Beresin, E. V., Berman, A., Gorelick, S. M., Helfgott, J. B., & Tobin, C. (Participants). (2014). Celebrities through violence: The copycat effect and the influence of violence in social media on mass killers (Published roundtable discussion). *Violence and Gender, 1*(3), 107–116.

O'Toole, M. E., & Häkkänen-Nyholm, H. (2012). Psychopathy and violent crime. In H. Häkkänen-Nyholm & J. Nyholm (Eds.), *Psychopathy and the law* (pp. 139–158). Chichester, West Sussex, UK: Wiley-Blackwell.

O'Toole, M. E., Logan, M., & Smith, S. (2012). Looking behind the mask: Implications for interviewing psychopaths. *FBI Law Enforcement Bulletin, 81*(7), 14–19.

O'Toole, M. E., Smith, S. S., & Hare, R. D. (2008). In J. R. Meloy, L. Sheridan, & J. Hoffmann (Eds.), *Stalking, threatening, and attacking public figures: A psychological and behavioral analysis* (pp. 215–243). New York: Oxford University Press.

Page, M. A., Ruben, J. (Producers), & Ruben, J. (Director). (1993). *The good son* [Motion picture]. USA: Twentieth Century Fox.

Palermo, G. B. (2011). Psychopathy: Early and recent clinical observations and the law. *International Journal of Offender Therapy and Comparative Criminology, 55*(1), 3–4.

Palermo, G. B. (2013). Psychopathic aggression: Will or determinism? In J. B. Helfgott (Ed.), *Criminal psychology* (Vol. 2, pp. 355–380). Santa Barbara, CA: Praeger.

Palmer, R. B. (1994). Hollywood's dark cinema. New York: Twayne.

Pardue, A. D., Robinson, M. B., & Arrigo, B. A. (2013). Psychopathy and corporate crime: A preliminary examination, Part 1. *Journal of Forensic Psychology Practice, 13*(2), 116–144.

Pardue, A. D., Robinson, M. B., & Arrigo, B. A. (2014). Psychopathy and corporate crime: A preliminary examination, Part 2. *Journal of Forensic Psychology Practice, 13*(2), 145–169.

Partridge, G. E. (1930). The problem of psychopathics. *Psychiatric Quarterly, 10*, 53–99.

Patrick, C. J. (2001). Emotional processes in psychopathy. In A. Raine & J. Sanmartin (Eds.), *Violence and psychopathy* (pp. 57–77). New York: Kluwer/Plenum.

Patrick, C. J. (Ed.). (2006). *Handbook of psychopathy*. New York: Guilford Press.

Patrick, C. J. (2007). Getting to the heart of psychopathy. In H. Herve & J. C. Yuille (Eds.), *The psychopath: Theory, research, and practice* (pp. 207–252). Mahwah, NJ: Erlbaum.

Patrick, C. J. (2013). Conceptualizing psychopathy. In J. B. Helfgott (Ed.), *Criminal psychology* (Vol. 2, pp. 278–310). Santa Barbara, CA: Praeger.

Patrick, C. J. (Ed.). (2018a). Cognitive and emotional processing in psychopathy. In C. J. Patrick (Ed.), *Handbook of psychopathy* (2nd ed., pp. 422–455). New York: Guilford Press.

Patrick, C. J. (Ed.). (2018b). *Handbook of psychopathy* (2nd ed.). New York: Guilford Press.

Patrick, C. J. (Ed.). (2018c). Psychopathy as a masked pathology. In C. J. Patrick (Ed.), *Handbook of psychopathy* (2nd ed., pp. 3–21). New York: Guilford Press.

Patrick, C. J., Fowles, D. C., & Krueger, R. F. (2009). Triarchic conceptualization of psychopathy: Developmental origins of disinhibition, boldness, and meanness. *Development of Psychopathology, 21*, 913–938.

Patterson, J. (Director), & Siegel, R. T. (Producer). (1991). *Sins of the mother* [TV movie]. USA: Corapeake/Polson Company; New Films International/CBS.

Paulhus, D. L., Neumann, C. S., & Hare, R. D. (2017). *Self-Report Psychopathy Scale* (4th ed.) (SRP 4). North Tonawanda, NY: Multi-Health Systems.

Peaslee, D. (1993). *An investigation of incarcerated females: Rorschach indices and psychopathy checklist scores.* Unpublished doctoral dissertation. Fresno: California School of Professional Psychology.

Pechorro, P., Goncalves, R., Maroco, J., Nunes, C., & Jesus, S. (2014). Age of crime onset and psychopathic traits in female juvenile delinquents. *International Journal of Offender Therapy and Comparative Criminology, 58*(9), 1101–1119.

Peck, S. (1991). Healing human evil. In J. Abrahms & C. Zweig (Eds.), *Meeting the shadow: The hidden power of the dark side of human nature* (pp. 176–180). Los Angeles: Jeremy P. Tarcher.

Pemment, J. (2013). Psychopathy versus sociopathy: Why the distinction has become crucial. *Aggression and Violent Behavior, 12*, 458–461.

Pemment, J. (2015). The reappearing psychopath: Psychopathy's stain on future generations. *Aggression and Violent Behavior, 25*, 237–242.

Pera-Guardiola, V., Contreras-Rodríguez, O., Batalla, I., Kosson, D., Menchón, J. M., Pifarré, J., & Soriano-Mas, C. (2016). Brain structural correlates of emotion recognition in psychopaths. *Plos One, 11*(5), 1–17.

Peretz, I. L. (1973). The golem. In I. Howe & E. Greenberg (Eds.), *A treasury of Yiddish stories* (pp. 245–246). New York: Schokin Books.

Perkins, K. (2010). *Surviving a sociopath.* Morgan Hill, CA: Bookstand.

Perri, F. S. (2011). White collar criminals: The "kinder, gentler" offender? *Journal of Investigative Psychology & Offender Profiling, 8*, 217–241.

Petrila, J., & Skeem, J. L. (2003). An introduction to the special issues on juvenile psychopathy and some reflections on the current debate. Juvenile psychopathy: The debate. *Behavioral Sciences and the Law, 21*, 689–694.

Pettitt, J. (2016). Popular psychopaths and holocaust perpetrators: Fiction, family, and murder. *The Journal of Popular Culture, 49*(6), 1301–1319.

Pfohl, S. J. (1985). *Images of deviance and social control.* New York: McGraw-Hill.

Phillips, J., Phillips, M. (Producers), & Scorsese, M. (Director). (1976). *Taxi driver* [Motion picture]. USA: Columbia Pictures.

Phillips, K. D. (2013). Empathy for psychopaths: Using fMRI brain scans to plea for leniency in death penalty cases. *Law & Psychology Review, 37*, 1–48.

Phipps, P., Korinek, K., Aos, S., & Lieb, R. (1999, January). *Research findings on adult corrections' programs: A review.* Document No. 99-01-1203. Olympia, WA: Washington State Institute for Public Policy. Retrieved from http://www.wsipp.wa.gov/ReportFile/1309/Wsipp_Research-Findings-on-Adult-Corrections-Programs-A-Review_Full-Report.pdf

Phoenix, J. (2004). An analysis of women's involvement in prostitution. In D. A. Dabney (Ed.), *Crime types: A text/reader* (pp. 292–306). Belmont, CA: Wadsworth.

Picart, C. J., & Greek, C. (2003). The compulsion of real/reel serial killers and vampires: Toward a gothic criminology. *Journal of Criminal Justice and Popular Culture, 10*(1), 39–68.

Pike, A. (2011). *Danger has a face.* Denver: Outskirts.

Pinizzotto, A. J., & Davis, E. F. (2000). Offenders perpetual shorthand: What messages are law enforcement officers sending to offenders? *Law Enforcement Bulletin, 69*(7), 1–6.

Pinizzotto, A. J., & Finkel, N. (1990). Criminal personality profiling: An outcome and process study. *Law and Human Behavior, 14*(3), 215–233.

Piquero, A. R. (2017). "No remorse, no repent": Linking lack of remorse to criminal offending in a sample of serious adolescent offenders. *Justice Quarterly, 34*(2), 350–376.

Polaschek, D. L. L., & Skeem, J. L. (2018). Treatment of adults and juveniles with psychopathy. In C. J. Patrick (Ed.), *Handbook of psychopathy* (2nd ed., pp. 710–731). New York: Guilford Press.

Porter, S., Brinke, L., & Wilson, K. (2009). Crime profiles and conditional release performance of psychopathic and non-psychopathic sexual offenders. *Legal and Criminological Psychology, 14*(1), 109–118.

Porter, S., Fairweather, D., Drugge, J., Herve, H., Birt, A., & Boer, D. P. (2000). Profiles of psychopathy in incarcerated sexual offenders. *Criminal Justice and Behavior, 27*(2), 216–233.

Porter, S., & Porter, S. (2007). Psychopathy and violent crime. In H. Herve & J. C. Yuille (Eds.), *The psychopath: Theory, research, and practice* (pp. 287–300). Mahwah, NJ: Erlbaum.

Porter, S., & Woodworth, S. (2006). Psychopathy and aggression. In C. J. Patrick (Ed.), *Handbook of psychopathy* (pp. 481–494). New York: Guilford Press.

Porter, S., Woodworth, S., & Black, P.J. (2018). Psychopathy and aggression. In C. J. Patrick (Ed.), *Handbook of psychopathy* (2nd ed., pp. 611–634). New York: Guilford Press.

Porter, T. (2015). Cesarean kidnapping: Maternal instinct, malingering, and murder. *Research Gate.* Retrieved from https://www.researchgate.net/publication/267260633_Cesarean_Kidnapping_Maternal_instinct_Malingering_and_Murder

Poy, R., Segarra, P., Esteller, A., Lopez, R., & Molto, J. (2013). FFM description of the triarchic conceptualization of psychopathy in men and women. *American Psychological Association, 26*(1), 69–76.

Prado, C. E., Treeby, M. S., & Crowe, S. F. (2016). Examining the relationships between sub-clinical psychopathic traits with shame, guilt and externalisation response tendencies to everyday transgressions. *The Journal of Forensic Psychiatry & Psychology, 27*(4), 569–585.

Prentky, R. A. (2003). A 15-year retrospective on sexual coercion: Advances and projections. In R. A. Prentky, E. S. Janus, & M. C. Seto (Eds.), *Sexually coercive behavior: Understanding and management* (pp. 13–32). New York: New York Academy of Sciences.

Prentky, R. A., & Burgess, A. W. (2000). *Forensic management of sexual offenders.* New York: Kluwer/Plenum.

Prentky, R. A., Janus, E. S., & Seto, M. C. (Eds.). (2003). *Sexually coercive behavior: Understanding and management.* New York: New York Academy of Sciences.

Pulkkinen, L. (2013, December 29). Serial rapist Kevin Coe demands he be freed. *Seattle Post-Intelligencer.* Retrieved from https://www.seattlepi.com/seattlenews/article/Serial-rapist-Kevin-Coe-demands-he-be-freed-5097070.php

Quayle, J. (2008). Interviewing a psychopathic suspect. *Journal of Investigative Psychology and Offender Profiling, 5*(1–2), 79–91.

Quinney, R. (1970). *The social reality of crime.* Boston: Little, Brown.

Quinsey, V. L. (1995). The prediction and explanation of criminal violence. *International Journal of Law & Psychiatry, 18*, 117–127.

Rader details how he killed 10 people. (2005, June 28). *CNN.com.* Retrieved from http://www.cnn.com/2005/LAW/06/27/btk/index.html

Radzinowicz, L. (1966). *Ideology and crime.* New York: Columbia University Press.

Radzinowicz, L., & Wolfgang, M. E. (1971). *The criminal in confinement.* New York: Basic Books.

Rafter, N. (2004). The unrepentant horse-slasher: Moral insanity and the origins of criminological thought. *Criminology, 42*(4), 979–1008.

Rafter, N. (2006). *Shots in the mirror: Crime films and society.* Oxford: Oxford University Press.

Rafter, N. (2007). Crime, film, and criminology: Recent sex-crime movies. *Theoretical Criminology, 11*, 403–420.

Rafter, N., & Brown, M. (2011). *Criminology goes to the movies: Crime theory and popular culture.* New York: New York University Press.

Rafter, N. H. (1997). Psychopathy and the evolution of criminological knowledge. *Theoretical Criminology, 1*(2), 235–259.

Raine, A. (1993). *The psychopathology of crime: Criminal behavior as a clinical disorder.* Cambridge, MA: Academic Press.

Raine, A. (2013). *The anatomy of violence: The biological roots of crime.* New York: Pantheon.

Raine, A., & Dunkin, J. (1990). The genetic and psychophysiological basis of antisocial behaviour: Implications for counseling and therapy. *Journal of Counseling & Development, 68*, 637–644.

Raine, A., Fung, A. L. C., Portnoy, J., Choy, O., & Spring, V. L. (2014). Low heart rate as a risk factor for child and adolescent proactive aggressive and impulsive psychopathic behavior. *Aggressive Behavior, 40*, 290–299.

Raine, A., Meloy, J. R., Bihrle, S., Stoddard, J., Lacasse, L., & Buchsbaum, M. S. (1998). Reduced prefrontal and increased subcortical brain functioning assessed using positron emission tomography in predatory and affective murderers. *Behavioral Sciences and the Law, 16*(3), 319–332.

Raine, A., & Sanmartin, J. (Eds.). (2001). *Violence and psychopathy.* New York: Kluwer Academic/Plenum.

Raine, A., & Yang, Y. (2006). The neuroanatomical bases of psychopathy: A review of brain imaging findings. In C. J. Patrick (Ed.), *Handbook of psychopathy* (pp. 278–295). New York: Guilford Press.

Ramsland, K. (2013, May 29). Psychopath analysis: The early days. *Psychology Today.* Retrieved from https://www.psychologytoday.com/us/blog/shadow-boxing/201305/fledgling-psychopaths

Ray, J. J., & Ray, J. A. B. (1982). Some apparent advantages of subclinical psychopathy. *The Journal of Social Psychology, 117,* 135–142.

Reid, C. L. (1998). A balanced review of Yochelson-Samenow's theory of "the criminal personality." *The Justice Professional, 10*(4), 333–360.

Reid, W. H. (Ed.). (1978). *The psychopath: A comprehensive study of antisocial disorders and behaviour.* New York: Brunner/Mazel.

Reid, W. H. (1985). The antisocial personality: A review. *Hospital and Community Psychiatry, 36,* 831–837.

Reid, W. H., Dorr, D., Walker, J. I., & Bonner, J. W., III. (1986). *Unmasking the psychopath.* New York: Norton.

Reidy, D. E., Kearns, M. C., DeGue, S., Lilienfeld, S., Massetti, G., & Kiehl, K. A. (2015). Why psychopathy matters: Implications for public health and violence prevention. *Aggression and Violent Behavior, 24,* 214–225.

Reidy, D. E., Shirk, S. D., Sloan, C. A., & Zeichner, A. (2009). Men who aggress against women: Effects of feminine gender role violation on physical aggression in hypermasculine men. *Psychology of Men & Masculinity, 10*(1), 1–12.

Rendell, J. A., Huss, M. T., & Jensen, M. L. (2010). Expert testimony and the effects of a biological approach, psychopathy, and juror attitudes in cases of insanity. *Behavioral Sciences and the Law, 28*(3), 411–425.

Report of the Committee on Serious Violent and Sexual Offenders. (2000). Retrieved from http://content.iriss.org.uk/throughcare/files/pdf/longterm/lt4_risk2.pdf

Ressler, R. K., Burgess, A. W., & Douglas, J. E. (1988). *Sexual homicide: Patterns and motives.* New York: Simon & Schuster.

Rhineberger-Dunn, G., Briggs, S. J., & Rader, N. (2016). Clearing crime in prime-time: The disjuncture between fiction and reality. *American Journal of Criminal Justice, 41,* 255–278.

Rhodes, L. A. (2002). Psychopathy and the face of control in supermax. *Ethnography, 3*(4), 442–466.

Rhodes, L. A. (2004). *Total confinement: Madness and reason in the maximum security prison.* Oakland: University of California Press.

Rhodes, L. A. (2009). Supermax prisons and the trajectory of exception. *Studies in Law, Politics, and Society, 47,* 193–218.

Richman, J., Mercer, D., & Mason, T. (1999). The social construction of evil in a forensic setting. *Journal of Forensic Psychiatry, 10*, 300–308.

Rieber, R. W., & Green, M. (1989). The psychopathy of everyday life: Antisocial behavior and social distress. In R. W. Rieber (Ed.), *The individual, communication, & society* (pp. 48–89). Cambridge: Cambridge University Press.

Rieber, R. W., & Vetter, H. J. (1995). The language of the psychopath. In R. W. Rieber (Ed.), *The psychopathology of language and cognition* (pp. 61–88). New York: Plenum Press.

Riech, K. B. (2014). Psycho lawyer, qu'est-ce que c'est: The high incidence of psychopaths in the legal profession and why they thrive. *Law & Psychology Review, 39*, 287–299.

Robinson, M. B. (2004). *Why crime? An interdisciplinary approach to explaining criminal behavior.* Upper Saddle River, NJ: Prentice Hall.

Robinson, M. B., & Beaver, M. B. (2009). *Why crime? An interdisciplinary approach to explaining criminal behavior* (2nd ed.). Durham, NC: Carolina Academic Press.

Robinson, R. A., & Ryder, J. A. (2013). Psychosocial perspectives of girls and violence: Implications for policy and praxis. *Critical Criminology, 21*, 431–445.

Roche, M. J., Shoss, N. E., Pincus, A. L., & Menard, K. S. (2011). *Sexual Abuse: A Journal of Research and Treatment, 23*(2), 171–192.

Rodger, E. (n.d.). *My twisted world.* Retrieved from https://www.documentcloud.org/documents/1173808-elliot-rodger-manifesto.html

Rogers, R., Jordan, M. J., & Harrison, K. S. (2007). Facets of psychopathy, Axis II traits, and behavioral dysregulation among jail detainees. *Behavioral Sciences & the Law, 25*(4), 471–483.

Romney, L. (2006, July 25). Killer who sparked 3-strikes law survives overdose. *Los Angeles Times.* Retrieved from http://articles.latimes.com/2006/jul/25/local/me-klaas25

Ronson, J. (2011). *The psychopath test: A journey into the madness industry.* New York: Riverhead Trade.

Rosan, A., Frick, P. J., Gottlieb, K. A., & Fasicaru, L. (2015). Callous-unemotional traits and anxiety in a sample of detained adolescents in Romania. *Journal of Evidence-Based Psychotherapies, 15*(1), 79–95.

Rosenberg, A. D., Abell, S. C., & Mackie, J. K. (2005). An examination of the relationship between child sexual offending and psychopathy. *Journal of Child Sexual Abuse: Research, Treatment, & Program Innovations for Victims, Survivors, & Offenders, 14*(3), 49–66.

Rosenberger, J. S., & Callahan, V. J. (2011). The influence of media on penal attitudes. *Criminal Justice Review, 36*(4), 435–455.

Ross, J. (2014, March 31). Willmar trial: Man allegedly admitted he killed friend's grandmother. *Star Tribune.* Retrieved from http://www.startribune.com/local/253300061.html

Rossmo, D. K. (2000). *Geographical profiling.* Boca Raton, FL: CRC Press.

Rotenberg, M., & Diamond, B. L. (1971). The biblical conception of psychopathy: The law of the stubborn and rebellious son. *Journal of the History of the Behavioral Sciences, 7*(1), 29–38.

Ruben, J., Page, M. A. (Producers), & Ruben, J. (Director). (1993). *The good son* [Motion picture]. USA: 20th Century Fox.

Rudin, S., Coen, E., Coen, J. (Producers), & Coen, J., Coen, E. (Directors). (2007). *No country for old men* [Motion picture]. USA: Miramax Films, Paramount Vantage.

Ruffles, J. (2004). Diagnosing evil in Australian courts: Psychopathy and antisocial personality disorder as legal synonyms of evil. *Psychiatry, Psychology, and Law, 11*(1), 113–121.

Rule, A. (1987). *Small sacrifices: A true story of passion and murder.* New York: New American Library (NAL Books).

Rule, W. (2013). *Born to destroy: Psychopathy in females: A life story.* Moscow, Russian Federation: Winefred Rule.

Runevitch, J. (2018, May 8). Franklin man accused of soliciting teens for sex—again. *WTHR.* Retrieved from https://www.wthr.com/article/franklin-man-accused-of-soliciting-teens-for-sex-again

Sade, Marquis de (1966). *Justine* (H. Weaver, Trans.). New York: Capricorn Books.

Sade, Marquis de (1968). *Juliette* (A. Wainhouse, Trans.). New York: Grove Press.

Sadeh, N., Javdani, S., Finy, M.S., & Verona, E. (2011). Gender differences in emotional risk for self- and other-directed violence among externalizing adults. *Journal of Consulting and Clinical Psychology, 79*(1), 106–117.

Salekin, R. T. (2006). Psychopathy in children and adolescence: Key issues in conceptualization and assessment. In C. J. Patrick (Ed.), *Handbook of psychopathy* (pp. 389–414). New York: Guilford Press.

Salekin, R. T., Rogers, R., & Sewell, K. W. (1996). A review and meta-analysis of the Psychopathy Checklist and Psychopathy Checklist–Revised: Predictive validity of dangerousness. *Clinical Psychology: Science and Practice, 3*(3), 203–215.

Salinger, J. D. (1945, 1951). *The catcher in the rye.* Boston: Little, Brown.

Samenow, S. E. (1984). *Inside the criminal mind.* New York: Times Books.

Samenow, S. E. (2013). The criminal personality. In J. B. Helfgott (Ed.), *Criminal psychology* (Vol. 1, pp. 209–225). Santa Barbara, CA: Praeger/ABC-CLIO.

Sanders, C. R., & Lyon, E. (2005). Repetitive retribution: Media images and the cultural construction of criminal justice. In J. Ferrell & C. R. Sanders (Eds.), *Cultural criminology* (pp. 25–44). New York: New York University Press.

Sandys, M., Pruss, H., & Walsh, M. (2009). Aggravation and mitigation: Findings and implications. *The Journal of Psychiatry & Law, 37,* 189–235.

Sargeant, J. (1996). *Born bad: The story of Charles Starkweather and Caril Ann Fugate.* London: Creation Books.

Schimmenti, A., Capri, C., La Barbera, D., & Caretti, V. (2014). Mafia and psychopathy. *Criminal Behaviour and Mental Health, 24,* 321–331.

Schmalleger, F. (2004). *Criminology today: An integrative introduction.* Upper Saddle River, NJ: Pearson/ Prentice-Hall.

Schouten, R., & Silver, J. (2012). *Almost a psychopath: Do I (or someone I know) have a problem with manipulation and lack of empathy?* Hazelden, MN: Harvard University Press.

Schwark, J. D. (2015). Toward a taxonomy of affective computing. *International Journal of Human-Computer Interaction, 31*, 761–768.

Schwartz, S. H. (1990). Individualism-collectivism: Critique and proposed refinements. *Journal of Cross-Cultural Psychology, 21*, 139–157.

Scott, C. L., & Resnick, P. J. (2006). Violence risk assessment in persons with mental illness. *Aggression and Violent Behavior, 11*(6), 598–611.

Scott, R. (2014). Psychopathy—An evolving and controversial construct. *Psychiatry, Psychology and Law, 21*(5), 687–715.

Scully, D., & Marolla, J. (1984). Convicted rapists' vocabulary of motive: Excuses and justifications. In P. A. Adler & P. Adler (Eds.), *Constructions of deviance: Social power, context, and interaction* (pp. 261–277). Belmont, CA: Wadsworth.

Secret confessions of BTK. (2005, August 12). *Dateline NBC.* Retrieved October 24, 2005, from http://www.msnbc.msn.com/id/8917644/#story Continued

Sedeh, N., Javdani, S., Finy, M. S., & Verona, E. (2011). Gender differences in emotional risk for self- and other-directed violence among externalizing adults. *Journal of Consulting and Clinical Psychology, 79*(1), 106–117.

Seigfried-Spellar, K. C., Villacís-Vukadinović, N., & Lynam, D. R. (2017). Computer criminal behavior is related to psychopathy and other antisocial behavior. *Journal of Criminal Justice, 51*(1), 67–73.

Selznick, D. O. (Producer), & Fleming, V. (Director). (1937). *Gone with the wind* [Motion picture]. USA: MGM.

Serin, R., & Kennedy, S. (1997). *Treatment readiness and responsivity: Contributing to effective correctional programming.* Research Report R-54. Ottawa, Canada: Correctional Service of Canada.

Serin, R. C., & Amos, N. L. (1995). The role of psychopathy in the assessment of dangerousness. *International Journal of Law & Psychiatry, 18*, 231–238.

Serin, R. C., Peters, R. D., & Barbaree, H. E. (1990). Predictors of psychopathy and release outcome in a criminal population. *Psychological Assessment: A Journal of Consulting & Clinical Psychology, 2*, 419–422.

Seto, M. C., Harris, G. T., & Lalumière, M. L. (2016). Psychopathy and sexual offending. In C. B. Gacono (Ed.), *The clinical and forensic assessment of psychopathy: A practitioner's guide* (2nd ed., pp. 403–418). New York: Routledge.

Seto, M. C., & Lalumière, M. L. (2010). What is so special about male adolescent sexual offending? A review and test of explanations through meta-analysis. *Psychological Bulletin, 136*(4), 526–575.

Setoodeh, R. (2011). Crazy chick flicks. *Newsweek, 157*(6), 43–45.

Sevecke, K., Lehmkuhl, G., & Krischer, M. K. (2009). Examining relations between psychopathology and psychopathy dimensions among adolescent female and male offenders. *European Child & Adolescent Psychiatry, 18*(2), 85–95.

Shariat, S. V., Assadi, S. M., Noroozian, M., Pakravannejad, M., Yahyazadeh, O., Aghayan, S., Michie, C., & Cooke, D. (2010). Psychopathy in Iran: A cross-cultural study. *Journal of Personality Disorders, 24*(5), 676–691.

Shaw, J., & Porter, S. (2012). Forever a psychopath? Psychopathy and the criminal career trajectory. In H. Häkkänen-Nyholm & J. Nyholm (Eds.), *Psychopathy and the law* (pp. 201–222). Chichester, West Sussex, UK: Wiley-Blackwell.

Shepherd, S. M., Campbell, R. E., & Ogloff, J. R. P. (2016). Psychopathy, antisocial personality disorder, and reconviction in an Australian sample of forensic patients. *International Journal of Offender Therapy and Comparative Criminology, 62*(3), 609–628.

Sheridan, T. (2011). *Puzzling people: The labyrinth of the psychopath.* Velluminous Press: www.velluminous.com.

Sherman, L. W., Gottfredson, D., Mackenzie, D., Eck, J., Reuter, P., & Bushway, S. (1997). *Preventing crime: What works, what doesn't, what's promising.* Report to the U.S. Congress. Washington, DC: U.S. National Institute of Justice—Office of Justice Programs. Retrieved from http://cjcentral.com/sherman/sherman.htm

Shestack, J. (Producer), & Dahl, J. (Director). (1994). *The last seduction* [Motion picture]. USA: October Films.

Shipley, S. L., & Arrigo, B. A. (2004). *The Female homicide offender: Serial murder and the case of Aileen Wuornos.* Upper Saddle River, NJ: Pearson.

Shou, Y., Sellbom, M., Xu, J., Chen, T., & Sui, A. (2017). Elaborating on the construct validity of triarchic psychopathy measure in Chinese clinical and nonclinical samples. *Psychological Assessment, 29*(9), 1071–1081.

Silverman, D. C., Kalick, S. M., Bowie, S. I., & Edbril, S. D. (1988). Blitz rape and confidence rape: A typology applied to 1,000 consecutive cases. *The American Journal of Psychiatry, 145*(11), 1438–1441.

Silverstone, P. H., Krameddine, Y. I., DeMarco, D., & Hassel, R. (2013). A novel approach to training police officers to interact with individuals who may have a psychiatric disorder. *Journal of American Academy of Psychiatry and Law, 41*, 344–355.

Simon, G. K. (2010). *In sheep's clothing: Understanding and dealing manipulative people.* Little Rock, AR: Parkhurst Brothers.

Simon, G. K. (2011). *Character disturbance: The phenomenon of our age.* Little Rock, AR: Packhurst Brother's.

Simourd, D. J., & Hodge, R. D. (2000). Criminal psychopathy: A risk-and-need perspective. *Criminal Justice and Behavior, 27*, 256–272.

Simpson, P. L. (2000). *Psychopaths: Tracking the serial killer through contemporary American film and fiction.* Carbondale, IL: Southern Illinois University Press.

Skeem, J. L., & Cooke, D. J. (2010). Is criminal behavior a central component of psychopathy? Conceptual directions for resolving the debate. *Psychological Assessment, 22*(2), 433–445.

Slate, R. N., Buffington, J. K., & Johnson, W. W. (2013). *The criminalization of mental illness: Crisis and opportunity for the justice system.* Durham, NC: Carolina Academic Press.

Smilanski, S. (2007). Determinism and prepunishment: The radical nature of compatibilism. *Analysis, 67*(4), 347–349.

Smith, R. J. (1978). *The psychopath in society.* New York: Academic Press.

Smith, R. J. (1985). The concept and measurement of social psychopathy. *Journal of Research in Personality, 19,* 219–231.

Smith, R. J., & Griffith, J. E. (1978). Psychopathy, machiavellianism, and anomie. *Psychological Reports, 42,* 258.

Smith, S. R. (1989). Mental health expert witnesses: Of science and crystal balls. *Behavioral Sciences and the Law, 7*(2), 145–180.

Smith, S. R., & Meyer, R. G. (1987). *Law, behavior, and mental health: Policy and practice.* New York/London: New York University Press.

Smith, S. S., O'Toole, M. E., & Hare, R. D. (2012). The predator: When the stalker is a psychopath. *FBI Law Enforcement Bulletin, 81*(7), 9–13.

Smith, S. T., Edens, J. F., Clark, J., & Rulseh, A. (2014). So, what is a psychopath? Venireperson perceptions, beliefs, and attitudes about psychopathic personality. *Law and Human Behavior, 38*(5), 490–500.

Sokmensuer, H. (2017). Killer moms: Susan Smith, Diane Downs, and others. *People Crime.* Retrieved from http://people.com/crime/killer-moms-susan-smith-diane-downs-and-others/diane-downs

Somma, A., Borroni, S., Drislane, L. E., & Fossati, A. (2016). Assessing the triarchic model of psychopathy in adolescence: Reliability and validity of the triarchic psychopathy measure (TriPM) in three samples of Italian community-dwelling adolescents. *Psychological Assessment, 28*(4), 36–48.

Spalt, L. (1980). Hysteria and antisocial personality: A single disorder? *The Journal of Nervous and Mental Disease, 168,* 456–464.

Sparks, C. G., & Sparks, C. W. (2002). Effects of media violence. In J. Bryant & D. Zillman (Eds.), *Media effects: Advances in theory and research* (pp. 269–285). Mahwah, NJ: Erlbaum.

Sparks, R. (1992). *Television and the drama of crime: Moral tales and the place of crime in public life.* Philadelphia: Open University Press.

Spaulding, E. (1923). *An experimental study of psychopathic delinquent women.* New York: Rand McNally.

Spice, A., Viljoen, J. L., Douglas, K., & Hart, S. D. (2015). Remorse, psychopathology, and psychopathy among adolescent offenders. *Law and Human Behavior, 39*(5), 451–462.

Spidel, A., Greaves, C., Cooper, B. S., Hervé, H. F., Hare, R. D., & Yuille, J. C. (2007). The psychopath as pimp. *Canadian Journal of Police and Security Services, 4,* 205–211.

Sprague, J., Javdani, S., Sadeh, N., Newman, J. P., & Verona, E. (2012). Borderline personality disorder as a female phenotypic expression of psychopathy? *Personality Disorders: Theory, Research, and Treatment, 3*(2), 127–139.

Stalans, L. J. (2004). Adult sex offenders on community supervision: A review of recent assessment strategies and treatment. *Criminal Justice and Behavior, 31* (5), 564–608.

Stanković, M., Nešić, M., Obrenović, J., Stojanović, D., & Milošević, V. (2015). Recognition of facial expressions of emotions in criminal and non-criminal psychopaths: Valence-specific hypothesis. *Personality and Individual Differences, 82*, 242–247.

State of Washington v. Ridgway [Videorecording]. (2004). Prepared on behalf of King County Prosecutor's Office. Seattle: Chameleon Data.

Steadman, H. J., Monahan, J., Appelbaum, P. S., Grisso, T., Mulvey, E. P., Roth, L. H., Robbins, P. C., & Klassen, D. (1994). Designing a new generation of risk assessment research. In J. M. Monahan & H. J. Steadman (Eds.), *Violence and mental disorder: Developments in risk assessment* (pp. 297–318). Chicago: University of Chicago Press.

Stein, H. (1989). The indispensable enemy and American-Soviet relations. *Ethos, 17*, 480–503.

Stermac, L. E., Segal, Z. V., & Gillis, R. (1989). Social and cultural factors in sexual assault. In W. L. Marshall, D. R. Laws, & H. E. Barbaree (Eds.), *Handbook of sexual assault* (pp. 143–159). New York: Plenum Press.

Steuerwald, B. L., & Kosson, D. S. (2000). Emotional experiences of the psychopath. In C. B. Gacono (Ed.), *The clinical and forensic assessment of psychopathy* (pp. 111–135). Mahwah, NJ: Erlbaum.

Stevens, G. F. (1994). Prison clinicians' perceptions of antisocial personality disorder as a formal diagnosis. *Journal of Offender Rehabilitation, 20*, 159–185.

Stout, M. (2005). *The sociopath next door.* New York: Broadway Books.

Strand, S., & Belfrage, H. (2005). Gender differences in psychopathy in a Swedish offender sample. *Behavioral Sciences & the Law, 23*(6), 837–850.

Stratton, J., Kiehl, K. A., & Hanlon, R. E. (2015). The neurobiology of psychopathy. *Psychiatric Annals, 45*(4), 186–194.

Stone, H., & Dellis, N. (1960). An exploratory investigation into the levels hypothesis. *Journal of Projective Techniques, 24*, 333–340.

Sullivan, E. A., Abramowitz, C. S., Lopez, M., & Kosson, D. S. (2006). Reliability and construct validity of the Psychopathy Checklist—Revised for Latino, European American, and African American male inmates. *Psychological Assessment, 18*(4), 382–392.

Sullivan, E. A., & Kosson, D. S. (2006). Ethnic and cultural variations in psychopathy. In C. J. Patrick (Ed.), *Handbook of psychopathy* (pp. 437–458). New York: Guilford Press.

Surette, R. (1990). Estimating the magnitude and mechanisms of copycat crime. In Surette, R. (Ed.), *The media and criminal justice policy: Recent research and social effects.* Springfield, IL: CC Thomas.

Surette, R. (2002). Self-reported copycat crime among a population of serious and violent juvenile offenders. *Crime & Delinquency, 48*(1), 46–69.

Surette, R. (2006, 2014). *Media, crime, and criminal justice: Images and realities.* Belmont, CA: Wadsworth.

Surette, R. (2013). Pathways to copycat crime. In J. B. Helfgott (Ed.), *Criminal psychology* (Vol. 2, pp. 251–276). Westport, CT: Praeger.

Sutherland, E. H. (1949). *White collar crime.* New York: Dryden.

Sutherland, E. H. (1950). The sexual psychopath laws. *Journal of Criminal Law and Criminology, 40*(5), 543–554.

Sutton, S. K., Vitale, J. E., & Newman, J. P. (2002). Emotion among women with psychopathy during picture perception. *Journal of Abnormal Psychology, 111*(4), 610.

Svedholm-Hakkinen, A. M., Ojala, S. J., & Lindemann, M. (2018). Male brain type women and female brain type men: Gender atypical cognitive profiles and their correlates. *Personality and Individual Differences, 122,* 7–12.

Swanson, J. (2016). Sexual liberation or violence against women? The debate on the legalization of prostitution and the relationship to human trafficking. *New Criminal Law Review, 19*(4), 592–639.

Sykes, G. M., & Matza, D. (1957). Techniques of neutralization: A theory of delinquency. *American Sociological Review, 22,* 664–670.

Tamatea, A. J. (2015). "Biologizing" psychopathy: Ethical, legal, and research implications at the interface of epigenetics and chronic antisocial conduct. *Behavioral Sciences and the Law, 33*(5), 629–643.

Tavris, C., & Wade, C. (1984). *The longest war: Sex differences in perspective.* New York: Harcourt Brace Jovanovich.

Terkle, S. (2008). *The inner history of devices.* Cambridge, MA: MIT Press.

Terkle, S. (2011). *Alone together: Why we expect more from technology and less from each other.* New York: Basic Books.

Terry, L. (2010, December 10). Notorious kicker Diane Downs must wait 10 more years before she applies for parole again. *The Oregonian/OregonLive.* Retrieved from http://www.oregonlive.com/pacific-northwest-news/index.ssf/2010/12/notorious_child_killer_diane_downs_must_wait_10_more_years_before_she_applies_for_parole_again.html

Thompson, K. M. (2007). *Crime films: Investigating the scene.* New York: Columbia University Press.

Thornton, D., & Blud, L. (2007). The influence of psychopathic traits on response to treatment. In H. Herve & J. C. Yuille (Eds.), *The psychopath: Theory, research, and practice* (pp. 505–539). Mahwah, NJ: Erlbaum.

Transcript of Homolka Interview. (2005, July 4/Updated 2018, April 22). *The Globe and Mail.* Retrieved from https://www.theglobeandmail.com/news/national/transcript-of-homolka-interview/article20423757

Triandis, H. C. (1990). Cross-cultural studies of individualism and collectivism. In J. J. Berman (Ed.), *Cross-cultural perspectives* (pp. 41–134). Lincoln/London: University of Nebraska Press.

Turvey, B. E. (1999, 2002, 2011). *Criminal profiling: An introduction to behavioral evidence analysis* (4th ed.). San Diego: Academic Press.

Tütüncu, R., Kılıç, S., Başoğlu, C., Ateş, M. A., Algül, A., Balıbey, H., & Cetin, M. (2015). The reliability and validity of the Turkish version of Psychopathy Checklist–Revised. *Bulletin of Clinical Psychopharmacology, 25*(2), 118–24.

Ullrich, S., & Marneros, A. (2007). Underlying dimensions of ICD-10 personality disorders: Risk factors, childhood antecedents, and adverse outcomes in adulthood. *The Journal of Forensic Psychiatry & Psychology, 18*(1), 44–58.

Umbach, R., Berryessa, C. M., & Raine, A. (2015). Brain imaging research on psychopathy: Implications for punishment, prediction, and treatment in youth and adults. *Journal of Criminal Justice, 43*(4), 295–306.

Umbreit, M. S., Coates, R. B., & Vos, B. (2004). Victim-offender mediation: Three decades of practice and research. *Conflict Resolution Quarterly, 22*(1–2), 279–303.

Utt, K., Saxon, E., Bozman, R. (Producers), & Demme, J. (Director). (1991). *The silence of the lambs* [Motion picture]. USA: Orion Pictures.

Uzieblo, K., Verschuere, B., Van den Bussche, & Crombez, G. (2010). The validity of the Psychopathic Personality Inventory–Revised in community sample. *Assessment, 17*(3), 334–346.

Vachon, D. D., Lynam, D. R., Loeber, R., & Stouthamer-Loeber, M. (2012). Generalizing the nomological network of psychopathy across populations differing on race and conviction status. *Journal of Abnormal Psychology, 121*(1), 263–269.

Vaidyanathan, U., Hall, J. R., Patrick, C. J., & Bernat, E. M. (2011). Clarifying the role of defensive reactivity deficits in psychopathy and antisocial personality using startle reflex methodology. *Journal of Abnormal Psychology, 120*(1), 253–258.

Valdez, A., Kaplan, C. D., & Codina, E. (2000). Psychopathy among Mexican American Gang Members: A comparative study. *International Journal of Offender Therapy and Comparative Criminology, 44*(1), 46–58.

Valentis, M., & Devane, A. (1994). *Female rage: Unlocking its secrets, claiming its power.* New York: Carol Southern Books.

Van Honk, J., & Schutter, D. J. (2006). Unmasking feigned sanity: A neurobiological model of emotion processing in primary psychopathy. *Cognitive Neuropsychiatry, 11*(3), 285–306.

Van Voorhis, P. (1994). *Psychological classification of the adult male prison inmate.* New York: State University of New York Press.

Van Voorhis, P., Wright, E. M., Salisbury, E., & Bauman, A. (2010). Women's risk factors and their contributions to existing risk/needs assessment: The current status of a gender-responsive supplement. *Criminal Justice and Behavior, 37*(3), 261–288.

Vaughn, M. G., & DeLisi, M. (2008). Were Wolfgang's chronic offenders psychopaths? On the convergent validity between psychopathy and career criminality. *Journal of Criminal Justice, 36*(1), 33–42.

Veen, V. C. (2011). Cross-ethnic generalizability of the three-factor model of psychopathy: The Youth Psychopathic Traits Inventory in an incarcerated sample of native Dutch and Moroccan immigrant boys. *International Journal of Law and Psychiatry, 34*(2), 127–130.

Venables, N. C., & Hall, J. R. (2013). Forensic assessment of psychopathy. In J. B. Helfgott (Ed.), *Criminal psychology* (Vol. 2, pp. 311–340). Santa Barbara, CA: Praeger/ABC-CLIO.

Verdun-Jones, S. N., & Butler, A. (2013). Sentencing neurocognitively impaired offenders in Canada. *Canadian Journal of Criminology & Criminal Justice, 55*(4), 495–512.

Verona, E., Bresin, K., & Patrick, C. (2013). Revisiting psychopathy in women: Cleckley/Hare conceptions and affective response. *Journal of Abnormal Psychology, 122*(4), 1088–1093.

Verona, E., & Vitale, J. (2006). Psychopathy in women: Assessment, manifestations, and etiology. In C. J. Patrick (Ed.), *Handbook of psychopathy* (pp. 415–436). New York: Guilford Press.

Verona, E., & Vitale, J. (2018). Psychopathy in women: Assessment, manifestations, and etiology. In C. J. Patrick (Ed.), *Handbook of psychopathy* (2nd ed., pp. 509–528). New York: Guilford Press.

Verschuere, B., van Ghesel Grothe, S., Waldrop, L., Watts, A. L., Lilienfeld, S. O., Edens, J. F., & Skeem, J. L. (2018). What features of psychopathy might be central? A network analysis of the Psychopathy Checklist–Revised (PCL-R) in three large samples. *Journal of Abnormal Psychology, 127*(1), 51–65.

Vess, J., Murphey, C., & Arkowitz, S. (2004). Clinical and demographic differences between sexually violent predators and other commitment types in a state forensic hospital. *Journal of Forensic Psychiatry & Psychology, 15*(4), 669–681.

Vidal, S., & Skeem, J. L. (2007). Effect of psychopathy, abuse, and ethnicity on juvenile probation officers' decision-making and supervision strategies. *Law and Human Behavior, 31*, 479–498.

Viljoen, S., Cook, A. N., Lim, Y. L., Layden, B. K., Bousfield, N. K., & Hart, S. D. (2015). Are psychopathic and borderline personality disorder distinct, or differently gendered expressions of the same disorder? An exploration using concept maps. *The International Journal of Forensic Mental Health, 14*(4), 267–279.

Villar, G., Arciuli, J., & Paterson, H. M. (2014). Remorse in oral and handwritten false confessions. *Legal and Criminological Psychology, 19*, 255–269.

Vincent, G. M., Vitacco, M. J., Grisso, T. G., & Corrado, R. R. (2003). Subtypes of adolescent offenders: Affective traits and antisocial behavior patterns. *Behavioral Sciences and the Law, 21*(6), 695–712.

Visser, B. A., Pozzebon, J. A., Bogaert, A. F., & Ashton, M. C. (2010). Psychopathy, sexual behavior, and esteem: It's different for girls. *Personality and Individual Differences*, *48*(7), 833–838.

Vitacco, M. J., Lishner, D. A., & Neumann, C. S. (2012). Assessment. In H. Häkkänen-Nyholm & J. Nyholm (Eds.), *Psychopathy and the law* (pp. 17–38). Chichester, West Sussex, UK: Wiley-Blackwell.

Vitacco, M. J., Neumann, C. S., & Jackson, R. L. (2005). Testing a four-factor model of psychopathy and its association with ethnicity, gender, intelligence, and violence. *Journal of Consulting and Clinical Psychology, 73*, 466–476. doi:10.1037/0022-006X.73.3.466

Vitale, J. E., Baskin-Sommers, A. R., Wallace, J. F., Schmitt, W. A., & Newman, J. P. (2016). Experimental investigations of information processing deficiencies in psychopathic individuals: Implications for diagnosis and treatment. In C. B. Gacono (Ed.), *The clinical and forensic assessment of psychopathy* (2nd ed., pp. 54–72). New York: Routledge.

Vitale, J. E., & Newman, J. P. (2001). Response perseveration in psychopathic women. *Journal of Abnormal Psychology, 110*(4), 644.

Vold, G. B. (1958). *Theoretical criminology*. New York: Oxford University Press.

Vold, G. B., & Bernard, T. J. (1986). *Theoretical criminology*. New York: Oxford University Press.

Wahid, N., Novaditya, R., Thoyibi, M. S., Fatimah, S., & Hum, A. M. (2016). *The psychopath phenomenon reflected in Gillian Flynn's Gone Girl novel (2012): A psychoanalytic approach* (Doctoral dissertation). Universitas Muhammadiyah Surakarta.

Waldman, I. B., Rhee, S. Y., LoParo, D., & Park, Y. (2018). Genetic and environmental influences on psychopathy and antisocial behavior. In C. J. Patrick (Ed.), *Handbook of psychopathy* (2nd ed., pp. 335–353). New York: Guilford Press.

Wall, T. D., Wygant, D. B., & Sellbom, M. (2015). Boldness explains a key difference between psychopathy and antisocial personality disorder. *Psychiatry, Psychology and Law, 22*(1), 94–105.

Wallace, J. F., Schmitt, W. A., Vitale, J. E., & Neman, J. P. (2000). Experimental investigations of information-processing deficiencies in psychopaths: Implications for diagnosis and treatment. In C. B. Gacono (Ed.), *The clinical and forensic assessment of psychopathy* (pp. 87–109). Mahwah, NJ: Erlbaum.

Wallis, C. (2016, August 12). Of psychopaths and presidential candidates. *Scientific American*. Retrieved from https://blogs.scientificamerican.com/mind-guest-blog/of-psychopaths-and-presidential-candidates

Walsh, A., & Beaver, K. M. (Eds.). (2009). *Biosocial criminology: New directions & theory in research*. New York: Routledge.

Walsh, A., & Vaske, J. C. (2011). *Feminist criminology through a biosocial lens*. Durham, NC: Carolina Academic Press.

Walsh, A., & Wright, P. (2015a). Biosocial criminology and its discontents: A critical realist philosophical analysis. *Criminal Justice Studies, 28*(1), 124–140.

Walsh, A., & Wright, P. (2015b). Rage against reason: Addressing critical critics of biosocial research. *Journal of Theoretical and Philosophical Criminology, 7*, 61–72.

Walsh, A., & Wu, H. (2008). Differentiating antisocial personality disorder, psychopathy, and sociopathy: Evolutionary, genetic, neurological, and sociological considerations. *Criminal Justice Studies, 21*(2), 135–152.

Walsh, T., & Walsh, Z. (2006). The evidentiary introduction of Psychopathy Checklist–Revised assessed psychopathy in U.S. courts: Extent and appropriateness. *Law and Human Behavior, 30*, 493–507.

Walsh, Z., & Kosson, D. S. (2007). Psychopathy and violent crime: A prospective study of the influence of socioeconomic status and ethnicity. *Law and Human Behavior, 31*(2), 209–229.

Walters, G. D. (1990). *The criminal lifestyle.* London: Sage.

Walters, G. D. (2003). Predicting institutional adjustment and recidivism with the Psychopathy Checklist factor scores: A meta-analysis. *Law and Human Behavior, 27*(5), 541–558.

Walters, G. D. (2004). The trouble with psychopathy as a general theory of crime. *International Journal of Offender Therapy and Comparative Criminology, 48*(2), 133–148.

Walters, G. D. (2008). Self-report measures of psychopathy, antisocial personality, and criminal lifestyle. *Criminal Justice & Behavior, 35*(12), 1459–1483.

Walters, G. D. (2012). Psychopathy and crime: Testing the incremental validity of PCL-R-measured psychopathy as a predictor of general and violent recidivism. *Law and Human Behavior, 36*(5), 404–412.

Walters, G. D. (2013). Psychopathy's role in the criminal justice system: Five empirical controversies in search of answers. In J. Horley (Ed.), *Critiques of psychopathy* (pp. 37–59). Hauppauge, NY: Nova Science.

Walters, J. (2015). Fetal abduction: Brutal attacks against expectant mothers on the rise in the US. *Guardian.* Retrieved from https://www.theguardian.com/us-news/2015/dec/02/fetal-abduction-attacks-expectant-mothers

Wang, E. W., & Diamond, P. M. (1999). Empirically identifying factors related to violence risk in corrections. *Behavioral Sciences and the Law, 17*, 377–389.

Wang, P., Baker, L. A., Gao, Y., Raine, A., & Lozano, D. I. (2012). Psychopathic traits and physiological responses to aversive stimuli in children aged 9–11 years. *Journal of Abnormal Child Psychology, 40*(5), 759–769.

Ward, T. (2010). Psychopathy and criminal responsibility in historical perspective. In L. Malatesti & J. McMillan (Eds.), *Responsibility and psychopathy: Interfacing law, psychiatry and philosophy* (pp. 7–24). Oxford, UK: Oxford University Press.

Warner, R. (1978). The diagnosis of antisocial and hysterical personality disorders. *The Journal of Nervous and Mental Disease, 166*, 839–845.

Warr, M. (2016). Crime and regret. *Emotion Review, 8*(3), 231–239.

Washington Post. (1992, February 6). Psychiatrist calls Dahmer a sane killer. *Washington Post.* Retrieved from https://www.washingtonpost.com/archive/politics/1992/02/07/psychiatrist-calls-dahmer-a-sane-killer/91cb4a83-0190-4e21-8b00-15e4d3d899d8/?utm_term=.77aa153289ab

Weber, D. C. (1999, August 26). Warrior cops: The ominous growth of paramilitarism in American police departments. *Cato Briefing Papers, 50*, 1–13.

Weibe, R. P. (2012). Integrating criminology through adaptive strategy and life history theory. *Journal of Contemporary Criminal Justice, 28*(3), 346–365.

Weisman, R. (2008). Remorse and psychopathy at the penalty phase of the capital trial—How psychiatry's view of "moral insanity" helps build the case for death. *Studies in Law, Politics, and Society, 41*, 187–217.

Weisman, R. (2009). Being and doing: The judicial use of remorse to construct character and community. *Social & Legal Studies, 18*(1), 47–69.

Weizmann-Henelius, G., Grönroos, M., Putkonen, H., Eronen, M., Lindberg, N., & Häkkänen-Nyholm, H. (2010). Psychopathy and gender differences in childhood psychosocial characteristics in homicide offenders: A nationwide register-based study. *The Journal of Forensic Psychiatry & Psychology, 21*(6), 801–814.

Wells, R. (1988). A fresh look at the muddy waters of psychopathy. *Psychological Reports, 63*, 843–856.

Wernke, M. R., & Huss, M. T. (2008). An alternative explanation for cross-cultural differences in the expression of psychopathy. *Aggression and Violent Behavior, 13*(3), 229–236.

Westen, D. (1985). *Self and society: Narcissism, collectivism, and the development of morals.* Cambridge: Cambridge University Press.

Wheeler, S., Book, A., & Costello, K. (2009). Psychopathic traits and perceptions of victim vulnerability. *Criminal Justice and Behavior, 36*(6), 635–648.

Widiger, T. A., & Crego. C. (2018). Psychopathy and DSM-5 psychopathology. In C. J. Patrick (Ed.), *Handbook of psychopathy* (2nd ed., pp. 281–296). New York: Guilford Press.

Widom, C. S. (1977). A methodology for studying noninstitutionalized psychopaths. *Journal of Consulting and Clinical Psychology, 45*, 674–683.

Widom, C. S. (1978). A methodology for studying non-institutionalised psychopaths. In R. D. Hare & D. Schalling (Eds.), *Psychopathic behaviour: Approaches to research.* New York: Wiley.

Williams, J. B. W., & Spitzer, R. L. (1983). The issue of sex bias in DSMIII: A critique of "A woman's view of DSMIII" by Marcie Kaplan. *American Psychologist, 38*, 793–798.

Williamson, S., Hare, R.D., & Wong, S. (1987). Violence: Criminal psychopaths and their victims. *Canadian Journal of Behavioral Science, 9*(4), 455–462.

Williamson, S., Harpur, T. J., & Hare, R. D. (1991). Abnormal processing of affective words by psychopaths. *Psychophysiology, 29*, 260–273.

Wilson, J. Q., & Herrnstein, R. (1985). *Crime and human nature.* New York: Simon & Schuster.

Wilson, M. J., Abramowitz, C., Vasilev, G., Bozgunov, K., & Vassileva, J. (2014). Psychopathy in Bulgaria: The cross-cultural generalizability of the Hare psychopathy checklist. *Journal of Psychopathology and Behavioral Assessment, 36*(3), 389–400.

Wilson, N. J., & Tamatea, A. (2013). Challenging the "urban myth" of psychopathy untreatability: The high-risk personality programme. *Psychology, Crime, & Law, 19*(5/6), 493–510.

Wilson, P., Lincoln, R., & Kocsis, R. (1997). Validity, utility and ethics of profiling for serial violent and sexual offenders. *Psychiatry, Psychology, and the Law, 4*(1), 1–12.

Wilson, W. (1999). *The psychopath in film.* Lanham, MD: University Press of America.

Winslow, E. K., & Solomon, G. T. (1989). Further development of a descriptive profile of entrepreneurs. *The Journal of Creative Behavior, 23*, 149–161.

Wishnie, H. (1977). *The impulsive personality.* New York: Plenum.

Wogan, M., & Mackenzie, M. (2007). An inmate classification system based on PCL:SV factor scores in a sample of prison inmates. *Journal of Offender Rehabilitation, 44*(4), 25–42.

Wolfgang, M. E., Figlio, R. M., & Sellin, T. (1972). *Delinquency in a birth cohort.* Chicago: University of Chicago Press.

Wolman, B. (1987). *The sociopathic personality.* New York: Brunner/Mazel.

Wong, S., Gordon, A., Gu, D., Lewis, K., & Oliver, M. (2012). The effectiveness of violence reduction treatment for psychopathic offenders: Empirical evidence and a treatment model. *The International Journal of Forensic Mental Health, 11*(4), 336–349.

Wong, S., & Hare, R. D. (2005). *Guidelines for a psychopathy treatment program.* North Tonawanda, NY: Multi-Health Systems.

Woodworth, M., Hancock, J., Porter, S., Hare, R. D., Logan, M., O'Toole, M. E., & Smith, S. (2012). The language of psychopaths: New findings and implications for law enforcement. *FBI Law Enforcement Bulletin, 81*(7), 28–32.

Woodworth, M., & Porter, S. (2002). In cold blood: Characteristics of criminal homicides as a function of psychopathy. *Journal of Abnormal Psychology, 111*(3), 436–445.

World Health Organization. (1978). *Manual of the international statistical classification of diseases, injuries, and causes of death* (9th ed.) (ICD-9). Geneva: Author.

World Health Organization. (1992). *Manual of the international statistical classification of diseases, injuries, and causes of death* (10th ed.) (ICD-10). Geneva: Author.

World Health Organization. (2015). *Manual of the international statistical classification of diseases, injuries, and causes of death* (10th ed.) (ICD-10). Geneva: Author. Retrieved from http://apps.who.int/classifications/icd10/browse/2015/en#F60.2

Wright, E. M. (2009). The measurement of psychopathy: Dimensional and taxometric approaches. *International Journal of Offender Therapy and Comparative Criminology, 53*(4), 464–481.

Wulach, J. S. (1988). The criminal personality as a DSMIII-R antisocial, narcissistic, borderline, and histrionic personality disorder. *International Journal of Offender Counseling and Comparative Criminology, 33*, 185–199.

Yakeley, J., & Meloy, J. R. (2012). Understanding violence: Does psychoanalytic thinking matter? *Aggression and Violent Behavior, 17*, 229–239.

Yang, Y., & Raine, A. (2018). The neuroanatomical basis of psychopathy: A review of brain imaging findings. In C. J. Patrick (Ed.), *Handbook of psychopathy* (2nd ed., pp. 380–400). New York: Guilford Press.

Yildirim, B. O. (2016). A treatise on secondary psychopathy: Psychobiological pathways to severe antisociality. *Aggression and Violent Behavior, 31*(1), 165–185.

Yildirim, B. O., & Derksen, J. J. L. (2015). Clarifying the heterogeneity in psychopathic samples: Towards a new continuum of primary and secondary psychopathy. *Aggression and Violent Behavior, 24*(1), 9–41.

Yochelson, S., & Samenow, S. E. (1976). *The criminal personality* (Vols. 1–3). New York: Jason Aronson.

Young, L., Koenigs, M., Kruepke, M., & Newman, J. P. (2012). Psychopathy increases perceived moral permissibility of accidents. *Journal of Abnormal Psychology, 121*(3), 659–667.

Young, M., Justice, J., Gacono, C. B., & Kivisto, A. J. (2016). The incarcerated psychopath in psychiatric treatment: Management or treatment? In C. B. Gacono (Ed.), *The clinical and forensic assessment of psychopathy: A practitioner's guide* (2nd ed., pp. 374–387). New York: Routledge.

Zehr, H. (1990). *Changing lenses: A new focus for crime and justice.* Harrisonburg, VA: Herald Press.

Zehr, H. (2002). *The little book of restorative justice.* New York: Good Books.

Zhong, L. (2013). Internalism, emotionism, and the psychopathy challenge. *Philosophy, Psychiatry, & Psychology, 20*(4), 329–337.

Zimbardo, P. (2007). *The Lucifer Effect: Understanding how good people turn evil.* New York: Random House.

Zinger, I. (1995). The misuse of psychopathy in Canadian court proceedings. *Issues in Criminological and Legal Psychology, 24,* 157–159.

Zinger, I., & Forth, A. E. (1998). Psychopathy and Canadian criminal proceedings: The potential for human rights abuses. *Canadian Journal of Criminology, 40,* 237–276.

Zona, M. A., Palarea, R. E., & Lane, J. C. (1998). Psychiatric diagnosis of the offender-victim typology of stalking. In J. R. Meloy (Ed.), *The psychology of stalking: Clinical and forensic perspectives* (pp. 69–84). San Diego: Academic Press.

Zweig, C., & Abrams, J. (Ed.). (1991). *Meeting the shadow: The hidden power of the dark side of human nature.* New York: TarcherPerigee.

Index

Notes are indicated by n following the page number.